FUNERALS
Consumers'
Last Rights

FUNERALS
Consumers' Last Rights

The Consumers Union Report on
Conventional Funerals and Burial
...and Some Alternatives, including
Cremation, Direct Cremation,
Direct Burial, and Body Donation

BY THE EDITORS OF CONSUMER REPORTS

Consumers Union, Mount Vernon, New York

Acknowledgments for permission to reprint previously copyrighted
material are given in Permission to Quote, pages 319–321.

Consumers Union wishes to acknowledge the assistance of
Ruth Mulvey Harmer, author of the pioneering book on the funeral
industry *The High Cost of Dying* (1963), and former president
of the Continental Association of Funeral and Memorial Societies.
She was the source of useful research and ancedotal material.

Library of Congress Catalog Card Number: 77-86468
International Standard Book Number: 0-89043-006-3
Manufactured in the United States of America

Funerals: Consumers' Last Rights is a special publication of Consumers Union, the nonprofit organization that publishes CONSUMER REPORTS, the monthly magazine of test reports, product Ratings, and buying guidance. Established in 1936, Consumers Union is chartered under the Not-For-Profit Corporation Law of the State of New York.

The purposes of Consumers Union, as stated in its charter, are to provide consumers with information and counsel on consumer goods and services, to give information and assistance on all matters relating to the expenditure of the family income, and to initiate and to cooperate with individual and group efforts seeking to create and maintain decent living standards.

Consumers Union derives its income solely from the sale of CONSUMER REPORTS and other publications. Consumers Union accepts no advertising or product samples and is not beholden in any way to any commercial interest. Its Ratings and reports are solely for the information and use of the readers of its publications.

Neither the Ratings nor the reports nor any other Consumers Union publications, including this book, may be used in advertising or for any commercial purpose of any nature. Consumers Union will take all steps open to it to prevent or to prosecute any such uses of its material, its name, or the name of CONSUMER REPORTS.

Contents

6

A First Word

Most people would agree that death is a difficult subject to think about or to discuss with others, particularly when it concerns those closest to us—a spouse, a parent, a child, a friend. Even more difficult may be consideration of one's own death and disposition. Few of us are prepared to confront the inevitability of death and to plan for it in a practical way. Few have even had much experience with death. The time has long since passed when people died at home and family and friends were intimately involved in preparations for the funeral. Ours is a nation where the dying are kept out of sight for the most part and where euphemisms for death—and everything connected with it—are commonplace. We have lost the ability to accept death as an integral part of life.

The 1970s have seen a new interest in the topics of death and dying. More and more articles and books on these subjects are being published. Colleges and other institutions are offering an increasing number of death education courses. Despite this trend, most people continue to evade the fact of death as an inescapable part of life. In a society that places great value on youth and good health, death becomes real only when it directly affects us or those close to us.

Yet, prudence would suggest that some thought and preparation for death occupy at least a small part of our lives. Perhaps, it could be argued, mature people ought to assume the responsibility for making plans for their own disposition, if only to spare their survivors some of the confusion and expense that so often follow death. *Funerals: Consumers' Last Rights* is a guide for people who wish to do just that, as well as for survivors faced with an immediate need to make funeral arrangements.

This book has two purposes. One is to help readers to become better informed about conventional funerals and burial (and how to arrange for them, at a saving, where possible), as well as less costly alternatives. The other purpose is to provide practical information about the choices and the decisions that most survivors must face only a few hours after death has occurred.

Funerals: Consumers' Last Rights is divided into four parts. Part I offers a general discussion of the funeral industry, what is involved in arranging for a funeral, and a brief description of other options. These several options are discussed in detail in individual chapters later in the book. Part II, intended for those who prefer a conventional funeral and burial, examines the funeral transaction in detail. These chapters explore the five major components of a funeral and burial: the coffin, embalming, items considered as "extras," the vault, and cemetery. For those who want to consider alternatives to a conventional funeral and burial, Part III discusses cremation, direct (immediate) burial or cremation, and the donation of one's body to medical science. Part IV considers two ways of prearranging for disposition: joining a memorial society or making financial arrangements in advance through a preneed plan. Throughout the book we have included information on costs of merchandise and services, and relevant legal information.

Our purpose was not to write an exposé of the funeral industry, although we find good reason to be critical of it. Consumers Union does recognize the undertakers' unique role. Without doubt, undertakers perform tasks that most of us would not want to carry out ourselves. We do not question the industry's right to honest profits; in a free enterprise system undertakers are entitled to operate profitable businesses. What we do question is the unreasonably high cost of funerals and burial. We also question the failure of many undertakers to provide consumers with explicit information, particularly price information, about goods and services and low-cost alternatives. Nor can we ignore the efforts of some undertakers, under a cloak of respectable professionalism, to exploit people when they are most vulnerable.

Citing a "compelling need" for intervention, the Federal Trade Commission in 1972 began an investigation into the funeral industry that resulted almost three years later in a proposed trade regulation rule. The FTC pointed to widespread abuses in the industry, and put forward a number of requirements and regulations for funeral homes that would make possible less expensive funerals and more informed choices for consumers. Consumers Union supported the FTC proposed rule in general, although, in detailed comments about the rule submitted to the commission, we also expressed reservations about some provisions and suggested alternatives to others. The funeral industry's resistance to the FTC proposed rule has been strenuous, as expected, and it will be some time—if ever—before the rule is fully effective. But even if the rule is eventually implemented and enforced, there will still be a need for consumers to have a clear idea of what to expect when arranging for a funeral and burial or other disposition.

Indeed, if there can be said to be an underlying theme in *Consumer Reports* and other Consumers Union publications, it is: Be informed. Even when appropriate governmental regulation exists, the consumer still must be knowledgeable. This is especially true in the funeral marketplace. There, where shock and grief abound and judgment often falters, there is no better protection for the consumer than knowledge.

Part I

The American Funeral: An Overview

1
The High Cost
of Funerals and Burial

Charles A. Lindbergh displayed the same foresight and determination in matters of death that he had shown in life. Only days before he died of cancer on August 26, 1974, he planned all the details of his own funeral. Informed by his doctors at New York City's Columbia-Presbyterian Medical Center that death was imminent, Lindbergh asked to be flown to his home on the island of Maui in Hawaii. There, he made careful arrangements for his funeral and burial. He asked that Hawaiian cowboys, employed on nearby cattle ranches, construct a roughhewn coffin out of eucalyptus wood and that his body be dressed in ordinary work clothes. At his request, the pallbearers also wore simple work clothes. A few hours after his death, Lindbergh was buried in a grave on a cliff overlooking the Pacific, and a brief, simple prayer he had helped to compose was read at the graveside.

Lindbergh's desire to work out the details of his own funeral and burial is rare in the annals of the American way of death. Most people find it difficult to contemplate the reality of dying,* let alone arrange the particulars of their own funeral and burial. Although Americans in recent years have begun to discuss and write about death more openly and realistically, many psychiatrists, sociologists, and members of the clergy believe

---

*Robert J. Kastenbaum, superintendent of Cushing Hospital in Framingham, Massachusetts, told Consumers Union of an experiment he had conducted at the hospital in 1968. Twenty-one mature women, divided into three groups, were asked to come to the hospital on several occasions to interview a patient. Although the man appeared healthy, he was presented to them as a hospital outpatient needing a diagnostic work-up. When women in two of the three groups (the third was a control group) were informed before a visit with the patient that his condition was uncertain, they reacted warmly to him. When, however, prior to another visit, they were told that the patient had been diagnosed as terminally ill, they avoided eye contact with the "dying" patient and found it difficult to communicate with him. Even those who had previously expressed open attitudes toward dying found it difficult to cope with a person they believed did not have long to live.

15

that people generally have a long way to go in accepting death—their own and that of others. It is one thing to consider death in the abstract, they point out; it is another to come to terms with it and even to plan for it. Few Americans are ever prepared emotionally for death.

Lindbergh, by keeping his funeral and burial as simple as possible, arranged for services that were in stark contrast with those of the conventional American funeral and burial. Lindbergh, of course, did not need to worry about an expensive funeral and burial imposing a financial burden on his family. Most Americans, however, are not that fortunate; yet many pay little attention to costs when they arrange for a loved one's funeral. They seem to think that money is not a proper concern at such a time. Perhaps the closest some people come to providing for funeral (and burial) expenses is by purchasing a life insurance policy. For others, the problem of such costs has no immediacy, presenting itself as a vague, remote expense belonging in the far-off future. They are too concerned with day-to-day economic problems to think ahead about expenses connected with death. Yet nearly 2 million people die in the United States every year, and their deaths affect millions of others, both emotionally and economically.

It is a reality of American life that for many people the cost of buying a funeral and burial for a family member is one of the largest single expenses a family will have to bear, exceeded only by the cost of a house, a car, a college education, and (perhaps) a catastrophic illness. For low-income consumers, payment of funeral and burial costs may be the largest expenditure they will ever have to cope with—often a financial disaster that can result in years of economic hardship. Among low-income people, the elderly are especially vulnerable. Of the nearly 2 million Americans who died in 1975, almost 1.25 million were sixty-five and over, according to the National Center for Health Statistics. In 1975, the median income for families whose heads were sixty-five and older was less than three-fifths that for all families. Living on fixed incomes, with few financial reserves, most older citizens are in no position to pay costly funeral and burial expenses for a spouse or other family member.

The case of a seventy-nine-year-old Pittsburgh woman was reported in 1972. Although her annual income was only $1,892 from Social Security benefits and interest on a small savings account, it cost "Mrs. J." $2,263 to bury her husband. Because Mrs. J. had requested a "modest" funeral, the undertaker gave her a discount of $57 on the $1,600 funeral home price. But he stipulated that to get the discount she would have to pay the bill by a certain date. "He told me that was the best he could do for me," she said. "I made inquiries at other funeral homes and they said it was very reasonable." In addition to the funeral home costs, she paid $150 for a burial plot and $570 for a headstone.

For those with only marginal financial security, funeral and burial costs can drastically affect the quality of life: A house may have to be sold; a young person may have to go to work instead of to college; life savings may be wiped out and large debts incurred.

Such devastating financial hardships are not ordinarily associated with other large consumer expenditures. Why is it, then, that funeral and burial costs can be so economically ruinous for so many people? One reason is that the majority of survivors are likely to be those least able to afford major expenses: the elderly, and widows and children who, in many cases, have lost the family's main wage earner.

Lack of time, too, may force survivors to make hasty and costly decisions. Most funeral buyers have little choice in making the purchase, for they find themselves facing a crisis that requires prompt resolution. Unlike other large purchases, which can be made after some thought and preparation (including, perhaps, comparison shopping), a funeral and burial are not usually planned for, and decisions typically must be made within a matter of hours.

Another explanation for the high cost of funerals and burial can be found in the unique nature of the transaction. In no other situation involving a major purchase is the buyer in such a vulnerable condition. Stress, shock, and even moments of irrationality, as well as the pressure of time and the lack of knowledge about the goods and services offered, can severely affect judgment. All too often, survivors rely entirely on the undertaker's opinions and let the undertaker make the decisions.

When prospective buyers look at a house or a car, it is possible for them to compare prices and talk over alternatives with different sellers. Usually, there is some knowledge of or familiarity with the items for sale. But most people are unfamiliar with the prices of funeral goods and services* and with cemetery costs. In transacting everyday business, consumers are usually not in an abnormal emotional state. With survivors, however, grief and, often, guilt may play an important part in the purchase of a funeral and burial, and these emotions may contribute to overspending.

The conventional American funeral—with open coffin and viewing of the body for two or three days—requires a number of purchases of funeral services and merchandise from undertakers. And the survivors of about 75 percent of those who die choose the conventional American funeral. The majority of survivors seem to agree with undertakers that a funeral with

---

*Members of a research project, undertaken in 1974 by the New York State College of Human Ecology, Cornell University, interviewed 489 adults living in both urban and rural areas of central New York State about funerals and found most of them uninformed. "Most respondents had attended more than ten funerals; yet less than half had ever made arrangements for a funeral. Urban and rural respondents of all ages and levels of education showed little knowledge of the laws, practices or pricing policies of the funeral industry."

the body present and an open coffin is the best way to pay tribute to the dead,* even though such a funeral may be financially prohibitive for some.

But Are Funeral Costs Too High?

Undertakers maintain that they do not charge too much for funerals, although they concede that in the funeral industry, as in every field, there may be a few unscrupulous practitioners. Industry members point out that a huge financial investment is required to maintain a funeral establishment. (The U.S. Department of Commerce noted in 1975 that investment in facilities and equipment can range from about $120,000 for a firm conducting fewer than a hundred funerals a year to more than $600,000 for one with more than three hundred funerals a year.) Spacious facilities—including visitation rooms and, often, a chapel—a site in a populated area where land can be expensive, parking accommodations, trained personnel, and expensive equipment such as hearses and limousines all contribute to high overhead expenses. In addition, staff, equipment, and premises usually have to be available twenty-four hours a day.

A brochure distributed by a chain of New Orleans funeral homes in 1976 stressed the high operating costs necessary to maintain a funeral establishment:

> A funeral home must be constructed to handle a "maximum requirement." That is, it must be able to accommodate the largest predictable number of possible arrangements. To put it bluntly, "people can't wait in line" when they need the services of a funeral director and a funeral home. In this sense, a funeral home is similar to a hospital. The result is a facility that can seldom be used to capacity, but one which must be air conditioned, heated, furnished, and maintained as though it were.

It has been estimated that a funeral home staff spends roughly seventy to eighty hours arranging for and conducting a funeral. Undertakers say they perform between sixty and ninety different functions for each funeral. An undertaker in Yonkers, New York, pointed out in 1976 that the personnel in his establishment included a manager, several undertakers providing twenty-four-hour service, receptionists, and office workers. "The overhead is very high," he said. "If there were really big money in funeral homes, less desirable people would soon be in the business."

In spite of the unique and essential services they provide, undertakers do not earn high profits for funerals, according to the largest trade association, the National Funeral Directors Association (NFDA).** The average

---

*A 1974 survey for the Casket Manufacturers Association of America found that more than 80 percent of the 1,060 respondents believed that "the casket should be open during calling hours."

**The NFDA has a membership of about 14,000. The next two largest trade associations are the Federated Funeral Directors of America with 1,100 members and National Selected Morticians with about 860 members. Smaller trade associations include the

profit per funeral in 1975, according to NFDA statistics, was $53 (or 3.5 percent of operating income) before income taxes. Federated Funeral Directors of America (FFDA), another trade association, said that the average profit per adult funeral (see page 25) in 1975 was about $168 (or 12.3 percent of the average sale) before income taxes. National Selected Morticians (NSM), a third trade association, said the average profit for funerals in 1975 was $44 (or 3.8 percent of the average retail sale) before income taxes. Both the NFDA and NSM state that between 1967 and 1975 the increase in funeral prices was well below the rise in the general cost of living, even though taxes, fuel, utilities, wages, repairs, and other costs steadily increased. According to the NSM, "Profit percentages for the funeral director have not increased in that period, but the cost of doing business has greatly multiplied." Few other business enterprises, the NSM says, "derive such a low profit margin compared with the total amount of investment required to equip, maintain and operate a modern funeral firm." (It must be noted, however, that other measures of profitability, such as return on equity or return on investment, may be more relevant. It is not possible to calculate these from available data.)

Furthermore, the funeral industry claims that the recession of the early 1970s, high unemployment levels, and generally tight money conditions caused delays in customers' payment of funeral bills. According to the NFDA, only 2 or 3 percent of all survivors pay the total bill at the time the funeral is arranged. Because it takes an average of forty-five days for survivors to collect insurance or liquidate assets, funeral homes say they have to wait at least that long for settlement of their funeral bills.

It is one thing to "document" high operating costs to justify high prices; more difficult is the question of what constitutes a fair price for disposing of the dead. Undertakers view their role as indispensable since they provide a service for society that few people want to perform themselves. Thus, providing a funeral cannot be described as a normal business transaction. Not many people realize, undertakers say, the kind of special services they are called upon to perform, services for which there can be no price tag: preparing for burial the maimed, often mutilated bodies of suicides, accident and disaster victims, and those who have died from disfiguring illnesses. Undertakers also perform another civic service, they point out, when they provide funerals for welfare and charity cases and for the indigent for far less money than is charged for the average funeral—often at a financial loss. And undertakers maintain they offer other benefits to survivors: They extend credit for some funeral and burial costs, and they counsel the bereaved.

It is problematical, according to many funeral industry representatives

National Funeral Directors and Morticians Association (with a mostly black membership) and the Jewish Funeral Directors of America.

and consultants, whether one can even estimate the monetary worth of a funeral. If an expensive ceremony is what survivors want, if it fulfills deep needs, who can say that it costs too much?

Two sociologists (one of whom is also an undertaker) concluded in a 1970 study of funeral expenditures in a small Northeastern college town that the amount of money spent on a funeral was not just the "mere exchange of cash between two agents" but a "secular ritual" that assumed significance because it displaced "diminishing ceremonial observances for the dead." In other words, high expenditures for funerals represent *"a secular and economic ritual of payment formerly performed by more religious customs and ceremonies."* (Authors' emphasis.) The sociologists added:

> Our view is that *because* people increasingly lack both the ceremonial and social mechanisms and arrangements that once existed to help them cope with death, monetary expenditures have taken on added importance as a means for allowing the bereaved to express (both to themselves and others) their sentiments for the deceased. For with so few modes of expression remaining to the bereaved, funeral expenditures serve as evidence of their concern for both the dead and the conventional standards of decency in their community of residence.

Edgar Jackson, a minister whose writings about grief and funerals are widely distributed by the NFDA (he is an unpaid consultant), pointed out in his book *For the Living* that it is wrong to judge whether funerals are good or bad on the basis of how much money is spent. Ceremony is important to human beings, he noted. If survivors gain personal satisfaction from elaborate funerals, who can judge their choice? Jackson wrote:

> A man and woman can be just as legally married by obtaining a license and having a justice of the peace mutter a few words, yet few people are satisfied with that. They choose instead to spend hundreds or even thousands of dollars that might otherwise be invested or used for furnishing the home to have a big wedding with many friends in attendance, a gay reception with an expensive dinner and flowers, gowns, and much, much more. They take pictures of it so that they will never forget this wonderful moment. None of this wedding ceremony is legally necessary, but it serves an important purpose in the lives of the participants. They seek to surround a most important event in their life with all the meaning, dignity, tradition and joy they can employ.

If survivors have to go into debt to pay for funerals, according to Jackson, then they are merely following a widespread American practice. Every year, he said, Americans go into debt for billions of dollars to buy cars, homes, appliances, and vacations. As for funerals, Jackson added:

> The important matter to be considered here is not so much the matter of the incurring of the debt itself as what can be done to help persons effectively meet the crises of their lives. If debt is an aid in doing that, the debt may be good. If it becomes a deeply depressing burden, then it is not good.

20

Clearly, many funeral buyers are indeed willing to go into debt to obtain the kind of funeral they want. A number of people do choose elaborate and expensive funeral services. But one wonders if as many people would choose costly funerals if simple and inexpensive alternatives were readily available. It is still quite difficult to obtain a low-cost funeral in many areas of the United States today.

At the heart of the problem is a startling phenomenon: There is an oversupply of funeral homes. With a relatively inelastic market, the country has almost ten times the number of funeral establishments it needs, according to some students of the funeral business. At present there are about 22,500 funeral homes;* yet some estimate that approximately 2,500 firms could handle the total number of funerals held each year. Testifying in 1964 at Senate subcommittee hearings on the funeral industry, the late Wilber Krieger, NSM managing director, said that "2,500 firms operating multiunit establishments strategically located could serve the demand."

A total of nearly 2 million deaths annually works out to an average of about eighty-eight services per funeral establishment, but the actual distribution of funeral home clients falls in an uneven pattern. Some large funeral home chains have an annual business of thousands of funerals. Other, smaller establishments (and there are many of these throughout the country) handle fewer than twenty-five. Half of all funeral homes arrange about sixty funerals a year, averaging a little more than one a week.

How do the marginal operators survive? Do they advertise lower prices in an attempt to compete against the large firms? On the contrary, competitive price advertising is not common within the funeral industry. The majority in the industry long regarded price advertising as unethical. Indeed, the NFDA Code of Ethics until recently provided that all members "refrain from price advertising." Howard Raether, executive director of the NFDA, addressing a 1963 NFDA conference, noted: "Funeral directors are colleagues, not competitors, and should be viewed as such within the profession. . . . The use of competitive weapons weakens the entire structure of the profession, as benefits are sought by a few to the detriment of many."

Raether has pointed out that nothing is gained by funeral establishments when they advertise: Advertising "does not create new markets or expand old ones." At best, he has stated, it only "shifts" the market or helps some firms maintain their portion of it. There is more than one NFDA member in most communities, according to Raether. "How can [the NFDA] comply with the objectives of its constitution and safeguard the common interests of its members by fostering competitive weapons?"

The NFDA maintains that if firms, seeking to gain more customers,

*The precise number of funeral establishments is difficult to ascertain. The 22,500 figure is most frequently cited. The U.S. Department of Commerce says that there were 20,854 funeral home locations in 1972 (the latest date for which statistics are available).

advertise reduced prices, a price war could result. Many in the funeral business greatly fear such a possibility, believing it would decimate the industry. Thus, recognizing their common interest—survival for all—undertakers generally do not use price advertising to compete against each other. This does not mean that each funeral home is not eager to attract a high volume of business. Nor does it mean that all establishments charge the same prices for funerals. There is, in fact, a wide disparity in funeral prices, which leads critics of the industry to question exactly how funeral prices are arrived at. But because most funeral establishments do not routinely advertise prices, consumers usually have little idea of what funerals can cost.

A 1973 Federal Trade Commission (FTC) funeral price survey* of funeral homes in Washington, D.C., noted that a "shroud of secrecy" has been thrown over funeral prices by the funeral industry. In 1974, the New York Public Interest Research Group (NYPIRG), a statewide consumer research and advocacy organization, came to the same conclusion. NYPIRG conducted a telephone survey** of sixty funeral homes, twenty cemeteries, and four crematories in the New York City area to obtain price information about funerals and burial. Almost two-thirds of the funeral homes refused to give prices over the phone or were generally uncooperative, according to NYPIRG. (All the cemetery representatives, however, were willing to give price information over the phone.)

Many undertakers maintain that each funeral is unique with its own requirements, so that exact prices can be quoted to consumers only when they are actually arranging for a specific funeral service. Any other form of price disclosure is generally looked upon by the funeral industry as advertising.

Locked in an industry that tends to be noncompetitive and overcrowd-

---

*The results of the Washington funeral home survey, carried out in October and December 1973, were published by the FTC under the title *FTC Survey of Funeral Prices in the District of Columbia.* The survey, which included a limited survey of burial costs as well, was part of a larger ongoing investigation, begun by the FTC Bureau of Consumer Protection in 1972, into funeral industry practices and consumer abuses. After several months of inquiry, the Bureau submitted to the commission a staff memorandum entitled Unfair Practices in the Funeral Industry: A Planning Report to the Federal Trade Commission. This unpublished report was to form part of the basis for the FTC's proposed trade regulation rule—a rule intended to offer greater consumer protection and to bring about sweeping changes in American funeral practices. The proposed FTC rule, the culmination of nearly three years of investigation, was published by the FTC in August 1975 under the title *Funeral Industry Practices: Proposed Trade Regulation Rule and Staff Memorandum.* Thereafter, public hearings were held by the FTC in major cities throughout the country, at which people and organizations interested in the proposed rule presented testimony, both written and oral. The public proceedings were held between April and July 1976 in New York, Chicago, Seattle, Los Angeles, Atlanta, and Washington. The FTC presiding officer reported his findings in July 1977, based on the proceedings as well as written testimony. He suggested no substantial changes in the proposed rule and recommended that the FTC proceed with its promulgation.

**The results were published in the pamphlet "A Death in the Family."

ed (in some sections of the country), and limited to a market that expands very little if at all, many undertakers who have analyzed the economics of their trade have begun to think in terms of expanding their services in order to increase their income. That way they can continue to raise prices and to realize a profit by selling consumers increasingly luxurious and expensive goods and more and more elaborate and costly professional services (such as "grief counseling"). On the other hand, some undertakers look to a volume business as the key to higher profits. To attract clients they prefer to experiment with low-cost package funerals and price advertising.

The Puzzle of Funeral Industry Statistics

There is some question about how increases in funeral prices in recent years compare with changes in the general cost of living. As mentioned earlier, funeral industry representatives claim that price increases for funerals were well below those in other sectors of the economy. They cite Bureau of Labor Statistics data,* which show that whereas the Consumer Price Index in 1975 had risen 67.1 percent since 1967, funeral home prices for adult funerals rose only 48.3 percent during that period.

Annual statistics obtained in NFDA surveys of funeral homes show a somewhat similar pattern. Compiling average prices based on the funerals selected at all the reporting firms each year,** the NFDA noted that while an average adult funeral in 1967 cost $850, it cost $1,285 in 1975, an increase of 51.2 percent. Howard Raether has pointed out, however, that because of the nature of the NFDA survey, there is no way to ascertain whether the average adult funeral in 1967 included the same components or used precisely the same goods and services as the average adult funeral in 1975. In any case, none of these figures necessarily tells the whole story about actual total sales rung up by the funeral industry.

Getting the whole story about funeral industry sales is not easy, despite the fact that two major government departments—Commerce and Labor—publish statistics concerning funerals and the funeral business. Both departments rely heavily on trade associations and individual funeral establishments for their information. The U.S. Department of Commerce, for example, makes extensive use of NFDA data in its presentation on the funeral industry in *U.S. Industrial Outlook,* a yearly publication. The Bureau of Labor Statistics gets its data directly from the funeral industry when it computes the Consumer Price Index and collects other statistics about the

---

*The Bureau of Labor Statistics surveys a relatively small sampling of specific funeral homes in fifty-six areas of the country for price information on a year-round basis. In larger cities, such as Chicago, Los Angeles, and New York, it uses about eight price quotations; in smaller cities, about three or four.

**In 1975, the NFDA received completed questionnaires from 1,148 firms, which reported on a total of 151,942 funerals.

industry. Critics question the validity and comprehensiveness of statistics provided by the funeral industry. Indeed, the FTC has said that statistics supplied by the NFDA may not be complete or completely accurate.

The sketchiness of industry and government statistics seems to be borne out by data from independent surveys and reports. These tend to reflect generally higher sales than the figures published by government agencies.* The specific components of the annual figures released by Commerce and Labor further invite skepticism. They give but a skeletal picture of the actual dimensions of the funeral industry. What's more, even the limited number of expenditures for goods and services that are included in the data are not defined in consistent fashion.**

The crucial omissions from Commerce and Labor statistics on the funeral industry suggest that the American public is not being informed about how much it actually spends each year on funeral goods and services. It is certainly clear that total expenditures listed by Commerce and Labor for the funeral industry in any given year do not tell the whole story. Cemetery costs, for instance, often come to $600 to $800 for one burial. Yet the government does not appear to collect separate data for these expenses. The Department of Commerce considers cemetery plots a form of real estate that does not properly belong under funeral costs. Commerce

*For example, in 1973, the Department of Commerce said that expenditures for "funeral service" were approximately $2.472 billion. According to other sources, this figure fell far short of the actual amount of funeral industry sales. This is understandable, since Commerce's figures did not include such crucial items as cemetery costs. In 1974, *Media & Consumer*, a now-defunct consumer journalism review, taking cemetery expenditures into account, came up with total industry sales for 1973 of more than $4 billion. The sales breakdown:

Funeral homes	$1.6 billion
Florists	800 million
Cemeteries	739 million
Monuments	450 million
Coffins	354 million
Vaults	305 million
	$4.2 billion

**The Department of Commerce says that expenditures in 1975 for "funeral services and crematories" (projected at $2.830 billion) cover some of the goods and services provided by "establishments primarily engaged in preparing the dead for burial, conducting funerals, and cremating the dead." Not included by Commerce are charges for vaults and other coffin enclosures, certain cemetery costs, and a few cash-advance items (see Chapter 12), such as newspaper notices and clergy's honoraria—items that funeral buyers frequently want. To make matters worse, the Commerce total specifically excludes receipts from crematories operated in conjunction with cemeteries; such crematories represent about 80 percent of those in the United States.

The Department of Labor, in its Consumer Price Index for funeral services, defines expenditures its data cover as follows: "Fee for a regular adult funeral service, including the cost of the casket; professional and staff service; preparation and casketing of body; and use of funeral home and other facilities." Excluded are the price of vaults and other coffin enclosures, cemetery charges, and cash-advance items, as well as crematory costs.

also points out that many plots are purchased years before need and cannot accurately be listed as an expenditure for the year in which death occurs. But what of other cemetery costs? The Department's Bureau of Domestic Commerce, which compiles funeral data, concedes that funeral and burial cost statistics are hard to obtain and that the various categories and classes of services are not clearly defined. Commerce hopes that, after the 1977 census, statistics will be more complete and more clearly categorized. Maybe then consumers will finally be given a firm statistical basis on which to assess how much is actually spent on funerals and burial in the United States each year.

How Much Does a Funeral Cost?

One of the most frequently cited sources for funeral costs is *Facts and Figures*, an annual statistical study of funeral home income and expense data, published by the NFDA. This survey is based on responses to a questionnaire sent every year to NFDA funeral establishments; the findings are prepared by a "research and analysis consultant."* Critics of the funeral industry question the funeral price figures published in *Facts and Figures*, claiming they are too low and not a true reflection of actual funeral prices. The low figures might be partly explained by the size of the firms that respond to the NFDA questionnaire. According to the 1976 *Facts and Figures*, "there is a slight over-representation of firms conducting a large number of services." Because of this over-representation of larger firms, which tend to charge somewhat less than smaller establishments, the overall statistical results may be affected. With this pattern of response, according to the FTC, "the NFDA has a built-in tendency to underestimate the true costs."

In 1975, according to the NFDA, the average charge for all types of funerals was $1,127. This figure included the 18.68 percent of services conducted for welfare recipients and for children as well as "partial-adult services."**

As noted earlier, an average total-adult funeral (with "adult" defined as those over fifteen years of age, because of the size of coffin required), including standard funeral services, cost $1,285 in 1975, according to the NFDA.

---

*The 1976 survey and those for the five previous years were prepared by Vanderlyn Pine, Ph.D., a sociologist. Pine, who is also an undertaker, is the author and editor of several books distributed by the NFDA.

**A "partial-adult" funeral is one in which no single funeral home provides the total goods and services for a funeral. For example, if a person dies outside his or her community and the body is returned to that community, the undertaker in the area where death occurred might embalm the body, provide a coffin, and accompany the deceased to the point of departure. The undertaker who receives the body in the decedent's community may then make all remaining arrangements for the funeral. Neither undertaker has provided an entire funeral.

Approximately 81 percent of all those who die in the United States are given a "total-adult funeral."

From the consumer's viewpoint, the NFDA figure may be misleading on two counts. First, the $1,285 figure represents what the undertaker charges for only the standard, basic goods and services provided by the funeral home—what is described in many mortuaries as a "complete" funeral (see page 33). Not included is what consumers may pay for vault, flowers, burial clothing, newspaper notices, clergy's honorarium, and transportation of the body to another community. In addition, there are crematory or cemetery costs (grave plot, opening and closing the grave, monument or marker). Thus, the actual total price that most consumers pay for the entire funeral and burial process is much more than funeral industry statistics indicate.

Other sources list higher costs than the NFDA's figures. A Veterans Administration price survey in 1972 of eight regional offices "indicated that the average funeral cost 'for veterans' had increased to approximately $1,300," cemetery expenses not included. In 1973, the secretary of the New Jersey State Board of Mortuary Science reported that the average cost of a funeral in that state was $1,500 to $1,600, exclusive of cemetery charges, which ranged from $100 to $800. The FTC investigation of the funeral industry (see footnote, page 22) has stated that the average adult funeral and burial in the United States cost close to $2,000.°

°In its 1973 survey of Washington, D.C., funeral homes, the FTC found the total price of a "typical" funeral and burial to be $1,886. The FTC noted that this figure was "in general accord with a number of other cost studies and estimates from around the country." In listing "typical," or standard, funeral and cemetery expenses, the FTC noted that all the "extra" expenses it included (items in addition to such standard goods and services as the coffin, embalming, etc., which are covered in the "complete" price) were chosen by the majority of funeral buyers, although hundreds of consumers chose in addition— or exclusively—other extras not included, such as burial clothing, hired pallbearers, a nurse, a hairdresser for the deceased, flowers, and an extra limousine. The FTC breakdown:

"Complete" adult funeral	$1,137
Interment receptacle (vault or grave liner)	136
Newspaper death notice	20
Clergy's honorarium	15
Transcripts of death certificates	5
Flower wagon	25
Organist	15
Single grave site	160
Opening and closing of grave	150
Marker or monument	178
Washington, D.C., sales tax	45
	$1,886

Some of the typical costs that make up the nearly $1,900 total are fairly low, so the FTC figure may be considered a conservative estimate.

In 1973, a Washington, D.C., management consultant firm conducted an extensive study of private funeral and burial costs for the Veterans Administration. The total average expense for a funeral and burial, it found, was $1,907. The management consultants took regional differences into consideration and divided the United States into five major regions. They further broke down costs into urban and rural-suburban groups. Their findings for average funeral and burial costs per death included:

	Urban	Rural and Suburban
Northeast	$2,350	$2,165
Southeast	2,120	1,806
Midwest	1,690	1,788
Central West	1,764	1,666
Far West	2,154	1,214°

In 1976, the Federated Funeral Directors of America reported on the results of its survey of 1975 funeral costs for 113,000 funerals conducted in seventeen Midwestern and Eastern states. The total or gross cost to the consumer of the average adult funeral, the FFDA said, was $1,899.11, exclusive of cemetery or crematory costs. However, it considered $1,369.75 to be the average 1975 funeral home price for a typical "complete" adult funeral. It arrived at this figure by deducting $209.39 for cash-advance items (such as flowers, clergy's honorarium, and newspaper notices), which it defined as nonprofit items,°° and an additional $319.97 for vault or other coffin enclosure, extra cars, clothing, and so on, which the FFDA did not consider to be components of a typical "complete" adult funeral.†

Rising Prices

Indications are that funeral and burial costs will keep rising, since inflation affects the funeral and cemetery industries, too. The Department of Commerce estimates that funeral home and crematory costs will increase at an average annual rate of 8.5 percent between 1975 and 1985. Coffin manufacturers have warned that the prices of steel, hardwood, and softwood are increasing drastically and that there will be "runaway inflation" for the raw materials needed to construct coffins "for years to come."†† A

°Average costs for the Far West were the lowest because the region has the nation's highest number of cremations—approximately 20 percent of the annual total. Cremation generally costs less than burial.

°°For a discussion of profits on cash-advance items, see Chapter 12.

†The FFDA noted that the cost of an average adult funeral has more than doubled since 1955, although the funeral home's net profit has "moderately" declined. The adult funeral that cost $1,369.75 in 1975 cost $643.16 in 1955 and $849.76 in 1965. And, says the FFDA, whereas in 1965 only one client out of fifty purchased a funeral over $1,500, in 1976 nearly one out of three funerals cost more than $1,500.

††In 1977, the Casket Manufacturers Association of America estimated that cost increases for labor, energy, and shipping would contribute to further coffin price increases.

Long Island undertaker stated in 1975 that before long he expected coffin manufacturers to ship their products with suggested retail prices on them, as automobile manufacturers do. "When that happens," he said, "we will have to increase our funeral arrangement charges. We try our best to keep prices down, but with your casket manufacturers you have three unions to contend with, and we get three increases a year." Cemetery costs have also gone up sharply in recent years. And the cost of labor continues to rise. On the basis of such trends, it seems safe to predict that by 1980 the charge for an average adult funeral and burial in the United States will amount to more than $2,500.

Yet many American funeral buyers will never have a clear idea of why they are paying the price they do for a funeral and burial. Because of the price-quotation methods used in many funeral establishments, purchasers are frequently not told the precise costs of many goods and services they choose. There are no standard prices for goods and labor such as those found in other industries. What's more, goods and services included in one mortuary's "complete" funeral figure may be considered extras in another's. The same coffin can vary in price from firm to firm and sometimes even from customer to customer within the same funeral home. And prices differ greatly in geographic areas as well as with different funeral establishments.

The late Wilber Krieger, when NSM managing director, made this point: "You can bring ten or 1,000 funeral directors together, give them all the same set of cost factors, and probably no two of them will arrive at the same selling price. Neither will they follow the same procedure in reaching their respective selling prices."

These inconsistencies have created widespread suspicion among investigators that the price quoted by a funeral home, more often than not, is geared to the individual funeral buyer and to whatever money is available or can be found—in short, to what the traffic will bear.*

---

*Insurance companies and labor unions have long complained that as soon as death benefits rise, so do beneficiaries' funeral costs. Testifying before 1964 Senate subcommittee hearings on the funeral industry, Harry Haskel, director of the Death Benefit Department of the International Ladies' Garment Workers' Union (ILGWU), noted: "At the fund's inception in 1937 the death benefit was $150 but it was raised to $500 in 1947 and to $1,000 in 1950 in the expectation that it would be sufficient not only for funeral expenses but also to help meet, in part at least, the cost of a plot or a headstone or to take care of an unpaid medical bill or help toward the support of a minor child. However, each successive increase in the death benefit paid by our union was invariably followed by increases in funeral charges which have now practically absorbed the entire death benefit."

This dilemma continues for the ILGWU. According to the union's Death Benefit Department, well over half the decedents in 1972 (the latest year for which data were compiled) had only $1,000 in ILGWU death benefits. Yet the average cost of a union member's funeral that year was $1,378, exclusive of cemetery expenses and transportation.

Funeral Home Pricing Methods

How do funeral establishments set prices for funerals? In a study of funeral pricing for the NSM in 1974, Alfred Rappaport, an accounting professor at Northwestern University, distinguished between funeral "pricing" and "quotation." Pricing, he said, is the means or method by which prices are established by the funeral home. Quotation is the method used to communicate prices to the consumer.

There are two basic approaches to the pricing of funerals. With the first—the "average-overhead-per-funeral" method—each funeral is expected to recover a share of out-of-pocket expenses, a constant dollar share of the fixed expenses, or overhead, and to contribute a percentage to the business's profit. With the second method, called "graduated recovery," the undertaker develops a pricing structure in which expected total revenues of all funerals cover costs plus overhead and profit. Under this method, each single funeral is not expected to yield uniform cost recovery and profit contribution. Rather, the proportion of costs and overhead is graduated at each funeral price level. Thus, a low-cost funeral is not expected to recover an average cost and overhead amount; an expensive funeral is priced to compensate for that.

In 1975, according to the NFDA's *Facts and Figures*, the average operating expenses for a funeral (including child, partial-adult, welfare, and total-adult services) was $960. For total-adult services, including welfare, average operating expenses were $1,073. (See table, next page.) The FFDA says the average operating expense allocated to each adult service in 1975 was $948. Yet the range of costs leading to these average figures is not identified. Thus there is no way of knowing what the precise operating costs for a $500 funeral are when compared with those for a $1,500 funeral.

Some observers of the funeral industry believe that overhead costs cited in industry surveys are too high. In 1966, in an article on funeral industry pricing based on his doctoral thesis, Roger Blackwell suggested that "the industry may be operating at price levels which are based upon the cost curves of the many small firms rather than upon the cost curves of large firms which can spread overhead costs over large volume."* Many smaller firms, with a low volume of business, are inefficient in the sense that although labor and equipment must always be available, the funeral homes are not in constant use. Blackwell calls this "excess capacity" and notes that

---

*For example, two giant funeral home conglomerates, Service Corporation International and International Funeral Services, each of which owns more than a hundred funeral establishments, draw on a central pool of services in cities where they own more than one funeral home. Teams of embalmers, undertakers, chauffeurs, and salespeople are sent where they are needed, and a fleet of funeral coaches supplies transportation. This arrangement allows the organizations to serve, say, six funeral homes with only twice the number of cars they would need for one firm. A central telephone takes calls at night.

HOW THE FUNERAL INDUSTRY
CLASSIFIES OPERATING EXPENSES

The NFDA breaks down funeral service expenses into eight major classifications and lists operating expenses for total-adult funerals in 1975 as follows:

Personnel	$ 513	47.8%
Facilities and Equipment	186	17.3
Automobile	93	8.7
General	92	8.6
Taxes	68	6.3
Direct Funeral Expenses	50	4.7
Promotion	47	4.4
Collection (collection agency and attorney fees for collecting overdue accounts, losses on uncollectable accounts, and discounts allowed on accounts)	24	2.2
	$1,073	100.0%

The FFDA breaks down operating expenses for an average adult funeral in 1975 as follows:

Salaries	$444.34	46.9%
Funeral Home and Facilities	364.83	38.5
Promotion	62.52	6.6
Supplies	27.84	2.9
Business Service (postage, office supplies, legal fees)	27.78	2.9
Sales (bad debts, discounts on sales)	15.86	1.7
Miscellaneous	4.94	.5
	$948.11	100.0%

The NSM breaks down average operating expenses for a funeral in 1975 in percentage terms only:

Salary Expense	36.5%
Cost of Funeral Artifacts	18.9
Administrative and Operating Expense	18.7
Building Occupancy Expense	11.0
Automobile Expense	5.5
Profit before Income Tax	4.9
Advertising Expense	4.5
	100.0%

"in other industries, the incentive to absorb excess capacity would normally stimulate the use of highly competitive marketing tactics in order to enlarge the market share held by an individual firm." Since funeral establishments do not aggressively compete with each other, their excess capacity leads to higher costs for funeral merchandise and services. (Blackwell has since served as a consultant to the NFDA and the Casket Manufacturers Association of America.)

When undertakers quote funeral prices to consumers, they use one of two basic methods to communicate costs: (1) the unit approach, or (2) the fragmented approach. (See Chapter 10 for a discussion of unit pricing and methods of fragmented pricing.) With unit quotation, or "package pricing," as it is commonly known, the consumer pays a single price for all basic funeral home costs, including the coffin. Fragmented quotation is used under a variety of names. The bi-unit approach separates the cost of the coffin from all other charges. Tri-unit, or functional, pricing breaks down the funeral price into at least three categories: coffin, facilities, and standard services. Itemized pricing means that specific services and specific facilities, as well as the coffin and other goods, are priced separately.

2
Typical Adult Funeral and Burial

Some components of a conventional funeral may vary from undertaker to undertaker, but the usual standard items included in the price of a "complete" funeral are: removal of the body to the funeral establishment; use of funeral home facilities; embalming and restoration; dressing of remains; cost of coffin; use of hearse; various staff services; arranging for religious services, burial permit, death benefits, newspaper death notices; providing pallbearers (although the charge for their services is extra); arranging and care of flowers; providing guest register and acknowledgment cards; extension of credit.

But this list is far from inclusive. It covers only the standard goods and services of the funeral home and does not include, for example, a vault, which, especially when purchased from a funeral home, can be a major expenditure. Nor are such items as extra limousines, music, clergy's honorarium, flowers, burial clothing, and taxes included. The costs of burial, too, frequently add hundreds of dollars to the funeral bill. Often it is the undertaker who sells the vault (if one is to be used), assists survivors with the purchase of a cemetery plot, and arranges with the cemetery for the opening and closing of the grave. In effect, these matters become a form of cash-advance items, billed through the undertaker, who is then reimbursed by the survivors.

During the past ten years, charges for the undertaker's professional services have been increasing—part of a trend within the industry to shift emphasis away from funeral merchandise to the undertaker's services. Charges for "professional" or "administrative" services vary from funeral home to funeral home, but they can cost hundreds of dollars. Testifying before a New York State legislative hearing on the funeral industry in 1975, the president of a union representing 300 licensed embalmers in New York City stated that $450 was a fair median figure in the city for "professional services," but that "$825 is not an unheard-of-price." Like doctors' and lawyers' fees, such charges are decided at the discretion of the funeral home providing the service.

Apart from this arbitrary fee (about which consumers may have little say), the price of a typical adult funeral and burial is based on these five major components: coffin, embalming, extras, vault, and cemetery.

Coffin. The most crucial moment of a funeral transaction comes with the choice of a coffin (see Chapter 10 for a detailed discussion of coffins). It is the single most important element in the cost of a conventional funeral because it almost always determines the overall cost. (Many other goods and services provided by the undertaker are the same in both expensive and inexpensive funerals.) In many funeral establishments, the price tag on the coffin represents the cost of a "complete" funeral. But that price tag may be deceiving, for usually the "complete" funeral is anything but complete. It may include the standard items listed above, but usually it does not include "extras," a vault, and, of course, burial or cremation. When the cost of those additional items is billed, it can come as quite a shock to survivors.

The most common method—the one used by about half the undertakers in the United States—of arriving at the figure for a "complete" funeral is "unit pricing" (or "package pricing"). The funeral is purchased as a unit for one lump sum, and the standard goods and services provided are included in the single package price. (Many undertakers prefer this form of pricing because they claim that funeral buyers are not well enough informed to choose among the various goods and services available.)

Often, unit pricing is based on the wholesale cost of the coffin. This amount is multiplied by the ratio of the dollar amount of a year's gross sales to the cost of a year's coffins, which is usually five-to-one (see page 78). The result is the price of the funeral.

This method of determining a funeral's price on the basis of coffin cost originated around the end of the nineteenth century. Furniture stores were then the retail suppliers of coffins. Coffin makers advised the furniture dealers "to mark up the wholesale cost of the casket three times—once to recover the cost of the casket, once to cover overhead, and once for profit." (In earlier times, cabinetmakers or carpenters built a coffin when death occurred; survivors then performed the burial services.)

But the sale of coffins began to be affected by the growth of cities in the early twentieth century: Cemeteries were established farther away from the community. Since neither survivors nor furniture dealers could readily transport coffins to cemeteries, those providing transportation began to play a role in burial ceremonies. After World War I, as homes became smaller and more city-dwellers lived in apartments, bodies were "laid out" less often in the home. Furniture dealers provided space in their stores or converted their premises or other buildings to undertaking establishments. The business of undertaking thus developed as tasks formerly carried out by people in different trades were unified into a single occupation. Gradually, undertakers took on other services, and, as embalming became more common, undertaking developed into a full-time business. In this new situation, the old "markup" value of the coffin changed. "The ratio of one to three," according to the NSM's Krieger, "became one to four or five, depending upon overhead costs, which were the biggest factor in changing the ratio."*

Specific pricing techniques may vary among undertakers (see pages 78-79), but the multiple of five remains a reasonably accurate index. With such a pricing system, it is to the advantage of undertakers, of course, to sell expensive coffins: The greater the cost of the coffin, the higher the profit. Coffin manufacturers also pressure funeral establishments to sell "quality" models and to keep them moving briskly.

Embalming. Second in importance only to the coffin, from the undertaker's point of view, is embalming (see Chapter 11), which makes possible the open coffin and the extra costs that go with a "viewable" body. Embalming is not usually a separate or deductible item in funerals. The procedure is generally performed routinely, and most funeral directors include it in the total cost whether or not it is actually done. (Sometimes, when survivors ask that embalming not be done, the funeral home will add a charge for "preservation," i.e., refrigeration—and that can cost survivors as much as embalming.)

Undertakers consider crucial the ritual viewing at the funeral home, and the additional costs this entails. They stress that a funeral with the body on view is not only part of tradition and religious heritage, but psychologically healthy as well. In a 1971 essay Howard Raether, of the NFDA, noted that mankind has been viewing its dead for centuries. But some people, he said, "want to deny the death which has occurred." Raether added:

> One method of disguising this reality is failing to have the body present during the period of the funeral or not viewing the remains if they are present.
> But it is essential to admit to death's presence. This can be a painful experience. It also can be a helpful and rewarding one. Some say that they

---

*In his book, *Successful Funeral Service Management*, Krieger gave several examples of how firms employ unit pricing. He stressed that this method is based upon the undertaker's knowledge of costs, the firm's particular circumstances, and the nature of the community. The managers of one firm, according to Krieger, determined their prices this way:

1. Their last 12 months' gross sales (and they have exceptions or changes from year to year) were $120,000. Their net profits were satisfactory from their standpoint: $17,400.
2. The cost of the merchandise sold was $24,000.
3. Dividing the gross sales ($120,000) by the cost of the merchandise ($24,000), they found a multiple of five.
4. All wholesale casket costs were then multiplied by five to arrive at the unit price of the funeral.

wish to remember the deceased as he or she appeared alive. However, to view the body is one of the first steps of accepting the death. If the death was violent or the body wasted away, the skills of the funeral service licensee will be employed in such a fashion as to modify or erase the scars of violence or the ravages of disease. Preparation allows for an acceptable recall image of the deceased.

Undertakers also maintain that embalming protects the public health. "You have the responsibility," wrote Wilber Krieger, addressing himself to undertakers in *Successful Funeral Service Management,* "of protecting the sterilization of the dead human body. You and your associates stand between disease and the public. The embalming operation, properly and conscientiously performed, kills germs and prevents their spreading."

There is considerable question about whether embalming does indeed prevent the spread of contagious diseases, as many in the funeral industry claim. An embalming fluid company's advertisement in a mortuary trade journal stated:

The modern Funeral Director performs perhaps the most vital of all community functions ... guardianship of the public health. For without his dedicated service of embalming, contamination and disease would sweep unchecked throughout the land.

Yet nowhere in the United States is embalming required by law, except under special conditions. The practice has been frequently misrepresented by undertakers as required by law, and many funeral buyers assume this to be true.

Without embalming, the undertaker's services could shrink to two or three fundamental and simple tasks. It is not surprising, therefore, that the funeral industry spends large sums of money—in lobbying, advertising, public relations, and education materials—to promote funerals "with the body present."

Extras. Once the "complete" funeral with its standard goods and services has been selected, the funeral buyer must decide about the purchase of certain extra items (see Chapter 12) not usually included in the price. These extras can be the most puzzling of all funeral expenses because they vary from undertaker to undertaker, and often the buyer is not aware of what is and what is not included in the "complete" funeral price.*

Despite such inconsistencies, certain items and services can be considered "standard extras" in most funerals—just as there are "standard" components of a "complete" funeral. These "standard extras" include the cost of burial clothes, newspaper death notices, flowers, hired pallbearers, extra limousines, copies of death certificates, and out-of-town transportation

---

*In its 1973 survey of Washington, D.C., funeral homes, the FTC found some disparity in charges for extras. Costs for such major items as limousines for mourners, flower cars, and chapel music were considered part of a "complete" funeral package in some establishments but were extras in others.

of the body. Some of these items are also called cash advances or accommodations by undertakers, who usually arrange and pay for them on behalf of the funeral buyers and are reimbursed later.

Vault. The funeral vault, a container enclosing the coffin when it is placed in the ground, can be one of the costliest components of a funeral. There is no real evidence that a vault offers permanent or prolonged protection for a body, as vault manufacturers like to imply. In some cases, in fact, a "sealed, airtight" vault may actually hasten decomposition of the corpse. Nor is a vault required by law, as is frequently suggested by both undertakers and cemetery representatives.

A vault or other type of coffin enclosure, however, may be required by many cemeteries, which claim that a container keeps the ground from collapsing as the coffin gradually disintegrates. Some cemeteries sell their own type of coffin enclosures, usually grave liners, which are often made of concrete boxes or sections of concrete and are less expensive than funeral home vaults made of steel, concrete, or fiber glass.

Because of extensive promotion by vault companies and undertakers, and cemetery requirements, sales of vaults have risen astronomically in the past fifty years—to the point where, in 1975, 72 percent of all burials included a vault or other form of coffin enclosure.

Cemetery. The coffin enclosure—vault or grave liner—is only one of several expenses usually necessary for burial in a cemetery (see Chapter 14).* The others include the plot itself, opening and closing the grave, a marker or monument, and (sometimes) perpetual care of the grave site. In many cemeteries there is a charge for setting the monument or marker and for recording fees. Many funeral buyers, unaware that there will be extra cemetery costs in addition to the price of the funeral, are dismayed to learn that typical cemetery costs range from $400 to $800, and can run much higher.

Cemetery costs vary widely around the country and according to the type of ownership of a cemetery. But burial in most cemeteries involves a number of component costs that can sometimes be quite high. For example, a grave liner that costs the funeral buyer $100 can be manufactured for only a fraction of that amount. Opening and closing a grave (average charge, $175) can be done in twenty to thirty minutes in many cemeteries with a gravedigging machine. In addition, cemeteries have been accused of a wide range of deceptive and exploitative practices: tying in the purchase of their own monuments or markers to grave-plot sales; misinforming consumers about legal requirements for vaults or grave liners; failing to provide the perpetual care for which payment has been made; using deceptive methods in the "preneed" sale of burial plots.

---

*As an alternative to ground burial, some people choose entombment in a crypt in an above-ground community mausoleum.

Even so brief a summary of the five components of a conventional funeral and burial indicates how complex and difficult funeral and burial arrangements can be, how confusing the choices—and how costly the consequences. Yet costs are not the whole story. There are other elements in the purchase of funeral and burial services, intangible and often hard to pin down, that make it unique among consumer transactions.

3
Emotional Factors in the Funeral Transaction

Many bereaved survivors who come to funeral homes are emotionally vulnerable and not in a proper mental state to arrive at important decisions in a calm or rational way. Critics of the funeral industry point out that manipulation of survivors' guilt and grief is a common tactic of undertakers. They note that the funeral transaction is the most inequitable one imaginable. The undertaker is calm and collected, familiar with all the facts surrounding death, accustomed to dealing with survivors, and there for one purpose: to sell funeral goods and services for a profit. Buyers, on the other hand, are often totally at a loss to know what to do. They find it difficult to withstand calculated selling techniques and pressure to spend more money. Undertakers make no secret of the fact that they prefer family members, rather than intermediaries, to make funeral arrangements. Howard Raether, of the NFDA, has stated the association's policy: "It is good for those who survive to have the right and duty to make the funeral arrangements. It is part of the grief syndrome, part of the therapy of mourning. It is a positive hook upon which the hat of funeral service is hung."

And Edgar Jackson, in *For the Living*, saw no reason for the clergy to accompany survivors to funeral homes:

Usually the clergyman is not called upon to offer his judgments upon the purchases a family makes. We cannot imagine his going with them to a neighborhood automobile showroom when they buy a car, to protect them in the event that a sharp automobile salesman has entered the dealer's employ. He does not go with them when they buy a new home from their realtor in order to protect them from some overzealous real estate salesman. He does not help them select a hospital room during illness, nor does he offer financial advice on matters surrounding other religious ceremonials. Nor does he usually feel inclined to pass a judgment on the funeral director in his neighborhood by trying to protect a family from possible overzealous salesmanship on the part of the funeral director.

Moreover, Jackson maintained that undertakers do not benefit from survivors' sorrow. In thirty years of parish ministry, he said, "I have never personally known of any instance where the funeral director tried to take advantage of the grief of the bereaved for his personal advantage." On the contrary, he stated, "at a time when all was chaos and uncertainty, a calm gentleman stepped into the picture and began to bring order out of chaos."

Many undertakers believe that they perform a valuable function in helping grief-stricken survivors get through the difficult time immediately following death. Yet some observers point out that such solicitousness does not preclude exploitation. LeRoy Bowman,* in *The American Funeral,* supported this view:

> Grief on the part of the family is recognized by undertakers as a disabling factor, but the number of cases in which it leads them to moderation in recommendations for elaborate funerals seems to be very small. For the majority of them the vulnerability of the family due to grief is an advantage in the bargaining situation not to be neglected. Further, through their process of rationalization, the very grief of the family comes to be a reason for more expensive and elaborate funerals on the assumption that the larger the expenditure the greater the solace for the grieving.

Just as many undertakers are convinced that they help mourners to cope with death, so many funeral buyers undoubtedly subscribe to the theory that an elaborate, expensive funeral is therapeutic for grief. Yet the "traditional" funeral, which in most cases is arranged by an undertaker in a funeral home, is a comparatively recent phenomenon. In a 1976 essay, Vanderlyn Pine, the NFDA consultant, pointed out that until "the past thirty to fifty years death occurred at home in familiar surroundings in the presence of kin or close friends, and funerals were community events." With the change in the nature of funerals has come an astounding proliferation of the few items that were once required to bury the dead. Nowadays, a mortuary can provide as many as one hundred different goods and services for a funeral. Thus, it would seem that this relatively new "traditional" funeral can be regarded not just as a way of comforting survivors but also as a profit-making venture, created in large part by the funeral industry.

---

*A sociologist, Bowman developed an early interest in the role of funeral rites in urban, industrial society. (To help support himself while in college, he lived in a funeral home for two years, taking emergency calls and helping in the preparation of bodies for burial.) Combining scientific research with a philosophical and practical approach to simpler funerals, *The American Funeral,* published in 1959, was a pioneering work in the movement to change American funeral practices.

4
Alternatives to the Conventional Funeral

The average conventional funeral and burial cost $2,000 and up. But a number of alternatives are available to most people:

- Cremation
- Direct cremation or direct burial
- Donation of one's body to a medical school or to a scientific research center

What's more, with a minimum of time and effort, consumers can discover which low-cost choices are open to them and then make arrangements ahead of time for the type of disposition they prefer. There are two ways to facilitate such advance planning:

- Membership in a memorial society*
- Purchase of a preneed plan through a preneed sales firm or a funeral home or cemetery

Not all of these choices are of equal merit (for a detailed discussion of each, see Parts III and IV). Some will cost more than others. Some may not be acceptable to everyone. Nor do any offer absolute guarantees that a person's wishes will be carried out. Many preneed plans contain pitfalls. Following a conventional funeral, cremation—instead of burial—may not be as economical as direct cremation (cremation immediately after death, perhaps with a memorial service but with no funeral). Yet each alternative listed above may be preferable to being completely unprepared—and thus inflicting upon survivors the painful experience of having to make hasty arrangements in uncertainty and under stress.

---

*Memorial societies should not be confused with "burial societies," to which poor people, particularly in the South, belong. For pennies a week, usually paid over a long period toward a "burial policy," they seek to ensure a "decent burial" for themselves.

Planning in Advance

Planning can be the key to avoiding high funeral and burial costs and the emotional pressures that can force survivors into expensive decisions. Arranging in advance does not necessarily entail spending money before death. (Indeed, many inexpensive prearrangements would be covered by the $255 Social Security death benefit available to most Americans; see page 57.) Prearrangement does mean deciding in advance the kind of disposition desired, discussing plans with family and friends, putting instructions in writing* and filing them with the people who are likely to be responsible for carrying them out.

Those who choose a particular funeral home or, say, a fraternal organization that takes care of funerals, burial, and cremation for members, should be sure their instructions are also on file with the people responsible for the arrangements.

It is important that people prearranging their own disposition discuss their wishes in an open and frank manner with those relatives and friends closest to them. Many people will want to take into account the wishes of those who may survive them. (For example, a husband or wife may resist the prospect of a spouse being cremated.) Discussions in which all opinions and points of view are expressed can help minimize confusion when death occurs. (Appendix 2 contains a listing of what survivors may need to consider when death occurs. Use of these guidelines may also help to minimize confusion.) It can cut down as well on costs, which may be incurred because there were no clear instructions—for example, if there is agreement on a simple coffin before need, survivors may not purchase a costly one later.

It should be noted, however, that as a matter of law in almost every state survivors may disregard a decedent's wishes concerning final disposition—with the possible exception of donation of body or body organs. Survivors may choose additional goods or services; an undertaker may persuade survivors to have a more expensive funeral.

Cremation. An alternative to earth burial, cremation (see Chapter 15) often follows a conventional funeral. The obvious advantage of cremation over earth burial is cost. The expenses of a typical cemetery plot, a vault, opening and closing the grave, and a marker or monument are eliminated. Most crematories charge anywhere from $75 to $150 to cremate a body. Some crematories may require the body to be delivered in a coffin and both body and coffin to be placed in the cremation chamber or furnace (retort). But a "suitable container," that is, one made of pressed wood, fiberboard, composition cardboard, or plain wood, is all that is legally required in most

---

*In addition to a will, a last letter of instruction for survivors and attorney or executor can be of help. A separate letter is important since a will may not be located until it is too late to be of use in specifying funeral instructions. For information about what to include in a letter of instruction, see Appendix 1.

states. Remains may be buried, scattered on land or sea,* stored, or placed in an urn in a cemetery columbarium (an arrangement of recessed niches, indoors or outdoors, usually protected by a front of glass), or delivered to survivors. In some crematories, special equipment permits pulverization of remains.

If cremation follows a conventional funeral utilizing the facilities of a regular funeral establishment, the saving in cemetery expenses may somewhat reduce the overall funeral costs, but the total price will still be high. Some funeral homes offer special cremation plans that include modified conventional services.**

In 1976, just above 7 percent of those who died in the United States were cremated, but the number of cremations increases every year. As burial space becomes less available and more expensive, and as religious restrictions against cremation are eased, the number of people who choose this means of disposition will probably grow dramatically in coming years.

Direct Cremation or Direct Burial. As the terms imply, direct cremation and direct burial (see Chapter 16) mean quick, simple, inexpensive disposition of the dead. High-priced coffins, embalming, restoration, viewing, flowers, pallbearers, a procession to the cemetery—all are eliminated. With direct cremation or direct burial, the undertaker removes the body from the place of death, provides a simple container or plain coffin, and transports the body to the crematory or the cemetery. (Survivors usually have the choice of whether to accompany the body.) The entire procedure can be carried out in a matter of hours. A memorial service or meeting can be arranged for a later date, according to the wishes of the decedent or survivors.

Prearrangements for direct cremation or direct burial can be made through memorial societies (see Chapter 18), often the surest and least expensive way to arrange for disposition. But in communities where there are no memorial societies, other means must be sought. Most funeral establishments presumably will provide direct cremation or burial if asked. Some firms are now offering this less expensive service in addition to their standard services. A funeral home chain in New York City, for example, has been advertising that it makes arrangements for immediate cremation for $235 (plus $100 crematory charges). But many undertakers do not ap-

---

*At present, only one state (Indiana) prohibits the scattering of ashes.

**For $415, for example, one establishment in New York City offered in 1977 the following arrangement, described in its brochure: "PLAN III Cremation with Viewing and Attendance. This plan provides for the removal of the deceased from the place of death, securing and filing of all necessary affidavits and permits with the proper authorities, preservation and preparation of the remains, wood casket covered with embossed doeskin, reposing of the remains at our chapel for one day, conveyance to the crematory, crematory arrangements, crematory charges and delivery of the Cremains [ashes and bone fragments] in the crematory container, to the family."

prove of direct cremation or direct burial on principle.* Perhaps more important, direct cremation or burial, compared with a conventional funeral, is much less profitable for the undertaker, so that in a typical funeral establishment an undertaker may make exorbitant charges for the coffin or for transportation costs or staff services.**

In recent years, however, new types of mortuaries have begun to appear on the funeral scene—commercial businesses that specialize in low-cost direct burial and direct cremation. By maintaining unpretentious establishments, keeping overhead costs low, and doing a high volume of business, they are able to charge less than conventional funeral homes while still making a profit. Most of these low-cost firms are to be found on the East and West coasts of the United States and in some of the larger cities in other areas. They are less common in the South, the Southwest, and the Middle West. Despite stiff opposition from the established funeral industry, the number of these low-cost firms is growing.

Donation of Body for Medical Research. In some areas of the United States today, there is a shortage of bodies for medical school teaching and scientific research. (A number of dental schools also need bodies for teaching purposes.) In a few schools, the situation is critical. The number of unclaimed bodies in hospitals and morgues, bodies that were formerly given to medical schools, has declined because increased Social Security and welfare death benefits for the indigent have facilitated their burial. (In some areas, unscrupulous undertakers have claimed bodies for burial in order to collect the death benefits.) The number of unclaimed bodies in New York City, for example, dropped from six hundred a year in 1970 to two hundred in 1973, causing a severe shortage of cadavers in the city's medical schools.

Autopsies, too, performed by pathologists in hospitals, can provide valuable medical information: They can show the extent of a disease that was impossible to ascertain during life, allow surgical procedures to be

---

*Howard Raether and Robert Slater, in their essay "The Funeral with the Body Present: An Experience of Value," undoubtedly spoke for many undertakers when they said: "Memorial societies generally recommend immediate disposition of the body with a bodiless memorial service sometime thereafter. For most people, this is contrary to what has been learned about grief reaction. Death is a loss; and for the well-being of an individual and of society, it is important to acknowledge realistically the loss that has occurred and to give testimony to the life that has been lived. Some Americans, through the memorial society movement, attempt to sanitize their lives or intellectualize their emotions following a death by using euphemisms in their speech, disguising their behavior and sedating their emotions, as if to pretend that what has happened has, in fact, not occurred at all."

**For example, in July 1972, a funeral home in Great Neck, New York, charged $746 for an immediate burial with no services held in the funeral home. There was no embalming, although $60 was charged for preparation of the remains and $35 for use of the preparation room. Other fees included $165 for "arrangement and supervision" and $200 for use of the facilities.

evaluated, and, in some instances, add to the progress of medical research. There are other ways in which the dead can be of benefit to the living. Not only can bodies be bequeathed to medical schools but certain parts of bodies can be donated for particular needs: eyes to an eye bank; ear bones for research on deafness; kidneys, bones, and tendons for transplants; and pituitary glands for hormone extraction. As knowledge about organ and tissue transplants increases, there will be a growing need for human transplant material.

Donation procedures are simple (see Chapter 17). And bequeathal of body not only can be of value to medicine, but, in most cases, can eliminate funeral and burial costs, if desired. Memorial societies usually have information about the specific needs of medical schools and research centers in their communities, but many medical centers, hospitals, and research institutions can be approached directly.

Memorial Societies. One of the best ways a consumer can obtain information about prearrangement for death is by becoming a member of a memorial society (see Chapter 18). There are now about 150 of these groups in the United States—about 20 more are in Canada—with at least 750,000 members. Memorial societies are consumer movements, organized in reaction to high funeral and burial costs and the lack of effective legislation—on both state and federal levels—to regulate the practices of funeral establishments, cemeteries, and related industries. The societies stress simplicity, dignity, and economy in death, and the right of individuals to arrange the disposition of their own bodies. Many members choose direct cremation or direct burial; in those instances, family and friends often hold a memorial service for the deceased (a meeting without the body present).

These nonprofit organizations—usually affiliated with churches, ministerial associations, senior citizens centers, unions, or civic groups, and staffed almost entirely by volunteers—provide information about low-cost funerals, cremation, bequeathal to medical schools, and other pertinent facts relating to death arrangements. Many memorial societies have contracts or agreements with one or more undertakers to provide the society's members with prearranged services at less than regular costs. Some memorial societies without formal agreements have understandings with cooperating funeral homes and function in much the same way as the contract societies. Those without any arrangements, formal or informal, seek to provide helpful information about funeral facilities available in the area and to advise members about procedures. One great advantage of societies with contracts or cooperating undertakers is that they save members—at a time when it may be hard to make sensible choices—the difficult task of searching for moderate-cost facilities. These societies can provide preplanned services at moderate costs because their arrangements with morticians, in effect, guarantee sufficient volume to justify lower prices for members. In addition, members have reasonable assurance that their wishes will be carried out after death.

Anyone may join a memorial society; there are no restrictions. Those who become members pay a one-time fee (rarely more than $20 covering all members of the family). After reviewing the society's information, members decide what type of service is desired and fill out forms provided by the society. The forms are filed with the undertaker selected, the memorial society, and whomever else members designate, so that everyone who may be involved in arrangements after death can be aware of a member's wishes.

Preneed Plans. The term preneed (see Chapter 19) applies here to funeral or burial services that are prearranged and paid for, usually on an installment basis, in advance of need. At first glance, those who wish a conventional funeral may find a preneed plan attractive for a number of reasons. For example, it would seem to guarantee that one's wishes will be carried out, to spare survivors the distress and possible pitfalls involved in making arrangements at time of grief, and to ensure that a funeral and burial will be paid for without financial demands on survivors.

A closer look at preneed plans, however, may cause prospective buyers to have second thoughts, especially since the ostensible advantages of a preneed plan may be better realized in other ways. For instance, a major drawback with some preneed funeral plans is that buyers cannot be sure that the amount contracted for will be enough at time of death to cover the goods and services chosen. Since survivors will then be called on to make additional payment or less expensive goods and services will be substituted, a major purpose of preneed—choosing and paying for one's own funeral—may be defeated with some plans.

Those who wish to consider purchasing a preneed plan should be sure to do careful research on available plans and applicable state laws (some information on state laws is listed in Appendix 3) and, if possible, to consult an attorney. In any case, the contract should be read and the terms of the agreement fully understood prior to signing.

Each of the above summaries is intended to outline the options available to consumers who want to avoid expensive conventional funerals and burial. These alternatives are available through prearrangement for those who prefer to plan their own disposition. But prearrangement is not always required for each of the alternatives. Some may be useful for survivors who must act on short notice without the advantages of preplanning.

It is possible that these alternatives will not appeal to all readers, that some would not choose any of them for themselves or for deceased family members or friends. Some people may not want to think about or arrange for their own deaths. Others may feel that funerals are "for the living," as the NFDA says, and that it is therapeutic for survivors to make all the arrangements at the time of death. Others may prefer the conventional funeral and burial for those once close to them, believing that it fulfills unique needs at a time of grief and stress.

Part II, "Arranging for a Funeral and Burial," is intended for those readers who reject, for whatever reason, the alternatives to the conventional funeral and burial. Its purpose is to describe in detail existing practices in the selling of funerals, to show how it may be possible to minimize exploitative methods encountered in some funeral homes, and—most important—to suggest how it may be possible to avoid excessive costs for a conventional funeral and burial. Parts III and IV discuss in detail alternatives to conventional funerals and burial and ways of arranging for them.

Part II

Arranging for a Funeral and Burial

5
Finding
an Undertaker

Many people die in the hospital.* If death occurs elsewhere, bodies are often taken to a hospital to have death confirmed. It is here that difficulties can begin for survivors. Hospitals usually want dead bodies removed as soon as possible.** If someone dies at home where others reside, there may also be a feeling of urgency to remove the body quickly from the residence. In both cases, great pressure is felt to find an undertaker at once. But how to find one, where to turn?

For many people, the choice of an undertaker is haphazard, often based on social relationships. In small towns, a long-time funeral establishment may be chosen because the present undertaker's father years ago buried a relative of the deceased. It may be that the undertaker is a fellow member of the Elks, Rotary Club, or American Legion or active in the same church or synagogue. Even in large cities, some establishments may be known as "Catholic undertakers," "Jewish undertakers," or "the undertaker who does the funerals for the First Methodist Church." Often, survivors will choose an undertaker from their own ethnic group. Friends may recommend a firm, or survivors may remember a mortician who arranged a neighbor's funeral. The selection may depend upon the location of the funeral

---

*According to a 1970 nationwide survey of undertakers conducted by Robert Fulton, consultant to the National Funeral Directors Association, "the majority of funeral directors make most of their removals (70 percent or more of the time) from hospitals. The exception to this is in the Pacific region where only slightly more than 40 percent [of funeral directors] make that many removals from hospitals. The growth of nursing homes and other retirement centers in the Pacific area may account in great part for this one exception."

**In 1975, *Canadian Consumer* magazine reported the results of a survey on funerals by the Consumers' Association of Canada, and quoted one of the respondents: "In three separate instances the hospital wanted to know which funeral home within one-half hour of the death and what survivor has their wits sufficiently collected to think of shopping around! There are hundreds of people who don't know what to do and may even take advice from hospital personnel."

home. Sometimes, the choice is simply a matter of remembering a placard in a bus, a radio or television commercial, a newspaper advertisement, or a billboard. In some cases, hospital personnel will make a recommendation.

Sometimes, when "body-snatching" occurs, survivors have little choice. This practice, most common in low-income communities, usually involves an arrangement or understanding between unscrupulous hospital employees and undertakers. When a death occurs, the employees notify an undertaker, who, through ruse or solicitation, takes the body to the funeral establishment. It is against the law in all states to remove a body without a survivor's consent. In 1974, two such incidents occurred at New York City's Metropolitan Hospital; in one case, two hours after the death of a patient there, a funeral establishment notified his family of his death and stated that his body was being brought to the funeral home. Once a body is brought to a mortuary, it is difficult—sometimes impossible—to remove it. In most cases, survivors are discouraged from trying to remove the body. Usually, the undertaker demands payment for having removed the body from the hospital and for other services. Some undertakers insist, erroneously, that state law prohibits removing bodies from funeral homes. Some morticians hold the body unless survivors produce a court order authorizing its release.

Only rarely is an undertaker chosen because of reasonable prices. More often than not, survivors have no idea of what the funeral negotiation will entail, what services are offered, or how prices are determined.

Those consumers who try to find an undertaker in advance by comparing prices by telephone are usually in for a disheartening experience. When members of the New York Public Interest Research Group (NYPIRG) represented themselves as friends of a bereaved family and sought information from sixty funeral homes in the New York City area by telephone in 1974, two-thirds of the establishments refused to give prices over the phone or were uncooperative. Some of the responses were: "It's a policy"; "It is unfair to the family"; "It's not ethical"; "I don't know what you mean by a 'funeral.'" According to NYPIRG: "If every person arranging an actual funeral was discouraged from obtaining this information by telephone by two-thirds of the places contacted, the job would be exceedingly difficult."

A Pittsburgh consumer group—the Alliance for Consumer Protection—had equally discouraging results using the mails. In 1974 its members attempted to survey funeral prices in the Pittsburgh area with the intention of making the findings public. A three-page questionnaire was sent to fifty undertakers selected at random. Only five responded, and four of the five refused to allow the information they enclosed to be published. Yet the consumer group learned certain facts that could help consumers: Some of the funeral homes offered low-cost, full-service funerals, a few as low as $350.

But, said an Alliance spokesperson, the important information that such options were available in the Pittsburgh area, with specific names of firms and their prices, could not be given to the public. "It's just obvious," said the president of the consumer group, that "the funeral directors want to maintain the advantages they have over the consumer."

The Maryland Citizens Consumer Council (MCCC) had a similar experience in 1976. The MCCC phoned fourteen funeral homes listed in the Yellow Pages in Prince George's and Anne Arundel counties. Only five funeral home representatives were willing to give answers over the telephone in response to the MCCC survey. Those who refused to answer questions said they were too busy or could give the information only in personal interviews. Some doubted that the MCCC was an authentic organization; two funeral homes suspected that the MCCC callers were memorial society members.

Raymond Arvio, author of *The Cost of Dying*, notes how some New York City college students were told by an undertaker they were visiting, "Bring me the body and then I will discuss prices."

Given the problem of not being able to learn funeral prices before the need arises, what should survivors, looking for a moderately priced funeral, do when faced with the imperative of finding an undertaker as quickly as possible? There are a number of ways to seek advice and information.

Memorial Societies

For help in finding out where a low-cost funeral can be obtained in the community, it is usually best to call a memorial society (see Chapter 18). Most societies will provide nonmembers with information about types of services available and comparative costs. (Look under "Memorial Society" or "Funeral Society" in the White Pages of the telephone book; sometimes the name of the city or town will precede the title. In the Yellow Pages the society may be listed under "Associations" or "Social Service Organizations.") If there is no such society in the immediate community, one in a nearby city may know of undertakers in the area who are willing to provide low-cost funerals. To locate the nearest memorial society, it may be necessary to turn to the Continental Association of Funeral and Memorial Societies in Washington, D.C., the clearinghouse in the United States, or the Memorial Society Association of Canada in Weston, Ontario.

One possible problem with trying to reach a memorial society in an emergency is the limited hours that some societies keep. Because they are volunteer organizations usually operating out of private homes or churches, their telephones may not be staffed twenty-four hours a day (although some memorial societies do maintain a round-the-clock telephone answering service).

Churches and Synagogues

If survivors belong to a church or synagogue, the clergy can usually be called upon for help in arranging a funeral.

The American Lutheran Church urges its members to involve the clergy in funeral arrangements and has issued a leaflet containing comments and suggestions about what to do when there is a death:

> Notify the pastor immediately when a member of the congregation dies. . . . Enlist the experience and counsel of the pastor in making burial arrangements. He should be the first to aid the family in planning a Christian funeral. Final plans for the funeral should not be made until the pastor has been consulted.

When he testified before the 1964 Senate subcommittee hearings on the funeral industry, Howard Johnson, canon theologian of the Episcopal Cathedral of St. John the Divine in New York City, noted with regret that most people do not call the clergy when a death occurs:

> Because everything must be done in a hurry, there is seldom opportunity for the survivors to do any comparison shopping. Distraught, most people rush to the first mortuary they happen to know of or find in the Yellow Pages of their telephone directory. They do not know where to turn. Alas, few of them turn to the church. The minister, since he is not a clairvoyant, is usually the last to know. He is called by the funeral director when the funeral arrangements have already been concluded. Then, in most instances, it is too late.

But Coriolis, the pseudonym for a Canadian undertaker who wrote a book criticizing the funeral industry (*Death, Here Is Thy Sting*), does not think that the clergy are very effective in helping bereaved parishioners. Only a small minority, he says, will accompany survivors to funeral homes. The majority "are unwilling to get 'mixed-up' in the business transaction at all." Many, he says, are not informed about funeral prices and the availability of low-cost services. Although the clergy's help is desirable, he says, they are often unknowledgeable about the practical aspects of funerals.

This may often be the case. Yet many indications point to a growing movement in a number of faiths for the clergy to take the lead in urging a return to simpler funerals. A survey of undertakers by the National Funeral Directors Association, for example, found that "almost half of the respondents have noticed a change in attitude on the part of the clergy. The nature of these changes in attitude include: requests for briefer funerals (19%); closed caskets (11%); and church services (3.5%). . . . Almost a third (30%) of the respondents reported that the clergy appeared to be more helpful and more personal with respect to them and the survivors than ever before."

The Quakers as well as the Unitarians have long advocated simple, brief funeral and burial rites (the Unitarians favor cremation). The *Jewish*

Funeral Guide, prepared by the Joint Funeral Standards Committee of the Rabbinical Council of America and the Union of Orthodox Jewish Congregations of America, urges all Jewish congregations to follow the Jewish tradition of simple funerals. The funeral, according to the guide, "should in every respect express the dignity, sanctity, and modesty of a solemn religious service." Ostentation should be avoided, according to the guide. "Flowers and music have no place at the Jewish funeral service."

The Committee on Christian Faith of the United Church of Canada has issued a statement entitled "Christian Burial," which states:

> In life, a person's worth is not measured by the abundance of things he possesses. In death his worth is not to be calculated by the extravagance of his funeral or the elegance of his tombstone. Christian burials ought to be as simple as possible. Excessive expenditures on elaborate caskets, vaults and headstones are to be deplored. People should be on guard against being moved to commit themselves to such expenditures in a time of emotional stress."

Some congregations have founded societies for the purpose of helping members arrange for simple funerals. In Pittsburgh, John Baiz, rector of Calvary Episcopal Church, with members of his congregation started the Omega Alpha Society in 1965, which during the five years of its most active operation, served to aid church members confronted with a death in the family. For those who needed it, the society provided a funeral service, including undertaker's fee, for about $300. Recalling one funeral he had conducted in which the coffin cost $40,000, Baiz noted: "This seems to be, in general, not quite the Christian perspective of what to do with earthly remains." The church burial society was founded not only to counteract high funeral costs but as a protest against the "lifestyle" of funeral homes— "what it does to the whole Christian attitude toward what it means to die, to be dead," in Baiz's words.

In 1973, the St. Francis Burial Society was founded in Washington, D.C., by two Protestant clergymen, William A. Wendt and Robert Herzog (the organization is, however, nondenominational). The general unavailability of simple pine-box coffins was a motivating factor in starting the society, which sells funeral products at modest prices. Simple pine coffins and plain pine boxes (for cremated remains), crafted by cabinetmakers, can be ordered by mail (see Chapter 10).

The two clergymen also were concerned about society's attitude toward death and the inability of most people to deal with bereavement and grief. In their view, many current funeral and burial practices are death-denying as well as costly. Because of their concern for the psychological as well as the practical aspects of death, Wendt and Herzog expanded the activities of the St. Francis Burial Society. The organization now publishes a quarterly magazine, sponsors conferences on death and dying, and lobbies against restrictive burial laws and questionable funeral practices. The society also plans to offer counseling services for death-related problems for both individuals and groups.

Since the founding of the St. Francis Burial Society, a companion organization, The Forum for Death Education and Counseling, has been developed by Daniel Leviton, a professor at the University of Maryland who is a close associate of Wendt's. Primarily a professional counseling organization, the forum's purpose is to strengthen death education and improve the quality of counseling in dealing with death, dying, and bereavement. The forum works closely with the St. Francis Society and shares many of its goals. Both organizations see a need to help the clergy to be better equipped in death counseling and helping the bereaved.

Since 1976, Arnold Goodman, rabbi at a Minneapolis synagogue, has become involved with his congregation in planning funerals for members of the synagogue. Citing the twin needs to "deprofessionalize" funerals by "involving people more closely in their own destinies" and to simplify funerals, Goodman said that all funerals are now provided free and conducted according to religious requirements. Members of the "Society to Honor the Dead," he said, take care of the body, build an oak coffin, sew the cotton shroud, counsel the family, and provide a limousine. Neither embalming nor vaults are permitted. Survivors have to pay only for a cemetery plot and the cost of opening and closing the grave. Goodman told Consumers Union in May 1977 that eleven funerals had been held, at an average cost to the synagogue of about $400 per funeral.

Unions and Community Organizations

In some communities, labor union committees, consumer groups, civic organizations, and fraternal societies may be able to assist survivors with information about funeral and burial arrangements. Many such organizations are aware of high death costs, and a number of them try to help their members keep funeral and burial expenses down. For example, the Death Benefit Department of the International Ladies' Garment Workers' Union has been concerned for years about high death costs (see page 28). According to a spokesperson, the union does not unquestioningly pay its members' funeral and burial expenses, but checks each bill carefully to make sure it is accurate. Often the union can get a reduction in the amount initially charged. District 65 of the Distributive Workers of America in New York City provides a $500 death benefit for its members and keeps a list of funeral homes offering inexpensive funerals. It says it will call these establishments at the request of a member's family in an effort to arrange for a low-cost funeral and burial.

Even if a decedent was not a union member, a labor organization may be able to give helpful advice to survivors seeking information. Relatives or friends may also have access to union committees experienced in these areas.

Some consumer groups and community associations, familiar with the problems of high funeral and burial expenses, may have information about comparative prices for funeral homes, which establishments to avoid, and so on. Consumer groups may also be knowledgeable about state and local laws governing funeral sales and burial requirements.

A Word of Caution

Suppose, however, that all efforts to find a moderately priced establishment prove fruitless, or that survivors, feeling the pressures of time and responsibility, decide simply to go to the nearest funeral home and take their chances. Bereaved people under stress may well feel that an experienced, established mortician can best handle their problems, and provide the type of funeral they want. If this is the case, a number of precautions should be taken before and during the funeral transaction. Survivors should be aware of the death benefits that are available to them (see Chapter 6). They should know what to expect when purchasing a funeral, what options are open to them, what goods and services can be rejected, and what questions to ask the undertaker. They should know the legal requirements for funerals and burial in their community. They should have some idea of costs and funeral home pricing methods. (These and other important points are covered in ensuing chapters of this book.) Funeral buyers who are knowledgeable and informed will probably be able to avoid overspending. They may also be spared the resentment and anger some survivors experience when presented with unexpectedly high bills for a funeral and burial.

6
Death Benefits

As soon as possible after death occurs, survivors should find out what death benefits are available. Almost all benefits must be applied for; they are not sent automatically. Many people do not realize that they are entitled to certain benefits and so, unfortunately, money is lost when the time limit for application runs out. Among the most common benefits are life and casualty insurance, employer's payments (usually for severance pay, vacation time, and the like), and benefits from Social Security, Veterans Administration (VA), credit unions, trade unions, and fraternal organizations. But other benefits are also available to millions of Americans:

• If death "arises out of and in the course of employment," there may be Workmen's Compensation Insurance benefits.

• Federal, state, and some local governments award survivors' benefits to families of some of their civilian employees.

• Survivors of railroad employees, either active or retired (but depending on length of service), receive survivors' insurance benefits from the Federal Government Railroad Retirement Board.

• A number of states now have death benefits included in no-fault automobile insurance to cover funeral and burial expenses for someone killed in a motor vehicle accident.*

---

*At this writing, a bill for a nationwide no-fault law is before Congress. The bill, Standards for No-Fault Motor Vehicle Accident Benefits Act, includes a funeral and death benefit to survivors of a "reasonable amount," which may be limited to $1,000. When an earlier version of the bill was before the House of Representatives, the Continental Association of Funeral and Memorial Societies took a strong stand against a funeral allowance. Continental's statement noted in part: "It is our conviction that legislating a funeral benefit would have an inflationary effect and redound to the benefit of the funeral industry, not the general public. What is defined as a ceiling in a No-Fault Bill will become the base price charged the families of accident victims and, ultimately, we fear, all consumers of funeral industry products and services. As presently conceived, it would not constitute a benefit for survivors but would be a bonanza for the funeral industry. When

Social Security Death Benefit

A Social Security death benefit is available to the survivors of people who meet certain requirements. Every person who has worked under Social Security for forty quarters (ten years), or for six quarters (one and a half years) during the three years prior to death, is normally credited with a lump-sum payment of $255. Payment is made to a widow or widower living in the same household with the worker at the time of death and responsible for the funeral and burial expenses.* If there is no surviving spouse eligible for payment, the death benefit may be paid to any other survivor responsible for the expenses of disposition. Social Security will also send the payment directly to the funeral home. If there are any expenses related to the donating of a body to a medical facility, such as transporting the body, Social Security will reimburse for these costs, although this sum probably will not be the full $255. Those who apply for Social Security reimbursement should be sure to submit their claim within two years from the date of death.

If a decedent's funeral and burial costs are paid by an organization such as a fraternal or religious group, which, by prearrangement, is obligated to meet these expenses, then Social Security will pay the death benefit only to the surviving spouse. In other words, a survivor other than the spouse will receive the benefit only if he or she has paid for funeral and burial costs.**

Veterans Administration Death Benefits

Veterans and their dependents are eligible to receive various death benefits from the VA.† Any veteran who has served honorably in the armed forces, in wartime or peacetime, is entitled to a $250 death benefit plus free burial in a national cemetery. There are 103 VA cemeteries but, at this writing, grave sites are available in only fifty-five of them (see Appendix 4) in twenty-seven states and Puerto Rico.†† The VA is expanding the National Cemetery System.

---

added to existing Social Security benefits of $255 and Veterans benefits of at least $250, even the lowest proposed allowance of $500 will push minimum charges over the $1,000 mark. However if when reported out of your Committee, the legislation does contain allowance for funeral expenses, we urge that the maximum figure not exceed $500."

*If the expenses come to less than $255, however, the benefit would be only for the amount actually paid.

**Ernest Morgan, author of *A Manual of Death Education and Simple Burial,* has suggested that organizations offering death benefits for their members provide new kinds of arrangements or plans so that survivors can obtain both Social Security and organizational payments. "In fact," says Morgan, " 'death benefits' of all kinds should be replaced by 'survivor benefits.' "

†According to the director of the VA National Cemetery System, there are more than 29 million eligible veterans plus dependents, collectively a total of more than 50 million people or close to one-fourth of the total U.S. population.

††According to the VA, strict limitations have been placed on burial at Arlington National Cemetery. "In addition to the spouses, minor children, and dependent adult children of

The spouse and any minor child of a veteran are also entitled to free burial in a national cemetery. (If the spouse or minor child of the veteran dies first, he or she may be buried in a national cemetery if the veteran signs a paper confirming intent to be buried next to the spouse or minor child. If the veteran dies first and is buried in a private cemetery, the spouse and minor child of the veteran no longer have the right to be buried in a national cemetery.) Application for burial in a national cemetery should be made at the time of death of the veteran, or of an eligible dependent, by applying to the superintendent of the nearest national cemetery in which burial is desired.

If a veteran is buried in a private cemetery, $150 is available from the VA for cemetery expenses in addition to the standard VA $250 death benefit.

All veterans are entitled to a headstone and a U.S. flag. In some cases, transportation costs for the remains are paid by the VA. If a veteran dies in a VA facility where he or she was properly admitted for hospital, nursing home, or domiciliary care, the VA is usually required to pay the cost of transporting the body to the place of burial, either by hearse, common carrier, or both. The same benefit applies when the veteran dies en route while traveling under authorization of the VA for the purpose of examination, treatment, or care.

A veteran who dies of service-related disabilities receives a total of $800 in death benefits, plus free burial in a national cemetery, headstone, and flag.

Under certain conditions, members of the National Guard, Armed Forces Reserves, and Reserve Officers Training Corps also qualify for death benefits.

Application for the $250 death benefit must be made within two years following the veteran's death. Any VA office will provide information and other assistance in filing applications. At time of death, the VA will help survivors make immediate arrangements for a plot in a national cemetery, transportation, headstone, and flag. Some communities also have "veterans affairs" offices, which may provide information.

Using the Undertaker to File Claims

Undertakers are usually knowledgeable about death benefits available under both the VA and Social Security, as well as other claims, and most undertakers will help survivors fill out applications. It is, in fact, a common

persons already interred in the cemetery, members of the Armed Forces dying on active duty, and retired members of the Armed Forces who have performed active Federal service, who are carried on official service retired lists, and are eligible to receive compensation stemming from service in the Armed Forces, may be interred in the cemetery. Also, recipients of the Medal of Honor and persons having honorable military service who held an elective office in the U.S. Government or served on the Supreme Court or in the Cabinet or in an office compensated at Level II under the Executive Salary Act are eligible for interment in Arlington National Cemetery."

procedure for survivors to authorize the undertaker to file claims on their behalf so that death benefits can be applied against the funeral bill. If survivors prefer, however, they can file their own claims for death benefits. Upon request, both Social Security and the VA will send survivors the appropriate forms to be filled out. It can take up to four weeks for the death payments to arrive, once forms have been filed.

Filing for death benefits on behalf of survivors is a standard procedure in most funeral homes. If survivors decide to file their own claims, they should ask the undertaker whether this would entitle them to a deduction from the "professional services" charge that is a basic component of most funeral bills. If this service is not performed by the funeral home, survivors should not have to pay for it.

Necessary Documents and Papers

Whether survivors prefer to apply for death benefits themselves or to use the services of an undertaker, they will need copies of a number of documents and personal and business papers in order to prove death and receive benefits. (The number of copies needed for each document will depend on the number of claims submitted by survivors.) In some cases and with some documents, it is necessary to submit a copy that has been certified by the issuing agency. (Copies made on duplicating machines, for example, are not acceptable for some claims.) Survivors will need:

• At least ten certified copies of the death certificate to establish insurance claims, Social Security and VA benefits, as well as other claims.
• Copies of birth certificates of surviving spouse and minor children for Social Security and VA benefits.
• Copies of marriage certificate for Social Security and VA benefits for surviving spouse and minor children.
• Copy of W-2 form or federal income tax return for the most recent calendar year as proof of the decedent's employment record for Social Security benefit.
• Copy of veteran's discharge papers for VA benefits.
• Copies of receipted bill from funeral home for VA benefits—also for Social Security benefit if applicant is not the surviving spouse.

Survivors should know the Social Security number of the decedent to claim Social Security benefits. In addition to obtaining the necessary documents for death benefits, survivors should locate important papers such as bankbooks, stock certificates, real estate deeds and mortgages, credit card bills, installment loan and service contracts, and life insurance and mortgage policies. Sometimes, credit, loan, or mortgage insurance covers all or part of outstanding balances in case of death. Survivors should also get in touch with organizations and institutions the decedent worked for, belonged to, or had business dealings with, reporting the death and requesting information about any life or health insurance policies, special funds, or pensions to which the survivors might be entitled.

Canadian Benefits

The Canada Pension Plan (CPP)* (the equivalent of the Social Security system in the United States) pays a lump-sum death benefit to the estate of a person who has contributed to the plan for at least three calendar years since the plan's inception in 1966. The amount of death benefit depends on the amount contributed to the plan by the deceased; it is calculated on the basis of six times the monthly government retirement pension received by the decedent, or 10 percent of the earnings ceiling for the year of death, whichever is less. The maximum payment for the CPP death benefit in 1977 was $930. Application forms can be obtained from local offices of the Canadian Pension Commission, which administers the CPP. Documents that must accompany the application include: death certificate, deceased's birth certificate, social insurance number, and statement of contributory salary and wages.

Veterans Benefits. Death benefits for veterans in Canada are not guaranteed, as they are for those who fulfill the requirements in the United States. Veterans' survivors should inquire about possible benefits at their local office of the District Representative of the Department of Veterans Affairs; application for the benefits must also be made to that office. If a veteran, when alive, qualified for any veterans benefits, it is possible that survivors may qualify for some form of partial or full death benefits. Documents that may be needed with the application are: death certificate, marriage certificate, birth certificates of spouse and any children, and decedent's rank and serial number.

The Last Post Fund (see Appendix 5 for cities with offices throughout Canada) is a private Canadian organization that arranges funerals and burial for veterans who die without the means to do so for themselves. For such veterans the fund provides a coffin, the services of an undertaker, a cemetery plot, cost of opening and closing the grave, and a marker. The fund asks that a telephone call be made to the nearest fund office when the death of an eligible person occurs. Application should be made before burial; funds are not available thereafter.

---

*Residents of Quebec who contribute to the Quebec Pension Plan may be eligible for a death benefit under this plan, which is similar in most respects to the CPP.

7

Discussing
Funeral Costs
with the Undertaker

When survivors go to the funeral home, it is important for them to get *in writing* as much price information as possible—for the coffin, services, and other individual charges—before other matters are discussed with the undertaker. At the same time, one of the most important precautions for survivors is not to disclose to the undertaker the total amount of money available in death benefits. Undertakers will, of course, assume Social Security and, often, VA benefits. Indeed, many morticians display a proprietary attitude toward these benefits, as if they were automatically entitled to receive them from government sources.*

Certainly undertakers are entitled to know they will be paid promptly for their services. And they cannot be blamed for wanting some definite understanding about the method of payment.** But funeral buyers can protect themselves from the possibility of inflated costs by not revealing the actual amount of money earmarked for funeral expenses. Even so, undertakers usually have a good idea, from a number of indications, what sums are available or can be obtained (see page 66).

---

*This frequent assumption on the part of undertakers was questioned by a funeral buyer, angered over the high price ($645.28) charged by a Danbury, Connecticut, funeral home for a simple cremation. In an open letter sent in 1973 to the funeral home, newspapers, the FTC, and memorial societies in his area, the customer criticized the mortician's attitude: "On several occasions," he said, "you tried to 'justify' your high prices on the basis of Social Security and veterans death benefits—your inference being that it really wasn't costing me anything. Where do you think Social Security gets the money? Where do you think the Veterans Administration gets the money? From me and every other citizen—that's where they get it. Your repeated efforts on this point represent improper conduct designed to confuse and mislead the public."

** In *The American Funeral*, LeRoy Bowman pointed out that, unlike businesses selling automobiles or refrigerators, the undertaker cannot reclaim a casket or vault because of nonpayment after burial. "There is no question," Bowman wrote, "that he would be faced with many an unpaid bill of large dimensions if he did not protect himself.... The argument that everyone is entitled to a decent funeral does not logically lead to the conclusion that the funeral director should take risks in the matter of payment."

The wisest course of action for the prudent funeral buyer is, first, to request in advance of the actual purchase a detailed price estimate in writing of specific funeral goods and services as well as an estimate of cemetery costs. Then the undertaker should be informed that the total price must fall within a certain limit—a limit that survivors can afford and that will also take disposition costs into account. This advice is often difficult to follow because a detailed price breakdown is not always provided before the funeral. Even when it is, there is no guarantee that the undertaker's final bill will match the estimate.*

In dealing with a funeral home, price itemization** (see page 79) is one of the best protections for consumers. Not only are buyers told the specific charge for each funeral component, but they have a chance to consider the goods and services included by the undertaker and to reject those not desired, thereby possibly lowering the total funeral cost. At present, only six states—California, Colorado, Florida, Minnesota, New Jersey, and New York—have laws requiring some form of written itemization of charges. And, according to the FTC, only Minnesota comes near to having an adequate itemization requirement.† In California, the itemization law essentially requires only a bi-unit bill: a separate price for the coffin and one for "professional services." In Colorado and Florida, an itemized statement is provided only if the customer asks for one.

---

*A legal almanac on funeral and burial practices, *The Law of Death and Disposal of the Dead* by Hugh Bernard, discusses this practice: "For example, the New York State Funeral Directors Association (an NFDA affiliate) cooperated with the Attorney General of that state in an investigation of funeral practices [in 1964]. One of the abuses found was that a customer would be quoted a price in advance of a funeral, and after the service would be presented with a bill listing added services at extra cost that he had been led to believe were included in the original price as quoted. With this practice also was involved the widespread custom (nationwide in extent) of 'unit pricing,' that is, quoting the casket price as including an unspecified bundle or package of 'services' without itemizing them or ascertaining if the family desired all of them. A casket with 'complete services' in one funeral home would cost several hundred dollars more or less than the same casket and 'services' at another mortuary."

The almanac stresses that survivors should get a clear, concise estimate of funeral costs before deciding what to choose. Bernard writes, ". . . it behooves the person arranging the funeral to insist that the undertaker supply a breakdown of the services to be provided and the price of each. This should be done before coming to any agreement on the funeral to be contracted for. It is a wise precaution to insist that the list be in writing. Even in the case of thoroughly reputable, ethical, and honest funeral directors, the belief appears to be widespread that because an apparent majority of American families desire relatively elaborate, ceremonial, and costly funerals, all families do; and hence certain services (e.g., embalming, cosmetic and restorative treatment of the remains, a casket if the body is to be cremated, and the like) will be supplied automatically unless the family insists otherwise when making the arrangements."

**The FTC, in its 1975 proposed rule to regulate the funeral industry, would make price itemization mandatory in all funeral establishments.

†Even Minnesota's cost-itemization law, according to the director of that state's Office of Consumer Services, "has serious shortcomings, which the FTC regulations could remedy."

New Jersey requires price itemization of all funeral goods and services to be provided at the time arrangements are made. New York State's price itemization law requires that, at the time arrangements are made, the customer be given a statement showing the total cost of the funeral, together with an itemized list (*not* a price list) of the merchandise and services included in the total and a separate itemized statement of cash advances. (The New York law also requires that funeral home customers be given a complete description of the coffin, including manufacturer's name and model number and the type of material from which it is made.) According to the FTC, the New York law does not ensure that the written itemization will be given to the consumer *before* a particular funeral is chosen.

Twenty-six states require some form of written price disclosure but do not require that each funeral component be separately priced. Eighteen states and the District of Columbia have no price disclosure requirement.

The FTC points out that its proposed price-itemization requirement is a "significant departure" from the traditional way in which most undertakers have conducted their business and dealt with customers. Under the proposed FTC rule, funeral homes would be required to furnish customers with a printed or typed list of both goods and services and prices. At present, most funeral homes list in print only the names of the specific goods and services on their customers' bills. Prices are usually written in by the undertaker, which suggests that there are no standard fees but, rather, what the undertaker decides the traffic will bear in each transaction. The FTC's proposal would eliminate the practice of writing in prices. The proposed rule, says the FTC, "does no more than provide consumers with the basic data on prices and choices which [are] supposed to be available to all buyers to allow informed marketplace decisions."

There are several ways to finance a funeral. (According to the NFDA, only 2 or 3 percent of all survivors pay for the full amount of the funeral at the time arrangements are made. Many undertakers give a cash discount if the bill is paid in full promptly.) The majority of undertakers ask their customers to sign an agreement of payment or contract that carries no finance charge for the first three or four months. After that, interest is charged. This method recognizes the fact that it often takes a number of weeks for Social Security and VA benefits to arrive; the settlement of an estate may take much longer. A number of funeral homes offer installment plans, a fixed sum to be paid weekly or monthly. In smaller communities and in rural areas, where morticians are more likely to know their customers, the method of payment is often much more informal, a "pay me when you can" arrangement.

8

Some Psychological Aspects of the Funeral Transaction

Buying a funeral is complicated enough from a purely practical and financial perspective. But the purchase is often made even more complex by a number of attitudes and assumptions on the part of both survivors and undertaker. Funeral buyers may not realize how much these aspects of the funeral transaction can affect the choices and decisions that are made. The most overwhelming of these is the grief of the survivors, a debilitating factor itself, but one that is frequently compounded by other sentiments and reactions present during the negotiations.

One obstacle confronting consumers—and it can be a formidable hurdle for funeral buyers to overcome—is that undertakers generally feel that they are the ultimate authorities when it comes to the appropriate forms for the expression of mourning.* It is not solely for reasons of profit, LeRoy Bowman has observed, that undertakers suggest costly items. It is

*Columnist Goodman Ace described such an experience in *Saturday Review* magazine in 1970. Called upon to arrange the funeral of a member of the family—his first such experience—he wrote of the sense of alienation he felt in the funeral home seated before the desk of the man in charge, "a man who knew where everything and everybody belonged." Ace, on the other hand, felt he knew nothing, not even answers to simple questions.
  "Now what about flowers?" the undertaker asked.
  "We have asked that flowers be omitted," I replied.
  "No, I mean the spray on the casket. Do you want a spray?"
  "Well, I guess so."
  "They come in three sizes. There's the small piece placed in the center, or the three-quarter length, or the blanket of flowers that covers the entire casket."
  "Well, I don't know. What would you think?"
  "May I suggest the three-quarter length?"
  I nodded.
  He made the entry as he said, "Flowers, seventy-nine dollars. Now, what about music? Something classical?"
  "I suppose so."
  "Bach? Beethoven? Mozart?"
  "Yes," I replied, as I felt myself disintegrating.
  "Which one?"

64

also because of an ideal they want to see expressed in the funeral ceremony. They have their own sense of the fitness of things. Undertakers consider funerals their "creations," rituals that must be arranged in an appropriate manner, using the best materials available. Because of the undertaker's personal identification with the funeral, "he feels a sense of belittlement if his standards of excellence are not met. . . . The result is a distinct tendency to tell clients what they should do, or what 'is being done. . . .' "*

Implicit in this attitude is the belief that undertakers should be the final arbiters of what constitutes an appropriate ceremony. And, in many cases, that role extends to the undertakers' judgment of funeral buyers' social status. Many undertakers are convinced that survivors should purchase funerals commensurate with their income or standard of living; it can be an affront to the undertaker when buyers insist on paying less than the undertaker thinks they can afford.**

Coriolis, the Canadian undertaker-critic, calls the attitude that prompts such practices the "Cadillac theory"—the belief held by many undertakers that anyone who drives up to a funeral home in a Cadillac does not have the right to buy a "cheap" funeral. All arguments against the Cadillac theory are countered with references to the high overhead costs of most funeral homes; expensive funerals are needed, say the undertakers, to meet those costs. Yet imagine how frustrated an undertaker would be, says Coriolis, "if the proprietor of the corner store refused to sell him a ten-cent cigar on the grounds that a man of his stature could afford a larger contribution towards the overhead of his store! The comparison

---

"I don't know," I said, rising, unreasonably disturbed at my own inadequacy to answer a few simple questions.

As I paced, he remained calm and made a note on the form, and asked the next question.

"Now, what about clothes?"

I sat again in utter bewilderment. This was to be a cremation. What did it matter? I gathered it did from his next remark.

"We can furnish a suit, if you like. Or some prefer a robe or even pajamas."

He waited for my answer while I sat there thinking, "This too shall pass." But it didn't.

"I suggest pajamas," he offered.

I nodded.

He wrote, as he said, "Pajamas, twelve dollars and sixty cents." And then he added, "That includes the sales tax."

And there you have it—the two irrevocables, death and taxes.

*This point of view was expressed by a successful undertaker in Glen Cove, New York. The undertaker, whose funeral home serves a predominantly Catholic clientele, said he "feels a 'mission' to persuade patrons to make the funeral as religious as possible." "Clients," he noted, "are not aware enough to know what choices they have. If the funeral director doesn't do it, it doesn't get done."

**One Baltimore undertaker told a reporter writing about funerals in 1977: "There are people who can afford to pay their way but they want to save money. People who can dagnab well afford it but they just want as much as they can for the lowest possible nickel. No firm I know of can operate by serving people at a loss."

may sound ludicrous, but this is exactly what funeral directors are doing."

How does an undertaker know a customer's worth? Any number of signs offer clues to the adept seller. The way survivors dress or speak, their address, the car they drive—all are significant. Sometimes, an undertaker picks up the body at home or pays an initial call there, permitting a measure of financial status. Then, too, during preliminary discussions of funeral arrangements, an undertaker may have a chance to gauge a customer's affluence. For example, an undertaker often helps survivors to compose the decedent's obituary, which can reveal a great deal. Any of these indications can prompt the undertaker to decide that a higher-priced funeral is in order—and to charge accordingly.*

The appeal to status and the undertaker's disapproval of—and resistance to—the desire for simplicity and moderation can often sway the buyer's determination. Even people who are able to withstand blatant pressure to show their concern for the decedent by spending as much as possible for "the loved one" may still be susceptible to subtle suggestions. It might be hinted that they are stingy or that they are ignorant of prevailing funeral standards among "social leaders" in the community.

In 1976 at a hearing in Chicago on the FTC proposed rule, a resident of Highland Park, Illinois, testified that his first experience with a funeral home had resulted in "one of the most disgusting experiences that I believe I have ever had in my life." His father had just died, he said, and at the funeral home he told the undertaker that he wanted an inexpensive funeral. "It was obvious that he could not hear me," the man recalled,

> because the figures he began to quote me were astronomical, in the range of $3,500 and up. In the course of our conversation in selecting the casket, the gentleman stated that a person in my father's position, should have the very best bronze or metal casket. This statement was made, to the best of my knowledge, without the gentleman having any knowledge as to what my father did for a living or what his position in life was. In the further course of our conversation, this gentleman stated that I should spend as much money as possible on the funeral arrangements because this was the last act I could do for my one and only father.

---

*Bereaved buyers are rarely aware of such calculations on the part of the undertaker. But they can be alert to social pressures exerted in a funeral transaction. Ann Burnside Love, in a magazine article, described the social pressure she felt when arranging for her husband's funeral: "The most painful part of planning a funeral," she wrote, "is being led into a series of elegant rooms filled with caskets. While this experience by itself is difficult, the real blow comes, most widows find, when they suddenly realize that their relationship with their deceased husband is being measured in dollars and cents. Often, a widow senses a subtle implication that the cost of the casket not only reflects (or enhances) her husband's station in life, but also indicates the degree of her love. Even without pressure from the funeral director, a widow's own emotional response may lead her to feel she's making an evaluation about the worth of this person's life. But those feelings can't be resolved by spending money she can't afford—and which could be used more constructively elsewhere."

Survivors, no doubt, often shrink from the idea of a "cheap funeral," with its implications of tawdriness and ugliness. Yet a member of the Roman Catholic clergy writing to a funeral trade association publication in 1961 made clear that there is a distinction between "cheapness" and "simplicity":

> Regarding "cheaper funerals" and the loss of human dignity, let me say this: Contemporary English distinguishes between that which is inexpensive and that which is cheap, in the sense of being vulgar. Human dignity is never lost when man acts according to reason, with prudence and moderation, and thus according to his faith and his means. . . .
>
> When a poor man attempts to make a lavish display—with all the modern trappings of questionable taste—that is obviously beyond his means, it is then that he suffers a loss of dignity and has put on an expensive show that has been cheap and vulgar.

9
Two Decisions before the Funeral Transaction

When questioned, most people say they want inexpensive funerals. Surveys and polls report consumer disapproval of excessive charges by undertakers. But these responses are made under normal circumstances. When death occurs, and the same consumers are ushered into the undertaker's office, then they too become vulnerable funeral buyers who may very well succumb to the same pressures they had earlier deplored.

One reason for this is that many survivors are alone and defenseless when they meet with the undertaker. Even if an entire family goes to the funeral home, each member may well feel grief and stress—emotions that can affect good judgment. To help counteract this, survivors should always take with them to the funeral home a friend or acquaintance*—preferably one who has made funeral arrangements in the past—and, when appropriate, a member of the clergy. Not only can such associates offer consolation and support, but they are usually more willing to ask questions and less vulnerable to psychological pressures.

To minimize the likelihood of making arrangements with an undertaker without fully understanding their implications, survivors—and those accompanying or acting for them—can make two important decisions before they arrive at the funeral home. The first is to decide whether to have the coffin open for viewing or closed. The second is to resolve to be persistent, even aggressive, in asking for either (1) an itemized breakdown of costs or (2) the total price of an inexpensive or moderately priced funeral package with a list of what is included.

There can be a considerable difference in cost between funerals with an open coffin and those with a closed coffin. Without viewing, burial can usually take place sooner, and a number of expenses can thus be avoided: embalming, restoration and cosmetic work, other staff services, new burial

---

*Some survivors delegate friends or acquaintances to go in their stead.

68

clothes, and so on. If there is a closed coffin, some undertakers—when asked—will agree to omit embalming and to deduct this charge from the total bill.* Not all funeral buyers want a closed coffin, but they should be aware that it can mean a less expensive funeral.

Even when there is to be an open coffin, inquiries should always be made about deducting costs for goods or services not chosen. The option of deducting is rarely offered by the undertaker, yet certain extras (use of the chapel, limousine, organist, guest register, acknowledgment cards) in some funeral homes are deductible upon request, which can affect the final price.

Many mortuaries have a wide range of complete funeral packages, often including low-priced adult funerals.** Funeral buyers, however, are frequently unaware that inexpensive services are available.†

The difference in funeral costs, the FTC found in its 1973 survey of Washington, D.C., funeral homes, is the difference in the price of coffins. And, in noting this, the report stressed a significant point:

> Many consumers seem to believe that along with a "better" (costlier) casket, one gets a "better" or more inclusive set of services from the undertaker. The realization that this is usually untrue brings into focus the real question confronting the funeral buyer. Once he has chosen a funeral home, has decided that a casket is desired, and is pondering the choice of a particular casket, the revelant inquiry is whether a given *casket* is worth to him the price differential between that casket and its less expensive counterparts. Speculation that the choice of a casket will alter the assortment of services offered by the undertaker serves only to blur and confuse the choice that must be made. Judging from the survey results, in the absence of express indications to the contrary from the mortician, the consumer may safely

---

*There still may be a charge for "preservation," however, although it should be less than for embalming. Some homes charge extra for refrigerating the body. If there are no refrigeration facilities, other means of preserving the body (a plastic pouch, powders to mask the odor) can be used. These procedures may appear on the bill as "use of preparation room," "special sanitary care," "preparation of remains," and so on.

**The results of a 1974 survey of funeral homes in four cities showed that, although prices varied substantially, many funeral homes provided low-priced funerals. The prices included $250 in Charlotte, $495 in Cincinnati, $300 in Louisville, and $450 in San Francisco.

†For example, the 1973 FTC survey of Washington, D.C., funeral homes found that the majority of fifty-five respondents provided an inexpensive funeral package—some for as low as $210. Yet the FTC found that the actual number of low-cost funerals conducted in Washington in 1972 and 1973 to be very few. Ten funeral homes where inexpensive funerals were available had sold none at all. In twenty-six establishments, only 5 percent or less of all funerals sold were the least expensive available. In eight firms the percentage of low-cost funerals was greater than 5 percent of the total number of funerals, but for each firm the actual number came to under five a year. In only seven funeral homes did the least expensive funeral constitute at least 10 percent of all funerals. The FTC's conclusions: (1) Most consumers are unaware that inexpensive funerals are available in many establishments; (2) undertakers presumably do not inform their customers about them.

assume that the choice of a casket will not affect the concomitant services and facilities provided.

It is up to the consumer, then, when choosing between, say, a $600 and a $1,200 funeral, to decide whether the difference in the coffin is worth the additional $600—especially since there will be very few, if any, differences in the services provided by the funeral home.

10
A Crucial Choice: The Coffin

In 1974 a Minneapolis undertaker, David Lee, took large advertisements in the Minneapolis *Tribune* and the *Star* to inform people about his theory that a "fine funeral need not be costly." The advertisements stated:

> The most appropriate funeral is one that is within the means of the family. Even among the affluent a simple, unostentatious funeral is now considered in better taste than the ornate regalia common in the past. America has shown a healthy trend toward the tasteful and dignified, rather than the lavish and gaudy. Unfortunately, people have not always known where to find such a funeral.

The advertisements listed individual retail prices for a selection of coffins: a brocade-covered wooden coffin for $90; a steel coffin for $195; a solid oak coffin for $420. Lee's two funeral homes offered a full range of funerals, twenty-five in all, with the least expensive costing $275.

In addition, Lee's advertisements listed a complete cost breakdown for a moderate-priced funeral:

Professional staff services	$250
Embalming	65
Cosmetology	10
General use of facilities	70
Use of facilities for visitation	25
Use of facilities for funeral services	25
Initial transfer of deceased	35
Funeral coach	46
Acknowledgment cards	2
Visitor register	2

"For . . . complete price," the advertisements said, "deduct any item not needed and add the cost of the casket and burial vault, where required. Note: Price does not include the flowers, transportation, cemetery lot, telegrams and telephone calls, clergyman, special music, obituary notices, certified copies."

In publishing these advertisements, Lee violated a cardinal rule among undertakers: the restriction against price advertising. That action in itself was significant. More than that, he performed a service for consumers: The advertisements may have helped to spare some Minneapolis funeral buyers the ordeal of having to choose, without knowing what options and price range to expect, a coffin in the selection room of a funeral home.

The Selection Room

Of all the areas in a funeral establishment, the selection room, where coffins are displayed, is the most important to the typical undertaker. It is here that survivors are most vulnerable, under greatest pressure to make the "right choice." In many establishments, great attention and care are lavished on this room. Spaciousness is an absolute requirement—a minimum of forty square feet of floor space for each coffin (the expensive models often get sixty square feet). Wall-to-wall carpeting in a soft color enhances the room's atmosphere. Lighting is extremely important; it is designed to avoid shadows, and to bring out the luster and polish of the coffins on display.

A good deal has been written by people both inside and outside the funeral industry about the sales psychology of the selection room.* And, whether selection-room sales methods are criticized or defended, there is general agreement that the arrangement used in most funeral homes works. It is based on the "Keystone Approach" of Wilber Krieger of National Selected Morticians, who set down in *Successful Funeral Service Management* his classic plan for selling high-priced coffins.**

He constructed a system that would first help undertakers decide in what price range they should try to sell coffins. (Most people, obviously, will not buy the highest-priced models.) To accomplish this, it is necessary to find the "median sale"—the middle sales price of all caskets sold in the past year or two.† The next objective, Krieger said, should be to sell the

---

*Coriolis points out that "no stone is left unturned in the effort to achieve ideal sales conditions. There are instances in which thousands of dollars have been spent by funeral men to move doors or windows or to change the shape of the room in order to achieve the desired psychological goals."

**Krieger's formula, according to the FTC in 1975, is still recommended to undertakers in "how-to" trade manuals. The FTC noted: "Staff's visits to approximately 30 casket selection rooms, examination of trade publications, and interviews with funeral directors and customers all indicate that the overwhelming majority of funeral homes in the country establish their casket offerings and arrange their casket display rooms in accordance with the principles advocated by Krieger and his disciples."

†For example, if an establishment sold a hundred coffins in one year, the cost of each, from the lowest to the highest, should be listed. The price of number fifty, near the middle, is the median sale price. It is a better gauge of medium cost than the average

greatest number of coffins possible at a price that is just above the median price. The largest group of coffins displayed in the selection room should fall somewhere within that group. For instance, Krieger wrote, if there are thirty coffins in a selection room, three should be in the lowest price group, eight in the next, twelve in the group above the median, and seven in the highest. As a rule, undertakers do not expect to sell the costliest coffins; they are on display mainly for the purpose of trading up. (In the case of coffins at the top of the line, Krieger advised undertakers, "people *buy*, and your efforts toward selling in that area of your display are confined to giving information that is helpful to the buyer.") The more the highest-priced coffins cost, the higher the median is likely to be.[*]

Coffins, Krieger proposed, should never be placed in an ascending or descending order of price range but organized in a way designed to help the buyer "find his price level." Krieger's system involved placing coffins in intricate arrangements. If, for instance, a buyer is "embarrassed" by the high prices of some fourth-group coffins, the selection room should be so arranged that the buyer, Krieger wrote, then "tends to turn" to the cheapest ones on display. Here, Krieger admonished, there should not be too large a selection. "The unbalanced line with its heavy concentration of [low-cost units makes] it very easy for the client to buy in this area with complete satisfaction." Instead, just a few low-cost coffins could help direct the customer back toward higher-priced ones.

Coriolis describes one selection room that is arranged according to the methods used in most establishments. Directly beyond the most expensive coffins, at the end of the wide aisle Krieger called the "Avenue of Approach," centered at the far wall, is the third-group coffin (sometimes two or three coffins) the undertaker is chiefly interested in having the customer consider. This coffin is not the most expensive one but at the top of the third group, more expensive than the two coffins first seen when entering the room. If buyers pass this area and enter the narrow aisle Krieger called "Resistance Lane," they find themselves moving past on one side the least expensive models and on the other the most expensive. The contrast between the two is so glaring[**] that chances are buyers will in desperation choose one of the

---

sale, because a few very high sales, according to Krieger, could give a distorted average sale.

[*]A 1969 article in *Mortuary Management* by the executive director of the Casket Manufacturers Association of America supported this theory: "Many unthinking funeral directors," he wrote, "believe that they can buy cheaper and sell higher and a make a profit, when actually the opposite is true. For the higher quality caskets a funeral director buys the more profit he will make, as the casket determines his sales level. When he does not have a very obvious quality differential in the caskets in his salesroom, he will sell consistently at a low sales average. . . . It is literally impossible for a funeral director to pay too much for his caskets, but he can easily pay too little and end up in the red."

[**]A reporter writing about funeral homes in the Baltimore area in 1977 noted that the least expensive coffin in funeral homes is generally given "short shrift" when undertakers

most expensive models in the center of the room or one of the second- or third-group coffins on the right.

Coriolis notes "key sales points" in the showroom that directly influence choice. And he criticizes this sales technique:

> If you were aware that a car dealer used such merchandising tactics, you would go to another. If you knew that a particular furniture store was loaded with similar gimmicks, you would seek out its competition. This type of thing just described is universal, however. Every funeral home in [Canada] is up to most of these tricks, plus a few of its own.

Undertakers claim that pressure is never used to induce customers to buy expensive coffins and that frequently funeral buyers are free to inspect coffins alone in the selection room. But the carefully planned strategy of the display room, Coriolis maintains, allows as much freedom of choice as a "loaded gun."*

Raether cautions undertakers about the "traumatic effect" the selection room can have on survivors, confronted with an "overwhelming number" of coffins. The undertaker should precede survivors into the selection room to give them reassurance. "It is similar to a parent preceding a child into a strange or dark place." In an "orientation area," the undertaker can show a few examples of coffins, encouraging questions and comments. In guiding survivors through the rest of the room, he can encourage them "to touch and feel the different selections." The considerate undertaker, Raether says, will leave the room after a while so that survivors can discuss their preferences privately and arrive at a decision.

Once a coffin has been selected, the undertaker must decide its "appropriateness" for the needs—psychological, sociological, and financial—of the survivors. "If for some reason the [undertaker] finds the selection totally inconsistent with his evaluation of the family's *needs,* he may feel they should counsel further about it." Particularly important, says Raether, is that survivors do *not* exceed their financial ability to pay for the coffin they choose.** The conscientious undertaker should point out that al-

escort survivors through the selection room. "The casket," wrote the reporter, "normally a wooden box covered with gray cloth costs (with services) about $700-$800. It seems narrow, small and unattractive in the midst of grander models."

*In his book, *The Funeral Director and His Role As a Counselor,* Howard Raether, executive director of the National Funeral Directors Association, discusses techniques that undertakers can use with survivors in selling coffins. He suggests, for example, that the undertaker first explain the purpose of the coffin—that it is meant to receive the body of the deceased, that it should be "a part of the funeral ceremony itself," as well as part of the funeral procession. "This approach will serve to not only reassure the family of its usefulness but also bring proper focus on its importance in the funeral with the body present." The coffin, says Raether, is the "last material gift . . . that can be given to the body which was once a person." It should become apparent, Raether says, that for many survivors there is the desire that this gift be "aesthetically desirable and/or protective."

**Raether offers special advice to undertakers dealing with survivors who must arrange

though survivors feel it to be a wise choice at the time, they may question it later. If the undertaker thinks that survivors have chosen a less expensive coffin than they should, he may question this choice as well. However, if survivors demonstrate that their selection is based on "sound rationale," the undertaker should accept their decision. Raether is at pains to caution undertakers against any kind of coercion in the selection room. He does not believe, however, that survivors are very often under the kind of emotional pressure that would make coercion possible.

"When such is the case, there are usually at least two other persons present who can counterbalance the emotional instability of any one member of the party," according to Raether.

Types and Styles of Coffins

There are three main types of coffins: (1) the full couch (in which the entire body can be viewed); (2) the half couch (which shows the body from the waist up); (3) the hinge cap (which is the same as the half couch, except for variations in the placement of hinges on the molding and paneling of the coffin). Less common is the "lift-lid," the removable cover on the least expensive type of coffin, which Coriolis describes: "It is not hinged, but the upper half simply lifts right off the case, and often is left leaning against a nearby wall so as to appear grossly incongruous." The half-couch coffin is the type most frequently chosen by funeral buyers.

A considerable range of materials is used in the construction of coffins. Wilber Krieger noted that from fifteen to twenty different kinds and grades of wood are used, increasing in cost as they "move up the scale of hardness." The less expensive woods—pine, chestnut, cypress, red cedar—are usually covered with cloth. More expensive hardwoods—oak, birch, maple, cherry, mahogany, and various imported woods—are treated with "clear natural finishes . . . applied in the same manner as those used on fine furniture."

Metal is another major material used in the manufacture of coffins. Specially treated iron, steel, copper, and bronze, ranging in thickness from 20-gauge to 16-gauge, are the standard metals used.[*]

---

for a welfare, charity, or indigent funeral. For these services, it should be made clear that the funeral home supplies a "basic casket" and there is no access to the selection room. "If the selecting party asks to see other caskets, [the undertaker] should explain that such a procedure is not necessary since such selection is not a part of the service they are arranging. In the event that they are persistent, [the undertaker] should explain that if they are choosing not to use the welfare allowance then, of course, the regular selection room is available to them."

[*]"As you reach the top of the metal quality ladder," said Krieger, "you will find a copper casket produced by an electrolytic process that deposits a one-piece casket upon a form. The copper is one-quarter inch thick. Above this item in quality, you will find the cast bronze casket. This top-quality piece of merchandise is actually cast in a mold and is of one-piece construction."

According to the Casket Manufacturers Association of America in 1977, about 67 percent of adult caskets are made of steel, while 15 to 16 percent are hardwoods, and about 13 percent are wood covered with cloth. Others are constructed of aluminum, bronze, copper, fiber glass, stainless steel, and zinc.*

A wide variety of fabrics is used on the inside and outside of coffins. Linings range from muslin to transparent velvet. The coverings of less costly wooden coffins are made from inexpensive doeskin and broadcloth as well as from brocade and all-silk velvets.

Coffin Costs

The mystery of coffin prices—what is a fair price for a particular coffin?—is almost impossible to unravel. Wholesale prices of coffins are not readily available to anyone outside the funeral industry. The FTC has noted that "direct comparisons between the wholesale costs of coffins and their retail prices are extremely difficult because funeral directors guard wholesale prices as 'TOP SECRET' information." Members of the New York Public Interest Research Group, for example, called several coffin manufacturers listed in the Manhattan Yellow Pages in 1974 in an attempt to compare wholesale coffin prices with the few retail coffin prices researchers were able to get from funeral homes. "None would give any price information, claiming that only licensed funeral directors could be given prices."

That same year, however, an investigative reporter for the now-defunct journal *Media & Consumer* was given some 1973 average wholesale coffin prices by the Casket Manufacturers Association of America: steel coffins sold for $194; hardwoods (such as mahogany and oak), $267; expensive metals (bronze and copper), $709; and softwoods (pine), $91.**

But such average wholesale prices are difficult to evaluate because of the seemingly endless variety of certain features in coffins. "If all possible

---

*A coffin catalog used by a California undertaker features color photographs of one manufacturer's line of metal coffins—all half-couch models—and lists the undertaker's retail prices as ranging from $600 to $2,664. (The undertaker's standard funeral home service charge of $525 is added to the price of whatever coffin is selected.) An 18-gauge steel "royal palm" green model lined with "spray green Lorraine crepe" retails for $1,251. To the untutored eye, the "colonial silver" 20-gauge steel coffin lined with "ivory Drexel crepe," costing $600, may appear just as elegant as the $1,251 model. But differences in the thickness of the steel and design detail more than double the price. An 18-gauge bronze coffin costs $1,372, and the price of a 32-ounce solid copper model lined with velvet is $2,664.

**In New York City, the destitute and the indigent who die alone and often anonymously are buried in "shooks," the white pine boxes that are the coffins of potter's field. Shooks come in seven sizes, ranging from "0" to "6," the smallest being about twelve inches square, the largest about seven feet long. In 1977, the shooks ranged in price from 95¢ to $42.65. The most common size box is "5," which costs $22.60. Abbot & Abbot Box Corp., of Long Island City, New York, is the supplier; the firm would sell a "5" box to the general public for $32.65, a "6" for $60.75.

combinations of body styles, moldings, handles, corners, finishes, and interiors were set up," Wilber Krieger wrote, "it is my opinion that there would be more than 100,000 designs or styles." The Public Affairs Committee notes that differences in price are often based on minor differences in detail or decoration—the type of cloth covering in the less expensive models, or slight variations in upholstery. Among the metal coffins, "the lower-priced ones often are the same gauge of steel [as the higher] but may have merely a cotton mattress instead of a spring *and* mattress, rayon instead of silk covering, less shirring and piping, and plated extension handles instead of brass." Coriolis notes that "all round hardware," a continuous bar handle that runs completely around a coffin, is found only on the best models. Rounded lids—"swell-tops"—are another characteristic of the most expensive cloth-covered coffins, while a "rowboat"—an inexpensive cloth-covered coffin—has a flat top. *

Pricing Methods

Many undertakers maintain that a coffin is a "component part" of the entire funeral. Its retail price, they say, is not arrived at separately but is part of an undertaker's overall funeral price, which must take into account the total operating expenses of an establishment.

Those undertakers who do set a separate price for coffins, however, say they have a "onetime markup"** of coffins. The figure they cite most frequently is 100 percent. That is, if a coffin costs $100 wholesale, its retail price is $200. If it costs the undertaker $250, the consumer will pay $500. But undercover investigators for a New York State commission looking into funeral practices in 1974 said that the *minimum* increase for the retail price of coffins in New York City was about 150 percent, and that it was not unusual for the increase to go to 300 percent or more. Testifying in 1975 before a New York State Senate legislative hearing on the funeral industry, a member of the Memorial Society of Long Island said that the society's cooperating undertakers told members that increases of 300 percent to 500 percent are not uncommon in funeral homes.†

---

*In its 1973 survey of Washington, D.C., funeral homes, the FTC found that in a number of establishments the three least expensive funerals available included both metal coffins and cloth-covered wooden ones. It is generally assumed, the FTC said, that cloth-covered wooden coffins are less expensive than metal ones, but this is not always the case. A wooden coffin covered with a cloth that is of a better grade than doeskin or broadcloth cost more at wholesale than the minimum-priced metal coffin "(roughly $65 vs. $95.)". And some wooden coffins, covered with "plush" material, had a higher wholesale cost (about $150) than the least expensive metal coffins.

**The term markup, as used in the funeral industry, can be confusing. If the wholesale price of a coffin is $100 and the retail price is $200, some undertakers would describe this as a 100 percent markup. The executive director of the Casket Manufacturers Association of America, however, considers this a 50 percent markup, as do some economists.

†The executive director of the Casket Manufacturers Association of America defends

According to the FTC in 1973, "a rule of thumb for casket pricing is that retail cost is roughly five times the wholesale cost." The FTC noted that although some undertakers use a multiple under five and some more than five, five itself "remains as a remarkably accurate index of an undertaker's aggregate markup." Indeed, the multiple-of-five index "holds up uncannily across the entire industry," the FTC said. "Multiply the wholesale value of casket shipments by five, and you have the dollar volume of the funeral service industry."* Of course, as noted earlier, funeral industry financial data cited in industry and government statistics do not tell the whole story of how much consumers spend in the funeral marketplace.

In the majority of funeral homes, coffins on display in the selection room carry price tags or price cards. Depending on the method of pricing used by the firm, the price will be either for the coffin alone or for a "complete" funeral (which, however, covers only certain funeral home costs; see page 33).

There are four main methods of quoting or setting prices for funerals, although some undertakers use variations of all of them.

Unit Pricing. The price tag on the coffin includes the funeral home price for the funeral, minus vault and other extras covered by cash advances. For example, the "typical" funeral, as determined in the 1973 FTC survey of Washington, D.C., funeral homes, listed the price of a "complete" funeral as $1,137 (the price tag on the coffin). Additional funeral home costs (including a vault for $136,** newspaper notices $20, clergy's honorarium $15, death certificate transcripts $5, flower wagon $25, organist $15) brought the total price of the funeral to $1,358, not including burial costs and sales tax.

Bi-Unit Pricing. This method, sometimes called the service-charge method, separates merchandise from service. There is one price for the coffin and a separate one for the undertaker's services. Krieger noted that this method came into use because many funeral buyers—never really sure what

---

such "sharp markups" and says there are legitimate reasons for undertakers to double and triple the wholesale costs of coffins. He maintains that undertakers make low profits in other areas of their business and points out that there are a number of operating expenses involved in merchandising coffins, such as warehouse rent, display merchandise, and inventory expenses.

*The FTC noted that the total wholesale value of merchandise shipped by coffin companies to undertakers in 1971 was, according to the Casket Manufacturers Association of America, $331.6 million. This figure multiplied by five, according to the FTC, came to $1.658 billion "as an estimate of the dollar volume of the funeral service industry for 1971. And, in fact, the 1971 volume of the industry, extrapolated from Department of Commerce Figures [in *U.S. Industrial Outlook—1972, with Projections to 1980*], *was* $1.65 billion!"

**In the typical Washington, D.C., funeral cited by the FTC, the average cost of an interment receptacle was listed as $136. This, according to the FTC, was a "weighted average" of the average cost of a vault purchased from a funeral home, $311, and the average cost of a concrete liner or box, which cost about $85.

they are being charged for—think they are paying too much for coffins under unit pricing.

Functional Pricing or Tri-Unit Pricing. With this method, the price of the coffin is set separately; professional and staff services constitute another unit of charge; a third is the use of the funeral home and facilities. (Occasionally, an additional component, covering special automobiles, is used.)

Price Itemization. This method requires an exact rendering of the price of each item and service included in the funeral. Its main advantage for consumers is that they know exactly what they are paying for. It makes it easier for consumers to reject goods and services they do not want and to request that the total price of the funeral be reduced proportionately.

Although price itemization is the most desirable form of pricing from the consumer's point of view, it does not always provide the protection it should.* If a buyer rejects one item or service, the undertaker may arbitrarily raise other prices as compensation. Unscrupulous undertakers have even been known to switch price tags on coffins.**

Many funeral homes using the price-itemization method provide a printed list of goods and services (sometimes totaling fifty or sixty items), but prices are not printed on these lists. They are written in by the undertaker during the funeral transaction. Thus, consumers have no way of knowing whether they are being charged the same prices as everyone else.†

Sales Pressure Tactics

Although pricing methods may vary from funeral home to funeral home, the use of sales pressure tactics seems common to many. There is much

---

*Nor is the price itemization requirement always followed in the six states where it is the law. Many undertakers, taking advantage of consumers' lack of knowledge about the law, do not provide an itemized price list before the funeral takes place unless a customer requests it. The FTC noted in 1975 that only 48 percent of funeral homes in Florida—one of the six states—reported in a 1974 survey by the Florida State Investigation Committee that they itemized prices for customers. In 1976, the New York State Health Department levied fines on three funeral homes in the New York City area for failure to itemize costs for various services.

**The FTC says that it has knowledge of funeral homes where this is done before prosperous-looking survivors enter the selection room.
    Coriolis recounts that "while visiting a funeral director recently, I was treated to an amazing display of price switching, as he prepared for the arrival of a family to choose a casket. The shuffle involved the price tags on four caskets. My host explained to me that it was necessitated by the previous sale of a case [coffin], and the fact that he did not want to bother unpacking another to fill the gap. Imagine a car salesman who has sold his last $4,000 unit, raising the prices of his cheaper cars to fill the gap!"

†In its proposed rule, the FTC would require funeral homes to have available at all times and to provide customers with a printed or typed price list of goods and services. When such a list is made available to customers, there can be no question of arbitrary pricing during the funeral sale. The FTC would also require in its proposed rule that every funeral home provide a printed or typed coffin price list, giving "in ascending order" the prices of all coffins sold by the establishment, together with information to help customers identify which of the listed coffins are on display.

evidence from consumers—in books, articles, and letters columns—and from investigators, attesting to the fact that funeral buyers frequently feel strong pressure from funeral home personnel to buy expensive coffins.

In 1970, an employee of a national credit union association publication described an experience familiar to many funeral buyers. The employee reported what happened when he and his brother arranged their mother's funeral:

"We'll take the $650 casket."

"Yes, but she *was* your mother. Surely something in a better casket would be more befitting her memory. Now this $800 casket . . ."

Who would say no at a time like this? My mother had just died. The funeral director showed us the more expensive casket. The employee added: "Neither my brother nor I could say anything. We just nodded our assent at what burned in my stomach as a high pressure gimmick. Then, after the funeral, we were told the final amount. It had increased due to 'extra' services. The total happened to be a few dollars short of my mother's insurance policy."

A Unitarian minister wrote in his church's news bulletin in 1976: "Only last week a man sat in my office and told how he had said to the funeral director that he did not want an expensive casket for his mother, to which the undertaker responded, 'You mean to say you did not love your mother?'"

Consumers often feel coerced into purchasing expensive coffins because personnel in many funeral homes are themselves under pressure to sell costly merchandise and expensive funerals. Undercover investigators for the New York State commission looking into funeral practices in 1974 revealed that performance charts are posted in many large mortuaries and funeral home chains, giving details of sales and how much business has been brought in by staff members. The charts are used to evaluate the work of each employee. Those employees who have low sales figures are often reassigned to other tasks, such as embalming and cleaning bodies. In order to avoid transfer to "the pit," personnel use aggressive tactics to sell expensive coffins.*

The Batesville Casket Company provided a tape recording to funeral homes for personnel to use as an aid in selling coffins.** According to the

---

*The FTC notes that documents obtained from a large California mortuary reveal a "compensation system which penalizes salespersons for low-priced sales and rewards them for high-priced ones."

**Batesville, with headquarters in Batesville, Indiana, is the largest coffin manufacturer in the United States, selling 13 percent of the nation's coffins (net sales in 1975 were $78.5 million). Batesville informed its shareholders in its 1975 annual report that it was expanding its "customer service and educational activities." The report noted that business seminars involved 11,000 funeral directors in 52 locations and more than 1,000 funeral directors were brought to Batesville for educational programs. Batesville personnel demonstrated to students at mortuary science schools "the most current aids used in the funeral service profession," and a consumer education film program was prepared for undertakers, according to the report.

New York State commission investigators, some funeral home personnel privately admitted that the Batesville presentation is "one of the most blatant" on the market. The sales pitch puts heavy emphasis on the "protective" features of expensive coffins, with the apparent intent of instilling guilt feelings in survivors who, by not purchasing a costly, protective coffin, would expose the deceased person's body to the elements.

At the same time, many undertakers disparage inexpensive coffins. In some establishments, deprecatory terms are used to describe the cheapest coffins: "orange crates," "this box," "rowboats," "stovepipes," and so on.* According to the FTC, the techniques of disparagement "can range from the subtlest glance of disapproval to a direct statement that a certain selection is inappropriate and disrespectful."**

In many funeral homes the most inexpensive coffins cannot be found in the selection room; nearly half the Washington firms with selection rooms surveyed by the FTC in 1973 admitted that their least expensive coffin was not on display. A 1974 Florida survey of all funeral establishments in the state revealed that 23 percent of those responding did not display their lowest-priced coffins.

It is not uncommon for funeral buyers asking to see low-cost models to be led to a dimly lighted space under the stairs, to a small cramped storage room, to a basement, or behind curtains to view them. The coffins are hidden, not because of lack of space, but because many undertakers are afraid that too many will be sold. If an inexpensive coffin is displayed in the selection room, and sells too well, undertakers usually remove it.

There is evidence, too, the FTC reports, that "funeral directors and/or casket manufacturers deliberately vulgarize caskets so that the funeral buyer will purchase a more expensive model. Tactics include poor finishing, the use of tawdry lining material or fabric of garish colors, and the like."†

---

*A Rhode Island reporter described his experience in a Pawtucket funeral home in 1969: "The funeral director tapped his fingers lightly on the side of the gray metallic coffin on display in the well-lit and thickly carpeted 'selection room' of his Pawtucket funeral home and said, 'Don't buy this. It's nothing but a tin can,' he remarked. 'You wouldn't want to be walking up the steps of the church and have the bottom drop out of it. You'd be better off by getting something sturdier,' he advised as he moved on to a more expensive casket."

In 1972, a California reporter described an undertaker's reaction when asked for a simple funeral with the least expensive coffin. "What?" exclaimed the undertaker in horror, "You'd put your mom into a *pine* box?" When researchers with the New York Public Interest Research Group called funeral homes in the New York City area and asked for prices of the least expensive coffins, one response was: "The cheapest casket is $150, but you really wouldn't want it. For $300 and up, it is presentable."

**So prevalent does the practice seem that the FTC has included a provision in its proposed rule that would prohibit disparagement of any kind when a customer expresses concern about price.

†Coriolis notes that when he pointed out the "cheap grade of satin lining" in a coffin salesman's elm coffins, the salesman told him that was done to help sell something better. Inexpensive models in most establishments, Coriolis says, are "deliberately defaced in

A 1974 investigational hearing in Washington, D.C., according to the FTC, revealed that the least expensive coffin on display in a large Washington funeral home was "silver taupe (a color somewhere between lavender and pink)." It was admitted at the hearing that the color was chosen deliberately, to discourage people from buying the coffin.*

Protection for the Body?

Sixty-seven percent of all coffins sold in the United States in 1976 were steel. The popularity of steel coffins is undoubtedly due to coffin manufacturers' and undertakers' claims of durability and the implication in their selling that steel coffins preserve and protect the body. Some casket manufacturers offer a thirty-year or even a fifty-year warranty on their metal coffins and say they will replace those that prove defective during that time. Some manufacturers state in their warranties on a sealer coffin (a coffin that is tightly or hermetically sealed, often with a rubber gasket) that it offers "peace of mind protection" or "security through the ages."**

The NFDA's Howard Raether, however, cautions undertakers against using phrases such as "eternal protection," "last forever," and "indestructible" to describe coffins in the selection room. He notes the recent FTC regulations enacted to make warranties and guarantees less deceptive and to give consumers more protection. Raether warns undertakers: "The funeral director by virtue of presenting the manufacturer's warranty or guarantee becomes directly involved and liable, especially if the merchandise was defective or its handling affected the merchandise so that conditions of the warranty or guarantee were impossible to fulfill."

Yet many customers want to believe that an expensive sealer coffin will protect the body and somehow deter decay. The Casket Manufacturers Association of America's 1974 survey of attitudes toward death and funerals found that 67 percent of the 1,060 respondents rated "protection of the body" as "important" or "very important."

The question of whether coffins prevent decomposition of the body or provide long-term protection against the elements is one for which there is no ready answer. The number of occasions when it is possible to investigate

order that they would be overlooked by the purchaser in favor of a better-looking and more expensive casket."

*In its proposed rule, the FTC recommends that when coffins on display are available in other colors, funeral homes must post notices stating this fact. The rule also proposes that the three least expensive coffins available in a funeral establishment must be displayed in the selection room. (If there are fewer than twelve coffins in the selection room, then only one of the three least expensive must be on display.)

**According to an FTC attorney, "These manufacturers and their customer funeral homes will disingenuously guarantee that if the body is disinterred and is found to have decayed within the time limit of the warranty, the price of the casket will gladly be refunded. There is little likelihood, of course, that most customers would investigate that guarantee."

the state of a corpse that has been buried for any length of time is obviously limited. Medical examiners, coroners, and pathologists involved in legal investigations are those most likely to have the opportunity to judge whether an exhumed body has been well preserved. There are differing opinions about the efficacy of sealer coffins, vaults, and embalming. The consensus among pathologists seems to be that no one component in burial determines how long a body is preserved in the grave; the length of preservation depends on a combination of factors.

In 1976, a pathologist in the New York City medical examiner's office performed an autopsy on the body of a four-year-old girl who had died ten years earlier. The pathologist stated that the body was exceptionally well preserved because the coffin was watertight and airtight* and the body had been well embalmed. (For a discussion of embalming and the preservation of the body, see Chapter 11.)

Dr. Joseph Jachimczyk, for many years the coroner of Harris County in Texas, agrees that many variables can determine the condition of an exhumed corpse. He found that some bodies buried for eight years were better preserved than those in the grave for only eight weeks. The condition of bodies, he said, depends on the embalmer's art, the soil** in which the grave is located (high and dry ground slows decomposition more than marshy areas), whether there is seepage into the coffin, and whether there is a concrete vault enclosing the coffin.

Some medical authorities, as well as cemetery personnel, have had sharply different experiences and opinions. In *The American Way of Death,* Jessica Mitford quotes the chief pathologist of San Francisco General Hospital as saying, "If you seal up a casket so it is more or less airtight, you seal in the anaerobic bacteria—the kind that thrive in an airless atmosphere." The results are "pretty horrible," he said, adding that it would be better to be buried in a shroud than a coffin.

Investigators for the New York State commission looking into funeral practices in 1974 described a case in which a body was exhumed ten months after burial in a New York cemetery. Although the coffin had been sold with a fifty-year guarantee, it had collapsed under the weight of the earth, and decomposition was in an "advanced state." Funeral home informants told the investigators that expensive all-copper coffins "are known by those in the industry to be of such soft metal that they collapse soon after burial, although they are sold as protective caskets."

Offering sealer coffins with special mechanisms to keep them airtight for preservation and protection is an obvious psychological inducement to

---

*A Westchester County (New York) medical examiner told Consumers Union in 1976 that there is no such thing as an airtight coffin.
**One former cemetery worker told Consumers Union that sandy soil was an excellent preservative for coffins and bodies, while clay soil was poor.

bereaved survivors to spend more money. Evidence does suggest that coffins can be a factor, in some cases, in preserving bodies. But decomposition of the body is inevitable, eventually, and no one can accurately predict the rate of decay.*

Unconventional Coffins

Although it is unlikely that inexpensive cardboard or plastic coffins will ever be popular with many undertakers, some establishments have begun to sell them for use in funeral services. A mortuary in Yonkers, New York, Havey's Funeral Home, uses coffins made of heavy corrugated cardboard for services that precede cremation. The body reposes in the container (the "Creceptacle"), which in turn is placed inside a conventional coffin in the funeral home during viewing hours. The firm charges $785 for its Century Plan, which includes embalming or other preparation, "rental of formal decorative casket," "limited visitation at the funeral home," funeral services, transportation to the crematory, and scattering of the remains; the crematory fee is not included.

Ambrose Havey III told Consumers Union that he was the first to manufacture this type of cardboard coffin and that he has taken out a patent on his product. Sales of the cardboard coffin have increased to such an extent that the firm is having the coffins mass-produced in Florida.

Another recent variation of the conventional coffin is the "eternal rest bed vault," manufactured by a company in Iowa. This coffin, made of a light brown material called "styron 475" (usually described as fiber glass or plastic), is supposedly a combination coffin and vault. Its major advantage is that the purchase of a vault is not necessary; the coffin/vault is placed directly in the ground. The unit is actually a cylindrical two-piece container and lid, weighing about sixty pounds and theoretically capable of holding a three-hundred-pound body. Those who sell the unit claim it is even more resistant to the elements than the most expensive coffin.

At the funeral home, the body is viewed in the bottom half of the eternal rest bed vault, which fits inside a "catafalque," a special coffin with a handsome exterior, but no bottom, which is used each time the eternal rest bed vault is included in the funeral. To all outward appearances, this combination looks like any other coffin. When the body is taken to the cemetery, it is sometimes transferred temporarily to another container. The lid of the eternal rest bed vault is put in place and sealed only at the cemetery. Some firms transport the catafalque and eternal rest bed vault together to the cemetery. There, the coffin/vault is removed from the catafalque, and the lid put in place and sealed just before burial.

---

*The FTC requires in its proposed rule that funeral homes and coffin manufacturers refrain from claiming that coffins prevent decomposition or decay of a dead body and refrain from misrepresenting the preservative or protective function of a coffin.

The selling price of the eternal rest bed vault ranges from $695 to $795; according to industry sources, it costs about $100 to manufacture. The coffin/vault is sold primarily by cemeteries, but some funeral homes also sell the unit. And in some parts of the country it is sold door-to-door by salespeople on a preneed basis (purchasers can keep the unit in their home or have it stored for them).

In Orlando, Florida, the owners of a mortuary and cemetery offer a complete funeral and burial with the eternal rest bed vault for $1,695 (as opposed to $3,000 for their services for a conventional funeral). Soon after they began to offer this special plan, the owners said, 180 orders for the eternal rest bed vault were received, as well as inquiries from funeral homes throughout Florida. The president of two cemeteries in Virginia Beach, Virginia, who also owns a mortuary, reported selling between four hundred and five hundred eternal rest bed vaults within the first seven months after he began to merchandise them for funerals. A funeral with the coffin/vault, excluding cemetery expenses, cost $1,330.

Sales of the eternal rest bed vault by some cemeteries, however, have met with opposition from many undertakers, since this unconventional burial container means fewer sales of both coffins and vaults by funeral homes. In Virginia Beach, a suit was brought by the state against a local undertakers' trade association. The suit charged, under the state's 1974 antitrust law, that members of the association had conspired to prevent competitors from selling the eternal rest bed vault by their refusal to handle funeral services using the product. The attorney for the undertakers' association maintained that undertakers could be liable for lawsuits when the body is exposed at the graveside, especially when the deceased or the survivors had specifically requested that the body not be exposed. "I wouldn't want my wife or mother lying out there," the attorney said, "while five or six gravediggers are messing around trying to get that lid on."

Even though the eternal rest bed vault appears to be unique in some respects, questionable sales methods—most notably "tie-in" sales—may be involved when the coffin/vault is sold by cemeteries. For example, at the two cemeteries in Virginia, eternal rest bed vaults were sold only to people who purchased burial plots from the cemeteries. And at the cemeteries in both Florida and Virginia where the coffin/vault was sold as part of a complete funeral package, prices were high. One of the advantages of purchasing an eternal rest bed vault is said to be the saving to the consumer in the cost of a vault. Yet $1,695 for a funeral and burial and $1,330 for a funeral alone are not insubstantial sums.

Coffins by Mail?

Those who would like to economize on the cost of a coffin may wish to consider buying a plain pine coffin by mail. Coffins can be obtained from the

St. Francis Burial Society (3421 Center Street, N.W., Washington, D.C. 20010), which offers two types of assembled coffins—the contemporary (rectangular) design at $160 and the traditional (hexagonal) design at $180. The society also offers coffin kits for assembling; included are all necessary parts, hardware, and instructions. The contemporary coffin kit costs $95; the traditional coffin, available only upon special request, sells for $99. The society also offers plans for a completely do-it-yourself coffin; the price is $2.50. According to the society, there are practical everyday uses for coffins around the house. For example, they can serve as blanket chests, coffee tables, wine racks, or even pool cue holders. Once purchased, the coffins can be stained or painted.

Those who would like to provide their own coffin for burial or cremation should be aware that this procedure could create problems for survivors who use the services of a funeral home. Because coffins are usually a major source of profit for conventional mortuaries, undertakers may object to using a coffin provided by customers. Some may refuse, even though supplying one's own coffin would seem not too different from providing one's own burial clothes—a common enough occurrence in funerals. Inquiries among funeral homes in the area may lead to an undertaker who is willing to accept a coffin not sold by the funeral home. If such an establishment is found in advance of need, a useful precaution would be to send a letter of instruction to the funeral home, stating that a coffin will be provided.

Some Guidelines for Choosing a Coffin

• In some communities there are mortuaries that have no coffin selection room on the premises. In general, these funeral homes tend to have lower average funeral prices than firms with selection rooms.* Customers can choose coffins from a catalog, photographs, slides, or are taken to a coffin wholesaler who displays a wide range of models. Although the undertaker without a selection room may have to pay a higher price for coffins because of buying them on an individual basis,** saving on overhead tends to lower the overall cost of the funeral for the consumer.
• Sometimes, even in funeral homes that have selection rooms, it is possible, if a consumer so requests, to choose a coffin from a catalog or pictorial display. Such a method avoids the sense of pressure some people may feel when looking at the actual models in the selection room.

Customers who enter the selection room should remember that it is fre-

---

*The 1973 FTC survey of Washington, D.C., funeral homes found that undertakers without selection rooms generally save overhead expenses because they do not need to maintain an inventory of coffins or large areas of mortuary space in which to display them.

**New York State commission investigators were told in 1974 that coffins purchased on an as-needed basis are sometimes sold at higher prices through a "gentleman's agreement" between coffin wholesaler and undertaker.

quently necessary to ask to see the least expensive coffins; these models are often kept elsewhere. If a moderately priced or inexpensive coffin is in an unattractive color, customers should ask whether it is available in other colors. If a particular color is not available at the funeral home, the undertaker should be asked if it can be obtained from a wholesaler within the time available and at no additional cost.

• If there is to be a closed coffin during funeral services, survivors who wish to buy the least expensive unit might consider covering the coffin with a pall (a heavy cloth used to cover a coffin, hearse, or tomb) or, if the decedent was a veteran, with a flag, or placing the coffin behind a screen. In this way, no one attending the funeral services need be in a position to ascertain the price of the coffin. The Episcopal Church encourages the draping of a pall over all coffins—whether the simplest pine or most expensive bronze—during funeral services to emphasize the democratic spirit within the church.

• Compared with a gleaming copper model or highly burnished mahogany, inexpensive coffins can appear drab. And it is when making the comparison that survivors often falter and choose a more expensive model, rationalizing that the deceased perhaps "deserves something better." At this point, funeral buyers might remember that the contrast between expensive and low-cost coffins is, for the most part, a deliberate merchandising tactic designed to make consumers spend more money.

• If funeral buyers are made to feel guilty or ashamed for insisting on a low-cost or moderately priced coffin, it may help to remember that undertakers are in business to sell goods and services; they are not moral judges or arbiters of taste. Funeral buyers have the right to choose freely and without pressure the product they want. If necessary, an undertaker should be reminded of the code of ethics that most trade association members subscribe to. The Code of Professional Practices of the National Funeral Directors Association states that the undertaker "shall provide the necessary services and merchandise in keeping with the wishes and finances of the family or their representative." And the Code of Good Practice followed by National Selected Morticians promises "to assure each purchaser complete freedom to exercise his preference in selecting a funeral service within his means."

• Some people question whether a coffin can be a true expression of love and respect for the dead. As religious leaders and lay people concerned about funeral practices have pointed out, love and respect for the dead can be demonstrated in other ways, according to the beliefs and wishes of survivors—through religious ceremonies, memorial services, gatherings of family and friends, or contributions to charity. The funeral industry has been remarkably successful in convincing millions of people that a commercial product—and the higher its price the better—is the preferable expression of affection and esteem.

11
To Embalm
or Not to Embalm

Embalming is the process whereby preservative and disinfectant fluids (the most common is formaldehyde) are injected into the arterial system and body cavities of a corpse. (For a detailed description of the embalming process, see Appendix 6.) The procedure entails, essentially, the substitution of embalming fluid for blood, and it is usually carried out very soon after death. Theoretically, embalming is performed for sanitary and public health reasons (disinfection) and for temporary preservation* of the body. Without embalming—or refrigeration—a body will begin to deteriorate; a characteristic odor may be detected soon after death. (The National Selected Morticians cites eight hours as the maximum time that can elapse if embalming is to arrest the process of decomposition.)

There can be little question of the need to embalm when the body is not to be buried until several days after death and refrigeration facilities are not available. There is disagreement, however, about the significance of embalming for public health reasons (see pages 91–98). As for the length of time that embalming preserves the body, no general estimate can be given. Many variables can affect the rate at which a body decomposes in the grave (see page 83).

But most funeral homes do not embalm just for the sake of preservation and disinfection. They embalm also because it is the necessary prelude to "restoration," the process by which embalmers attempt to give a more true-to-life appearance to the corpse. With embalming, followed by restoration,

---

*For those interested in long-term preservation, cryonics—the procedure by which bodies are immersed in liquid nitrogen or liquid helium and frozen—may be the answer. The purpose and hope of cryonics are that the frozen bodies can be reanimated at a future date—for example, when science discovers a cure for cancer or old age. The leading apostle of the cryonics movement is Robert C. W. Ettinger, whose book *The Prospect of Immortality* proposes that it may be possible to meet one's own descendants a thousand years from now.

88

a funeral establishment can offer survivors the ritual of viewing the body, a practice peculiar mainly to the United States and Canada. Survivors, through the combined procedures of embalming and restoration, may see the corpse looking remarkably lifelike after features and limbs are suitably arranged and various cosmetics are applied. In some cases, where there has been disfigurement, restoration may require surgical reconstructive procedures. (For a description of the restoration process, see Appendix 6.)

Why Embalming and Restoration?

Embalming and the companion art of restoration have long been essential components of the conventional American funeral. Since the turn of the century, Americans have been viewing their embalmed dead in open coffins, many believing that the custom is part of a "traditional" religious ceremony. It is difficult to document this belief, for it has no roots in either the Christian or Judaic religions. (In fact, it is contrary to Orthodox Jewish law.) Nor is embalming common outside the United States and Canada.

The practice of embalming began in this country during the Civil War, when embalmers prepared soldiers' bodies for shipment home. They became aware that the practice was profitable. Since that time, the embalmed "viewable body" in the open coffin has helped make funerals more expensive. This is acknowledged by C. Strub and L. Frederick in their basic embalming text, *The Principles and Practice of Embalming*. They write that embalming "forms the foundation for the entire funeral-service structure. It is the basis for the sale of profitable merchandise, the guardian of public health, the reason for much of our professional education and our protective legislation. . . ." Coriolis, the iconoclastic Canadian undertaker, states unequivocally that there is only one reason for embalming:

> So when Uncle Mort dies, the primary concern of the burial men is ensuring that he is put on display so that Aunt Minnie's "sense of the proper" will prompt her to buy the best casket she can afford in which to place him on display. Throughout the industry there is an accepted axiom that closed caskets result in the sale of lower-priced goods. This, then, is the reason for embalming; there is no other.

That rationale for embalming is undoubtedly furthest from the minds of survivors who come to funeral homes to arrange for services. As Strub and Frederick point out in their embalming textbook: "Actually, it is the surface appearance—the 'cosmetic effect'—rather than the tissue preservation itself that makes embalming an important and necessary part of the modern American way of life. No bereaved relative ever asks the embalmer if the deceased has been thoroughly disinfected and preserved; they are interested only in the naturalness of the appearance." A number of people both within and without the funeral industry have expressed objections about the propriety of "restoring" corpses and of trying to make them appear as

89

they did in life. But those who defend the practice interpret it as a necessary part of the funeral ritual.

In *For the Living*, Edgar Jackson addresses himself directly to the question and asks: "What about putting make-up and cosmetics on a dead body?" His answer is that this effort to reconstruct a resemblance to the living person not only shows reverence for the deceased but is a necessary step toward "wise grief management." "Proper respect for the body," says Jackson, "determines that it should not be made ready for viewing in an unkept and disheveled condition. So the hair is combed and the face shaved." Even eyeglasses and dentures are important factors in re-creating the dead person's living appearance.°

Cosmetics, eyeglasses, dentures are what Jackson calls "important functions of clear identity" that help survivors accept the reality of death. When the identity of the corpse is unmistakable, says Jackson, then survivors cannot deny what they see and must come to terms with death.

Misconceptions about embalming are shared by many people who believe it is (1) a legal requirement, (2) a public-health measure, or (3) a means for preservation of the body. Embalming is a legal requirement only under certain conditions. And its value as a public-health measure and a means of *long-term* preservation of the body is open to question (see pages 91–100).

Is Embalming Required by Law?

Legal requirements concerning embalming vary greatly from state to state, and a few states have no legal requirements at all. In many states embalming is required if the body is not buried or cremated within a certain time limit. In some states, among them Florida°° and Pennsylvania, the time period is twenty-four hours; in others it can be thirty, thirty-six, or forty-eight hours. Embalming is usually required if the body is to be transported interstate by common carrier; some states even require embalming intrastate if a body must be transported away from the community where death occurred. Embalming is usually mandatory when death is caused by a communicable disease. These are the main conditions under which state laws say a body must be embalmed. Some states stipulate that embalming is not required if refrigeration is used. And in some states the body need not be embalmed if it is enclosed in a tightly sealed outer container; in others, if

---

°Should the remains be laid out with glasses on?" asks Jackson. His answer: "It is quite obvious that putting glasses on the dead body serves no purpose as far as the body is concerned. Its eyes do not see and never will again. The practice of putting glasses on the dead body is primarily so that the familiar image of the person will be reenforced. . . . To use a comparison, we might say that it is foolish to place dentures in the mouth of the dead person because he will never eat again. The only purpose for using dentures is to give a more recognizable appearance to the face."

°°In Florida, however, the law states that cremation cannot take place before forty-eight

embalming cannot be performed because of decomposition, an airtight container is also required. (See Appendix 7 for a state-by-state listing of the legal requirements concerning embalming.) For Canadian requirements, see footnote below.*

Does Embalming Protect the Public Health?

Despite the relatively few state and provincial laws specifically requiring embalming, the practice—as well as the custom of viewing that it makes possible—has become so crucial to the entire funeral industry that many undertakers may well exaggerate the need for embalming. Some overstate the case for embalming not only to consumers in funeral homes but in publications and public statements. For example, Edward A. Martin, a mortician, wrote in his 1970 book, *Psychology of Funeral Service:* "Today's embalmer has done more to prevent the spread of disease in his community than most people realize." And a 1976 brochure distributed for consumers by a group of funeral homes in New Orleans says this about embalming:

> One question raised in recent years is that of the necessity of embalming a body if it is to be cremated. Embalming is necessary in the disposition of all remains for one reason—protection of the living. It is a sanitary measure that prevents the spread of infections and communicable diseases. There have been a number of cases where unembalmed bodies have caused serious illness.

In response to a letter requesting information about specific documented cases in which unembalmed bodies caused illness, the president of the New Orleans funeral homes was able to give no specific data, although he cited "a fearful yellow fever epidemic" in New Orleans as a precedent for embalming regulations, "as well as the typhoid fever which is also a dread disease always evident in some of the statistics in Louisiana." He suggested a query to the New Orleans Health Department. In response to an inquiry from Consumers Union, the chief of communicable diseases in New Orleans said: "I have no case documentation of unembalmed bodies

---

hours after death. Thus embalming (or refrigeration) is required prior to cremation.

*At present, Canadian provinces allow far more latitude in requirements for embalming than do U.S. state governments. In Quebec, embalming is not required under any circumstances. Under normal conditions of death, embalming is not required in any of the other provinces. When transportation is involved, five provinces require embalming only when transport takes more than seventy-two hours, and then there is a choice between embalming and a hermetically sealed container. In Newfoundland, embalming is mandatory if transport takes more than thirty hours; in Ontario and Saskatchewan, there is no time limit on transport, but either embalming or an airtight container is required for transport. Seven of the ten provinces have no embalming requirements in case of death by communicable disease. In Alberta, bodies must be buried within thirty-six hours; in Manitoba, within forty-eight. Saskatchewan has no embalming requirements for specified communicable diseases, but either embalming or a metal-lined coffin, hermetically sealed, is required for unspecified communicable diseases.

being a source of infection to others. There are, probably, such documenta-
tions in the historical literature, but I have not researched this." He pointed
out, however, the need for sanitary precautions when death occurs from
communicable disease. "Viable disease-causing organisms may be present,
for variable lengths of time, and be capable of being spread to others, either
by direct contact or by insect vectors."

Consumers Union's review of the literature found that there have been
very few controlled scientific studies on the efficacy of embalming or even
about the incidence and effects of microorganisms in the body after death.
An article entitled "Postmortem Bacteriology"* notes the dearth of published reports on the subject:

> Except for the handful of recent studies . . . postmortem bacteriology appar-
> ently has been either totally neglected in most institutions, or performed to a
> limited degree at best. From 1929 to 1958 only two articles appeared per-
> taining specifically to autopsy bacteriology. Moreover, virtually none of the
> current texts in microbiology even mention the subject.

In contrast to the kind of absolute claims made by many undertakers that
embalming prevents the spread of disease, the scientific and medical communities are usually objective, considered, and cautious in comments about
embalming. A letter from the U.S. Public Health Service's Center for Disease Control in Atlanta to Consumers Union in October 1974 stated:

> We have yet to see any data indicating that there is a significant public
> health problem associated with unembalmed or ineffectively embalmed
> cadavers. If there is a disease risk, it seems to us that it would be by far most
> likely among those individuals who handle such cadavers (*e.g.* pathologists,
> undertakers)....
>
> Embalming does not sterilize (sterilization is a complete destruction or
> removal of all microbial life) a cadaver, but rather embalming disinfects
> (reduces the level of microbial contamination) it.

Reviewing the Evidence

In 1959, Elizabeth Ives, M.D., now head of the Department of Pediatrics at
University Hospital, University of Saskatchewan, in Saskatoon, wrote her
Doctor of Public Health dissertation on embalming and came to the conclu-

---

* "Postmortem Bacteriology" is not about embalming or even about the dangers of infection to those who handle cadavers. Its purpose is to examine available research in an
attempt to understand more about bacteria and microflora in dead tissue, primarily in the
first forty-eight hours after death. (Such studies are of increasing importance because of
the growing practice of tissue transplants and organ transplantation—see Chapter 17.)
The article asks a number of pertinent questions, among them: "Is there visceral bacterial
dissemination after death; and, if so, how soon post mortem?" "Are the viscera of man
sterile?" " What is the visceral distribution of microorganisms?" On these and other questions the author concludes that "a complete interpretation of the results obtained" is not
possible; "the final picture," he says, "is still fuzzy."

sion that "under normal circumstances the possible risk of infection from a newly dead body [i.e., unembalmed] is slight." Her dissertation stated:

> if it could be shown that a fresh body is a potential danger and that embalming effectively combats that danger then, this alone would be sufficient to make immediate embalming advisable in 100% of deaths. However, it is by no means established that such a danger exists and any danger is probably slight since the mortality amongst undertakers is no greater than that for the community as a whole.*

In 1973, in a letter to Richard Middleton, M.D., a prominent member of the Memorial Society Association of Canada and chairman of the Anatomy Committee, Memorial University of Newfoundland, Ives wrote to reaffirm her earlier views: "I doubt if any evidence has come to light which would materially alter my comments made at that time."

This is not to say that cadavers are without hazards, even bodies whose death is not caused by infectious diseases. Ives, in her dissertation, noted that "it is well known that, after death, normally innocuous but potentially pathogenic bacteria spread from the bowel into all the tissues of the body. ... This spread of bacteria is probably a great deal more rapid than is commonly believed."** However, Ives continued, "the skin surface appears to be a reasonably efficient barrier for some time after death and, providing it remains intact, there is little danger from this wide dissemination of bacteria in the tissues." Ives noted in addition that with the cessation of breathing and speaking after death, the risk of "nasopharyngeal organisms" being released into the atmosphere is reduced. Nonetheless, Ives was careful to point out, "little is known about the survival of viruses in the body after death."†

Not all investigators agree that embalming may not be necessary for

---

*Coriolis echoes Ives's impression when he notes that life insurance firms would undoubtedly raise their rates for embalmers if they thought there was the risk of contagion from dead bodies.

**According to "Postmortem Bacteriology," however, even this assertion is in question. The authors note that "the dictum that bacteria invade and disseminate within the body soon after death originated with a few early workers around the turn of the century who considered this explanation the most logical for their observed high rate of positive postmortem blood cultures. However, the data presented in some of the recent publications used for this review establish reasonably clearly that postmortem invasion does not occur, probably at least for the first 24 hours after death."

†Ives's full comments here were: "Also, although contents of bowel, bladder, stomach and lungs may be extruded after death, they are probably no greater a source of infection than they would have been during life. Despite these facts, however, it is important to realise that a body is not entirely lacking in danger and that all risk of infection does not die with the body. There is a very well established risk that the body of a person dying from an infectious disease can transmit that disease to the living and little is known about the survival of viruses in the body after death. Generally speaking, however, there is no reason why a body immediately after death should be a greater source of infection than that same body during life; there is a slightly increased possibility of infection after a post mortem examination has destroyed the integrity of the skin."

public health reasons. An article by Jerome F. Frederick, Ph.D., reproduced and circulated by the NFDA, states unequivocally that pathogenic
bacteria in bodies survive for a long time. In "The Public Health Value of
Embalming," Frederick writes:

> the present form of embalming is of exceptional importance insofar as
> the general health of a population is concerned. There is little doubt that the
> injection of a dead body with disinfecting and preserving solutions material-
> ly decreases the number of pathogenic organisms in our immediate environ-
> ment. . . .
>
> Those that stress the idea that the dead human body should be interred
> without embalming, are surely not aware of the fact that bacteria, and par-
> ticularly pathogenic bacteria can survive in the earth and soil for long
> periods of time, remaining viable and capable of causing infectious disease.
> This has been recognized for a long time. . . .
>
> Therefore, the interment of a body, without prior disinfection via em-
> balming, is essentially, the placing of a vast culture medium containing
> billions of pathogens, into a soil which probably will not kill off the patho-
> gens and may even stimulate the growth of these organisms!

Gordon Rose, Ph.D., of the Department of Mortuary Science, Wayne State
University, concurs with Frederick's opinion. In a laboratory study (for
which support was received from the NFDA), Rose came to the conclusion
in 1970 that unembalmed bodies are a health hazard. Noting that samples
were taken from various anatomic sites in cadavers at different postmortem
time intervals up to seventy-two hours, the abstract of Rose's paper, "The
Microbiologic Evaluation and Enumeration of Postmortem Specimens from
Human Remains," states in part that "several recognized and potential
pathogens, both bacterial and mycotic, were recovered consistently from
body fluids and/or aspirates withdrawn from human cases certified to have
died from causes other than an infectious disease." The abstract of Rose's
paper concludes:

> These studies indicate that unembalmed human remains are capable of con-
> tributing a multitude of infectious doses of microbial agents to a body han-
> dler, the body storage area, or to the environment adjacent to the body stor-
> age area.

Another view supporting the public health role of embalming is described
in a pamphlet published by the Embalming Chemical Manufacturers Association. The association retained Foster D. Snell, Inc., an independent
group of consulting microbiologists, to conduct laboratory tests in order
to determine the efficacy of embalming chemicals and topical disinfectants
on human remains. "Microbiologists at the Snell Laboratories," the pamphlet relates,

---

*Frederick, a biochemist, is director of chemical research at the Dodge Chemical Com-
pany, one of the country's two largest makers of embalming products.

performed a series of tests on two groups of human remains. One group was embalmed, the other was not. Microbial counts were made on all subjects at a number of sites—including the heart, lung, colon, bladder, mouth, and nose. Counts were made immediately prior to embalming half of the test group, and at intervals thereafter of two, four, eight, and twenty-four hours.

The scientists at Snell concluded: "The embalming fluids were found to be highly active in reducing the microbial flora in human remains. It was determined that the microbial population was reduced greater than 99 percent at every site two hours after embalming. The control bodies (those that had not been embalmed) demonstrated, as anticipated, a continuous microbial growth pattern.

Hailing Snell's findings, *The American Funeral Director* in its August 1973 issue published an editorial entitled "A Definitive Study Proves That Embalming Safeguards Public Health," which stated:

The long-debated question as to whether or not embalming is necessary to safeguard public health has been settled once and for all. . . . These findings are of great significance to members of the funeral service profession and to all others concerned with public health. We suggest that you secure a copy from your embalming fluid supplier, read it carefully, and keep it handy for reference. The report constitutes a decisive response to those misinformed critics who are unaware of the possibilities for rampant contagion that every unembalmed body presents.

Most of the literature supporting embalming emphasizes the possibility of danger to public health when the procedure is omitted. But none attempts to present evidence of the spread of contagious disease when embalming is *not* carried out.* Nowhere in the United States is embalming mandatory before twenty-four hours has elapsed after death (longer in some states)—except when the decedent was infected with a communicable disease. That fact would seem to support the view that there is little health peril in unembalmed bodies not infected with a communicable disease. And other common-sense factors tend to invalidate the claim that embalming helps to check disease and epidemics. In *The Law of Death*, Hugh Bernard notes:

Orthodox Jews and other religious groups that do not have the remains embalmed . . . have for many years successfully interred their dead without menace to the public health or injury to the sensibilities of the bereaved and their friends.

Bernard is careful to point out, however, that "One characteristic of their funerals is, of course, prompt burial." In sum, there is no question that most

---

*Commenting on the claims that embalming checks the spread of disease, Coriolis notes: "India and China do not have embalmers, and their population-increase figures lead one to believe that they have not yet succumbed to this plague. In England, France, and Germany, embalming is negligible, yet there are still signs of human life. Even Russia is struggling along without a stalwart mortician in every commune."

dead bodies contain potentially pathogenic microorganisms. But is embalming essential for cadavers that have not contracted infectious diseases before death? The evidence is still inconclusive. Not enough research has been carried out in this area.

Embalming and the Spread of Infectious Disease

Authorities have noted that epidemics and plagues have been caused by inadequate city planning, faulty engineering, and poor sanitation systems. When these abuses were corrected, infection that had been spread by rodents and seepage from graves into water supplies ceased. Subsequent improvements in the public health occurred not just in the United States and Canada, where embalming is common, but also in western Europe, where embalming is rare.

What about the spread of infections today? In the case of death by infectious disease—i.e., smallpox, diphtheria, tuberculosis, anthrax, hepatitis, and so on—there seems to be no question about the need for regulations mandating certain health measures, although these need not necessarily require embalming. The Center for Disease Control has stated: "Contact with cadavers that were infected before death with smallpox, tuberculosis, and possibly other infectious diseases, might transmit these diseases." Will embalming prevent such transmission? Even here there is room for doubt. In 1976 the deputy minister of health, Community Health Programs, in British Columbia, noted:

> It is our view that the process of embalming serves no useful purpose in preventing the transmission of communicable disease. In those few cases where a person dies of a highly infectious disease, a far better procedure would be to wrap and securely seal the body in heavy plastic sheeting before removing it from the room where death occurred.

Physicians in the City of Vancouver Health Department stated in 1976: "There does not seem to be any indication that embalming is necessary from the public health point of view, except when it is necessary to preserve the body for some time, for example, to permit its shipment abroad for disposal."

Despite the common assumption in the United States that embalming reduces most of the risk of infection, at least one laboratory analysis refuted that supposition more than twenty-five years ago. The 1951 study, "The Isolation of Pathogens from Tissues of Embalmed Human Bodies," reported that many common pathogens as well as viable tubercle bacilli were present in twenty-two out of twenty-three cadavers that had been embalmed for twenty-four to forty-eight hours.

"It is significant," the authors said, "that the tubercle bacillus was isolated from the tissues of 22 bodies and from several lesions in many of them. The significance is much greater when it is realized that most of the lesions from which these organisms were isolated were not those with a thick fibrotic wall, but were well-vascularized lesions into which embalming fluid should be expected to penetrate, since all the embalming was done by the arterial method."*

In her 1959 dissertation on embalming, Elizabeth Ives commented on the effect of embalming on infectious diseases:

> Such risk as does exist is probably diminished but not entirely removed by embalming. Under circumstances where the risk of infection is well established—namely most of the notifiable diseases—embalming is of very doubtful value and in the specific case of tuberculosis almost none at all.

In addition to tuberculosis, Ives noted that other bacilli tend to resist disinfection. She cited the smallpox virus, which is "virtually unaffected by embalming," as well as spore-bearing organisms such as anthrax, tetanus, and gas gangrene. These bacteria, she said, "almost certainly will survive the effects of embalming and remain viable in such a treated body."

Ives was careful to note, however, that over a period of time after death "embalming will eventually sterilise the body," an especially important consideration, she said, if subsequent anatomical dissection might be necessary.

This is a significant consideration for medical education and research. But what about disease-infected bodies buried in cemeteries? Is the public health protected because they are embalmed? Or is it safeguarded because cemeteries are set apart from the rest of the community in segregated areas removed from the water supply? There is still no clear answer.

Ives concluded that the removal of dead bodies to funeral homes, which isolates them from public contact, is probably of greater value as a public health precaution than the embalming process itself. What, then, of the hazards to embalmers and the funeral home staff? What risks do they face? Seemingly very little. "To see embalmers at work," said Ives in her 1959 dissertation, "and witness the complete indifference with which, apparently without ill effect, they can treat such obvious dangers as an abdomen full of pus, is to become really convinced of the small size of the risk

---

*The authors concluded: "It is thus apparent that emphasis is placed on the aesthetics of embalming, and not on the disinfection of the remains, although in most states the legal requirements pertain primarily to the elimination of contagion. However, apparently no practical studies have been made on tissues from embalmed bodies to indicate that substances or combinations of substances will produce the 'perfect sanitation of remains.' . . . Since we were able to isolate virulent tubercle bacilli from the tissues of 22 of 23 embalmed bodies in which there was sufficient evidence that viable organisms were present, it would appear that embalming as such, as ordinarily done by the arterial route, does not render the tissues free of contagion in a short time. It would also appear important to re-evaluate the practical value of embalming if it is used to free the body of contagion.
"The relationship of such ineffectiveness of embalming to certain aspects of public health is evident."

likely to be associated with a dead body under normal circumstances."*

In 1972, the Board of Directors of the Memorial and Funeral Planning Association of Newfoundland wrote to the provincial minister of health, pointing out that Ives's opinion in her 1959 dissertation—"that embalming is of no value for sanitation and public health"—had never been questioned in medical circles. The letter stated that the Newfoundland organization and the 200,000 members of the Memorial Society Association of Canada

> support recent expert opinion that modern medical procedures and shipping techniques have completely obviated any need for embalming for purposes of sanitation or of public nuisance. . . . Refrigeration is more efficient, and in the long run less costly, in postponing putrefaction and indeed in maintaining the appearance of the dead within such time and purposes as is required for customary funeral arrangements.

Does Embalming Ensure Preservation?

Some undertakers genuinely believe that embalming is the key to long-term preservation. In a 1972 interview, Norman G. Heard, a Pittsburgh undertaker and chief spokesman of the Allegheny County Funeral Directors Association, was asked how long a properly embalmed body would last. "If a body is embalmed properly," he said, "and put into a casket that keeps out moisture, the body will last thirty to forty years."

Heard told Consumers Union in 1977 that he still stands by this statement and knows one instance in which a grave was opened after thirty years because of a lawsuit. The body was found to be in good condition.**

---

*Coriolis also tells of the head pathologist at Toronto General Hospital who said to a group of embalming students that, as far as the dangers of disease are concerned, doctors and nurses "are exposed to far more viruses in the course of a day than funeral men come in contact with in months."

The deputy minister of health in British Columbia stated a similar view in 1976: "To my knowledge, the transmission of bacterial or viral infections from people who have not died from an infectious communicable disease to people who handle or view the bodies is not a problem. Certainly, no such cases have been reported to this health department in the last twenty years, and I have never seen this means of transmission cited as a problem in the public health literature. Hospital pathologists and morgue attendants, who would be at greatest risk, are trained in the proper procedures and wear protective apparel."

**Rarely does a lay person have the opportunity to learn about the effects of embalming on a body months or years after death. But one such account was given in Jessica Mitford's *The American Way of Death*. The author described an interview she had with Jesse Carr, M.D., chief of pathology at the San Francisco General Hospital and professor of pathology at the University of California Medical School. Mitford questioned Carr about the efficacy of embalming as a means of preservation. "'An exhumed embalmed body is a repugnant, moldy, foul-looking object,' said Dr. Carr emphatically. 'It's not the image of one who has been loved. You might use the quotation "John Brown's body lies a-moldering in the grave"; that really sums it up. The body itself may be intact, as far as contours and so on; but the silk lining of the casket is all stained with body fluids, the wood is rotting, and the body is covered with mold.' The caskets, he said, even the solid mahogany ones that cost thousands of dollars, just disintegrate. He spoke of a case where a man was

Heard said that long-term preservation depends on a number of conditions: the work of a skilled embalmer, the type of casket, and, most important, the kind of soil in which the coffin is buried. Conceding that the chances for ideal conditions are rare, "almost nil," Heard nonetheless maintained that bodies can survive in good condition for a long time, particularly in certain kinds of soil.

Howard Raether, in public testimony in 1976, said, "No reputable funeral director would imply that there is an everlasting preservation of the body resulting from embalming." Yet many undertakers tend to capitalize on the fact that survivors, feeling acute grief for someone who has just died, are unwilling to accept the reality of the body's decay. In their bereaved state, many mourners prefer to believe undertakers' implied assurances that the body will survive in the lifelike condition in which they viewed it at the funeral home. Undertakers often encourage this belief by stressing themes of "eternal preservation" and "peace-of-mind protection" in the sale of particularly sturdy—and costly—coffins and vaults.

While it is true that bodies can be preserved intact for a long time if strong chemicals are used, the type of embalming done in most funeral homes does not ensure lasting results.* Mortuary embalmers use a dilute embalming fluid to keep the corpses looking lifelike and natural, with only enough preservative (which tends to distort and bloat the face) in the embalming fluid for the body to last a short time.* *

In cases where long-term preservation is required, stronger chemical

---

exhumed two and a half months after burial: 'The casket fell apart and the body was covered with mold, long whiskers of penicillin—he looked ghastly. I'd rather be nice and rotten than covered with those whiskers of mold, although the penicillin is a pretty good preservative. Better in fact than embalming fluid.'"

A somewhat different description of an exhumed, embalmed body appears in Thomas Thompson's *Blood and Money*, published in 1976. This account described an autopsy performed by the late Milton Helpern, for many years the chief medical examiner in New York City. The procedure was done on the body of a thirty-eight-year-old woman. A detailed description of the state of her body was given. Five months after burial, the "overall state of preservation was good." Although the facial features were mostly intact, black mold covered the cheeks and nose. Greenish-black mold also covered parts of the torso and one hand. "Tissues of the upper and lower extremities were soft." Although the body was generally intact, "everywhere the flesh was softening, soon to pull away from the bones, destined to disappear." Inside the body was a "gray, mushy mucosa material, product of the passage of time and the breaking down of the flesh by nature's forces."

*Embalmers use a wide range of fluids. Different embalming chemicals are selected for different conditions of the body. (Jaundice, for example, requires special fluids.) There are pre-injection solutions, arterial fluids (which come in different strengths), water softeners, and fluids for cavity embalming. In a typical embalming procedure, more than one type of fluid is used. In an establishment that handles about 100 to 125 bodies a year, the annual cost of embalming fluids can be about $1,500.

* *Often the proportion of preservative in the embalming fluid can be a source of anxiety in funeral establishments. Coriolis says that "There is constant talk among funeral men about the appearance of the deceased; always they wonder whether a body will 'keep'; one often hears them considering whether it will smell."

solutions are used. For instance, a pathologist affiliated with the College of American Pathologists told Consumers Union in 1977 that the type of embalming done in most funeral homes would not be suitable for bodies used in medical school teaching. Since these cadavers may be used in teaching for months, tissues must be firm, and both the procedure and the embalming fluid used are different from those used in mortuaries.*

No matter what amount of preservative is used in mortuary embalming, the length of the preservation of the body in the grave can never be predicted with certainty. As was noted in an earlier chapter (see page 83), a number of varying factors can affect the condition of a body: the type of soil, the coffin, the vault, and the embalming itself.

S. R. Gerber, M.D., the executive secretary of the International Association of Coroners and Medical Examiners, told Consumers Union in 1977 that there have been cases in which exhumed bodies were in as good condition as they had been when they were buried—sometimes even after two years. This can happen, he said, when a body is well embalmed and enclosed in a strong, protective vault in a section of the cemetery where drainage is excellent. The most important factor, said Gerber, is the burial ground and the amount of water seepage. If a vault is made of porous material and not well manufactured (if, for instance, the lid does not fit tightly), then no matter how well embalmed the body, there will be more rapid decomposition. In Gerber's experience, vaults rarely withstand seepage.

Should a Body Be Embalmed?

In general, bodies begin to decompose rather rapidly after death, usually within four to eight hours, accompanied by the typical odor of decomposition. Decomposition is not always that rapid, however. Some bodies may remain in a state of natural preservation for several days. A number of factors can affect the rate of deterioration, including the cause and circumstances of death, the age of the decedent, the weather (high temperatures and humid air can hasten decomposition), and the differing rates of decay of the vari-

---

*Jack Davies, M.D., chairman of the Department of Anatomy at Vanderbilt University School of Medicine, informed Consumers Union in 1977 that the type of embalming performed on cadavers in medical schools takes several days to complete (compared with several hours in funeral homes) because it is done slowly and meticulously. Only one small incision of about two inches is made in the groin of the cadaver. No pumping machines are used; the principle of gravity, in which the fluid finds its own way to all the body recesses, is relied on. Seven gallons of fluid are used to embalm one body. The mixture consists of formaldehyde, the dominant element, phenol (carbolic acid), which prevents mold from forming, and a very small amount of glycerine to keep the cadaver moist. Morticians also use formaldehyde and glycerine but in small amounts because of their concern for appearance. Once embalmed by a medical school, a cadaver can last almost indefinitely, although schools generally use bodies only from three to nine months for teaching purposes. (See Chapter 17 for information about donating bodies to medical schools.)

ous organs. As a rule, though, funeral homes must cope with the effects of rapid decomposition of the bodies. One of the most important reasons mortuaries give for embalming is that most personnel do not like to handle unembalmed bodies because of concern about odor and infection. The NFDA explains it this way:

> The body is subject to quick deterioration. Problems resulting therefrom are decomposition, bloating, purging and the presence of maggots unless properly cared for immediately. Sometimes cleansing, disinfecting and placing the body in a refrigeration unit may or may not avoid serious problems. If the body is to be present for the period of the funeral, including the visitation or wake and for the funeral service. It should be embalmed. If it is not [embalmed], offensive odor, sanitation and appearance problems will exist.

If there is to be a two- or three-day period, or even longer, between death and the final disposition of the body, a genuine dilemma can exist for a funeral home without refrigeration—and the majority of mortuaries in the United States do not have refrigeration facilities. This is not hard to understand since most establishments (more than 95 percent) are small businesses for which refrigeration units would be a major expense.* (In the two years since the proposed FTC rule was published, however, purchases of refrigeration units rose slightly. Representatives of two suppliers of refrigeration units told Consumers Union in 1977 that they thought mortuaries were waiting to see whether the FTC rule would be promulgated and what provisions it would contain concerning embalming.)

A delay of several days before burial can occur for a number of reasons. Among these, viewing of the body is the most common; if this is desired and refrigeration is not available, then embalming is usually necessary. If the body is held in the funeral home for a day or two but without viewing, there is less need for embalming. Even with visitation—with the coffin closed—embalming need not be necessary; the body can be placed in a heavy plastic pouch within the coffin. Some funeral homes employ what they call "sanitary care," that is, the use of powders and odor-cover-up techniques on unembalmed bodies. In some communities, when it is necessary to hold a body for a period of time (for legal or other reasons), it is possible to use the refrigeration facilities of a hospital or a medical examiner's morgue. There is often no fee for this service.

If Death Occurs in a Nursing Home

Preservation of the body, by embalming or refrigeration, can present a special problem when death occurs in a nursing home, where procedures are different from those in a hospital. This is particularly true when death oc-

---

*Prices for one-body units may range from $3,400 to $5,039, according to representatives of two suppliers of refrigeration units.

curs late at night. In a hospital, a resident physician is usually available—no matter what the hour—to sign the death certificate, a necessary prerequisite for removal of the body. But if a death occurs at 2 A.M. in a nursing home, most personal physicians will not come at once to sign a patient's death certificate. It can be many hours, sometimes ten or twelve, until the necessary medical and legal requirements are taken care of.

The director of a nursing home in Westchester County (New York) described some of the difficulties involved when a patient dies at night. Often, the physician's answering service refuses to deliver the message immediately. If the doctor is out of town, the covering doctor frequently is reluctant to assume responsibility for a colleague's dead patient. On those few occasions when no doctor will come and there appears to be no other alternative, the nursing home will call the office of the local medical examiner and arrange to have the body transferred to the county morgue.

The Westchester nursing home also has an arrangement with a local funeral establishment in case there is a long delay before funeral plans can be made. This sometimes happens when survivors cannot be located right away or when they have to travel a great distance. Since the funeral home has no refrigeration, bodies must be embalmed for preservation. This can cause problems for survivors. First, a body may be embalmed without their permission if a sufficient period of time elapses before authorization could be obtained. Second, survivors may want to use a different funeral home or to hold the funeral in another community. In such cases, they will undoubtedly have to pay for some of the services performed at the first funeral home.

Viewable Bodies: Grief Therapy?

A major argument for embalming, advanced by undertakers and their supporters, is the desirability of "viewable bodies." Survivors, they say, benefit emotionally and psychologically from viewing the dead. The majority of undertakers believe that this ritual is a healthy, therapeutic way to deal with death. A letter to Ann Landers in 1974 is typical:

> Dear Ann Landers: I am a funeral director who disagrees with "Edith in Nebraska." First of all, embalming, which she calls "barbaric," is for sanitation purposes as well as for temporary preservation. Second, the viewing of the deceased, especially for members of the family, serves a vital psychological need and helps them accept the finality of death. Finally, the funeral service is for the living, not the dead. I believe the music, sermon and all decisions connected with the funeral should be made by those who are making the arrangements, and not by the one who has passed on. The individual's wishes and preferences can, of course, be discussed with the family before death occurs, but if the family disagrees, the wishes of those left behind should take precedence, since they are the ones who are affected.

Representative of the funeral industry's thinking, a current NFDA pamphlet, "With the Body Present," quotes the late Erich Lindemann, M.D., professor of psychiatry at Harvard Medical School, on the subject of viewing the body:

When asked, "What do you consider to be the most useful part of the whole funeral process?" [Dr. Lindemann] responded, "The moment of truth that comes when living persons confront the fact of death by looking at the body." When questioned further why he thought this was true, he said, "People tend to deny painful reality. They tend to marshal their mental and emotional resources to deny the fact that death has occurred. But when they experience that moment of truth that comes when they stand before the dead body, their denials collapse. They are facing reality and that is the first important step toward managing their grief. When it is done with other people, the reality is confirmed and at the same time they are encouraged to face the feelings that are basic to the grief response. Grief is a feeling. If you deny it you have difficulty coping with it, but if you face it you start the process of healthful mourning.

Edgar Jackson in *For the Living* says, "It is far better to fix the image clearly in one's mind, perhaps by standing quietly beside the casket in the funeral home hour after hour, until the full emotional meaning of the death is grasped." Without the body, something is lacking, undertakers say, "some acceptable image for recalling the deceased." Indeed, the NFDA's "With the Body Present" states, "Seeing helps us to believe. Often much time, effort and money are expended to recover a missing body for the purpose of confirming the fact that the death has occurred." Only with the body present is there a "meaningful symbol" on which to focus attention and "stimulate emotions and memories."

Viewable Bodies: Costly Illusion?

Paradoxically, those who oppose funerals with open coffins interpret the same symbol—the dead body—in exactly opposite terms. By concentrating on a cosmetically made-up corpse that appears to be resting or sleeping, they say, survivors are refusing to face the fact of death. In their opinion, undertakers engage in a kind of illusion that tends to deny death and stresses the lifelike preservation of the body. Emphasis should not be on the deceased's remains, it is argued, but on the spiritual qualities of the one who has died and on the opportunities for maturing and growing that death brings to survivors' lives. In *A Manual of Death Education and Simple Burial*, Ernest Morgan describes what he believes to be the failures of the conventional funeral: "First, it tends to be much harder on the survivors; second, preoccupation with the lifeless shell from which the breath of personality has departed almost inevitably diminishes the attention which is given the ongoing aspects of that personality and thus loses much of the

103

opportunity for positive value; third, it is generally much more costly."

A Unitarian minister in Los Angeles, Peter Hans Christiansen, commented on an open-coffin funeral:

> As far as I'm concerned, a commercial funeral for anyone is out; I'll never do another. But a *memorial* service is essential. A memorial service is for the people who are left alive, and the best service is one where there's no coffin at all. The immortal things which people leave on earth are their friends, their children, their relationships. Those are things that have nothing to do with a . . . lifeless carcass. As far as I'm concerned, the custom of the open coffin is not only an economic atrocity, which adds hundreds to every funeral bill, it gives terrible pain to the survivors. I can't count the times I've had to coax sobbing widows or parents or children away from an open coffin, and for *what*?

LeRoy Bowman, author of *The American Funeral,* supported this view:

> Parting with the tangible remains of the deceased must come soon after death. The sooner it happens the fewer memories will be clouded by unnecessary and unpleasant associations and the freer the mind will be to form satisfying recollections of other days. In any case, goodbye is said in no real sense to the lifeless form; it was sensed in the last communication between the living persons, or will be expressed in reminiscences of the coming weeks and years.

Among psychiatrists and other mental health professionals involved in counseling, death education, and therapeutic practice, there is no unanimity about the value of viewing in the grief process. Ann Kliman, a psychologist in Westchester County (New York) and a consultant to the NFDA, has been involved in crisis-situation counseling for many years. She strongly believes in the therapeutic value of a funeral with an open coffin, and maintains that viewing is a crucial factor in beginning the process of mourning, especially when death is sudden or unexpected. According to her, viewing provides the opportunity to accept the fact of death and to say the last good-byes to the deceased.

Children, too, Kliman says, should participate in the funeral and viewing. Most of her colleagues who are child therapists, she says, support this position. Because children indulge in a great deal of fantasy and magical thinking, the reality of the open coffin is often less frightening than misconceptions about death. And children are not then isolated or cut off from those close to them at a difficult time. Thus they do not experience the "secondary psychological loss" of family and friends at the time of death. But, she cautions, children should be properly prepared for what to expect and for the particular style of mourning they will encounter.

This view is not shared by Daniel Leviton, Ph.D., of the University of Maryland, who founded The Forum for Death Education and Counseling. Leviton pointed out to Consumers Union that viewing could be traumatic for a child. He cited the hypothetical example of a child taken to view a beloved grandparent who had died of a devastating illness. Even though prepared for what to expect, the child could be traumatized by the experience.

Leviton believes that there are so many variables in a person's reaction to death that no single factor can effect a "good" bereavement. Some people can have a good "grief experience" despite a bad funeral. A good bereavement, Leviton says, usually happens when survivors receive support in the community from family, friends, neighbors, coworkers, and clergy. Empathy and understanding on the part of all these people can help a person return to normal life. Like many of his colleagues who teach death education, Leviton points out that there are no studies to support the contention that viewing aids bereavement, only anecdotal evidence.

Avery Weisman, M.D., professor of psychiatry at Harvard Medical School, also told Consumers Union that there is no evidence that viewing is necessary to begin the grief process. He said that statements about the therapeutic need for open coffins and viewing are simply "informed opinions not subject to research." Pointing out that grief and bereavement are complicated individual processes just beginning to be studied, Weisman said that no one even knows how long normal grief lasts. In his view, it would be premature to say that open coffins facilitate grief. No one can back up such statements with any acceptable research, because there is no controlled research on the subject. Nor, for that matter, he said, is there any research to demonstrate the opposite point of view.

Weisman stressed the importance of a "person-oriented" funeral, one that takes into account the needs and wishes of survivors and does not impose a uniform procedure upon them. In his opinion, a funeral ceremony is important to the grief process because it affirms the reality of death, but it does not matter whether the coffin lid is open or closed. It should be left to the survivors themselves to decide what is best for them, Weisman said.

How best to express grief for the dead is a question for which there can be no precise dictates. Each individual must discover what forms of mourning, what tributes to the dead are most meaningful when death occurs. For survivors, it is a matter, finally, of personal choice. But that choice should be based on an awareness of the available options and an understanding of what is involved in each choice.

In short, the practice of embalming raises a number of complex questions—scientific, psychological, and financial—and all of them affect the decisions that people must make when involved in death arrangements. Some people may agree with the NFDA that "the funeral with the body present provides a proper climate for mourning as it permits grief to be expressed directly." For them, any "radical" departure from familiar burial rites long accepted as a "proper" tribute to the dead could cause acute discomfort. For those who choose a conventional funeral and an open coffin there may indeed be emotional fulfillment—but there will also be higher financial costs.

The FTC Proposed Rule on Embalming

Included in the 1975 FTC proposed rule for the funeral industry is a provision concerning misrepresentations about embalming in funeral homes. (Two other provisions in the same section, 453.3, prohibit claims that embalming prevents decomposition or decay or that it preserves the body.) The provision on misrepresentation requires that funeral homes furnish to customers a printed or typewritten statement that includes this information:

> To avoid purchase decisions based on misconceptions about legal or public health requirements, the following statements are provided for your information. Please ask for an explanation of any statement which is not clear.
> Embalming is not required by law except in limited circumstances. It is not to be performed without authorization from a legally responsible individual except in those instances where it is required by law.

The FTC's proposed provision restricting embalming has aroused considerable opposition among undertakers. The fact that they would not be allowed to embalm without permission, say funeral trade association representatives, could cause a wide range of difficulties and problems for mortuaries. National Selected Morticians' official position on the FTC provision was submitted by its legal counsel to a 1976 government hearing in Washington on the FTC proposed rule. Part of its statement said:

> National Selected Morticians cannot support this provision as written, as the provision ignores a number of practical reasons, including impacts on small businessmen, and also several psychological reasons why embalming without explicit permission is performed by funeral directors. The FTC staff has misinterpreted embalming without permission as a purely exploitative practice conducted for the financial gain of the funeral director.
> Preparation and preservation of a dead human body are standard procedures in funeral service, unless there are instructions to the contrary during the initial death call because of religious beliefs or known requests for immediate disposal. It is not, as the FTC contends, an overt attempt to create a captive consumer family to select merchandise. Embalming is an act to prevent decomposition as soon as possible. In spite of FTC opinion to the contrary, embalming does provide bactericidal action in sanitizing the body, halts putrefaction, and preserves the remains for an undetermined period of time.

The NSM cited a number of reasons why undertakers must embalm. It pointed out that when death occurs in a nursing home or in a sudden accident, the undertaker might have difficulty in locating a "responsible member of a dispersed family." The same would be true when someone dies suddenly and "the only relative with authority to give permission is away on a trip." A delay of more than four to eight hours without refrigeration, according to the NSM, can seriously impair the embalming procedure, with the result that survivors would be denied "their customary right to a traditionally religious oriented or humanist service." The delay in obtaining family approval "could allow rapid decomposition of a body to reduce it to a state of unpleasantness not conducive to customary funeral rights [sic]." The NSM also pointed out that many families do not wish to be called upon by an undertaker for several hours after a death. Thus, if someone dies during the night, and the undertaker phones for permission to embalm, the request for authorization "could disturb or further aggravate the shock. . . ."

The NSM says that this FTC requirement could cause additional expenses for funeral homes, most notably, "expensive refrigeration equipment." And, according to the association, "there will be increased costs in overtime labor required to obtain timely authorization, particularly where a death occurred during the night. The man hours required in many instances to track down the family to obtain permission would be a burden on the firm with a small staff, particularly since it would be inappropriate to charge the purchaser for such time. . . . Even though the purchaser cannot be charged directly for such efforts, the funeral home's overhead will be increased."

In 1976 the NFDA's Howard Raether testified before a subcommittee of the House Committee on Small Business looking into the FTC proposed rule. He maintained that "critics of the funeral with the body present have deliberately distorted the embalming issue," and said that the public has not been made aware of the necessity to embalm when there is "a wake or viewing period." As the NSM had done, Raether warned that funeral homes and extended-care facilities such as nursing homes would be forced to install and maintain refrigeration units at great expense.*

Effects of the FTC Rule

In their objections to the FTC proposed provision, undertakers stress unusual cases—for example, when survivors cannot be located or the body

---

*In a statement to the FTC about the proposed rule, the NFDA said this on the subject of embalming: "Proposed Rule 453.2(a) states the usual practice presently followed by funeral directors. If possible it is always desirable to obtain permission; however, the Rule can become a hardship in cases where the next of kin are not available or are not known and where there is no other adequate form of preservation of the body for the purposes of funeralization if it should be the desires of the family when contacted. The Rule would hamper the activities of law enforcement officials and would create an undue hardship on nursing home facilities and hospitals and other facilities which house the elderly."

must be held for an inordinate length of time before arrangements can be made. Situations like these, however, are the exception. In most cases, a responsible survivor can be reached by funeral home personnel.

Nonetheless, should the proposed provision go into effect, the FTC would have to take into consideration these unusual situations. For example, if an undertaker were unable to locate survivors and the body had to be held for a length of time that made embalming desirable, the FTC would take the circumstances—including the undertaker's "good faith efforts" to locate survivors—into consideration in deciding whether there had been a violation.

If embalming is restricted by the FTC rule, some firms may well incur additional costs. There are a number of ways in which the burden of extra expenses could be lightened. For example, one refrigeration company representative commented that in areas where funeral homes tend to cluster, it might be economically feasible for several establishments to share in the purchase and use of a refrigeration unit. Or refrigeration equipment could be leased instead of purchased. Since most funeral homes with a refrigeration unit charge customers an additional fee for use of the unit, that income could help compensate for leasing charges.

The Decision about Embalming

• Unless the proposed FTC rule goes into effect, many undertakers will undoubtedly continue to embalm bodies routinely soon after receiving them, frequently without permission from survivors. Accordingly, survivors should discuss the question of embalming with the undertaker as soon as possible after death occurs. The undertaker should be informed *before* the body is taken to the funeral establishment whether embalming is desired. If embalming is not desired, survivors should ask the undertaker to deduct the cost from the bill. (If the funeral home has refrigeration, there is usually a charge for "preservation.")

• Some undertakers will tell survivors that embalming is required by law. Embalming is, however, legally required only under certain circumstances, primarily: (1) if the death occurs from a communicable disease; (2) if the body is to be transported by common carrier; and (3) in some states, if disposition does not take place within a certain time limit. Survivors should acquaint themselves with the laws governing embalming in their state (see Appendix 7). Three good sources for this information are local memorial societies, the state board of undertakers and embalmers, and the office of the state attorney general. Local or state health departments may also be able to provide this information.

• If there is to be an open coffin and viewing in the funeral home for two or three days, embalming, in almost every case, will be necessary. If the funeral establishment has refrigeration facilities, however, it is possible to

have viewing without embalming. The body can be held in the mortuary refrigerator for about twenty hours, taken out for two or three hours of viewing, returned to the refrigerator, and brought out again for another two or three hours on the second day.*
• If the funeral is to be held with a closed coffin and no viewing, with burial or cremation following soon after, there may be no need to embalm. The question then arises: What form of remembrance and expression of grief best fulfill survivors' needs? A great many factors will influence the choice. The type of ceremony will depend on the wishes or religious beliefs of survivors, on the age and character of the person who died, on the people who attend. Whether there is a ceremony with the closed coffin present or a memorial service after burial or cremation will be determined by a number of practical considerations: the condition of the body at the time of death; the state's time requirements for burial or cremation without embalming; whether certain family members, friends, and associates can be present soon after death.
• Many approaches are possible in rites for the dead, but, essentially, the funeral or memorial service should suit the circumstances and personalities involved and have unique meaning for family and friends. Memorial societies stress that ceremonies should illuminate the special qualities and values that characterized the life of the deceased, which have now become part of the lives of those who live after. It could be said that these aims, after all, are not too different from what survivors seek to express in conventional funerals. Yet the differences are great, not only in psychological emphasis but in the saving of hundreds—even thousands—of dollars.

---

*One funeral home owner pointed out to Consumers Union that this method could present problems for some viewers. Many visitors, he said, want to touch the body, and the very cold skin could be shocking to the touch. There could also be a problem with appearance, such as skin discoloration.

12

Extras Add Up

Some years ago, when Ann Landers, in her syndicated column, objected to the practice of taking photographs of open coffins in funeral homes, she received complaints from readers, calling her "hardhearted" and "cruel." One reader wrote: "I wouldn't take a million dollars for the pictures I made of my husband laid out in his blue suit. He looked better in that box than he had anytime in the last ten years."

The photographs of her husband in his coffin,* for which the widow had gladly paid the funeral home an additional fee, came under the heading of extras, one of many available in funeral homes—particularly when the funeral includes an open coffin and viewing.

Some undertakers prove ingenious in finding ways to "enhance" funeral procedures with expensive extras. Years ago, one funeral home provided a viewing scene of singular imagination, as described by a clergyman (in 1964 to a Senate subcommittee investigating the funeral industry). He had gone to a funeral home to pay his last respects to a woman parishioner:

> On arrival at the funeral parlor, Mr. McAdoo [a fictitious name], the wid-ower, and I were greeted by a well-marcelled receptionist who smiled demurely and said, "Mrs. McAdoo will see you now"—as if we had come to make a social call. The receptionist escorted us into a room where we had expected to find a body decently laid out for burial. Instead, we found our-selves in a tastefully furnished lady's boudoir, complete with vanity table, mirror, combs, and brushes, together with other requisites of the feminine toilette; and, on a canopied, four-poster bed, propped up on silken pillows and clad in a negligee was Mrs. McAdoo.

---

*In recent years, the funeral industry has thought up a new embellishment in the art of viewing-room portraiture: "portrait memorialization"—"an original portrait in oil" made from a photograph of the corpse. A 1973 advertisement in *Mortuary Management* told funeral directors the portrait was "an added service of good will. A substantial and extra avenue of income for you."

110

"It would be unfair to suggest," the clergyman added, "that this kind of hideous vulgarity and maudlin bad taste is typical of the majority of funeral directors. Yet it does exist and can be bought, if you care to foot the bill."*

Boudoir settings and portrait memorialization are bizarre examples of extras sold in funeral homes. Many of the "regular" extras, however, are usually accepted by survivors as necessary items in a conventional funeral. Although the definition of funeral extras can vary from establishment to establishment, there is usually a fairly standard group of goods and services not included in the cost of a "complete" funeral. These items are billed separately—hence the term extra.

The most common extras are: flowers, burial clothing, additional limousines, flower vehicle, clergy's honorarium, newspaper death notices,** hired pallbearers, transcripts of death certificates, music, prayer cards, memorial books and cards, sympathy cards, acknowledgment cards, gratuities, sales tax, and transporting the body to a distant community. The latter can be by far the most expensive extra, one incurred in about 10 percent of all funerals.

Besides these fairly conventional extras, an enterprising undertaker may suggest a number of additional items that survivors may wish to select: death masks, crucifixes, Bibles, memorial flag cases, cemetery lights, veils, boutonnieres, or Mass card holders. Funeral homes have even been known to provide—neatly prepackaged in a vial or sack—the handful of earth (sometimes, sand) that may be thrown into the grave.

Extras fall into different categories. There is merchandise, often sold at a substantial profit over wholesale costs, and there are special services—by clergy, musicians, pallbearers, hairdressers,† and, occasionally, nurses to attend mourners. Less common merchandise and services include ship-

---

*Another variation on conventional viewing customs was put into practice several years ago by an undertaker in Atlanta, who said the idea came to him in a dream one night. He transformed his funeral home into a "drive-in" mortuary, with five large windows behind which coffined bodies were on display all hours of the day and night. According to the owner, the drive-in concept offered advantages for relatives and friends. People who didn't like to get dressed up and those pressured for time could drive by, view the deceased lying in a lighted window, "and just keep going." The undertaker observed that many people liked to view bodies after midnight. A similar drive-in viewing window was installed in a Louisiana funeral home in 1976. Drivers could view the body reposing in front of a small cross with a blue neon border. By leaning slightly out of the car window, they could sign an outside guest register. The owner of the funeral home acknowledged that some protests had been made in the community about this unorthodox method of viewing. But she defended the practice, explaining, "Some people feel it's an honor."

**Death notices are regarded as advertisements because they notify people about visiting hours, time of interment, etc.; they must be paid for in most newspapers. Obituaries are usually considered news (although in some communities newspapers charge for them).

†A long-established funeral home in Washington, D.C., offers such cosmetic services for the dead as shampooing and waving or trimming hair, shaving and manicuring, and plastic surgery, if required.

ping cases and long-distance telephone calls and telegrams.

Some survivors request police motorcycle escorts for the funeral cortege; in many communities police escorts are provided for funerals free of charge at the request of the undertaker. The police chief in Baton Rouge, Louisiana, declared in 1977, however, that he would begin charging a fee for funeral cortege escorts. He estimated that in 1976 it had cost the police department $100,000 to provide escorts for 1,459 funerals. "I feel it is now time for funeral homes to pick up the expense," he said.*

Norman G. Heard, the Pittsburgh undertaker, has defended the expensive fancy extras offered by the funeral industry, claiming that funeral homes offer consumers what they want. "The public doesn't have to buy it. It's the same as everything else.... If the public's not going to buy it, you're going to go out of business. Right?" Heard claimed that the funeral industry has upgraded its older, simpler funeral merchandise and services to better serve the public. "A funeral director's job is basically to the living," he said. "Once we've properly cared for the dead, then our entire services are to those who are left. Therefore, in an effort not to be considered old fashioned or passé ... we have changed things and bettered things in our way of thinking." People do not want a funeral home to be morbid, said Heard; they want to be comfortable, and they want superior goods.

Cash Advances or Accommodations

Many of the extra goods and services in a funeral are listed on the undertaker's bill as "cash advances" or "accommodations." Funeral homes frequently advance the funds on behalf of funeral buyers for certain goods and services that must be paid for before or immediately after the funeral but are not provided by the undertaker. These advances are repaid later by the customer. Not all extras are cash advances—for example, burial clothing sold in the funeral home or additional limousines provided by the undertaker. And not all cash advances are extras. Occasionally, undertakers advance money for vaults, cemetery or crematory charges, and memorials.

Undertakers claim that they make no profits, or only small ones, on the funeral extras they sell to survivors. This is undoubtedly true if one compares the profit made on the coffin or major services with the profit made on, say, burial clothing. However, the selection of an assortment of extras by survivors can prove a considerable source of income to a funeral establishment and significantly raise the amount of the customer's bill. Because undertakers frequently obtain discounts from sellers of cash advance items, such extras can yield more profit to the undertaker than

*One enterprising mortuary in Los Angeles provided a motorcycle escort of six full-time riders, with another nine on call, for its own funerals as well as those of other mortuaries. The motorcycles and uniforms were similar in appearance to those used by the police department.

112

extras sold directly by the funeral home. But the NFDA does not condone profits on cash advances. It has informed the FTC that survivors should benefit *in toto* from all discounts and rebates from accommodations. According to the FTC, however, it is not uncommon for funeral homes to make substantial profits on cash advances, either by increasing the price or by not passing along to funeral buyers discounts or rebates on certain items.* (In some cases, according to the FTC, funeral homes receive kickbacks from the people who provide the services.) The FTC estimates that overcharges alone come to approximately $40 million a year and that about $18 million of this amount is from overcharges on flowers and death notices, for which many undertakers get trade discounts on large-volume orders.

Crematory charges, payments for pallbearers, clergy, and obituary notices may also be misrepresented on customers' bills. In 1975, the president of a union representing three hundred licensed embalmers in New York City testified before a New York State legislative hearing that one large funeral establishment in New York City used its regular employees as pallbearers for funerals. The firm paid each of them $4 per funeral, although it billed customers $16 for each pallbearer. In 1972, a Pittsburgh woman told of having been billed $56 for death notices in two newspapers, although the total cost had come to only about $21.

The matter of payment for clergy's services can be problematical, too. Some clergy find it distressing that funeral homes charge customers for honoraria. But, to make matters worse, the payment is sometimes not even passed on to the clergy by the undertaker. A California minister reported in 1972 that he had been bitterly reproached by a widow for charging so much for his part in her husband's funeral. "I not only never *charged* that poor woman anything," he said. "I'd never been *paid* anything by the funeral home!" He added that when he checked with other families for whom he had conducted funerals, he found that four of them had been charged from $20 to $50 for his services—although in all four cases the funeral homes had not transmitted the money to him.

The FTC has pointed out that undertakers justify their pocketing the difference in charges by claiming that this money is compensation for their services in handling arrangements. In fact, however, undertakers charge a

---

*Testifying before a 1974 House investigational hearing, J. Thomas Rosch, director of the FTC Bureau of Consumer Protection, said: "We have developed some evidence that at least in some instances in the District of Columbia, the amount of cash actually advanced by the mortuary is less than that which is represented on the statement." Rosch mentioned discounts to undertakers for crematory charges, for flowers, and for death notices, and that "when the charge is made on the consumer's bill, it appears as though what this consumer is being charged is actually what was paid out by the mortician, and which is in fact not true." He noted that the practice had turned up "on a spot basis" in the 1973 FTC investigation of Washington, D.C., funeral homes, and that he could not say how widespread it was.

separate fee for professional services, which supposedly include arranging for cash advances.

Undertakers also defend the practice of not passing on trade discounts to consumers by arguing that these are volume discounts available only to funeral homes and would not be available to individual funeral buyers making their own arrangements. Yet, as the FTC notes, consumers retain undertakers as their agents, with the understanding that undertakers will act in the best interests of consumers. For undertakers to deny consumers the benefits of their expertise and special business connections would seem to be a breach of faith.*

Flowers

The conventional American funeral typically includes about twenty floral displays in addition to those provided by survivors. Sales of floral tributes for funerals constitute a sizable sum. Even though the selling of "sympathy flowers" remains the virtually exclusive province of the approximately twenty thousand retail establishments in the flower business, the retail florist industry claims not to know the dollar value of funeral flower sales.**
In fact, no one is sure precisely how much money is spent on flowers for funerals. Such data are not collected by the government, which is content to publish only total retail sales of florists ($1.605 million in 1972, according to the latest available government statistics).

An independent analyst, who is an outspoken critic of the floriculture industry's failure to make sales information public, has monitored sales over the years and compiled his own statistics. According to data he made available to Consumers Union, retail florists in 1977 will gross an estimated $2.250 billion. About 40 percent of that total—$900 million—will be spent on sympathy orders. The average retail establishment will ring up sales of between $450 and $500 for a single funeral.

A questionable procedure that can directly affect the amount of money consumers spend on funeral flowers is the pressure exerted by the floriculture industry on newspapers in the United States and Canada to cut from death notices such phrases as "please omit flowers" or "in lieu of flowers." The Society of American Florists objects to charities or memorial funds

---

*In 1976, Service Corporation International, the largest funeral home chain in the United States, entered into a consent order with the FTC. SCI agreed, among other things, not to overcharge customers for cash advances and to make restitution for them.

**In 1963, according to Jessica Mitford in *The American Way of Death,* $246 was spent on flowers for an average funeral. The Canadian undertaker Coriolis, in 1967, stated that the average Canadian funeral had approximately twenty-five floral pieces costing about $15 each—$375 worth of flowers. Coriolis noted that "if only one-fifth of this money, or $75, was redirected from the florist's pocket to the always-needy coffers of the Canadian Cancer Society or the Ontario Heart Foundation, it would have amounted to nearly $4,000,000 in the year of 1965, in Ontario alone."

siphoning off money that might have gone for flowers. Representatives of florists' trade associations regard the insertion of "please omit" as evidence of an "antibusiness" attitude; they say it smacks of a boycott of a specific product. Industry sources estimate that such prohibitions may cut in half the usual number of floral displays. Furthermore, they claim, when survivors friends and acquaintances request in newspaper notices that donate to a specific charitable cause, the survivors are dictating how sympathy should be expressed.

Because members of the retail florist industry are potential newspaper advertisers, their objections carry some weight with newspaper publishers and advertising departments; the result is that a number of newspapers in this country and Canada prohibit survivors from including in death notices a request to omit flowers.*

How do undertakers actually feel about flowers at funerals, since arranging and transporting floral pieces can mean extra work hours in their establishments? In a 1973 survey of undertakers reported in *Florist* magazine, "97 percent either 'agreed' or 'strongly agreed' that flowers serve a useful purpose at funerals." And 96 percent "feel flowers provide significant comfort to close survivors." No doubt, flowers are an integral part of the conventional funeral ritual—in the viewing room, on the coffin, at the grave; without them, the total "memory picture" effect that undertakers strive for would be diminished.**

But despite efforts by florists to keep sales of funeral flowers high, there is some indication that they may be declining somewhat in the United States. According to the *Florist* magazine survey, nearly one-quarter of the respondents stated that a "major problem facing their industry was the increase in cremations, memorial services, etc. where funeral directors are not required to provide complete services." Other respondents cited changing public attitudes, a trend to "less ceremony," and "less concern about others." The survey found that many undertakers believe that the funeral industry and florists "have a common interest in trying to combat the trend towards 'less formalized funerals.'"

---

*In 1975, the editor of the Pittsburgh *Press* refused to meet with members of a consumer organization in Pittsburgh about the newspaper's ban on "please omit flowers" in its death notices. The *Press* said it could not support a policy of boycotting a particular product.

**Yet, floral tributes can represent real transporation problems when there is no flower car, according to one undertaker in East Hampton, New York. (If a flower car is used between the funeral home and the cemetery, it is almost always an extra expense, ranging in cost from $25 to $50 or more, depending on mileage.) The East Hampton undertaker usually tries to transport about ten floral pieces in the hearse, but, he said, "We're thinking of adding a 'decoration charge' for the churches that allow all the flowers people want." Some churches, he pointed out, limit the number of floral pieces at the church service.

Burial Clothing

Burial clothing is another extra that sells well in funeral establishments. Many funeral buyers seem to feel that an entire new outfit is required for burial (even though the clothing of the decedent may be suitable and the lower part of the coffin may be kept closed). Most sizable mortuaries display garments for the dead: shoes, stockings, underwear or lingerie, shirts, suits, tuxedos, dresses, negligees, pajamas, as well as shrouds often used for Jewish decedents.* The cost of special burial clothing is not negligible, in part because of the kind of fabric in many outfits (i.e., silk and satin in women's clothing), in part because burial clothing is often made to meet the special needs of undertakers. It is difficult to clothe a corpse—the limbs tend to be rigid and untoward movement must be avoided or the effect of the set features or a carefully contrived restoration may be destroyed. To make the task easier, mortuary clothing, especially women's, often comes with slits or openings in the back. Presumably, the deceased's own clothing could be adjusted in similar fashion, since any necessary alterations would not show.

Several manufacturers of burial garments explained to Consumers Union that there are generally more sales of women's clothing** than of men's. One firm reported manufacturing five basic styles for men and more than 250 for women, exclusive of custom orders. About eighty of the standard dress styles are offered in a variety of colors—one crepe model is available in twenty colors (pale blue is the most popular). In addition to the firm's basic styles for men, there is a deluxe suit, described as completely finished, pockets and all, ready for street wear. As with conventional clothing, prices of burial clothes vary according to style, fabric, and the relationship of retail prices to wholesale prices. As a rule, undertakers add on about one-third of the wholesale price to arrive at the retail price.

Announcements in trade journals inform morticians about the latest trends in burial clothing. A few years ago, *Casket & Sunnyside* announced one firm's "new-season" line of burial fashions for women featuring "dyed-to-match crepe-and-lace creations":

> Also included in the new collection is a satin-n-sheer negligee dress consisting of a shimmering satin gown with a complete, flowing sheer coat on top.

---

*Many funeral homes serving the Jewish community sell shrouds to fulfill the religious requirement that the body be wrapped in a cloth or sheet for burial. The 1973 survey by the FTC of Washington, D.C., funeral homes reported the average cost of a shroud to be $37 in one establishment and $65 in another.

**An owner of one burial-garment business, however, told Consumers Union that she regularly advises widowers not to buy a new gown but to use a high-necked, long-sleeved dress, perhaps one bought for an anniversary celebration or a family wedding. (She herself expects to be buried in her own clothes.) For those who cannot or do not want to make such a choice, she manufactures gowns in a range of materials, including a polyester dress and matching jacket retailing for about $50.

Provided are matching satin ribbon detailings, topped with an embroidered floral bouquet in delicate contrasting shades.
These items . . . may be returned . . . if in the purchaser's judgment they do not meet the fashion requirements of his clientele.

The highest quality of merchandise is emphasized: "Handmade original fashions—styles from the best in life for the last memory." Manufacturers also have their specialties: "New Bra-Form. Post-Mortem Form Restoration." And burial shoes are offered with special features: "Soft cushioned soles and warm luxurious slipper comfort* . . . true shoe smartness."

Transportation

Transportation of the body can be one of the costliest funeral extras. This is true even when the funeral and burial take place in the same community, if the cemetery is beyond a "fixed-service" radius. Transportation is especially costly when out-of-town travel is necessary (see below). Extras such as the ambulance or "first-call" car (which picks up the body and takes it to the funeral home), the hearse, flower cars, limousines for survivors and other mourners all help raise the overall price of funerals. The reason: Funeral vehicles are expensive.

A hearse that cost $13,000 in the late 1960s was priced at $18,000 in 1976. Ambulances are so expensive that many undertakers use first-call cars instead. And funeral automobiles cannot be classified as long-term investments; they quickly become obsolete. According to Norman Heard, the Pittsburgh undertaker, it's important to funeral home clients to ride in shiny, up-to-date vehicles.** "People want to drive in a limousine to the cemetery. They want a new hearse to take grandpa to the grave site." Most undertakers feel that no self-respecting establishment can afford to keep a funeral vehicle for more than two years—three at the most. And the resale value of these vehicles is limited; there is not a large market for used hearses.

About 60 percent of funeral homes own a small fleet of vehicles; other

---

*The FTC is critical of funeral industry advertising that explicitly or implicitly stresses "comfort" for the deceased. "A person free from bereavement is able to see the absurdity in purchasing particular funeral merchandise on the basis of its comfort for the deceased," the staff planning memorandum stated, "but a bereaved person beset by feelings of grief and guilt is not." Funeral buyers, the memorandum continues, should, of course, be able to purchase Beautyrest orthopedic coffin mattresses, satin pillows, "Ko-Zee" burial footwear if such merchandise provides solace, but undertakers and manufacturers should be prohibited from "making comfort claims as a basis for selling products for a dead person."

**To encourage new sales, vehicle manufacturers take full-page color advertisements in trade journals and praise their products in glowing prose. Hearses are given names like "Sovereign," "Regency," "Baronet," "Eterna," and "Crown Sovereign." One model was described in *Mortuary Management* as "exquisitely designed to provide that special, awesome dignity that only the finest coach can add to a funeral."

establishments may lease or rent. Owned, leased, or rented, such vehicles often show up as a separate item in funeral buyers' bills. Generally, only the hearse and one limousine are included in the price of a "complete" funeral. (In many states undertakers have a monopoly over the transportation of human remains.*) Charges for extra limousines to the cemetery vary, but usually run about $50 per car.

Out-of-Town Transportation

In 1974, a reader of *Consumer Reports* wrote to his senators, representative, and Consumers Union to protest, among other things, unusually high transportation costs charged by a Miami undertaker. The reader stated in part:

> My father recently died in Miami, Florida, and the funeral was in New York. The funeral director in Miami charged $250 to move the body to the airport, while the one in New York charged $35 to move it from the airport. [The customer was billed only once, by the New York undertaker, who included on his bill the charges incurred in both the Miami and New York funeral homes.] When I requested an explanation of the difference in cost for the same service, and an adjustment of the charges, the funeral director in New York threatened to sue me and had his attorney send me a dunning letter. . . . My father's funeral was very modest, yet it still cost almost $2,000 after the funeral home added in all their "little" charges. . . .

Transporting remains to another community can add greatly to the cost of a funeral, as the experience of the *Consumer Reports* reader demonstrated. In that instance, there were payments for airline shipping charges from Miami to New York ($101.74) and for the services of two undertakers as well.

Every year an estimated 200,000 bodies in the United States are transported by air, rail, or hearse to out-of-town locations. The arrangements for services vary: In some cases, the funeral is held in the community where death occurred, with burial elsewhere; in other cases, when a person dies away from his or her own community, both the funeral and burial are held at the place of destination. Either way, two funeral establishments are usually involved, since, in most cases, an undertaker transports the body to the terminal and another picks it up at the destination point after shipment by air or rail.

Transportation rules for shipping remains are normally set by the

---

*For example, in Massachusetts, according to the FTC planning memorandum, a corpse must be transported in a hearse-type vehicle, with one licensed funeral-coach operator aboard. "Since virtually all such licenses are held by persons in the employ of the funeral industry, morticians enjoy a state-conferred exclusive charter," the FTC said. The Massachusetts law preventing an ambulance from doubling as a hearse is especially puzzling in view of the fact that many people die in ambulances or are pronounced dead on arrival at a hospital after being transported in an ambulance.

state. New York State's Sanitary Code, for example, provides that no body can be transported by common carrier without a transit permit, signed by an undertaker, specifying, among other things, the method used for preparation of the body. A transit label, to be attached to the outer box or case, is also required. The Code specifies that the body be placed for shipment in a watertight container—either a sealed metal transfer shipping case or a coffin inside a strong, tightly closed outer box. For shipping by air, there is some leeway permitted in the type of outer container. Many funeral homes provide shipping containers, although some airlines have their own.* Canvas covers, or "bags," cost from $35 to $50. Containers made of sturdy plywood or corrugated cardboard—often called air trays—cost about $20.

Today, most bodies being shipped any distance are sent by air. The rates for shipping bodies by air are anywhere from 175 percent to 250 percent more than those for other air freight, depending on weight, what airline is used, and the distance. In addition, as already noted, the undertaker's charge for transporting the body in each community can be substantial.

It has been estimated that approximately 25,000 bodies a year are transported by air from Florida, where many older, retired people live. Bodies are flown mostly to the Northeast and the Midwest. This transportation service is an annual $3.2 million industry in Florida. Nationwide, the major scheduled domestic airlines** carry at least 67,500 bodies a year (exact figures are difficult to obtain without a central clearinghouse for the data). In addition, regional scheduled airlines and operators of "air hearse" services transport human remains. A number of undertakers also have gone into the air transport business and carry corpses in their own aircraft. One organization, the Flying Funeral Directors of America, founded in 1960, has nearly two hundred undertaker members.

Transporting human remains by rail is becoming less common in the United States and Canada, although transportation by air costs more. The National Railroad Passenger Corporation (Amtrak) ships human remains through its express service to many cities in the United States. There is a basic charge of $30 plus express charges between the points of shipment.

---

*In Florida, the owner of Sky-Pak, an air-freight company that transports bodies, designed a special corrugated cardboard container for coffins.

**One of the major airline carriers of human remains in the United States has developed a system to facilitate the shipment of coffins. In every city where it has offices (approximately fifty-seven), there is a "Jim Wilson desk." This department handles all the details of transporting bodies: "Jim Wilson" is the code name for this service.

The airline bases its air freight rate on weight plus distance. Thus, in 1976, it cost $71.05 per 100 pounds to ship human remains from New York to Los Angeles, plus 5 percent sales tax; if the combined weight of body, coffin, and container were 250 pounds, the cost would be $186.50. From New York to Chicago, the rate was $33.10 per 100 pounds, and from San Francisco to New York $64.65 per 100 pounds. In addition, the airline supplies, for $20, the "Jim Wilson Air Tray," its specially designed coffin container.

The cost of transportation is based on a minimum weight of four hundred pounds, unless a specific weight is stipulated by the sender. For example, remains shipped from New York City to Washington, D.C., would cost a total of $46 ($30 handling charge and $16 transportation charge). At one time, it was necessary to pay passenger rates to ship a body in the United States, but now railroad agents handle shipment at each end. An undertaker usually delivers and picks up the body at each railroad station.

The extra expense incurred in the transportation of bodies is something that many people do not consider when they make known a wish to be buried in another city or state or country after death or if they purchase a cemetery lot on a preneed basis and then move to another area. And yet this obligation imposed upon survivors to pay additional transportation costs frequently can represent great financial hardship.

If survivors should find themselves in a situation where it is necessary to arrange for transportation of human remains over a considerable distance within the country, one cardinal rule should be followed: If a relative or friend dies in a strange locality but is to be buried in another locality, never call a funeral home in the place where death occurs. Always call the funeral home in the community where the funeral and burial are to take place. The undertaker there will make arrangements with a funeral home in the community where the death occurred, and, although there will still be extra expense, overall costs should be less and time saved. Even though the funeral home in the strange community may charge too much,* as did the undertaker in Miami, the bill should not be as high when it is clear to all concerned that another undertaker is arranging the funeral.

Survivors should also compare prices of the different kinds of transportation available. If the place of destination is less than three hundred miles away, it may actually save on transportation costs to hire a funeral coach or hearse rather than use an airline in addition to a hearse at each terminal.

Lowering the Cost of Extra Items

The best way to decide which extras to include in a funeral is to begin by discussing the cost of each item and service with the undertaker in advance. Unfortunately, this is frequently impossible because of the widespread practice of package or unit pricing and because undertakers in forty-four states are not legally required to draw up an itemized bill before the funeral. New York is one state where funeral directors are required to provide a written statement, including itemization of costs, when funeral arrangements are made. The following bill, submitted for an actual funeral in 1973,

---

*It is not uncommon for survivors to be charged for a funeral service by both funeral homes—in the strange community and at the place of destination.

is one example of what funeral buyers in that state were entitled to be told before a funeral takes place.

Mahogany casket	$804
Enclosure, pine	85
Removal of body	25
Embalming	125
Preparation room use	20
Use of funeral home—two days	250
Arrangements, supervision	175
Hearse from funeral home to church to cemetery	53
Limousine from funeral home to church to cemetery	47
Mass of the Resurrection	60
Memorial prayer cards	14
Register book	5
Acknowledgment cards	13
Four pallbearers at $15	60
Death notice in newspaper	17
Twelve transcripts of death certificate at $2	24
Gratuities	8
Headstone	300
Two-plot grave	200
Opening grave	60
Blanket of roses	50
	$2,395*

Even for funeral buyers who must cope with the common practice of unit pricing, it is still advisable and desirable to ask in advance (1) what goods and services requested by survivors are not included in the total funeral package price; (2) the individual prices of those extras; and (3) whether the specific goods and services included in the package price will actually all be needed. The FTC recommends that buyers be persistent, even aggressive, in seeking the information. Items and services considered as extra costs vary with each funeral establishment, but the alert buyer may find that some undertakers will deduct certain costs if the goods and services are not desired. This information is usually not volunteered, so sur-

---

*Members of the clergy and other residents of Westchester County, New York, where the funeral took place, considered this overall funeral price modest and below the general standards of the community. Many families, they noted, would have chosen a more expensive coffin, a costlier vault than the pine enclosure selected, and a larger headstone. In this bill, certain extras were not chosen, among them burial clothes and floral wreaths. The $60 for the Mass of the Resurrection would probably cover the costs of the music and an offering for the clergy.

vivors should make a point of requesting a reduction in the overall price.*

Some extras are unavoidable for nearly all survivors when death occurs, whether or not they arrange for a conventional funeral; certified copies of death certificates, for example, are usually required in order to file for death benefits. For those who use the services of a funeral home, other extras may be necessary, such as newspaper death notices, hired pallbearers, and cars for mourners. But a number of goods and services are unnecessary in a simple funeral service. For example, burial clothing, flowers, flower car, and various funeral home cards are all expendable when survivors want an inexpensive funeral.

No matter the type of funeral desired, funeral buyers should understand *before* they sign a contract that specifies payment for certain extras that these items and services are added expenses not included in the "complete" funeral. When asked, reputable undertakers will at least explain which extras are in addition to the package price, even though they may be reluctant to discuss specific costs of extras.

---

*The FTC cited as an example a funeral home in Washington, D.C., that deducts $40 from the package price if clients do not use the mortuary chapel and a $21 deduction for those who do not have a church service.

13
Vaults and
Other Coffin Enclosures

"What About Funeral Costs?" is a current National Funeral Directors Association pamphlet, issued "in the public interest." Published to give funeral buyers some idea of what to expect in arranging for a funeral and of the costs involved, it manages to steer the consumer in the direction of goods and services that can be expensive and perhaps unnecessary.

Heading the pamphlet's list of "categories of charges" for funerals are the services of the undertaker and staff, use of facilities and equipment, and "the casket and vault selected." The matter-of-fact inclusion of the vault in this section suggests that a vault is a standard part of the funeral package. The implication is that a vault (which is a type of coffin enclosure) is as much a burial requirement as the coffin itself.* There is no mention in the NFDA pamphlet that a vault, unlike a coffin, is rarely included in the package price for a "complete" funeral, that it may be an optional choice, or that its equivalent—for example, a grave liner—is generally available at less cost from most of the cemeteries that require a coffin enclosure. (Not all cemeteries sell grave liners, however, and some cemeteries sell vaults as well as liners.) Not until the third page, under "Burial Enclosures," does the pamphlet suggest that vaults are not universally chosen and that there are alternatives to vaults:

> For earth burial, many people wish the casket and remains to be placed in an outside enclosure. Outside enclosures, providing protection against

---

*Testifying before a House investigational hearing in 1974 about a proposed law requiring that all Washington, D.C., funeral homes submit itemized bills in advance to funeral buyers, J. Thomas Rosch, director of the FTC Bureau of Consumer Protection, objected to a special itemization category for vaults. "We believe," he said, "that a separate category for a burial vault is undesirable because it might foster the mistaken impression that vaults are in some way required. We know from our investigation that many consumers now buy burial vaults because of this misconception. A law aimed at giving funeral buyers more information and more choice should not operate, we feel, to reinforce erroneous beliefs as to the legal or other necessity for vaults."

the elements, are known as burial vaults. They are made of concrete, steel, fiberglass and solid copper. Burial vaults range in price from about $175 up, and are generally sold through funeral directors.

For those who do not use a protective vault, many cemeteries require the use of some type of outside enclosure to reduce the possibility of a grave cave-in.

Protection of the Body

"Protection against the elements" is a recurring theme in vault manufacturers' and undertakers' advertising. A few years ago, a vault company described its products in an advertisement in *Casket & Sunnyside* as "The Legacy of Ancient Egypt Fulfilled in 20th Century America":

> The Pyramids of Egypt: they stand as awesome reminders of the great wealth and power of ancient kings and their search for timeless interment. Today, through the miracle of 20th Century technology, you can provide this kind of everlasting protection for every man.

And a brochure put out by another company stated that its vault

> —placed over the casket in the grave—is built to protect against water in the ground, to make the last resting place of a loved one dry. And what priceless peace of mind this brings, throughout the years, to those who are left behind.

The FTC points out in its 1973 planning memorandum that while it may be true that a vault will protect human remains from the weather for, say, thirty years, "far more destructive forces than rainwater" will be at work.

Coriolis, the Canadian undertaker, also expresses skepticism about vaults in *Death, Here Is Thy Sting*:

> In a recent conversation with a family in the selection room, I was pointedly asked what the advantages of a concrete vault were. Immediately I was confronted with a dilemma which I often face. Should I tell them what I believe to be the truth—that the vault is nothing more than a source of sundry income to the funeral director—or does my responsibility to my employer necessitate that I sing loud hosannas to the virtues of the vault? Striking a compromise, I explained that the vault ensured that the grave did not continually settle, as it does when pine shells disintegrate after a few years. I assured them that it would last as long as they would, and I evaded the question of the protection it affords.

As far back as 1937, the FTC promulgated trade practice rules for the concrete burial vault manufacturing industry. Rule 9 stipulated that manufacturers were not to say that vaults "remain air-tight, water-proof or sweat-proof when such representations, statements, assertions or claims are not true in fact, or are misleading, or are not known to be true, with the tendency, capacity or effect of misleading or deceiving any purchasers or prospective purchasers of burial vaults. . . ." Such claims, the FTC asserted,

124

constitute "an unfair trade practice." Whether, indeed, vaults afford extra protection for the body is difficult to ascertain. Few survivors would want to investigate the claims that vault manufacturers make for their product.

Cemeteries May Require a Vault

The fact that thousands of tons of concrete and metal are being buried in the ground every year is a source of alarm to many people, even to some members of the funeral industry. A manufacturer of "molded fiber glass casket-vaults"—a combination coffin-vault weighing only one-fourth to one-seventh as much as concrete vaults—has pointed out that a concrete vault usually weighs more than a ton and that there are substantial labor costs involved in transporting it to the cemetery. "It takes more and more people (labor is increasingly expensive) and equipment," he says, "to do the job." Furthermore, he adds, "conventional casket and vault combinations have become so unwieldy and the heavy equipment so damaging to the landscape" that cemeteries are finding them increasingly difficult to accommodate. In 1974 an industry representative pointed out to *Media & Consumer* an additional liability to the durable combination of metal coffins and concrete and metal vaults: lack of erosion. "It is ecologically wrong to fill the ground with materials that don't erode," he said; "vaults are superfluous."

Yet most cemeteries in the United States require some kind of coffin enclosure, according to the executive director of the National Concrete Burial Vault Association, who stated in a letter to Consumers Union:

> We do not know of any cemeteries that require a *vault*, but cemeteries do require, in most areas, that an outer receptacle be used—sometimes called sectionals, grave liners and rough boxes, either of wood or concrete. Their only purpose is to prevent sunken graves and a large percentage of the cemeteries in the country would require this.

Cemetery representatives maintain that as time passes coffins disintegrate and the ground above them begins to cave in. This, they say, makes cemetery upkeep difficult, especially when power gardening equipment is used to tend the grass around the plots. Cemeteries also stress the possibility that without coffin enclosures the ground could become uneven and visitors could stumble or trip at the grave site.* Cemeteries could thus be liable for lawsuits.

In its 1973 planning memorandum the FTC noted that "no one has ever checked the validity of the cemetarians' claims for the necessity of vaults." The FTC pointed out, however, that American cemeteries in general dig

---

*"A cemetery requires a vault," according to a cemetery president in Virginia Beach, Virginia, "so that you can be assured that when you step on a spot you're not going to fall through and break your leg. With elderly people their bones break easily anyway and they're the ones who frequent the cemeteries. . . ."

graves closer to each other than in other countries (where vaults are virtually unknown) and that this, together with the use of power gardening equipment, may justify the requirement of vaults. In comments supporting its 1975 proposed rule, the FTC stated:

> As we noted in our initial planning memo, there is some doubt as to the necessity for burial vaults, and the claim should not go unchallenged. The staff has not, however, recommended any direct attack on cemeteries requiring vaults because the factual question is a close one and there may be a sufficient basis for the practice. ...

Types of Enclosures

When interviewers from the New York State College of Human Ecology, Cornell University, surveyed 489 adults in central New York State in 1974 about funeral practices, they found that a number of those interviewed were confused about the definition of a vault. The word vault itself may be a source of confusion, since it also means an arched structure of masonry, or a room or space—sometimes resembling a mausoleum—covered by an arched structure. Some respondents defined vaults as above-ground mausoleums used for storing bodies in coffins when the ground is frozen. (Mausoleums are above-ground structures in which one or more bodies are placed or sealed in crypts.)

The prefabricated two-part coffin enclosures of steel and concrete sold by undertakers are called vaults; the concrete grave liners or sectional boxes sold by cemeteries, although of much more roughhewn construction, are sometimes referred to as vaults, too.

A grave liner generally has, in addition to a concrete bottom, two concrete end pieces and two concrete side pieces; grooves in these pieces permit them to be fitted together to form an enclosure for the coffin. The concrete lid is usually supported by the side pieces. Holding the side pieces in position and going around the length of the concrete box are two steel "straps" about an inch wide. Some cemeteries use, instead of the sectional box, a "bell liner." This is a reinforced concrete receptacle, shaped like a vault but without a lid. A machine is used to lower the bell liner—open side down—over the coffin.

Prices of Coffin Enclosures

Nowadays, about 72 percent of all coffins are placed in some type of enclosure at burial. Sales for concrete vaults in 1976 came to about $295.5 million, an increase of only about $3 million since 1973.* Concrete vaults, averaging $200 each at retail, account for the major portion of vault sales, with metal

---

*The executive director of the National Concrete Burial Vault Association told Consumers Union that there has been a slight reduction in the number of units sold in recent

vaults, averaging $300 to $350, representing just a small fraction of the total.

About four out of every five coffin enclosures manufactured are sold through funeral directors. According to a vault industry representative, however, there is an increasing trend to sell to cemeteries. He expressed his preference for doing business with funeral directors because "cemeteries aren't interested in offering the best possible product to the customer."

A Midwest burial vault firm, selling almost exclusively to funeral directors, offers reinforced concrete vaults in nine price brackets. The top six come with a personalized nameplate and in a variety of colors, some in as many as eleven "enhancing finishes to complement any casket selection." The least expensive concrete vaults retail at about $125 to $150; they are made of natural unpainted concrete. Metal vaults sold by the firm include steel, stainless steel, and copper models, available in eight different price brackets. (The company also sells, on request, plastic and fiber glass models, because the client should have a full "range of choices.") Vaults are priced up to $2,000,* with the average sale $300.

Prices for grave liners generally range from $70 to $125. The 1973 FTC price survey of funeral costs in Washington, D.C., found that about 75 percent of funeral consumers there bought a concrete liner or sectional box from a cemetery at a cost of about $85. About 22 percent bought a burial vault from a funeral home for an average price of $311. Some cemeteries offered a wooden container for as little as $50. Vaults, on the other hand, cost, on the average, between $250 and $350, although consumers paid as much as $700 to $1,500 for stainless-steel or copper-lined models. NFDA literature generally states that the price of a vault sold through a funeral home begins at $175.

The FTC says that the "wholesale to retail mark-up" on vaults is seldom less than 100 percent and sometimes as much as 500 percent to 600 percent. "Thus, it is not surprising that the funeral director prefers that the customer buy an interment receptacle from him rather than from a cemetery and that he buy an expensive burial vault rather than a liner."

In its proposed rule, the FTC would have funeral homes give customers a separate price list for coffin enclosures. The rule states that the list would include "the price for each outer interment receptacle available from the funeral home for purchase by the customer, together with a brief

---

years, in part because of an increase in the number of cremations and, to some extent, the growing use of mausoleums.

*Writing about vaults in *The American Way of Death*, Jessica Mitford observed: "They are getting more beautiful by the year, may be had in a variety of colors including polished stripes, and are frequently decorated with all sorts of lovely things—foreverness symbols like Trees of Life or setting suns—leading one to speculate as to whether the time may not be ripe for the introduction of a sur- or super- or supra-vault to protect the vault. And so on and on, like those little wooden eggs-within-eggs we used to find in our Christmas stockings."

description of each enclosure, and an effective date for the prices specified."
Furthermore, the FTC rule would require that funeral homes inform customers that a vault may not be necessary. The proposed FTC vault requirement notice would read:

> Some cemeteries require that an outer enclosure be placed around the
> casket in the grave, while others do not. Where such a requirement exists,
> it can usually be satisfied by either a burial vault or a grave liner, usually
> less expensive than a burial vault. Outer interment receptacles are often
> sold by cemeteries as well as by funeral homes. Before selecting any outer
> enclosure you may want to determine any applicable cemetery require-
> ments as well as the offerings of your cemetery and funeral home.

This FTC proposal prompted strong objections from the industry. The
NFDA's Howard Raether, testifying in 1976 before a subcommittee of the
House Committee on Small Business looking into regulatory agencies and
the funeral industry, stated: "This is inviting individuals to get the facts
from the competitor of the funeral home." Pointing out that a number of
cemeteries have funeral homes on their cemetery grounds, Raether noted
that survivors might be persuaded to have the funeral there rather than at
the funeral home they first went to. He also pointed out that "nothing thus
far released by the FTC indicates that cemeteries are going to be required to
point out to families that call upon them that some of what they have to
offer might be available from funeral homes."

The House subcommittee, in its published report on the hearings, was
especially critical of this provision of the proposed rule, calling it "abhor-
rent to free enterprise and a requirement not imposed upon any other line
of business." The report further added that requiring an undertaker to
"advise customers to contact competitors demeans any honest, reputable
businessman." An FTC attorney conceded at the hearings that such a provision might not be "a good precedent." But, he added: "I think this, or
something like it, is necessary."

Questionable Practices

Cemeteries, which profess to be more interested in the utilitarian aspects
of coffin enclosures for the prevention of grave cave-ins, are in direct and
increasing competition with undertakers for the sale of coffin enclosures.
And, in the case of some unscrupulous proprietary (for profit) cemetery
owners, there have been dishonest practices in the sale of vaults. (Some
proprietary cemeteries have sales teams that sell not only plots but vaults
and grave markers on a preneed basis.) The North Carolina attorney general
issued a warning in 1972:

> Complaints have come to us from people who signed a contract to buy
> vaults and grave markers on a preneed basis. The cemetery ownership

changed before the products were delivered and the new owners will not honor the contracts of the former owners. When this happens, payment could be made twice: once by the deceased person who bought the products during his or her lifetime, and again by the decedent's estate.

The North Carolina attorney general urged consumers "to use caution" in buying such merchandise in advance of need. "When delivery is needed at some time in the future, the company which collected the money may be out of business or financially unable to provide the merchandise."

Other abuses—notably, misrepresenting vaults as a legal requirement —have also been recorded. Indeed, the FTC says that misrepresentations of law about burial vaults are common. In 1969, a Rhode Island newspaper reporter wrote that "some funeral directors and cemetery representatives quoted the law inaccurately. The reporter was told several times that . . . a grave liner or vault is required by state law." In 1973, the Montgomery County (Maryland) Office of Consumer Affairs filed a lawsuit including the allegation that a local cemetery was fraudulently representing vaults as a legal requirement. In 1974, the manager of a Kansas City, Kansas, cemetery assured Consumers Union that "our state laws require the use of vaults. . . ." In response to a query, a Kansas assistant attorney general informed Consumers Union that there is no law in the state of Kansas requiring vaults.

A Vault Is Not Always Necessary

The FTC says it is aware of no state law requiring vaults or grave liners, although it notes that "in some cases vaults may be required by city or county ordinance."

In 1974, a spot check by Consumers Union among cemeteries in various parts of the country—Kansas City (Kansas and Missouri), sections of New Jersey, New York City, Miami (Florida), and Milwaukee—found that most cemeteries queried required some form of coffin enclosure for their graves. Nonetheless, the survey showed that it is possible to find cemeteries that do not require coffin enclosures—for example, some municipal cemeteries and some smaller rural cemeteries. Consumers Union's survey indicated that no coffin enclosures are required in some sections of a large cemetery in a New York City suburb, while a 500-acre Catholic cemetery just outside New York City, where more than 2 million bodies are buried, does not require coffin enclosures.

For many years, the Veterans Administration National Cemetery System did not provide vaults or grave liners in its cemeteries. But in 1975 a test program using government-supplied grave liners was begun in ten of the active cemeteries in the system to see if maintenance problems of sunken graves and tipped headstones could be solved. According to the director of cemetery service, the test results were so favorable that now thirty-four of the fifty-five national cemeteries use grave liners.* Grave liners are specified for the new national cemeteries now nearing completion.

Guidelines for Selecting a Coffin Enclosure

If the decedent had purchased a cemetery plot in advance, survivors, in most cases, will be obliged to follow the requirements of the cemetery where the plot is located. But if cemetery arrangements are to be made after death has occurred, the question of whether a coffin enclosure is required may affect the choice of cemetery. Of course, survivors will also have to consider the costs of other components associated with burial—principally, the plot, the marker, and the opening and closing of the grave. (For a discussion of cemetery costs, see Chapter 14.)

Survivors who call cemeteries in the area should inquire whether coffin enclosures are mandatory. (Most cemetery personnel, unlike many undertakers, will discuss requirements and costs over the phone.) If so, the funeral buyer should ask whether one can be bought from the cemetery, and what the prices are. Whenever possible, a vault should not be bought from an undertaker; it is almost always less costly to purchase a grave liner from a cemetery. A vault should normally not be purchased on a preneed basis, since a decedent may be buried in a cemetery that does not require vaults, may be cremated, or donation of the body to medical science may be decided.

---

*In the other twenty-two they are not required. The director of cemetery service noted that for those cemeteries there were no bids from firms providing vaults, or the bids submitted were excessive, or contracts were not justified for small cemeteries in isolated areas with few burials.

14
Cemeteries

In Nashville, Tennessee, what is billed as a twenty-story, $12 million sky-scraper, the nation's tallest community mausoleum,* with 258,000 crypts, is under construction. Three floors are completed; two more are planned for the first stage of construction. Owned by H. Raymond Ligon, who has been in the funeral business for more than half a century, the Woodlawn high-rise mausoleum—"with luxurious carpeting, fine furniture, and meaningful pieces of art and fine sculpture"—has been called the "Death Hilton." The building is in the shape of a cross. The crypts (or burial chambers), about 12,900 to a floor, are made of three-inch-thick reinforced concrete, covered with slabs of marble, and they stand seven high on every floor (there are "companion" crypts for couples and sections for families). In contrast to prices in high-rise buildings for the living (where the top-level apartments cost the most), crypts on the mausoleum ground floor are the most expensive. The higher the level of a crypt, the lower its cost. The same principle applies to the seven stacked crypts on each floor: "Heart-level" (midway) and "heaven-level" (ceiling height) crypts do not cost as much as those at "prayer-level" (floor and kneeling height).

The Woodlawn mausoleum, like most others, is built on cemetery grounds. The entire complex consists of several units, with complete facilities for funerals, conventional burial, cremation, and entombment. (Burial above ground—the placing of the coffin in and sealing of the crypt— is frequently referred to as entombment.) Purchased in advance on a preneed basis (see Chapter 19), funeral home services for two are priced at $1,495 (including two steel caskets and two vaults). For conventional burial for two, the preneed price is an additional $1,495 (including two grave sites,

---

*Unlike private mausoleums, with space for one individual or for families, community mausoleums—usually two or three stories high—hold multiple crypts that are sold to various purchasers.

opening and closing the graves, and a bronze marker for two). A funeral for two plus entombment is priced anywhere from about $3,400 to $6,500, depending on the size and location of the crypts.

One reason why Woodlawn has been able to keep the costs of its less expensive entombments at a price so close to those of conventional funerals and burial is the relatively inexpensive coffin Ligon designed to slide into the mausoleum crypts. Called the cross repose, it costs around $700, and, according to *The Wall Street Journal*, consists of a "bed-like bier" and a "fiberglass shell":

> After the body has been viewed on the bed it is covered with the shell, which connects with a frame around the foam-rubber mattress. The coffin is then lifted off the bed and taken to the adjoining chapel for the funeral service, thence to the mausoleum elevator and entombment.

Evening funerals, as well as evening visiting hours, which Ligon believes are more convenient for most working people, can be arranged. There is a religious grotto, the "Garden of Jesus," adjoining the mausoleum, where funeral guests can rest, before or after services, near an underground spring and close to "a replica of the Tomb of Christ," built from "actual stones from Jerusalem."*

Ligon constructed a community mausoleum—a two-story building—in 1969; its 30,000 crypts are about 80 percent filled. He began construction on the skyscraper primarily for economic reasons. The high cost of land in Nashville (some of the undeveloped land in Ligon's cemetery is worth $40,000 to $45,000 an acre, according to a Woodlawn representative) plus the shortage of cemetery space convinced him that a mausoleum was the best solution for the future. Woodlawn contains enough space for interments for about fifteen years. Ligon points out that 192 acres would be needed to bury the 129,500 bodies that the mausoleum can house on only seven acres.

Even before construction on the new mausoleum began, there was a $750,000 advance sale for crypts. By the middle of 1973, preneed purchases totaled $2 million. Woodlawn anticipates sales will reach a total of $3.5 million by mid-1978 and reports that about half the space on five floors is

---

*Woodlawn literature describes the origin of the grotto as follows: "In contemplating the Woodlawn high-rise mausoleum it was decided to give it the form of a cross as a symbol of Christ's sacrifice for all mankind. The structure was engineered to withstand the ages and the earth upon which it stands was tested for fitness and unseen fissures. Construction was well under way when a powerful underground water stream was discovered and emerged to the surface.

"This called for immediate and severe changes in the engineering plans with sealing away from the rest of the building so that the water might be contained. The result was that an elongated area was created without any apparent use.

"While being viewed by Woodlawn officials, a simultaneous expression of opinion came to the three observers as if they had been inspired. 'This is it—the place to create a religious grotto....'"

132

already sold. What is the appeal of high-rise burial? Survivors, Mr. Ligon says, find "a warm, dry, protected" mausoleum crypt more comforting than "a dark, damp hole in the ground."* He sometimes shows prospective customers a color photograph of an open grave and asks them if they really want to put their loved one in there. The answer is usually no.

Shortage of Cemetery Space

For all the popularity of mausoleums like Woodlawn, most Americans still expect an earth burial when they die. But the very success of conventional burial has created a problem: a lack of cemetery space. The National Association of Cemeteries has estimated that the average unfilled capacity of cemeteries of all types is sufficient to provide for ground burial of the population of the United States for about ninety-two more years. This estimate, of course, does not apply to all cemeteries or all geographic areas. As of 1977, for example, 48 of the 103 cemeteries in the Veterans Administration National Cemetery System were closed for interment, except for plots previously reserved, second interments in single graves, or cremated remains. Only fifty-five national cemeteries (see Appendix 4 for a list of active national cemeteries) in twenty-seven states and Puerto Rico have space available for new interments, although the Veterans Administration is currently planning to develop new cemeteries in various regions of the United States.**

Cemeteries in urban and suburban areas are also experiencing a critical lack of grave space. In New York City's Calvary Cemetery, more than 2

---

*Mausoleum managers stress this point in their advertising and promotion. A 1977 advertisement for two mausoleums in the New York City area read: "Burial in a majestic above-ground mausoleum—traditional resting place of the rich and the famous—now costs less than in a dismal, water-filled grave in an overcrowded, tombstone-cluttered cemetery." A 1976 advertisement for the same mausoleums read: "And of course you escape the emotionally disturbing problems of below-ground burial. Most everyone finds unfriendly elements of the earth, water-filled or sunken graves, defaced or knocked over head-stones, overcrowded weed-filled or snow-covered plots . . . offensive and depressing."

**In 1975, the director of the National Cemetery System warned that the Los Angeles National Cemetery, the last one open in that part of the country, would run out of space by the end of that year, that space was running out in national cemeteries near Philadelphia, New York, Chicago, and Detroit, and that space was "almost nonexistent" in retirement areas like Arizona and Florida. The thirteen national cemeteries in Virginia (not including Arlington National Cemetery) were all closed. A VA study in 1973 estimated that there were only about 1 million actual and potential grave sites in the National Cemetery System for about 29 million veterans and their spouses and eligible children. The new cemeteries, when they begin to open in 1978, should relieve some of the immediate pressure for veterans and their families.

The new cemeteries will be located near Riverside, California (scheduled to open in November 1978); Cape Cod, Massachusetts; Calverton, New York (scheduled to open in August 1978); Indiantown Gap, Pennsylvania; and Quantico, Virginia. The 1978 federal budget includes allocations for site selections for two additional cemeteries to be located in the Midwest and South.

million bodies are buried in 500 acres; plots are no longer for sale and interments take place only in graves previously deeded. The superintendent of one of Boston's largest cemeteries warned a number of years ago that within a quarter of a century there would be no more room for burials in that city. "It's something people just don't want to face," he said. In Westchester County, north of New York City, where several large cemeteries are located, some cemeteries are running out of space for ground burials. Representatives of several cemeteries in the area say they expect all their unused land space will be filled within ten to twenty-five years. One of the largest cemeteries just below Westchester, Woodlawn (400 acres and 257,000 interments), has only about fourteen unused acres. Available land, according to a Woodlawn representative, will be exhausted in about fifteen years.*

City officials in Calgary, Alberta, are "seriously concerned" about future land requirements for cemeteries in their community. Because of increasing land costs, the city cannot continue to set aside large tracts of land for future use as cemeteries. Therefore, Calgary city planners are promoting the idea of cremation, as well as the practice of two burials in one grave. In older Calgary cemeteries, families are encouraged to use the same grave a second, or even a third, time, if many years have passed since the last burial.

John Baiz, rector of Calvary Episcopal Church in Pittsburgh, who started a burial society with his congregation in 1965 to provide simple funerals for members (see page 53), has said that if current burial practices continue, "the first thing you know the whole country is going to be nothing but a vast cemetery." Baiz predicted that eventually, under certain circumstances, cremation might be mandated by law.**

What Can Be Done about the Shortage of Cemetery Space?

In 1975, D. W. Peabody noted in a *New York Times* article that one of the country's largest insurance companies had stated that unless new burial procedures are adopted, within five hundred years every acre in the United States will be taken up by cemeteries. The writer asked what is to be done with the bodies of the deceased in the future: "The ideal thing," he said,

---

*As a result, officials at Woodlawn have drawn up a long-range plan to set aside sites for additional community mausoleums. Woodlawn's first community mausoleum was created in 1967 by converting receiving vaults at the cemetery entrance to crypts and to niches for cremation urns. Subsequently, two new mausoleums were constructed. A year after the first was completed, 60 percent of its available space had been sold. The second mausoleum was designed to contain more than 1,200 crypts as well as niches.

**This thought was echoed by a respondent to a survey conducted by the Consumers' Association of Canada: "When land is so much in demand as at present and it promises to get worse, I believe the sensible humanitarian procedure to adopt is cremation. I believe it is criminal to have human beings forced to live in cramped conditions when thousands of acres of land are reserved and rendered unusable other than for burying corpses."

"would be to bury them immediately after death, without embalming them, in places where they could disintegrate naturally and the elements return to their respective cycles."

Malcolm Wells, an architect in Cherry Hill, New Jersey, has drawn up plans for such a cemetery in which coffins and vaults would be banned. Bodies would be wrapped in shrouds or burial cloths and be buried in the earth. The cemetery Wells envisions would resemble a park with trees planted as grave markers and inhabited by birds and animals. "Such a cemetery will never have to expand to make room for more and more concrete burial vaults," he points out. "There will be almost no limit to the number of burials. Human compost, like all other kinds, returns very quickly to life again. The new cemetery can quite literally become the transitional repository for an endless number of lives."

Between 1977 and the year 2000 approximately 46 million Americans will die (if the current annual figure of about 2 million deaths remains stable). In view of diminishing grave space, Wells's plan may seem sensible and imaginative to some people. But it probably will never be adopted in this country on a large scale, at least not until general attitudes toward burial practices change.

Mausoleums, on the other hand, even though they are above ground, are perhaps close enough in concept to conventional cemeteries to be acceptable alternatives. Nonetheless, the idea of massive or tall buildings filled with dead bodies does not appeal to everyone.

Cremation is an obvious solution to the shortage of graves. One reason cremation is now so common in England, Japan, and other heavily populated countries is that there is so little burial space left. But in the United States, cremation is far from popular,* although the number of cremations grows every year. In 1976, slightly more than 7 percent of all who died were cremated, an increase of almost 12 percent over 1975 figures.

Despite a steady trend toward cremation and a growing acceptance of mausoleums—whether high-rise or the more usual two or three stories—the conventional cemetery is still the prime choice of most Americans. Even though a plot of cemetery land is becoming increasingly expensive,** most people are willing to pay the price to be buried in the earth.

The Growth of Cemeteries

The traditional American cemetery in the eighteenth and early nineteenth centuries was set amid the living—in the middle of towns or in the church-

---

*According to a survey conducted for the Casket Manufacturers Association of America in 1974, 82 percent of the 1,060 respondents preferred earth burial for "loved ones" and 62 percent preferred it for themselves.

**One reason for the growing cost of available cemetery plots is that zoning laws in many areas prohibit establishment of new burial grounds.

yard, where burial was restricted to members of the congregation and their families. Because there was no money for upkeep (church sextons looked after the graves as best they could), many cemeteries fell into neglect. During the nineteenth century, as government authorities recognized the health hazards of such locations, and as space limitations grew more acute, cemeteries were moved to the outskirts of urban areas and to the suburbs. Gradually, municipalities began to assume more responsibility for burial grounds and enacted laws and regulations to govern them. In many states, burial grounds were supported by public funds. But not all cemeteries were publicly supported. Even today, private or small family cemeteries can be found in many parts of the country.*

Traditionally, both church and municipal cemeteries charged modest burial fees; in neither was burying the dead considered to be a profit-making enterprise. It was only in this century that developers began to buy land with the idea of making profits on the sale of grave plots. Because land costs were often low and property bought for burial purposes was tax-exempt, the cemetery business proved to be quite profitable. Each acre of land could be subdivided into numerous plots, and because of a cemetery's nonprofit status, owners did not have to pay income taxes on the proceeds from sales of grave plots.

How do developers and corporations in the business of owning cemetery land for financial gain fall into the category of nonprofit organizations? In *The Law of Death*, Hugh Bernard notes that although all states have laws regulating cemeteries, the language and coverage of the state regulations vary greatly. "Some," he says, "do not make clear distinctions between public and private cemeteries, and profit and nonprofit organizations.**

Modern memorial park cemeteries can be especially profitable because more room is available for bodies than in the traditional cemeteries. By eliminating monuments and paths, it is possible to bury 2,000 to 3,000 bodies in one acre. In some cemeteries, graves are dug very deep so that two—and even more—bodies can occupy what was once a single site.

Mausoleums can be even more profitable, since less land is needed and

---

*A number of states prohibit burial on private property. However, even in states where the practice is permitted, local authorities and appropriate agencies should always be consulted if this kind of interment is planned.

**Bernard cites Forest Lawn Memorial-Park in Southern California, which offers, in addition to burial plots, "complete undertaking services, churches, and other houses of worship, museums and gift shops, florists' wares, and much besides. Despite these ramifying activities, such cemeteries are often treated in law as non-profit, tax-exempt establishments. Many such enterprises," Bernard says, "are constructed on a complex of corporate entities, some to hold the land, others to handle the selling of lots, markers, mortuary services, etc.; many times such corporations are organized in states having more lax control devices than the state where the cemetery is located. Often state laws are ineffective in securing public disclosure of the records of such complex pyramidal corporate structures."

labor costs for maintenance are lower. A typical mausoleum built on three acres of cemetery land can hold about 8,000 bodies, whereas less than half that number could be buried in conventional graves in the same three acres.

Types of Cemeteries

It is difficult to establish the precise number of active cemeteries in the United States. Counting just the active nonfederal cemeteries, the American Cemetery Association (ACA) estimates the total to be 10,000 to 12,000. According to the National Association of Cemeteries (NAC), another trade association,* a more accurate total is between 50,000 and 55,000, including all cemeteries having at least one burial a year. (Many of the smaller cemeteries are rural, in small towns, or church-affiliated.)

According to the ACA and the NAC, nearly 25 percent of the country's cemeteries are publicly owned, operated by cities, counties, states, and local tax districts. About 17 percent are church-affiliated. A small fraction, about 2 percent, are owned by fraternal organizations and cooperatives. An additional 20 percent are operated by other types of nonprofit associations. The largest number—36 percent—are privately or corporately owned and managed; these proprietary cemeteries are operated for profit.

Basically, there are two types of cemeteries: (1) the traditional monument cemeteries, in which purchasers are generally free to choose the type of memorial or monument they want, and (2) modern memorial park cemeteries, where grave markers (usually granite or bronze) are set flush with the ground. Many modern cemeteries combine both types of burial grounds and also include mausoleums—both private ones, which serve as expensive monuments to individuals or families, and the larger community ones. There are two kinds of community mausoleums: indoor mausoleums, totally enclosed structures containing the crypts, and "garden" mausoleums, honeycomb-like structures with the crypts out in the open. Garden mausoleums may or may not have a protective overhang covering the crypts. Many cemeteries also have underground crypts (sometimes called lawn crypts, westminsters, or turf-top crypts)—preplaced concrete chambers or precast boxes, installed side by side or at multiple depth, which are then covered with earth and sod.

Cemeteries may also have a crematory on the grounds. In fact, most crematories are located on cemetery grounds. Some cemeteries also offer complete funeral services on their premises. According to the NFDA, in 1973 there were seventy-seven such funeral/burial establishments in twenty states; sixty-four of them were west of the Mississippi.

---

*The third major trade association is the National Catholic Cemetery Conference. A relative newcomer is the Pre-Arrangement Interment Association of America, founded in 1956. The association's representatives sell cemetery plots on a preneed basis, often by aggressive sales techniques.

Costs of Burial or Entombment

Cemetery costs usually cover three or four separate items:* (1) the plot of ground or the crypt; (2) for ground burial, the coffin enclosure—required by most cemeteries, but there are exceptions (see Chapter 13); (3) opening and closing the grave or entombment;** and (4) the memorial (marker, monument, or plaque).

Many cemeteries also charge for installing or setting the monument or marker at the grave site. Although some cemeteries charge an extra fee for perpetual care of the grave site or mausoleum crypt, others consider perpetual care to be part of the price of a lot or crypt and a certain percentage of the price is set aside in a trust fund for this purpose. Some states require such funding by law.

Cemetery costs vary widely throughout the United States and are generally higher in cities than in rural areas. In 1974, Consumers Union made a spot check of cemeteries in five areas—Kansas City (Kansas and Missouri), sections of New Jersey, New York City, Miami (Florida), and Milwaukee —that revealed a wide range of cemetery prices not only among different cities but among cemeteries within the same city, and even among different sections of individual cemeteries. The 1973 FTC survey of funeral costs in the Washington, D.C., area, which also included a limited check of burial costs, reported varying cemetery prices: Single graves cost from $205 to $400 in one cemetery, $100 to $300 in another (only a few $100 graves were available), and $175 to $275 in a third, which cited $225 as the average sale. Charges for opening and closing a grave ranged from $135 to $165. Prices of bronze markers at the three cemeteries started at $136, $177, and $275, respectively.

A survey of nongovernmental burial and funeral costs conducted for the Veterans Administration in 1973 showed cemetery costs to be somewhat higher. The average cost of a plot, or mausoleum crypt, or niche for an urn in a columbarium was $295 ($347 in urban areas, $243 in rural or suburban locations). Opening and closing the grave, or cremation, came to $124;

---

*Often, when survivors are making burial arrangements, they overlook—or are not told— that there will be cemetery expenses in addition to the cost of the grave plot. A reporter for the *Providence Journal* noted in 1969 that "other substantial cemetery costs were not mentioned until the reporter asked about them. For instance, the price of 'opening and closing' a grave, which is additional to the price quoted for the grave, was never mentioned by cemetery representatives until they were asked about them. Nor was the necessity to purchase a liner or vault for the grave mentioned until the cemetery representative was asked."

**It is not uncommon to tip gravediggers in cemeteries. On some itemized funeral home bills, "gratuities" is listed as a specific charge along with other goods and services; these gratuities are customarily paid to cemetery personnel. An investigator for a New York State commission looking into funeral and burial practices related in 1974 that unless the dispatcher at some New York cemeteries is tipped, funeral corteges will find themselves waiting "inordinate periods of time" before they are allowed to proceed to the grave site.

markers or monuments came to $187; coffin enclosures came to $147. Average additional miscellaneous cemetery expenses totaled $57. Thus the average total cost in 1973 of burial alone, according to the survey for the VA, was $810.

Cemetery costs have risen since then. In 1977 a "modest earth burial" in the Baltimore area was estimated to cost $1,300. And, according to the owner of a Maryland funeral home, "cemetery prices are going up almost every day. It's unbelievable." The $1,300 cemetery charge in Baltimore included $250 for the plot, $400 for a vault, $250 for opening and closing the grave, and $400 for a granite monument. In many cemeteries throughout the country, however, it would be possible to keep the price well below $1,300 by choosing a grave liner instead of a vault (assuming a coffin enclosure is required) and a flat marker instead of a monument.*

Indeed, it is possible to find cemeteries in many communities whose overall charges are low. In Baltimore, for example, where $1,300 was cited as an average cost for burial, one area cemetery charged only $200 for a burial. In 1977, at least two New Jersey cemeteries serving the New York-New Jersey metropolitan area provided relatively inexpensive burials. One charged only $65 for both the plot and opening and closing the grave; the other charged $170 for the same package.

Cemetery Lots

The results of Consumers Union's spot check in 1974 of cemeteries in several cities indicated that a typical price for a single grave plot in an urban area was between $225 and $250. But estimates of the average cost of a single plot vary widely. The FTC stated in 1973 that $250 for a grave plot "seemed high as a national average." But in 1974, *Media & Consumer* gave $325 as the average cost in or near cities and $175 in rural areas.**

The 1973 survey prepared for the VA cited slightly higher costs for grave plots in certain areas of the country. In Connecticut, the average cost of a grave site ranged from $200 to $300 and included perpetual care. In

---

*Average cemetery prices quoted to Consumers Union in 1977 by the three major cemetery trade associations for their member cemeteries ranged from $100 to $300 for a plot in metropolitan areas; in smaller communities and rural areas, plots ranged from $50 to $125. Opening and closing costs in metropolitan areas ranged from $115 to $185; outside these areas, the costs ranged from $75 to $150. The National Catholic Cemetery Conference said that average opening and closing costs for its member cemeteries in cities were $125, from $25 to $50 in smaller cities, and only about $25 in rural areas.

**The cost of a lot very much depends on the geographic area and the cemetery chosen. In Milwaukee, the lowest single-plot prices at three cemeteries were $105, $140, and $250. In Kansas City, the lowest prices at three cemeteries were $165, $175, and $187. Two New Jersey cemeteries quoted low prices of $150 and $175. The lowest price at a cemetery just outside New York City was $400 (for one or two bodies). Another cemetery in the New York City area offered a single plot for $150 in the memorial garden section and for $237.50 in "Tower Gardens," a higher-priced area. In Miami, the lowest prices at two cemeteries were $225 and $440 (for two).

the VA's Central West Region,* plots in urban areas cost, on the average, $368, and in rural and suburban localities, $262. A typical plot in Seattle cost from $225 to $500; prices were generally $50 less in other parts of Washington State.

Standard single-plot prices can go as high at $500, even higher; prices usually depend on the location of the grave in the cemetery. Many large modern cemeteries are laid out in sections, with the least expensive graves in the memorial park areas. Other sections have trees, shrubbery, landscaping, walkways, statuary, sometimes even a lake. Frequently, family plots can be purchased in these sections, and private monuments are allowed. The more elaborate and developed sections often have names such as Garden of the Apostles, Garden of Devotion, and Garden of Resurrection.

Some cemeteries offer bargains. The FTC said in 1973 that "package deals" were available in some Washington, D.C., cemeteries. One offered a grave plot, opening and closing, and a concrete vault for a total price of $230. Another sold grave sites and opening and closing (but not a vault) for $225. Usually, however, there are certain conditions attached to package deals. The grave must be bought for immediate use. There is no choice of location, since the graves are laid out in rows in special sections of the cemetery. If it is desired that the deceased be buried near spouse or relatives, a package deal may not be acceptable. Yet such an arrangement can offer a saving of $500 to $600 over regular cemetery costs.

Crypts

Crypts—both underground and in mausoleums—are generally more expensive than grave plots. Nonetheless, crypts seem to be growing in popularity. In 1977, a representative for a cemetery in Baltimore reported that 65 percent of all sales during the previous year were for mausoleum crypts. The Baltimore cemetery planned to add 8,000 more crypts to the 3,700 already completed. Crypts in the Baltimore mausoleum are priced according to level (there are six). "Heart" or "eye" levels cost $1,445; "heaven" level, about fifteen feet high, cost $950. Entombment cost $150. At the oldest cemetery in Baltimore, mausoleum crypts ranged from $875 to $2,200. Another cemetery charged $1,200 to $1,500 for a heart-level crypt, $85 for entombment, $75 for a bronze marker on the crypt, and $15 for a flower vase that can be attached to the crypt.

Both outdoor, or garden, mausoleum crypts facing lawns or gardens and below-ground crypts can begin as low at $450, according to the NFDA in 1976. But new garden crypts in one Baltimore cemetery were selling at a preconstruction price of $1,097 to $1,297. (Many cemeteries with mausole-

---

*Includes Arizona, Arkansas, Colorado, Idaho, Louisiana, Montana, Nevada, New Mexico, Oklahoma, Texas, Utah, and Wyoming.

ums located on their grounds sell crypts in advance at a discount while a mausoleum is being constructed; when it is completed, prices go up.) When the crypts are finished, they will cost between $1,597 and $1,797.* A letter received from a Milwaukee cemetery in 1974 offered below-ground crypts with "double depth vault, land, and a double bronze marker" at $1,395 for two. (Presumably, there would be additional cemetery costs at the time of interment.)

Many cemeteries also have sites where private mausoleums can be built to individual specifications. The manager of a cemetery in the New York City area reported in 1976 that fewer people buy private mausoleums now than in former years. The cemetery manager cited a recent purchase, in which the site cost $4,300 and the mausoleum—holding three crypts—cost $26,000.

Coffin Enclosures

Most cemeteries require outer enclosures for coffins in conventional earth burial. There is always a chance, however, that one or two cemeteries in an area will not.**

Vaults sold by undertakers (see Chapter 13), are almost always more expensive than coffin enclosures purchased at cemeteries. The price of a concrete grave liner purchased at a cemetery (and at some funeral homes) is usually in the range of $70 to $125, although here, too, prices vary widely. According to Consumers Union's spot check, one New Jersey cemetery charged only from $50 to $100 for its grave liners, while a cemetery in Kansas City, Missouri, charged $190 for what it called its "minimum requirement": an "outer case," described as a two-piece box. The 1973 FTC survey of Washington, D.C., funeral homes noted that about 75 percent of funeral buyers purchased a concrete liner or box at the cemetery, which cost about $85. Approximately 22 percent paid an average of $311 for a vault bought from an undertaker. The FTC noted, however, that a few Washington cemeteries would accept as an interment receptacle a wooden outer case costing about $50. Cemeteries that permit wooden enclosures, however, are in a small minority. Cemetery representatives point out that because wood deteriorates more rapidly than concrete or metal, ground shrinkage could

---

*In 1975, a large advertisement for a projected new mausoleum in the New York City area appeared in *The New York Times.* The builders noted that if prospective buyers reserve space before the start of construction they would save 30 percent on the price of crypts. As the construction program proceeds, the advertisement read, costs will rise. What if a person buys a crypt in advance and then dies before the mausoleum is in use? "Until construction is completed," the advertisement read, "suitable arrangements will. be made for temporary entombment."

**Consumers Union's 1974 spot check found that a large New York City cemetery did not require vaults; nor did a private cemetery in New Jersey or a municipal cemetery in Milwaukee.

occur sooner with wooden enclosures and the shrinkage could cause the graves to cave in.

Opening and Closing the Grave

In most cemeteries nowadays opening and closing a grave is done with a mechanically operated gravedigger, such as a backhoe. After the grave is opened, an automatic lowering device is frequently used to lower the coffin into the grave.* The opening and closing operation takes in all about thirty minutes and rarely costs the consumer less than $100. The actual cost to the cemetery for doing the work, the FTC has noted, is "a tiny fraction of the amount the customer pays." One Baltimore cemetery representative explained in 1977 that opening and closing fees help to cover other expenses that must be met by the cemetery, although he conceded that half the fee was "pure profit." Other cemetery representatives disagreed, however, citing increased labor costs. Some cemeteries say that opening and closing fees help "cover operating expenses." In 1977, one group of cemeteries raised its charge to open a grave in the Hartford, Connecticut, area to $200, citing this as the reason.**

In its 1973 survey the FTC listed $150 as the standard price for opening and closing a grave in Washington, D.C. In Consumers Union's 1974 spot check, two Kansas City cemeteries listed $160 and $165 for opening and closing; a third charged $100. One Milwaukee cemetery charged $235 and another, $140. The charge for opening and closing a grave was $95 at a cemetery in Miami. In Oregon, the cost of opening and closing ranged from a low of $75 to a high of $150. Opening and closing costs seem to be lower in many states of the Central West Region, according to the 1973 survey for the VA; the study indicated that $83 was the charge for urban areas while $41 was the cost for opening and closing a grave in rural and suburban areas.

Some cemeteries' charges for opening and closing vary according to whether a vault or concrete liner is used. The survey for the VA, for example, found that cemeteries in the Maryland and Washington area charged $195 for opening and closing if a vault was used; the vault itself

---

*"In the old days," says a gravedigger to Studs Terkel in *Working*, "it was supposed to be four men. Two on each end with a rope, keep lowerin' little by little. I imagine that was kinda hard, because I imagine some fellas must weigh two hundred pounds, and I can feel that weight. We had a burial about five years ago, a fella that weighed four hundred pounds. He didn't fit on the lowerin' device. We had a big machine tractor that we coulda used, but that woulda looked kinda bad, because lowerin' a casket with a tractor is like lowerin' anything. You have to respect ... We did it by hand. There were about a half dozen men."

**Baltimore undertakers were critical of opening and closing charges. "It takes them no more than 30 minutes to dig that grave with a backhoe," said one. "Unquestionably, not more than 45 minutes."

cost extra. With a concrete liner instead of a vault, and with the cost of the liner included in the cemetery price, the charge was $275; in the Seattle area, the charge was only $180.

Memorials: Markers, Monuments, and Plaques

Almost all cemeteries (and in some cases civil authorities) have strict regulations and restrictions governing the placement and size of monuments and markers.* Many cemeteries sell a standard size to be used for both single and double markers. Many also have rules about the kinds of material that may be used in memorials, usually granite, bronze, and marble. Cement, artificial stone, and iron are rarely prescribed. Mausoleums, too, may require a uniform type of plaque on their crypts. (Not all crypts have plaques. Some crypts have an outer facing of granite or marble, and the inscription is carved on that.) Cemeteries can even regulate to some extent the wording of inscriptions on memorials.

More and more of the new memorial park cemeteries require markers set flush with the ground. And an increasing number of cemeteries are selling their own memorials in competition with independent memorial dealers. In Studs Terkel's *Working*, a "memorial counselor" (cemetery salesperson) expresses the policy of many modern cemeteries when he says, "We have eliminated tombstones and monuments. We use level bronze memorials. You get away from this thing of a marble orchard—and the depression of cold, cold stone.** What you see are shrubs and flowers and trees. The beauty represents something for the entire community."

According to Monument Builders of America, a trade association of independent retailers, flat grave markers outsell monuments by a ratio of 3 to 2; this varies according to area. In urban centers, for example, there are more flat markers in cemeteries, but in rural areas monuments are more common.

The average price for markers, according to Monument Builders, is about $325—for monuments, $725—although prices vary at different cemeteries and in different parts of the country. Although both cemeteries and independent retail distributors sell monuments and markers, independent

---

*The FTC stated in its 1973 planning memorandum that many cemeteries "engage in a variety of unfair and deceptive acts" to promote the sale of their own bronze or granite markers. Noting that there are legitimate reasons for having certain uniform requirements to facilitate upkeep and care of grave sites, the FTC nonetheless reports that some cemeteries "impose stringent size, shape, and installation" regulations on purchasers, making it inconvenient for them to purchase markers elsewhere.

**A Milwaukee cemetery's brochure is typical of the trend: "NO TOMBSTONES. The depressing presence and coldness of tombstones are banned forever in favor of the democratic simplicity and classic beauty of dignified Bronze Memorials. . . . No substance known to man is more suitable for memorial purposes than bronze. Anchored in a heavy concrete foundation these plaques will endure forever. . . ."

dealers account for 85 percent of all sales, the trade association reports. In some cases, independent firms charge less than cemeteries do. In many areas, the cost of bronze and granite markers begins at $150. In addition to the material, the size, craftsmanship, and design of a marker or monument can affect the price, as well as the number of engraved letters in the inscription. The average size for markers is about two feet long and one foot wide; they vary in thickness from six to ten inches. Contemporary monuments are normally 2½ feet high, 3½ feet in width, and about 8 inches thick.

Most flat markers are made of granite or bronze, with granite markers by far the more common. In its 1973 funeral cost survey, the FTC said that one Washington, D.C., cemetery's lowest price for bronze markers was $275, while another offered two different types starting at $136 and $177. In another Washington cemetery, one section was set aside for bronze markers, costing $140, while another was reserved for granite markers, which cost from $124 to $185. Consumers Union's spot check of cemeteries in 1974 found one cemetery in Kansas City that used only granite markers, costing $190.

Other Cemetery Requirements

In addition to requirements concerning vaults and memorials, many cemeteries have other rules and restrictions affecting burial and entombment.

• In almost all cemeteries the opening and closing fee will be higher when interment or entombment takes place late in the afternoon, on Sundays, or on holidays.

• Embalming before entombment in above-ground crypts is a requirement in many mausoleums. Cemetery owners say there could be a problem of odor without embalming.*

• Most cemeteries have specific requirements concerning decorations, such as flowers, plants, urns, vases, as well as for ground changes or plot improvement. A number of cemeteries require that their own vases or urns

---

*Even when bodies in mausoleums have been embalmed, there can occasionally be problems with seepage and odor, according to a 1975 article in *Casket & Sunnyside*. A decomposing body, either because of poor embalming or "atmospheric conditions" (usually warm, humid weather) can exude gases that are trapped inside the crypt. Internal pressure builds up and cracks the marble facing, permitting the "liquid products of decomposition" to escape, stain the crypt, and cause putrescent odor. In some cases, the odor is so pervasive that people living in the neighborhood—some even thousands of feet away—complain to the cemetery. It is then necessary to remove the coffin from the crypt, clean and deodorize it, or even replace it, and embalm the body again. Before the body is returned to the coffin, a one-hundred-pound layer of dry cement covered with a layer of hardening compound is spread on the bottom of the coffin; then the body is placed in the coffin and covered with the same amount of cement and compound. These materials help to absorb and deodorize any fluids that might escape again. The coffin is then resealed within the crypt.

144

be used for crypts and at grave sites, and artificial flowers and wreaths are not permitted; fresh flowers are usually removed after a certain time has elapsed.

• Whether all cemeteries require bodies to be buried in conventional coffins is difficult to ascertain. (Few survivors, apparently, have put the question to the test.) Presumably, those who wish to be wrapped in a shroud and placed a few feet under the earth, as Malcolm Wells has suggested (see page 135), cannot have their wishes carried out in most American cemeteries.

• A cemetery in Louisville, Kentucky—and there may be others, elsewhere —requires that *all* bodies brought to it be embalmed, even when they are to be immediately cremated or immediately buried.

When the cemetery president was questioned in 1976 about the necessity for embalming prior to cremation, he answered that the cemetery was "sensitive about cremation because it's so final." Some survivors, he explained, might have second thoughts. The cemetery's embalming regulation gives survivors more time to decide whether cremation is what they really want. As for the extra embalming fee that survivors must pay, "I cannot believe," he said," that $75 is actually going to be that much to people at the time of passing of a loved one." Noting that forty-eight local undertakers bring bodies to the cemetery, the president added, "We have received nothing but compliments from funeral directors concerning this regulation."

Preneed Cemetery Sales

According to both the National Association of Cemeteries and the American Cemetery Association, there is a growing emphasis by cemeteries today on the preneed sale of cemetery plots and mausoleum crypts. Member cemeteries in both organizations are building up their sales forces, and the NAC says that preneed sales have increased tenfold. Both trade associations stress the importance of ethics and honest methods in the sale of cemetery plots, but questionable sales practices are not uncommon in all parts of the country. (For a discussion of preneed plans, see Chapter 19.)

Consumers should approach with caution any purchase of a grave plot or mausoleum crypt on a preneed basis, particularly if solicitations are made by mail, phone, or door-to-door salespeople using various promotional techniques, such as "gifts," "free goods," "special discounts," or artist's sketches of prospective cemeteries or mausoleums. In many cases, the cemeteries being promoted do not exist and in fact may never materialize. And, often, in addition to grave plots or crypts, salespeople are also selling vaults, markers, and even coffins on a preneed basis. Many sales promotion schemes are designed to get people to sign contracts that will ultimately bring in hundreds of dollars to the promoters. Some travel from community to community leaving behind dissatisfied and deceived customers who did not read their contracts carefully enough or were not sufficiently wary.

Hugh Bernard in *The Law of Death* warns that prospective buyers "confronted with colorful brochures and intensive sales efforts" should "look hard at the proposed sale in direct proportion to the sales effort being expended, especially if emphasis is placed on a 'non-profit' approach":

> Purely non-profit activities do not have funds to spend on high-pressure salesmanship and intensive advertising. The more eager the salesman is to make a sale, the more he stands to receive from the first payment the buyer makes, and the less therefore is available to pay for the actual goods, lands, or services in question. With regard to cemeteries, one is particularly warned against signing contracts for the purchase of lots in a projected cemetery where work has not begun or advanced to the point of reasonable assurance that the memorial park establishment will materialize as planned.

In many cases, only a part of the funds collected go to developing or improving cemetery land. A large proportion often goes to high sales commissions and profits.

In 1972, the *Consumer Protection Newsletter*, distributed by the attorney general of North Carolina, warned about high-pressure cemetery sales campaigns:

> There have been reported instances of outright purchase of cemeteries for such a purpose, or contracts made with cemetery owners who leave all sales activities in the hands of promoters. Some promotions have included the attraction of a "free" lot to one member of the family. The sales effort is then directed toward lots for other members of the family, and the vaults and markers.

The newsletter alerted consumers to a cemetery practice described as "reloading." Many new cemeteries, it said, undertake a campaign to sell grave lots, many of which are purchased with payments scheduled over a period of years. Some time after the lot program is ended, a new sales campaign gets under way to create additional profits for cemetery owners and salespeople. Representatives get in touch with those who bought lots in the first sales campaign, according to the newsletter, and offer them a package that includes "poured-in-place concrete vaults and grave markers. The charge is usually in excess of $1,000, and new time payment contracts often are obtained and sold to financing institutions."

The newsletter pointed out that in states where preneed laws do not protect purchasers of vaults and markers (some states have such legislation only for cemetery lots) the merchandise may never materialize if delivery is postponed until it is required. (See Appendix 3 for information on preneed laws.) Many contracts guarantee markers and vaults only at time of death, and by then the company "may be out of business or financially unable to provide the merchandise." Sometimes, the ownership of the cemetery changes, "and the new owners will not honor the contracts of the former owners. When this happens, payment could be made twice: once by the deceased person who bought the products during his or her lifetime, and again by the decedent's estate."

The questionable practices of two Virginia cemetery firms, Richmond Memorial Parks, Inc., and Margel Sales Corporation, led to their being fined the maximum under the law, $10,000 each, in U.S. District Court, on ten counts of mail fraud. According to a 1975 report published in *Consumer Reports*, the firms had sent out hundreds of thousands of postcards to both the general public and to veterans, advertising a "free" burial program. "Those who responded to the bait were visited by sales agents who sought, on the basis of false and deceptive literature and promises, to switch them to a full burial contract costing hundreds of dollars." Members of the general public were led to believe they had been "selected" for such awards. Veterans were given the impression that they were involved in a so-called Veterans Program, supposedly connected with the Veterans Administration.

Testimony was heard by the Senate Committee on Veterans Affairs in 1972 about a number of cemeteries throughout the United States that were engaged in deceptive practices affecting veterans. Typical schemes involved offering "free" graves to veterans (and, in some cases, their wives and other family members) on condition that they bought an expensive package of burial goods and services. Sometimes this resulted in veterans' paying more money overall.* Deceptive free-grave schemes for veterans became less common with the end of the Vietnam War and the 1973 National Cemeteries Act. That act provided increased burial benefits for veterans (see pages 57–58) and established the National Cemetery System within the Veterans Administration.

Apart from specific abuses and deceptions in cemetery sales, there are a number of misconceptions on the part of consumers about buying cemetery plots on a preneed basis. Many buyers look upon the purchase of a plot as something of a modest real estate investment. In case they move away or otherwise cannot use it, they reason, it can be sold, and probably for more than it originally cost. This is seldom the case. Because the owner of a plot is not, in a landholding sense, the real owner,** many cemeteries

---

*One outcome of the Senate hearings, and the adverse publicity that resulted, was the drawing up of a Consumer Code for Veterans Programs by the National Association of Cemeteries. The Code warned members of the cemetery trade association that strong disciplinary measures would be taken against violators.

**According to Hugh Bernard in *The Law of Death*, " the purchaser of a lot interest does not acquire a freehold right [i.e., absolute ownership] in the land itself, but only an easement entitling him to inter such number of bodies as the deed or other instrument pro-

will not buy back plots from purchasers. In certain states, the law prohibits cemeteries from buying back plots. Plot owners, therefore, must try to sell their grave sites on their own or through a cemetery broker. (And when the transfer is made, there is sometimes a cemetery charge—about $20—for recording the change in ownership of the plot.) In some states, such as New York, selling plots at a profit is against the law. Some cemetery sales agreements stipulate that the buyer may not sell the plot to anyone. In such cases, only the buyer can use the plot; a buyer who moves away can use it only by burdening survivors with the cost of transporting the body back from the place of death.

Some people buy a grave plot or crypt on a preneed basis as insurance against inflation, believing that they will spare their survivors a much larger expense years later. Many cemetery salespeople, the FTC has noted, made sales by emphasizing that buyers would avoid future inflationary costs. Often, buyers fail to note escalator clauses in their contracts, and sometimes when payments are made over a period of years, cemeteries raise the cost of plots to compensate for inflation.

Although some states have statutes regulating the sale of grave plots to ensure that money paid in advance goes into trust funds, strict supervision and enforcement of the laws is often lacking. In states where there is no legal protection, purchasers of preneed plots or crypts forego the use of their money, often for ten, twenty, or thirty years, and lose the advantage of spending or investing it elsewhere.

For some people, however, the sense of security in knowing that their place of burial is assured is worth the cost. While preneed plans involving prepayment of burial expenses are not the best arrangement for most people, in certain cases they may offer advantages—for instance, if an older person expects to remain in the area. Whenever cemetery lots or mausoleum crypts are bought in advance of need, family members should be involved in the decision and should be informed about all the particulars of the sale.

Guidelines for Choosing a Cemetery Plot or Crypt

Plot or Crypt. When buying a grave plot or crypt in advance of need, the first step is to make inquiries about the established cemeteries in the community, preferably those that are publicly owned, church-affiliated, or otherwise nonprofit. Some proprietary cemeteries, however, may have better bargains to offer than nonprofit ones. And such factors as the location of the cemetery in the community as well as the location of the plot within the cemetery may influence a buyer's choice. In some communities, there are

---

vides, subject to regulations of the cemetery or of public authorities as applicable. Since the right acquired is not a freehold . . . the usual incidents of ordinary landholdings do not apply."

combined mortuary-cemetery facilities, which might mean lower overall funeral and burial costs.* Before making a decision, a buyer should go to the cemetery to inspect the grounds, facilities, and upkeep, and the plot or mausoleum under consideration.

If a plot or crypt is to be purchased on a time-payment plan, as most are, a buyer should investigate the interest charged by the cemetery. Some cemeteries do not charge any interest at all. Among those that do, there can be wide diversity in interest charges, ranging from between 5 and 6 percent to as much as 18 percent on an annual basis. If the preferred cemetery charges a high interest rate, a buyer might be able to save money by taking out a lower-interest loan for the amount from a credit union or from a bank.

When buying a cemetery plot or crypt at time of need, all the precautions that should be observed when buying a plot or crypt in advance are even more crucial. Fortunately, it is usually easier to get information about cemeteries—costs and requirements—than it is to get facts and figures about funeral costs. Many undertakers are familiar with cemetery costs in their communities and should be able to give information about specific cemetery requirements and prices. Memorial societies, too, often have price information about cemeteries in their area. It is frequently possible for survivors themselves to obtain most of the information they need by telephone. (Most cemeteries are listed in the Yellow Pages of the telephone book.) Cemetery personnel are generally helpful and, if asked, will usually give prices over the phone.** Because of this, comparison shopping can be done in a relatively short time.

Perpetual Care. Some cemeteries include in the price of a plot or crypt a charge for its perpetual care. (Typically, 10 percent or more of the plot or crypt price is set aside for this purpose; municipal and other nonprofit cemeteries may allocate a larger percentage.) Others charge a separate fee. This money goes into what is called an endowment care fund, which is placed in trust; its earnings are used to maintain the grounds or mausoleums in perpetuity. Some states require such funding by law. A prospective buyer should ascertain whether the funds in the cemetery under consideration are sufficient to maintain the plot or crypt. In many cases, a state agency is responsible for the proper administration of the trust fund, and a buyer can check with the appropriate agency (the cemetery may be able to inform buyers which agency governs this fund) about the provisions for endowment care of cemetery property being considered.

If perpetual care is optional, a buyer should inspect grave sites with

---

*According to the National Association of Cemeteries, a reduction of 10 to 40 percent is possible with the elimination of the undertaker's services and transportation costs.

**In 1974, members of the New York Public Interest Research Group telephoned twenty cemeteries in the New York City area for price information. All the cemetery representatives called were willing to give prices over the phone.

and without the special care to determine whether it is worth a premium.

Coffin Enclosure. A buyer should ask whether interment of a coffin without a vault or grave liner, or with a simple wooden enclosure, is permissible. If an outer enclosure for the coffin is required and if the cemetery sells its own grave liners, a saving is possible since a grave liner almost always costs less than a vault. The type of outer enclosure selected may determine opening and closing costs.

Marker, Monument, or Plaque. A buyer should be sure to ask about the cemetery's requirements for markers and monuments, or for plaques or inscriptions if a crypt is to be purchased, since rules for this may determine the choice of a cemetery. Some cemeteries do not permit the installation of any memorial bought from an independent dealer but insist on selling their own, and they may have strict rules about the size, material, and style of markers they allow on graves. (Remember, the FTC warns that a cemetery with severely restrictive rules may be more expensive than others.)

In addition to the cost of the memorial itself, a number of smaller fees may be added on the purchase price. Installation (setting the memorial into a concrete foundation) can cost from $30 to $300. If a memorial is bought from an independent dealer, the cemetery may charge a higher installation fee than for its own markers and monuments. Although an independent dealer may charge less than a cemetery for a memorial, there may be an additional fee for delivery. In some cemeteries, there is an extra charge for maintenance of the memorial (in addition to the perpetual care of the plot). A buyer should insist on receiving the manufacturer's guarantee or warranty for a memorial so that a claim for repair or replacement can be filed if necessary.

Mausoleums. Many of the extra costs, requirements, and rules that apply to grave plots also apply to crypts in mausoleums. There is a charge for opening and sealing the crypt, as well as for perpetual care. Mausoleums also have requirements for the types of coffins that can be placed in crypts. Some mausoleums require a metal sealer coffin with a manufacturer's warranty attesting to the construction. If a coffin is not metal, it may have to be placed within a metal vault (another expensive purchase) in the crypt. Inscriptions on the face of the crypt are also subject to the approval of the cemetery management. Often, there are restrictions on the placing of flowers, wreaths, plants, and vases at the crypt.

Purchasing the Plot or Crypt

Once the decision to purchase a plot or crypt is made, buyers should carefully study the contract terms, including costs, with special attention to the section on perpetual care. If there are any doubts or problems about the terms of the contract, the appropriate state agency, or an attorney, should be consulted. After the purchase of the plot or crypt, the deed should be kept with other important papers, and copies of the deed should be available for family members and close friends.

The Option of Graveside Services

There is no question that when ground burial is chosen, the range of options, as far as expenses are concerned, is limited because of cemetery charges and requirements. There is not much one can do, for instance, about the cost of opening and closing the grave or charges for perpetual care. Unlike the option of choosing among different types of funeral services, which can mean a difference of hundreds, or even thousands, of dollars, the selection of a cemetery generally does not offer too much leeway in terms of cost.

One possible way to cut down on total funeral costs, however, is to hold a graveside ceremony for the deceased shortly after death instead of using a funeral home for services. Survivors may have to pay for a coffin* and the undertaker's services in picking up and transporting the body, but fees for embalming and the use of the funeral home for several days can be eliminated.

Indeed, for survivors who want a ceremony with the body present, but without viewing or religious services, a simple ceremony at the grave may be a logical and less costly procedure.

---

*A further economy at the graveside service could be the use of a mail-order coffin purchased in advance (see pages 85–86).

Part III
Some Alternatives to Conventional Funeral and Burial Arrangements

15
Cremation

The modern process of cremation goes back to the late nineteenth century when the first crematories were established in the United States. Today there are about 450 crematories in this country, approximately 80 percent of them owned by cemetery managements.* Some are owned by funeral establishments, and a few are government-owned. (In 1974 the Veterans Administration, noting a growing trend toward cremation among the general population, announced the construction of a "chapel/columbarium" at Arlington National Cemetery designed to handle 100,000 cremated remains.)

The Process of Cremation

The cremation chamber or retort is a special variety of furnace in which the body of an average-size adult can be reduced to from five to seven pounds of ashes and bone fragments. With the application of intense heat,** incineration usually takes about an hour and half. Natural or bottled gas is generally used; oil and electricity are less common. Because of the intense heat in the furnace and the special draft control, smoke and gases can be recirculated through the cremation chamber and usually do not escape into the open air in significant amounts. In some of the newer crematories, there is equipment that leaves less residue; this process is called pulverization.

Most crematory regulations require that the body be cremated in the

---

*There are no crematories in four states (Mississippi, South Carolina, South Dakota, and Wyoming).

**In his book *Cremation*, Paul Irion, a professor of pastoral theology at Lancaster Theological Seminary whose books about funerals are distributed by the National Funeral Directors Association, says: "Just as decomposition in the earth is oxidation, so cremation is a process of very rapid oxidation of the body tissues. The water content of the body is evaporated by the intense heat, the carbon-containing portions of the body are incinerated and the inorganic ash of the bone structure is all that remains."

container in which it is brought to the crematory. Wooden coffins, containers made of cardboard, fiberboard, or pressed wood, and some lightweight metal coffins are completely incinerated with the body. But when heavier metal coffins are used, the cremated remains (called cremains by many cemetery personnel) are taken from the burned-out coffin after the cremation chamber has cooled, and any remaining metal parts are then removed. Some metal coffins with a high melting point must be broken up with sledge hammers. The use of fiber glass or plastic coffins is discouraged by crematories since they can cause excessive smoke emission from the chamber.

Not all survivors choose to accompany the deceased's body to the crematory. (Many survivors prefer to hold a memorial service elsewhere at a later date if there has been no funeral.) When the body is unaccompanied, funeral home personnel will complete arrangements there. But for those survivors who accompany the body, most crematories have facilities that can be used for a final committal service for the deceased. Many crematories have chapels where services can take place. Services are sometimes desired by survivors even when services have been previously held at a funeral home. The committal room, usually between the chapel and the cremation chamber, is where surivors can, if they wish, witness the container being placed in the retort. In the wall between the committal room and the cremation chamber there is an opening large enough for the container to slide through. In some crematories, a specially designed structure in the committal room—called a catafalque—is mechanically equipped to facilitate the moving of the container from the committal chamber through the opening into the retort. In some of the older crematories, the cremation chamber is directly beneath the committal room, and the catafalque automatically lowers the container through an opening in the floor. For survivors who do not wish to view the container being placed in the retort but who wish to confirm that the cremation takes place a curtain is sometimes drawn between the survivors and the catafalque.

"Visitors," Paul Irion writes in *Cremation*, "are not permitted in the crematorium when cremations are in progress. Only witnesses designated by the family are allowed to be present when the process is begun." Correct identification of the remains is of primary importance. "The crematorium is also responsible for careful identification of the ashes so that they may be returned to the proper family. Most crematoriums do this by placing a registered numbered metallic disc in the cremation chamber with the casket to provide for subsequent identification of the ashes." The cremated remains are then placed in an urn or a special container and labeled.

The Growth in the Number of Cremations

In 1976 the total number of cremations in the United States was 140,052—slightly more than 7 percent of the 1,912,000 deaths that year. The 20,694 cremations in Canada in 1975 represented about 12 percent of the 170,500 deaths there that year. The number of cremations varies widely according to geographic location. Areas on the West Coast of both the United States and Canada have the highest number of cremations.* Of the total cremations in the United States in 1976, more than 40 percent (56,178) were in the five Pacific states (Alaska, California, Hawaii, Oregon, and Washington), whereas only 0.6 percent (862) were cremated in the East South Central states (Alabama, Kentucky, Mississippi, Tennessee) and 2 percent (3,168) in the West South Central states (Arkansas, Louisiana, Oklahoma, Texas). The Middle Atlantic and South Atlantic states accounted for nearly one-third (42,968) of all cremations in 1976.

British Columbia, on the West Coast of Canada, has the highest cremation rate in North America; almost 45 percent of those who died there were cremated. In Ontario, which has nearly three times the population of British Columbia, the cremation rate was just over 11 percent.

Cremation is far more common in a number of other countries, usually because of the scarcity of cemetery space, but also because of societal preference for this form of disposition. In Japan nearly 84 percent of those who died in 1973 were cremated (cremation is required by law in Tokyo).** The Cremation Society of Great Britain reported in 1975 that 59 percent of the dead in England, Wales, and Scotland were cremated. Cremation rates are also high in Australia (40 percent of all deaths in 1973, 66 percent in metropolitan areas) and New Zealand (42 percent in 1972). Cremation is widely practiced in the Scandinavian countries. In 1973 the cremation rate was 45 percent in Denmark, almost 43 percent in Sweden, and 26 percent in Norway.

Statistics show that the practice is increasing in the United States and Canada. According to a representative of the Cremation Association of North America (its membership consists of cemetery and crematory owners), the number of cremations in the United States and Canada rose 74 per-

---

*In an essay written in 1963, Robert Fulton, a consultant to the National Funeral Directors Association, sought to explain this high proportion: "The funeral itself is a gift—both given and received by the deceased and by his survivors. Once this is understood it is possible to account for the fact that over half of the cremations in this country every year take place on the Pacific coast. I propose to you that cremation in America could well be the result of anger, rather than of philosophy or economy. When we reflect upon the fact that some of the aged in this country are no longer welcome in the homes of their children and are no longer secure in the belief that with age comes respect, we can appreciate why they would uproot themselves from their families, friends, and their established place in the local community and flee in unprecedented numbers to retirement cities and other locales which on the Pacific coast are literally as well as figuratively on the edge of American society. By denying their children or other relatives the opportunity to give them the gift of the funeral at their deaths they give vent to their hostility and resentment toward a society that had rejected them."

**In 1968 there were 4,467 crematories in Japan, compared with 452 in the United States and 39 in Canada in 1976. Great Britain had 215 crematories in 1974.

cent during the ten-year period ending in 1974. In just one year, between 1975 and 1976, there was an 11.8 percent increase in cremations in the United States. The percentage of cremations is rising even faster in Canada; in 1975, for example, the Canadian cremation rate was up 16 percent over the previous year.

Even in the South, where cremation is less common than in other parts of the United States, more people are choosing it over burial. There was a 32 percent increase between 1975 and 1976 in the South Atlantic states plus Washington, D.C. The number of cremations in North Carolina doubled between 1963 and 1973. Out of more than 47,000 deaths in North Carolina in 1973, there were about 500 cremations, but that small number represented a significant increase. Moreover, before 1970 there were no private crematories in North Carolina (apart from university medical school facilities); by 1974 there were five.

There are four reasons for the increase in cremations: (1) cremation usually costs less than ground burial; (2) there is a growing shortage of cemetery space; (3) modern cremation methods are clean, quick, and efficient; (4) there is more religious tolerance—even encouragement—of cremation than in the past.

But Cremation Can Be Expensive

When cremation is chosen as an alternative to ground burial, some people still wish to include a conventional funeral service in their plans—whether for themselves or for the sake of their family, relatives, or friends. With such arrangements, the facilities of a regular funeral home are usually required and the costs will be higher than with direct cremation. With direct cremation, the undertaker removes the body from the place of death and, after obtaining the necessary permits, takes the body directly to the crematory. The whole procedure usually can be carried out within twenty-four hours. Some establishments specialize in this type of service (see Chapter 16).

Even when there is no funeral service and an undertaker is simply asked to pick up a body and arrange for cremation, charges can be high. In 1974 a man joined the Memorial Society of Greater Philadelphia, shortly after his son's death. He reported to the society on the bill submitted to him. The undertaker had picked up the body of the man's son in New York City, transported it to a crematory in Orange, New Jersey (about fifteen miles away), and later delivered the ashes in a small cardboard box to the son's widow, who lived one block from the funeral home. The undertaker submitted a bill for $939.50, including a charge of $595 for professional services, overhead, and merchandise.

Another case involving costly charges for cremation was reported in 1972 in the *Detroit Free Press*. Under the headline "$95 Cremation Costs Widow $897 Extra," appeared an account of an invalid woman's experience with an unscrupulous undertaker. Before Ethel Moore's husband died at the age of seventy-five, he had expressed the wish that his wife spend as little money as possible for death expenses. During the twenty years before his death, his medical bills had often come to half their meager monthly income, and he wanted his wife to have the insurance money that would be left to her.

Mrs. Moore, a sixty-year-old who was confined to a wheelchair most of the time, was notified of her husband's death by the hospital at 5:00 A.M. The widow was taken there immediately by a friend. "He was still warm," she told the *Free Press* reporter. "And they told me to get him out of there. They said I had to get him out right away." (Later, the hospital's executive director explained to the reporter that this was standard procedure. "If someone dies, the body is to be removed immediately. We are not a funeral home.")

The hospital phoned a funeral home and made arrangements for Mrs. Moore to meet a representative. He was waiting when she arrived at 6:00 A.M. and immediately took her to the coffin showroom. "I didn't think I had to have a casket," Mrs. Moore said later to the reporter. "I told them just to cremate him. But he said: 'Pick a casket.' Then I thought maybe you had to have a casket."

The owner of the funeral home told the reporter that no crematory in the Detroit area would accept a body without a "minimum" coffin. Moreover, the $750 model Mrs. Moore had chosen was not "much of a casket anyway." The coffin price also included a fee for embalming and displaying the body. A new suit, transportation, cremation, and other fees brought the total price to nearly $1,000. Most of the insurance settlement went to the funeral home, the rest to a neighborhood drugstore to pay the bills for medicine that Mr. Moore had needed. There was not enough money to pay for burying the ashes in a cemetery, so Mrs. Moore decided to keep them at home.

Five weeks later, in response to a call from Mrs. Moore, a funeral home representative delivered a cardboard box containing ashes and bone fragments in a plastic bag. Mrs. Moore, it seems, had not said she wanted an urn for the ashes. A medical authority who examined the contents of the plastic bag acknowledged that there was some validity in Mrs. Moore's shock at being handed a "bag of bones." Mrs. Moore then turned the ashes over to the Wayne State University School of Medicine, which finished the cremation, placed the ashes in an urn, and buried them at no expense to her.

Later she learned that the anatomy department would have handled her husband's cremation and burial free in return for the right to use his body first for teaching purposes (see Chapter 17). She said: "Why don't they tell you? They didn't give me a chance. I didn't know how they do those things. That's what he wanted to begin with, and now I don't think I did his wishes."

The Federal Trade Commission (FTC) commented in its 1973 planning memorandum that one reason cremation costs are so high in regular funeral homes is that morticians charge so much for their services and facilities.* Many people, according the FTC, want a simple cremation, which involves transportation to the crematory and the least expensive container. Even if the undertaker files a death certificate for survivors, the undertaker's role involves "little time or effort."**

It is not only morticians' individual charges that can make cremation expensive. Some states have statutes that automatically raise the cost. For instance, in some states (Florida is among them), by law, cremation cannot take place until forty-eight hours after death; yet, by law, if a body is not buried or cremated within twenty-four hours, it must be embalmed or refrigerated. Thus, when cremation is desired in those states, the cost of one of these two procedures must be incurred.

Some Exceptions

Not all undertakers overcharge for cremation. In 1974 a Miami undertaker was offering a $137.50 "cash and carry ashes" cremation service. "I believe that anyone who wants cremation is entitled to have it at the lowest cost possible," said W. L. Philbrick, a seventy-four-year-old mortician, in response to the criticism of his competitors. The reason he could offer cremation at such a low price, he said, was because of new refrigeration on his premises that could preserve bodies for the forty-eight-hour interval required by Florida law before cremation.

Some conventional funeral establishments offer a special modified plan that includes both a conventional funeral service and cremation. For example, one large funeral home chain in New York City has advertised cremation for $235, plus the crematory fee of $100—but with no viewing or use of the facilities. Firms that specialize in direct cremation and burial (see Chapter 16) are more likely to have reasonably priced cremation services, however, than conventional funeral establishments. One New York City funeral home specializing in low-cost cremation, for instance, offers two kinds of cremation services. The first type is direct cremation, which is priced at

---

*In 1972 a group of retired people in Miami worked out an arrangement with a funeral home for a special rate for cremation and the shipment of the remains to survivors. However, the cost worked out for each retired person's cremation was $1,000. Even though the retirees were saving approximately half of the $2,000 paid for an average adult funeral, their cremation arrangement was an expensive service in light of the fact that the average crematory charge is $100 and cremated remains can be mailed at ordinary parcel post rates (see page 171).

**"For the minimal services desired from the funeral director," the FTC noted, "charges of $20-$60 would be more than generous compensation. But in many cases where the consumer wants only minimal services from the funeral director, he is forced to pay a fee of $200-$400 or higher for the funeral director's services and facilities just as if a full-dress funeral service had been requested."

$235; the second type, "cremation with viewing and attendance," is priced at $415.*

Attitudes of Undertakers toward Cremation

Most undertakers, according to Paul Irion, writing in *Cremation*, "tend to be less than enthusiastic about cremation." But, in general, they cooperate with clients who want this form of disposition and will make the necessary arrangements. The authors of *The History of American Funeral Directing*, an industry-sponsored publication, consider undertakers to be less inimical to cremation. The inclination of morticians, they say, "is neither to encourage nor actively to resist the practice," but to carry out the wishes of survivors. The National Funeral Directors Association (NFDA) distributes books and literature on cremation, and its point of view appears to be neutral.**

In *The Funeral Director and His Role As a Counselor*, however, the NFDA's Howard Raether cautions undertakers against accepting "at face value" survivors' choices of "alternate forms of the funeral." Undertakers not only have a right but a responsibility to counsel survivors about whether such choices best meet their needs. "It is not inconceivable," says Raether, "that a member of the family not involved in the arrangements and unable to view the deceased might try to hold the funeral director liable for mental pain, anguish and suffering if that funeral director proceeded with the arrangers' wishes for an immediate disposition without counseling them as to what some of the after-effects might be. In another instance, if a funeral director does not counsel relative to the effects of certain procedures, he might be held liable for dereliction in his professional responsibility."

National Selected Morticians states in its literature that member undertakers will assist survivors in making arrangements for cremation. NSM

---

*The mortuary's brochure describes the latter plan: "This plan provides for the removal of the deceased from the place of death, securing and filing of all the necessary affidavits and permits with the proper authorities, preservation and preparation of the remains, wood casket covered with embossed doeskin, reposing of the remains at our chapel for one day, conveyance to the crematory, crematory arrangements, crematory charges and delivery of the Cremains, in the crematory container, to the family."

**"Considerations Concerning Cremation," a pamphlet published by the NFDA in 1974, even recognizes that cremation may be desirable for some survivors: "There may be a psychological advantage to cremation for some persons. The idea of a quick, clean incineration of the body is preferable to the slower process of reduction in a grave. They may prefer the immediate way in which the body is broken down to its basic components and then mixed with the elements of the earth, symbolizing a oneness with nature and the universe.

"For these families, cremation can lend support to the process of mourning by which one recovers from the traumatic separation of loss. An important aspect in this process is realizing, both emotionally and intellectually, that any further relationship with the deceased has ended and life must go on. Cremation may effectively symbolize this finality for some people."

members are "committed to clarifying and enacting your choices when death occurs," according to the NSM booklet, "A Helpful Guide to Funeral Planning." This extends to "simple disposition." "If, after careful consideration, you choose simply to remove the body of a loved one from its place of death and transfer it to its site for final disposition without ceremony, your funeral director can still be of assistance to you."

Critics of the funeral industry, however, say that individual undertakers do resist the idea of cremation. Morticians, say these critics, view proponents of cremation as would-be reformers of funeral practices and advocates of inexpensive and simple means of disposition. Many undertakers, according to the FTC, tend to discourage cremation.* The FTC notes in its proposed rule: "Funeral directors view the growing interest in cremation as a significant threat to the institution of the full-dress American funeral and to their livelihood. They recognize that they must provide cremation services if the public wants them, but try to discourage purchase of cremations or to increase the profit on them."

A Tennessee undertaker, who appeared in 1976 before a subcommittee of the House Committee on Small Business, which was looking into the proposed FTC rule, stated that customers of his funeral home rarely choose cremation:

> I've had three cremation cases in the last 25 years, this is not a problem in our area, in California it is. I'm not saying it's a problem, it's increasing more as a practice in California and Florida. But, out of the three cases, one was not embalmed, it was just a straight cremation. The wife didn't want anything done with him. She wanted his eyes given to the Vanderbilt Hospital. We are 65 miles west of Nashville. This man took his own life. When he was found he was carried to the local hospital. The wife got in touch with me and said, "I want him cremated, and I want his eyes given to the Vanderbilt Hospital."
>
> I said, "All I want for you to do is just sign this paper, and we'll be on our way."
>
> She said, "I want him cremated." I said, "Do you want embalming?" She said, "I don't want a thing, I don't want anything else." Here we go to Knoxville, Tenn., the nearest crematory, in 12 hours his eyes were taken to Vanderbilt Hospital; he was burned, and his ashes put in the garbage can. That's what she wanted, and that's what she got.
>
> The undertaker added: "She is living in mortal misery over what she has done to him, psychologically."

The executive director of the National Funeral Directors and Morticians Association of Chicago, representing 4,000 black undertakers, testified before the House subcommittee the same day as the Tennessee undertaker

---

*The 1973 FTC survey of Washington, D.C., funeral homes found that eleven undertakers either would not arrange for cremations or had never arranged for any.

and stressed the fact that black undertakers arrange for very few cremations:

> Blacks believe in respectful Christian service and burial for their loved ones.
> They don't care for cremation, no matter how cheap it might be financially.
> They want a church or chapel funeral. If you don't believe me, just check it
> out. For instance, the 100,000 cremations we had in this country last year,
> less than 500 of these were blacks.
>
> ... I checked with our funeral homes, and I can put my fingers on the
> three or four, or maybe eight black funeral homes that buried over 1,500
> persons, I checked with them to see how many cremations they had. And
> I would also like to say at this point until Dr. Martin Luther King came,
> you couldn't cremate a black in the South; his body had to be shipped
> North, cremated there, and his ashes had to be shipped back south because
> the crematoriums down there wouldn't cremate blacks. Therefore, we didn't
> cremate, and we are still not cremating.

If not all undertakers strongly disapprove of cremation, many would concede the possibility of survivors' spending less for funeral goods and services when cremation is chosen. This can be true even when a conventional
funeral precedes cremation. A vault, for example, is not needed. Usually
only immediate survivors go to the crematory; thus fewer limousines are
required. A flower car, which often accompanies mourners to the cemetery,
usually does not go to the crematory. Some survivors who choose cremation
may want a shorter viewing period. And knowledgeable customers may
know that, in the majority of cases, it is not necessary to buy a coffin: A
simple wood or cardboard container, costing from $10 to $50, is the only
requirement for most cremations. (See page 169 for the legal requirements
for a coffin used in cremation.)

One way an undertaker may seek to compensate for reduced profit
when cremation is chosen is to sell survivors an expensive coffin. And most
funeral buyers, because they are unaware that inexpensive containers are
usually available for cremation, do purchase coffins. The FTC, in its proposed rule, says that "the forced purchase of caskets for cremations appears
to be a significant problem, judging by consumer complaint letters, newspaper articles, and information from funeral directors and other sources."
In fact, the FTC says, it "received more complaints about caskets being required for cremations, by funeral homes and by crematories, than any other
kind of funeral complaint."

How can undertakers justify the sale of a coffin, particularly an expensive coffin, when it will be burned in the cremation chamber? Some falsely
claim that the purchase of a coffin is a legal requirement.* Some tell survivors that crematories have regulations requiring coffins. Some crematories
may have such a requirement, but many do not. In some cases, it is the

---

*That claim could be valid in only two states (see page 168).

funeral home itself that requires a coffin to be purchased for cremation.*

The FTC reports in its proposed rule that undertakers tend to encourage survivors to buy elaborate coffins.** Requiring consumers to purchase coffins for cremation, the FTC said, "is very much in the nature of a tie-in sale." The coffin is a separate item and one that is not necessary for disposition by cremation. Tying cremation and coffins together should be declared an unfair practice, according to the FTC.

Most survivors who arrange with a funeral home for cremation have little idea about requirements for cremation. They must rely on the undertaker for information. (A 1976 survey by the Maryland Citizens Consumer Council found consumers "astonishingly uninformed" about cremation requirements; nearly half those questioned either believed a coffin was necessary or did not know.) In this situation, the FTC points out, the undertaker becomes a "monopolist" who has "superior bargaining power" over bereaved survivors. Some may argue that undertakers have the right to determine the type of products they offer and that some consider it undignified to put a body in a non-coffin container; this, the FTC says, is invalid. Buyers are at the funeral home through necessity, not choice, and information about available options should be provided.

Religious Views on Cremation

A number of religions forbid cremation, among them Islam (the prohibition is for all Moslems, including Black Muslims in the United States), Orthodox and Conservative Judaism, and some Protestant denominations, such as the Missouri Synod of the Lutheran Church and some evangelical and fundamentalist sects. Other conservative Protestant denominations also tend to look with disfavor on the practice. Mormons may choose cremation, but it is discouraged by the church. The Eastern Orthodox churches do not favor cremation: The Greek Orthodox Church strongly opposes it, while the Russian Orthodox and Armenian Orthodox churches neither forbid nor approve.

---

*Four of the fifty-five Washington, D.C., funeral homes surveyed in 1973 by the FTC erroneously reported that a coffin for cremation was required by crematories, although none of the four major crematories in Washington, D.C., required coffins. Another funeral home said that coffins were mandatory, without stating why. Pointing out that this information was provided in sworn statements on a matter that could easily be verified by the commission, the FTC concluded that it was unlikely that the five firms had deliberately misstated the facts. "Rather," the FTC noted, "this appears to be an example of how the public may receive costly misinformation from funeral directors where there is no intent to deceive."

**In 1975 the license of a New Milford, New Jersey, undertaker was revoked by the State Board of Mortuary Science because he had substituted a $35 plain pine box for a $1,475 solid cherrywood coffin purchased for cremation. The body was cremated in the pine box. The undertaker then reclaimed the expensive coffin for resale. He was fined $1,000 and ordered to make full restitution to the customer.

The religions that permit cremation include most Protestant denominations, Roman Catholicism (under certain conditions), Reform Judaism, as well as Buddhism, Hare Krishna, and Hinduism.

When the movement to legalize cremation began in Europe and the United States in the second half of the nineteenth century, there was strong opposition from Western religions; they believed it was alien to the Judeo-Christian tradition.* Some Protestants argued that it was a "pagan" custom, antithetical to the traditional practice of burial. The Bible was cited as an authoritative source; it did not tell believers to cremate the dead. Another obstacle to the acceptance of cremation for both Protestants and Catholics was the doctrine of the resurrection of the body.** Those who accepted this belief in its literal sense maintained that it would not be possible for a body that had been cremated to be resurrected. According to the entry on cremation in the eleventh edition of *Encyclopædia Britannica*, this objection was answered by Lord Shaftesbury, the eminent Victorian reformer. "What would in such a case become of the blessed martyrs?" he asked, many of whom had been burned at the stake for their convictions.

Gradually, opposition to cremation among Western religions has diminished. As cremation has become more common and accepted as a dignified means of disposition, and as many churches have become more liberal in other ways, cremation has gained acceptance. The Church of England, for example, which once opposed cremation, has dropped its restrictions against the practice. Its support of cremation influenced, in turn, the Episcopal Church in the United States. Most American Protestant denominations, including Methodist, Presbyterian, the Society of Friends (Quakers), Christian Science, Seventh-Day Adventists, and Jehovah's Witnesses, permit cremation.

The Roman Catholic Position on Cremation

Until 1963, the Catholic Church was strongly opposed to cremation. Burial was the traditional method of final disposition, made more significant historically and spiritually by the burial of Christ. Cremation was not forbidden

---

*In his 1976 statement to the House subcommittee holding hearings on the proposed FTC rule, the president of the Missouri Funeral Directors Association said: "Just as disturbing is the emphasis of the Proposed Rule on the elimination of the memorial funeral from the American way of life and the fostering of a practice in which emphasis is given to disposal of the body immediately after death by either cremation or burial, and later memorialization only if necessary to satisfy the family. The ramifications of this practice upon the religious teachings of Christians, Jews and other religions who have established within their teachings a reverence for human life, a respect for those who died, and a belief in a life hereafter are appalling."

**According to a spokesman of the Roman Catholic Archdiocese of New York in 1976, this is still an obstacle for many Roman Catholics. "Cremation is becoming more common," he said, "but the change toward it among Catholics is not a significant one. People feel some concern about the resurrection of the body. A psychological problem exists."

by canon law until the late nineteenth century when the prohibition became official. Canon laws forbidding cremation were adopted in 1886 in response to the modern cremation movement, which the Catholic Church regarded as irreligious, anticlerical, and hostile to the belief in the immortality of the soul and the resurrection of the body. The church regarded proponents of cremation as "enemies of the Christian faith." Strong penalties—refusal of Christian burial and, in some cases, excommunication—were imposed on those who disobeyed the laws. Yet cremation was never opposed by the church on theological grounds; it was not considered contrary to dogma or divine law. The laws were largely a disciplinary measure. For this reason, the Pope had the power to rescind or change existing canon law.

For many years the International Cremation Federation sought the repeal of the canon laws on cremation. In 1962 the federation appealed to church representatives attending the Second Vatican Council to support the attempts to have the church reconsider its position. The council recommended that the question be studied. The church modified its opposition to the practice in 1963 and, today, Roman Catholics incur no penalties if they choose cremation under certain conditions.* These include: (1) if cremation is customary in a country, such as in India or Japan; (2) if there is danger of disease for reasons of epidemics, plagues, or war; (3) if a suitable grave site cannot be obtained because of cost or geographic distances; (4) if civil law requires cremation, as in Tokyo. Catholics who wish to be cremated must obtain permission from the chancery office of their diocese, which will decide whether the reasons for the request are acceptable to the church.

The church still urges its members to "religiously maintain" the custom of burial, however, and asks that bishops instruct Catholics not to choose cremation except for serious reasons. Many Catholics are still unaware that the church now allows cremation. A New York Archdiocese spokesman stated in 1976 that this information was made known in 1963 to bishops throughout the world. "If many Catholics do not know this," he said, "it is simply because bishops don't customarily make announcements."

Judaism's Position on Cremation

The three branches of Judaism in the United States have different views on cremation.

---

*The last rites, Catholic funeral services (such as a Requiem Mass), and burial in consecrated ground are no longer denied a person who chooses to be cremated, unless there is evidence that the request is motivated by denial of Christian dogma. And Catholics who specify they wish to be cremated are not denied the Sacraments while alive. However, official liturgical rites may not be performed by clergy at the crematory but must take place in the church before the body is removed. In England and Wales, this restriction was lifted at the request of the English hierarchy. The church also issued a special Order of Service for use by clergy in English crematories. Clergy in the United States may go privately to the crematory with mourners and recite nonliturgical prayers.

Orthodox Judaism considers cremation against Jewish law and follows a compilation of rules and procedures for burial based on Talmudic and scriptural interpretations, as well as ancient custom. According to Orthodox law, burial is the only proper way of disposing of the dead. If a body is cremated, the cremated remains cannot be interred in a Jewish cemetery, according to Orthodox Judaism.

Conservative Judaism also opposes cremation but allows cremated remains to be interred in Jewish cemeteries. According to the Committee on Jewish Law and Standards of The Rabbinical Assembly:

1) The position of the Committee is that the ashes may be buried in a Jewish cemetery. This permission does not indicate the Committee's approval of the practice of cremation. At the time of burial no religious service should he held.

2) A rabbi may officiate at a service at the funeral parlor or at the home of the deceased if it is known that the deceased is later to be cremated.

3) Urn should have an opening, so that the ashes come in contact with the earth.

Reform Judaism permits cremation as a legal practice and regards cremation and burial as equally acceptable. Reform Judaism permits interment of cremated remains in Jewish cemeteries. Irion, in *Cremation*, says that the acceptance of cremation by Reform Judaism is based on several points:

There is no biblical prohibition of cremation even though burial was clearly the customary practice of the ancient Hebrews. Burial is regarded as a way of respecting the human body and protecting it from desecration or indignity, a purpose served equally well by cremation. The Jewish laws which have been interpreted to make burial mandatory are seen as derived from traditional interpretations rather than from clear statements in scripture.

Legal Requirements

The laws governing cremation may vary from state to state. Rules and regulations may also differ from county to county and even from crematory to crematory. As a matter of law in almost every state—with the possible exception of bequeathing the body or body organs to medical science (see Chapter 17)—people cannot legally determine their final manner of disposition. A decedent's instructions to be cremated—either written or given verbally while alive—are not legally binding after death. The manner of disposition is decided by the next of kin, executor, or legal custodian. (For a discussion of the right to determine the disposition of one's own body after death, see page 41.)

Of course, many survivors are willing to carry out a decedent's wishes, but some assume that in order for cremation to be performed legally specific instructions must have been provided by the decedent. This is not so. The instructions of the next of kin or other person responsible for disposition are sufficient.

All states require a permit for burial or for transit for burial. But only a few require a special permit for cremation. (In most states, laws referring to cemeteries are interpreted judicially to include crematories, columbaria, and mausoleums.) Permits are usually issued by the county registrar of vital statistics. In some counties, the permission of the medical examiner or coroner is required; in others, a health department permit is needed.

Almost all states have specific laws designed to prevent the possibility that cremation could effectively conceal a crime. In every state a licensed physician must describe the cause of death on the death certificate. If the deceased was not under the care of a doctor, if the cause of death is unknown, or if a crime is suspected, a medical examiner or coroner must examine the body and issue a death certificate. No burial or cremation can take place without this document, which states the cause of death.

One of the reasons some jurisdictions require a medical examiner's permission is to ensure that cremation will not destroy evidence of foul play. With regular burial—unlike cremation—there is always the possibility of exhuming a body and performing an autopsy at a later date should there be suspicion of a crime as the cause of death. (Some states mandate a delay in cremation, presumably as a precaution against concealing a crime.)

In addition to the cremation (or burial) permit, written authorization of the next of kin or other person responsible for disposition is required by crematories. Forms must be filled out with complete instructions for the disposition of the cremated remains. Most states also have regulations governing record keeping at crematories, the sale of niches in which urns are kept, and perpetual care trust funds for the upkeep of columbaria.

Coffin Requirement for Cremation

Only two states—Massachusetts and Michigan—have laws that require coffins for cremation, but there is some question whether a standard coffin is actually required in either state. The Massachusetts regulation says: "In all cases of cremation a suitable casket must be used." Under Michigan's law, the body must arrive at a crematory "suitably casketed." Officials of both states, however, have informally indicated to the FTC that these regulations are not being enforced.

Most crematories around the country require a "suitable container." But what is suitable? The FTC found in its 1973 survey in Washington, D.C., that the crematories serving that area accepted bodies transported on a stretcher or in a cardboard container. In contrast, an undertaker in East Hampton, New York, stated in 1975 that the men at a local crematory "refuse to handle anyone who comes wrapped in a sheet."*

---

*In *The Law of Death,* Bernard points out that a family "may find itself against a stone wall if the crematory refuses flatly to accept an uncasketed body." If the crematory is the

The Cremation Association of North America urges crematories to accept bodies in a "suitable casket" or "acceptable container." What does it mean by suitable or acceptable? According to the trade association, the terms describe a container that protects the health and safety of crematory personnel, provides a proper covering for the remains, is of combustible material, and meets "minimum requirements for the maintenance of appropriate respect and consideration. . . ."*

In at least seven states (California, Florida, Maine, Maryland, Minnesota, New Mexico, and Wisconsin), according to the FTC, the law prohibits the requirement of a coffin for cremation. Yet even in those states the law is not generally enforced, and consumer complaints have been received.

In its proposed rule, the FTC would prohibit undertakers and crematories from requiring customers to purchase coffins for immediate cremation. The rule also stipulates that undertakers make available "suitable containers," that is, less expensive cardboard, knock-down-wood, pressboard, fiberboard, or composition containers.**

Disposing of Cremated Remains

Survivors who arrange for a cremation have several options in disposing of the cremated remains. They can (1) buy an urn and a niche in a columbarium (see page 172); (2) have the remains buried in a cemetery; (3) keep the ashes in a container at home; (4) in some states, bury the remains on private property; (5) in most states, either scatter the remains themselves on land or at sea or hire the operator of a plane or boat to do so. In only one state, Indiana, is there a statute forbidding the scattering of remains. Some communities may have local ordinances restricting the areas where cremated remains may be scattered.

In general, crematory and cemetery operators are opposed to the scattering of cremated remains, since their profits derive mainly from the sale of urns and columbarium niches or grave plots (the charge for cremation itself is relatively inexpensive). Unlike England and Europe, where the remains are pulverized into a fine ash, cremated remains in this country are usually left large and heavy enough to discourage strewing.† Under these circum-

---

only one in the area, says Bernard, or if "all such firms are uniformly adamant, little recourse is left to the bereaved family."

*The association suggests that survivors select a coffin the same way they would for burial, since, in either case, the coffin cannot be used again.

**The FTC cited a law proposed in the New Jersey General Assembly in 1974 that would have required undertakers to inform customers in writing that inexpensive containers were available in the funeral home for cremation and to provide them unless customers requested otherwise in writing.

†California instituted a procedure whereby pulverization is available for an additional charge upon request at crematories in that state. The Washington State legislature, acting in 1977 to permit pulverization, established a minimum size for particles of cremated remains.

stances, local authorities may consider scattered remains a public nuisance or hazard.

In California, despite strong opposition from crematory and cemetery operators and some religious groups, scattering cremated remains at sea is popular.* Some cemetery representatives offered reasons for their disapproval of the practice. "I just can't see someone sending mother out to sea in a cardboard box and then dumping her into the ocean," said the president of the Cremation Association of North America, who added that bones sometimes wash up on beaches. "It's kind of shocking," he said, "shocking to the people who find them and shocking to people who are members of the deceased's family."** The vice-president of the National Catholic Cemetery Conference criticized scattering of remains at sea because it precludes there being a permanent memorial. "It strikes me as being contrary to the whole concept of a Christian burial—with its proper disposition and care of remains."

The Cremation Association of North America has always opposed the scattering of cremated remains (the crematory operators discourage the term *ashes*, since the remains are technically fragments of bones).† It has no official policy on pulverization, which would make the scattering of remains more feasible, although several of its member crematories will pulverize on request.

The regulations of the local health department or other appropriate agencies should be consulted before scattering cremated remains. In some cases a permit may be required. If there is any doubt, a lawyer should be consulted.

Cremation Costs

Crematory Charge. The cost of the cremation process itself—the price that the crematory charges those who arrange for disposition—is low compared with the average cost of burial. Crematory charges can range from $35 to $150, with the average cost around $100 or so. In its 1973 survey of

---

*In 1972 the remains of 7,159 people were scattered over the Pacific—most from planes, although 1,879 "burials" were performed from boats.

**In reply to this criticism, one pilot engaged in scattering ashes from his own airplane said that he used a grinder to break down bone fragments to the consistency of heavy beach pebbles. None wash up on shore, he said, because ashes were strewn two miles or so off the coast.

†According to Paul Irion in *Cremation*, association members "have available pictures or specimens of cremated remains showing recognizable bone fragments several inches in length. This is intended to show that scattering is unsuitable because persons would see the portions of calcined bone or animals might carry them off. It is also pointed out that even with the drastic reduction of the body in cremation, there is still something of the person present which should be memorialized. The suggestion of spreading about five to seven pounds of fragments of bones of a loved one is naturally quite distasteful to many."

Washington, D.C., funeral homes, the FTC learned that of the four crematories doing most of the cremations in that area two charged undertakers $50, one $60, and the fourth $75. The FTC noted: But some funeral homes apparently billed customers for more than this amount.* When the Washington mortuaries were asked how much of the price they charged their customers for cremation represented the crematory's charge, fifteen of the forty-three respondents gave a figure different from the $50, $60, or $75 fees.

Eleven of the 15 reported figures of $100 or more, with highs of $195 and $200. These figures may indicate either great unfamiliarity with the actual charges of the local crematories or a mark-up applied to the crematory charge by the funeral director. Whatever the reason for the unusual figures reported to the FTC, they greatly overstate the actual crematory charges in the D.C. area.

Transportation of Body and Cremated Remains. In addition to the charge for cremation, most survivors will have to pay an undertaker for transporting the body to the crematory. In some cases, long-distance transportation will be involved, and the overall cost of cremation can be high.**

After cremation, if survivors choose not to have the cremated remains interred at the cemetery or placed in a columbarium but returned to them, the undertaker in many cases will pick up the remains and deliver them to survivors for an additional charge.† However, many crematories will mail the remains by parcel post in an ordinary container (for example, a metal canister within a cardboard outer case) to either the undertaker or the survivors.

Urns. Containers for cremated remains—urns—come in all sizes, shapes, and styles. They can be square, rectangular (in either horizontal or vertical styles), oval, or shaped like the classic Grecian urn. An urn with a capacity of 175 to 300 cubic inches can contain remains weighing from five to seven pounds, the average weight of bone fragments. A typical horizontal rectangular urn is about 6⅝ inches high, 8¼ inches wide, and nearly 4 inches deep. Urns are made of a variety of materials, ranging from wood to bronze

---

*In a 1975 consent order entered into with the FTC, Service Corporation International the largest funeral chain in the United States, agreed not to overcharge customers for cremation costs. The FTC considers this an unfair and deceptive practice.

**In South Dakota, for example, where there are no crematories, bodies from the western part of the state are customarily transported to Denver, Colorado; bodies from the eastern part of the state are shipped to Omaha, Nebraska, or to Minneapolis, Minnesota.

†The 1973 FTC planning memorandum noted that some crematories charge $25 for releasing ashes to survivors. Such a practice, the FTC noted, seems unfair. Pointing out that the crematory does not acquire any property rights in the cremated remains, the FTC said that "the right to dispose of the remains vests in the deceased's wife or next of kin according to state law. The crematory is paid separately for the cremation services it renders. The consumer gets no goods or services for the $25 or more he must pay to obtain the remains. Such a charge is nothing more than a ransom. . . ."

and other metals to ornamental marble. Bronze is the most common material for urns; the price of bronze urns ranges from fifty dollars to several hundred dollars. There are urns for the cremated remains of one person and those designed to hold the remains of several people (these cost considerably more than single urns—from $100 to more than $500). There may be an extra charge for inscriptions on urns.

Niche in a Columbarium. A columbarium is a special building (usually located on cemetery grounds) containing an arrangement of recessed niches to hold cremation urns. The price of a niche depends on its size, location, and the quality of the unit itself (for example, the type of materials used in its construction, the elaborateness of detail or design).

Niches generally have facings of glass (plain, etched, stained, layered, or faceted), bronze, marble, or other materials. If the niche is covered by a glass front, the inscription is usually on the urn inside. If the facing is bronze or other opaque material, the inscription is on the facing. Inscriptions are sometimes an additional expense and usually must be approved by the columbarium management. In many cases, the size, location, and material of the niche are considered in deciding what type of inscription will be allowed. Niches can cost as much as grave plots—from $50 to $750. (The oldest cemetery in Baltimore, for example, charges from $160 to $315 for a niche; two other cemeteries in that city charge from $210 to $375.) There are niches for single urns and large ones for several urns. Some columbariums have community niches, where, for example, urns are placed in a row on shelves in special rooms. Perpetual care costs are usually included in the purchase price of a niche, although some columbariums charge an extra fee.

Burying the Cremated Remains. Cremation urns can be buried in a family plot in the cemetery or in an "urn garden," a special section set aside for urns. In some states urns can be buried on private property, although permits from appropriate agencies may be required. The cost of a plot in an urn garden is usually less than a regular burial plot because less space is required. (In the New York City area, for example, a plot in an urn garden in city cemeteries is about $150; in smaller communities on nearby Long Island, it is about $55.) There may be additional costs for opening and closing the plot, perpetual care, and a memorial plaque. Some cemeteries require that urns—like coffins—be enclosed in a vaultlike container or enclosure for burial.

Scattering of Cremated Remains. There are a number of options open to survivors who want cremated remains scattered. The least expensive option—and for some people the most personal and meaningful—is to do it themselves. Many people scatter remains at sea, in a garden, in woods, or from a mountain.

Some crematories have "urn gardens" on their grounds for burial of cremated remains. If memorialization of the decedent is desired, a plaque may be placed on the grounds. Sometimes, there is a book of remembrance at the crematory in which the name of the decedent can be inscribed. A number of undertakers will scatter remains.*

In several cities commercial pilots scatter cremated remains. The fee charged by one pilot in New York City in 1977 was $270 (the fee may be somewhat lower in other parts of the country). Survivors may accompany him, although few choose to do so. He notifies them by letter when he has completed his flight. Another New York City pilot, who charges $250 for scattering, sends survivors a gold-edged certificate on which are listed the wind velocity, altitude, latitude, and longitude at the spot where the remains were released.** A pilot in Portland, Oregon, takes along survivors and a member of the clergy. If survivors do not accompany him, he will photograph the spot where the ashes were scattered.

Guidelines in Arranging Cremation

People who desire cremation and do not want to spend a great deal of money have a number of options open to them. (Costs will vary, of course, depending on whether direct cremation is chosen—see Chapter 16—or whether there are funeral services prior to cremation.)

• If there is a memorial society in the community (see Chapter 18), the most inexpensive cremation is probably available through membership in the society. Members of most memorial societies can arrange for formal funeral services first, if desired, followed by cremation. Nonmembers usually may also obtain the names of cremation firms from memorial societies.

• Commercial firms specializing in simple direct cremation services are another alternative.

• If cremation is arranged through a regular funeral home and funeral services are desired, the choice of a simple container for the body can help to minimize costs. Survivors should make inquiries about the crematory's requirements for containers or coffins.†

• It is not always necessary to purchase an urn for burial. Cremated remains can be buried in the simple canister or special container in which

---

*An East Hampton, New York, undertaker, accompanied by a minister, scatters cremated remains once a year in the Atlantic Ocean off Long Island.

**On the subject of scattering cremated remains from an airplane, the pilot observed: "It crosses everybody's mind that it might be nice to, well, float around. . . . Not all the ashes fall to the ground, you know. There are tiny particles that maybe fly forever."

†Several Washington, D.C., morticians pointed out to the FTC during its 1973 investigation that it is possible to arrange for cremation after viewing without buying a coffin. The body, they said, could be placed on a couch or daybed for viewing, or the funeral home could provide a coffin during the period of viewing only. An inexpensive container would then be adequate for cremation.

they are placed after removal from the cremation chamber. Survivors may also provide their own urns, although if an urn is placed in a columbarium in a niche with a glass facing, the management may reserve the right to approve any special or unusual container.*

• Some crematories bury urns in unmarked areas on their grounds at low cost. Other crematories provide inexpensive permanent storage for urns in large vaults.

• Those survivors who want the most economical cremation can have the cremated remains mailed to them by parcel post and either keep the urn or container at home or scatter the remains themselves. In all cases, however, the appropriate agency—usually the local department of health—should be queried in order to make sure the procedure is legal.

---

*A priceless set of Ming vases and a Wedgwood urn—both behind glass—contain cremated remains in a columbarium in Hartsdale, New York.

16

Direct Cremation
and Direct Burial

For $250, as of 1977, the Telophase Society* in California will pick up a body immediately after death, cremate it, and take care of the necessary paperwork. It will also arrange to dispose of the cremated remains (if the survivors wish it), usually by having them scattered at sea. Telophase (which takes its name from the Greek term for the last stage in the division of living cells) was founded in 1971 and is thought to be the first commercial business in the United States specializing exclusively in low-cost direct cremation. Some of the firms that followed Telophase's lead offer low-cost direct burial as well, but Telophase has stayed with its single specialty.

Direct cremation, like direct burial, entails immediate disposition of the body, thus eliminating embalming, viewing, and other potentially costly features of the conventional funeral. Arrangements are simple and relatively inexpensive. Yet, many firms in the new business of direct disposition have found it to be profitable. Telophase, one of the most successful in the field, operates as a membership organization. To become eligible for Telophase's $250 cremation, people must pay a one-time membership fee of $15 per person or $25 per couple or family.** Nonmembers can also be cremated by Telophase but at a cost of $300 each.

By early 1977, according to its president and cofounder, Thomas B. Weber, Telophase had about 22,000 members, performed approximately 3,000 cremations, opened four offices in Southern California and branches in Portland and Seattle. Although Telophase began as a storefront operation, the firm currently grosses almost $400,000 a year—compared with a 1973 gross of $150,000. The reason for his firm's success,† Weber believes,

---

*Direct disposition firms that call themselves a "society" should not be confused with a nonprofit memorial society (see Chapter 18).

**Children under eighteen are included in a family membership.

†In 1974, Weber summarized what his business had already accomplished. "We have,

is that along with a growing trend toward cremation in the United States more and more people are reluctant to pay high funeral costs.

According to Telophase, its operation is simplicity itself. When a person dies, survivors need make only a single phone call to Telophase to come and take over. From there on survivors are relieved of making any further arrangements for disposition. (Telophase will also help with plans for a memorial service). The firm's brochure describes what happens next:

> The body is transported to the Society's repository, where it is held until the death certificate has been completed and signed by the attending physician or the Coroner. A cremation permit is secured and the body is taken directly to a state approved crematory. Final disposition of ashes is made in accord with prior instructions.

The Funeral Industry and Direct Disposition

Weber and two colleagues founded Telophase because they thought conventional funerals "barbaric" and far too costly. "Frankly," Weber told a San Diego County newspaper reporter in 1973, "I believe we have let the human element be replaced by the mechanics of burial, the expensive casket, the flowers, big cars and plot location. It really is all morbid and very foolish. It does nothing for the dead, and it drains the living." Telophase, he said, doesn't "bury anyone, we honor the memory of the dead person and not the cadaver.... In my view the proper way of doing this is to remember someone and get back to living as soon as possible."

Almost from its beginnings in 1971, Telophase met opposition from the established funeral industry in California. This is understandable for it was a big business indeed that Weber was cutting into: That year California's 847 licensed morticians had handled more than 160,000 funerals and taken in $200 million to $300 million. Telophase was sufficiently successful in attracting business away from the funeral establishment to inspire other firms —among them, the Neptune Society—to enter the fast-growing field of direct disposition. Founded in 1973, the Neptune Society maintains eight offices in California and two in Florida, with an office reportedly handling about twenty-five to thirty cremations a week (at a fee of $255 each).

Industry attacks against the Telophase Society were concentrated on marshaling the authority of governmental bodies to quash the firm. An early goal was to force Telophase to be classified as a conventional funeral home and therefore subject to the conventional rules and regulations imposed on such establishments by the state of California. Weber, who holds a Ph.D. in biochemistry, had never identified himself as a funeral director

in our nearly four years of existence, become self-sufficient. We have set up repositories with large walk-in refrigerators in each county. We have acquired our own crematory and internally do our own printing and much of the maintenance on our own equipment."

and, in accordance with his commitment to low-cost direct cremation, Telophase does not offer embalming services. A three-year lobbying effort secured passage of a bill to bring Telophase under the jurisdiction of the state Board of Funeral Directors and Embalmers (which was controlled by undertakers). One immediate change resulting from the law was the need for Telophase to recruit and hire licensed funeral directors for its centers. It is these undertakers who greet the public, sign up new members, answer questions—and explain why Telophase believes people should avoid undertakers and funeral homes.

Telophase has managed to escape other onerous restrictions. For example, its centers have not had to include provisions for embalming. Instead, the firm relies on refrigeration as a method of "holding" bodies. Even here it differs from conventional mortuaries; it is part of Telophase's basic credo that the place where bodies are held should be separate from the place where arrangements are made by survivors. Attempts to force Telophase to combine all its operations under one roof have come to nothing, and the storage units continue to be housed separately from areas used by the firm in dealing with its customers.

Crematory under Fire

By 1974, Telophase had arranged for its own crematory (the only one in California operated independently of a cemetery). But it had also acquired the makings of a major confrontation with a second state regulatory body, the Cemetery Board.* Through a succession of court actions, the Cemetery Board has tried to close down the crematory, on which Telophase has a thirty-year lease. Among other charges, the board claimed that Telophase was operating without a license (which the board then refused to grant), that Telophase was scattering cremated remains without proper authorization to do so (in fact, the firm delegates the task to an ecumenical church group), and that Telophase, to qualify for certification, would first have to comply with several complicated and costly requirements. That particular issue was resolved in Telophase's favor when a case brought by California's attorney general's office on behalf of the Cemetery Board was thrown out of court in 1976. In April 1977 a Superior Court judge ruled that Telophase was not in fact operating a cemetery, within the meaning of the law, and therefore had no need to apply for a certificate to operate a cemetery.

Weber will not be surprised to find Telophase under siege soon again. After all, he told Consumers Union, Telophase has faced several attempts by the state legislature to put the firm out of business and has survived ten court battles in five years. The funeral industry means business. "We are an

---

*Until recently, the head of the Cemetery Board was also the head of the vast Forest Lawn Memorial-Park in Southern California.

economic threat to their industry," Weber says. "People now have an alternative."

Other Reasons for Industry Opposition

The funeral industry in California has stoutly maintained that consumers do not need direct disposition firms as alternatives. According to *California Business* in 1972, there was near unanimity in industry circles that consumers in search of an inexpensive funeral would not be turned away by conventional mortuaries.*

But there are more than price issues involved in the funeral industry's strong opposition to low-cost direct disposition businesses. To some extent, industry objections to direct cremation and direct burial stem from divergent views about the purpose a funeral serves and how survivors can best handle grief. *California Business,* which touched on this issue, included an interview with the executive secretary of the California Funeral Directors Association, who objected to Telophase-type operations for offering "just a disposal service. You can't qualify that as a funeral service," he said. "They don't offer embalming or religious services. . . . It's a completely pagan method of disposing of remains." The chief executive officer of a corporation operating a number of mortuaries in California maintained that most people want a conventional "meaningful ceremony" and said that older people often confide in him their preference for making their own arrangements in advance because they don't trust what their children will do: Some people, he said, take revenge at the time of funeral arrangements for someone they didn't like. "They tend to buy a pine box or have a cremation."

Other concerns on the part of the funeral industry tend to be more prosaic. Will establishments like Telophase be held to sufficiently high standards** if such businesses are not controlled by regulatory boards? Weber and operators of other low-cost firms do not deny that there should be health regulations for their firms, but they want to be regulated by state health departments rather than embalmers' boards, which, they think, will harass them.

Less Trouble Ahead?

Since direct disposition firms operate in a state-regulated industry, supervised by boards largely composed of industry representatives, the firms are

---

*"Hundreds of people are buried every year at no cost at all," according to the executive director of the California Funeral Directors Association. The president of Pierce Brothers, which operates a number of mortuaries in the Los Angeles area, said that his company offers low-cost services to those who desire them. "We offer these programs at costs similar to the co-operative," he noted. "If people want low cost we don't try to talk them out of it."

**Opponents of Telophase have accused the firm of failure to enforce health and safety

involved in more than an ordinary price war. As Consumers Union has long pointed out, government regulatory bodies are often controlled by some of the very people they are supposed to regulate, and the licensing procedure becomes, in effect, a license to protect those regulated from, among other things, cost competition that might benefit consumers.

But there may be new cards in a deck seemingly stacked against direct disposition firms. In 1976 the California legislature took a hand in how regulatory boards are constituted. It mandated that each of the state boards falling under the jurisdiction of the Department of Consumer Affairs include a percentage of members from outside the regulated trade or profession (in most cases, public members must constitute two-thirds of a board).* Richard Spohn, who heads the Department of Consumer Affairs, believes that with the new public members the department will keep a closer watch on the activities of the regulatory boards. He called the Telophase case an example of how the use of regulatory power can protect established operators at the consumer's expense. "A 400 percent cost differential being enforced by a state agency captured by the established operators can hardly be said to be in the consumer interest," according to Spohn.

Different States, Same Problems

Even before the California legislature acted to restrict businesses such as Telophase by putting them under the state Board of Funeral Directors and Embalmers, New York State had already made its move against continued growth of direct cremation and direct burial firms. And, as in California, the New York rules were changed ostensibly to protect the public health. In February 1974 an amendment to New York State regulations imposed a "health requirement" on newly established funeral homes. Critics of the funeral industry suggest that funeral trade association lobbyists were instrumental in passage of the measure for economic as well as for possible health reasons. In the future, new funeral homes in the state would have to include on the premises chapels or reposing rooms, "containing at least 300 square feet," and preparation (i.e., embalming) rooms, "containing at least 120 square feet." Since many firms offering low-cost direct disposition have neither facility, and since such facilities are not necessary for their type of operation, the amendment is likely to curtail the number of new low-cost

---

standards. But Dr. J. B. Askew, head of San Diego County's Health Department, defended Telophase. "They are running a straight operation. They came to me before they started to ask my advice on how to proceed. They have bent over backwards to meet the law."

*The eight-member California Board of Funeral Directors and Embalmers, for example, already has one appointee under the new law: Robert Treuhaft, who is a critic of the funeral industry and the husband of Jessica Mitford, the author of *The American Way of Death*.

firms that will be opened in New York State. Those already in existence before 1974, however, have been allowed to continue operating as before.

Florida, too, has acted to impede the rapid growth of direct disposition businesses. One St. Petersburg-based direct cremation firm, the National Cremation Society, challenged—without success—the requirement that the firm hire a licensed funeral director and maintain a preparation room. So far, the setback has not dealt a significant commercial blow to the four-year-old firm; in the year ending February 1977, it grossed between $450,000 and $500,000. According to the general manager, "we are definitely a money-making operation."

Growing by 400 to 500 new members a month (1977), the National Cremation Society has a membership of more than 20,000; membership fees are $24 per person. About 1,200 cremations are performed a year, with $275 the member's fee for cremation and $299 for a nonmember. (Thus the total cost is the same for members and nonmembers: $299.) The firm operates its own crematory and maintains a refrigeration facility capable of holding fifty bodies. Since it lost its court case in June 1976, the firm reports, it complies with state regulations even though there is no need for the services of an embalmer. The preparation room the firm was forced to provide "is now just an expensive storage area for mops and brooms," according to the general manager.

The National Cremation Society says it has the support of the Pinellas County medical examiner and health officials, who do not seem to think the business presents any health problems. Evidently, the firm also has the support of two judges, one the chief justice, of the Florida Supreme Court.*

Florida's Board of Funeral Directors and Embalmers, which led the fight against the National Cremation Society, did not spare a rival direct cremation business, the State Society for Cremation, also located in St. Petersburg. In 1976 the board revoked the license of the funeral director of the State Society for Cremation, provoking an editorial writer for the St. Petersburg *Times* to call it "just the latest instance of an established profession serving its own interests ahead of the public interest."

How Direct Disposition Firms Operate

Not all "direct" firms approach immediate cremation and burial in the same way or charge low fees, although the underlying principles for body dis-

---

*Their minority dissent in the June 1976 case said, in part: "By requiring petitioners to be licensed, and therefore to hire or be 'embalmers,' the majority has placed its approval on a purely anti-competitive statute by accepting a superficial appeal to the 'police power.' Given that petitioners' premises are regularly inspected and approved by various health and sanitation authorities, I am unwilling to say, as the majority has done, that the police power may be invoked to require the employment or presence of an embalmer for the performance of an activity . . . which is unrelated to public health concerns."

position are generally the same for all. Triangle Cremation Services in Chapel Hill, North Carolina, for instance, according to Ernest Morgan, a close observer of funeral practices, charges rates far below those of other direct cremation firms. "Furthermore," Morgan notes, "its clients may choose only those services which they want. . . . Triangle has contracts with both memorial societies in that part of the state, giving them 10 percent discount. It has a memorial society member on its board."

Most direct cremation and burial companies price their services under $400. Omega Funeral Service Corporation, of White Plains, New York, for example, charges $250 for either direct cremation (plus $100 for crematory costs and urn) or direct burial (plus cemetery costs). For either type of direct disposition, Omega offers a "total service" (standard for these firms), which includes removal of body from place of death, securing and filing the necessary permits and affidavits with the proper authorities, transportation of body to crematory or cemetery, placing newspaper notices, scheduling a memorial service, and providing advice about life insurance, Social Security, veterans' benefits, and related matters. For direct cremation, Omega provides a plain coffin and transports the remains to the crematory (and scatters the remains, if desired). For direct burial, the arrangements differ only in that the body is brought in a plain coffin to the cemetery, and Omega assists with arrangements for interment.

The Direct Cremation Company in New York City charges an all-inclusive fee of $350 for its services. Survivors have four choices for the disposition of cremated remains: (1) they may be stored at the crematory; (2) they may be taken away in an urn (provided as part of the package price); (3) survivors may arrange for burial of remains in a cemetery; (4) survivors may sign an affidavit permitting the company to dispose of remains.

Disposition without an Undertaker

Should family, friends, or an organized group wish to carry out a funeral and burial or other form of disposition without an undertaker, they may encounter difficulties. In some states, the law stipulates that only licensed undertakers can transport bodies from one place to another. In other states, although there may be no law prohibiting private transportation, the regulations may be vague, and officials with whom survivors must deal may be uncooperative.

In 1976 in Freeport, Maine, a man died after requesting that his family and pastor handle all the arrangements for his cremation. At first, officials in charge of issuing documents—death certificate, burial or transit permit, and authorization for cremation—were dubious about the legality of dealing with anyone but an undertaker. However, when the pastor assured the officials that there was nothing illegal about the procedure, they issued the necessary documents. But the superintendent of the crematory, where the body

181

had been transported in a pine coffin by pickup truck, refused to accept the body from anyone but a licensed undertaker. When the two other crematories in Maine also refused to accept the body unless an undertaker accompanied it, the pastor was forced to have a mortician sign the necessary papers and present the body for cremation.

Members of the St. Francis Burial Society (see page 53) have been fortunate in this regard. They found a crematory in Maryland that accepts bodies brought by family members who want to bypass funeral homes completely. In 1976, accounts of how this was done ("How We Claimed Our Own") appeared in St. Francis's quarterly magazine. In each of two instances, the surviving spouse, accompanied by family members, friends, and clergy, took the body directly from the hospital to the crematory. Although some difficulties were encountered, the survivors found most hospital and agency officials cooperative.* From their experience, St. Francis members developed a checklist outlining the most efficient procedure to be followed when family or friends take the body to the crematory. The information is summarized in Appendix 8.

Because it is so unusual for anyone but an undertaker to handle funerals, burial, or cremation, those who wish survivors to make arrangements for disposition after their death should try to find out in advance whether this procedure will be possible in their community. If there is a memorial society in the area, it may be knowledgeable about legal considerations. The state board of undertakers and embalmers can also provide information about state rules and regulations, as can the office of the state attorney general. Community agencies responsible for issuing documents after death can be consulted, and crematories and cemeteries should be queried about their policies. If it is possible to make such arrangements, the procedure would then require careful advance planning by the individual involved, as well as by family and friends.

Choosing Conventional Firms for Direct Disposition

Despite the funeral industry's opposition to low-cost direct disposition firms, an increasing number of conventional funeral establishments appear to be willing, if not necessarily eager, to provide direct cremation and burial at lower prices than they charge for their usual services. A few established funeral homes state outright in their advertisements that they offer low-cost,

---

*The pastor who accompanied one spouse wrote: "In talking to physicians, hospital, crematory, cemetery and other officials, I spoke confidently of what we were about, to help them be responsive. What we were doing was new to most of them since they usually deal with a familiar commercial funeral establishment rather than the next-of-kin or a minister. Over twenty times I explained, 'The husband is the funeral director; I am calling for him,' refraining from being defensive. If officials resist or become tense, it is often because they do not fully understand the law and are confused as to how to respond. I reassured them that the law permits this procedure."

immediate cremation.* Others may not advertise such services, but will provide them if requested.

Some undertakers may refer to the services provided by low-cost firms as "quick disposal," "body disposal" or "cut-rate cremation." However, it is not just speed and economy that many direct cremation and direct burial firms emphasize, but also qualities of simplicity and dignity. For this reason, consumers who wish direct cremation or direct burial may be more comfortable making the arrangements with a firm—if they can find one—that specializes in inexpensive, immediate disposition of bodies than with a conventional funeral home. Even if a conventional establishment does offer direct disposition, consumers may be made to feel that they are choosing an inferior service and should be "doing more" for the deceased.**

Finding a "Direct" Firm May Be Difficult

Direct burial and direct cremation firms are found mainly in three states— California, Florida, and New York. In California there are more than thirty; their number was growing rapidly in Florida and New York before laws were introduced to discourage them. Many of the larger cities in other states, however, do not appear to have attracted these establishments (state funeral board regulations may have prohibited them).

In February 1975 Consumers Union surveyed some fifty memorial societies† in the United States in an attempt to learn whether direct disposition firms were being established in different areas of the country. Memorial societies in large cities such as Atlanta, Chicago, Cincinnati, Kansas City, Philadelphia, Pittsburgh, and St. Louis reported that there were no such businesses in their areas. The People's Memorial Association in Seattle reported that direct cremation firms were unknown in its general area (Alaska,

---

*The Greater Louisville Funeral Society, of Kentucky, in a letter to Consumers Union in 1975, noted: "There has been a trend in recent years for the funeral directors to be more cooperative as to pre-planning and lower cost services, even to the extent of advertising that they provide low cost services if desired. These low costs, however, are rarely below $600 or $700 unless the minister certifies that the family simply cannot pay more."

**Omega, a direct-cremation-and-burial company in White Plains, New York, discusses this problem in its brochure:
"Can my local funeral director provide all of the services you describe?"
"Yes, but since Omega specializes in this type of service, we are better able to pass along the benefit of our tact and our understanding of your wishes than is the funeral director who only occasionally provides this type of service. In addition, you may be assured you will not be encouraged to buy expensive merchandise or purchase additional services."
The Direct Cremation Company in New York City points out in its brochure: "Direct cremation is the transportation of the deceased from the place of death *directly* to the crematory, thus making it unnecessary for the family to hold services at a funeral home . . . services which often put an emotional strain and a financial burden on the grieving survivors."

†For a full discussion of memorial societies, see Chapter 18.

Hawaii, Idaho, Montana, Oregon, and Washington). Memorial societies in the southwest—in Arizona, Nevada, and New Mexico—said they knew of no low-cost firms. The same response came from memorial societies in Arkansas, Indiana, Iowa, and New Jersey.

In the period since the Consumers Union survey was completed, direct disposition may have been established in some or all of these locations, and elsewhere. Interested consumers should check their local Yellow Pages. Ironically, in Westchester County (New York) where Consumers Union has its headquarters, direct disposition firms appear in the Yellow Pages under "Funeral Directors."

As for the future, commercial direct cremation and direct burial firms may need more time to be accepted in communities where the conventional funeral is the norm. Thomas Weber, of Telophase, believes that "high volume, low-cost funeral arrangements are definitely the trend of the future. Canada and the United States are the only two countries in the world that still go for the 'archaic ritual.'" Within the next decade, Weber predicts, 90 percent of the population will choose "the moderate to cheap funeral."

17
Helping
Medical Science
after Death

In July 1977, in the rush to adjourn, the New York State legislature failed
to pass a bill intended to ease the shortage of cadavers in some of the state's
medical schools. The bill would have given medical schools greater access
to unclaimed bodies—bodies sorely needed for medical education. The
failure was nothing new; similar attempts had been made before. The let-
down at the end was also familiar; as in the past, the bill's sponsors believed
they had been closing in on their elusive objective. But they had not anticipated the furor caused by a last-minute provision tacked on to the bill at
the urging of an Orthodox Jewish organization opposed to widespread use
of autopsy.

The amendment would have permitted the family of a decedent, or a
"religious representative," to limit the free hand of a medical examiner who
wished to conduct an autopsy. Early support for the principle of the bill—
to assist medical education—fast faded in the face of outraged protests
against the amendment from medical examiners. The chief medical examiner of Nassau County, for example, warned that the amendment would "set
us back a thousand years." He added:

It will put medical examiners out of business. Can you imagine what would
happen if we went to a husband who had murdered his wife and had to ask
him if we could have permission to conduct an autopsy. Why would any
perpetrator of a crime give such permission?

The medical examiners won their point, but the controversy over the
autopsy amendment killed any chance for the bill's passage that session.
The near-miss was a bitter disappointment to Burton Sherman, M.D., professor of anatomy at the Downstate Medical Center and chairman of the
New York State Anatomical Committee. He had also had high hopes for
the previous year's bill, which had made it safely through both houses of
the legislature, only to be vetoed by Governor Carey.

Sherman had been lobbying for several years for a bill that would allow

185

medical schools increased access to unclaimed bodies for dissection by medical students. By requiring a claimant to sign an affidavit, attesting to a special relationship to the deceased, before a body could be released for burial, the proposed legislation would have thwarted those undertakers who make it a practice to claim a body, bury it, and then bill the state or other funding source for the services provided. As a result, an increased number of unclaimed bodies could be available for medical education. According to Sherman, the state's schools suffered more acutely from a cadaver shortage than the schools of any other state, because New York has about 10 percent of the nation's medical schools and 15 percent of its medical students. At one New York medical school, he had explained, twenty or thirty students had to be assigned to one cadaver. Most medical educators believe the maximum use-ratio should be four students to one cadaver.

The shortage of cadavers has remained acute in the New York City metropolitan area. There, only ninety cadavers had been available for students in 1976; the minimum number required was six hundred. To meet the instructional need, cadavers had to be imported from out of state—some from as far away as California—at an average cost of $350 to $400 each. According to Sherman, the crisis is likely to continue—unless unclaimed bodies are made available for use in medical education.

The Need for Bodies

Thousands of bodies are needed every year to train future physicians and dentists. Some medical schools have active bequeathal programs and are dedicated to informing the public about the concept of bequeathal. (Few people think about the eventual donation of their body to a dental school, despite the need there for cadavers.) Although many medical schools have an adequate supply of cadavers, some schools experience a chronic shortage.* The institutions that experience the greatest need are usually either new schools or state schools in rural areas, or some schools in urban centers such as New York City and Washington, D.C.

Jack Davies, M.D., chairman of the anatomy department at Vanderbilt University School of Medicine in Nashville, Tennessee, conducts a periodic survey of the nation's medical schools to determine their need for bodies. (The survey is carried out for a committee on cadaver programs of the Association of Anatomy Chairmen.) Data from the June 1976 survey showed improvement over the previous year. There were even some schools with a surplus, able to share their excess with less fortunate institutions.

---

*For a listing of schools of medicine in the United States and Canada and of several American schools of dentistry and osteopathy, giving addresses, phone numbers, the degree of need for bodies, and transportation information, see *A Manual of Death Education and Simple Burial* by Ernest Morgan (8th ed., 1977, The Celo Press, Burnsville, N.C. 28714, $2), pages 61-63.

Specifically, of the 110 medical schools that responded to the survey, only 4 reported a severe shortage (11, in the previous year), and 11 a moderate shortage (14, in the previous year). Eighteen recorded more than a sufficient supply, with 12 of the 18 in a position to send bodies to other schools.

The reason why some medical schools receive more bodies than others is sometimes obvious. Prestigious medical schools rarely experience shortages. Yale, for example, cannot accept all the bodies that become available every year. In the Boston area, a large number of donors bequeath their bodies to Harvard Medical School, while the nearby medical schools of Boston University and Tufts are often ignored.* Similarly, the University of Michigan Medical School in Ann Arbor receives many bodies from donors, but Wayne State University in nearby Detroit must rely on unclaimed bodies from public hospitals and institutions. During a brief period every year, the University of California at Los Angeles receives bequeathals for all the bodies it needs for the entire year. Prospective donors are enrolled in the program only during that period.

In some areas, excess donations can assist the less fortunate schools. Emory University Medical School in Georgia is one of an increasing number using a bequeathal form that asks the donor's permission to transfer the body to another school in case of a surplus. In Virginia, a central state agency oversees the distribution of all unclaimed bodies and those willed to state medical schools. Illinois has had an effective system for centralized cadaver distribution for about fifty years.

The Donor Problem: Nothing New

Acquiring cadavers for study has long been a problem for students of medicine in the Western world. In the United States, Canada, Great Britain, and other countries, it is an indictable offense, liable to imprisonment, to offer "any indignity" to a dead body. And for centuries, autopsies and anatomical studies by medical students and doctors were considered indignities. Thus, in order to study the human body, anatomists and medical students had to resort to breaking the law. The robbing of graves for corpses was a flourishing business well into the nineteenth century. In order "to stem the wave of body-snatching and grave-robbing in the United States," says Hugh Bernard in *The Law of Death,* "beginning in 1831 with Massachusetts, most states passed 'anatomy laws' providing for the use in medical science and study of unclaimed dead bodies."

Later statutes in many states provided for the donation of bodies "by will, deed of gift, or other written instrument." In those states that did not have such statutes, it was not possible for people to will their body to sci-

---

* "The glamour of Harvard's name," according to a Tufts representative, "usually attracts more willed bodies than either Boston University or we do."

ence. Civil and common law in the United States and Canada hold that a dead body does not constitute "property." No one, according to the reasoning behind the laws (common law goes back to seventeenth-century England), can "own" a dead body. Therefore, a person cannot give it away. Survivors generally have the right of "possession" for purposes of disposition, but not of "ownership."

But even in the states where it was legal to bequeath one's body for scientific and medical research, the laws up until a few years ago were confusing, or incomplete, or otherwise inadequate. In many states the next of kin had to give consent to the donation after death. Frequently, permission was withheld. In some cases, problems of priorities could arise between the deceased, who may have expressed the desire *not* to have his or her body or parts of it donated, and survivors, who were asked to donate an organ for transplantation in order to save a life. Sometimes, there were conflicts between survivors regarding possible donation of a family member's body or organs, with some advocating it and others opposing. Problems arose with regard to open-ended donations, in which people willed their bodies for "medical research" but did not name a specific institution or a specific purpose for the donation. Sometimes, there were delays in obtaining donated bodies because of legal difficulties with wills. These and other problems frequently arose in the complex and uncertain process of body donations. The entire issue needed to be reviewed and clarified.

The Uniform Anatomical Gift Act

In August 1968, model legislation, the Uniform Anatomical Gift Act, received the endorsement of the American Bar Association. The act was designed to serve as the basis for legislation in the fifty states and to facilitate the donation and use of human bodies or individual parts—tissues and organs—for medical purposes. The final draft was a product of three years of intensive study by the National Conference of Commissioners on Uniform State Laws.* According to an article in the *Journal of the American Medical Association:*

> The Uniform Act is based on the belief that an individual should be able to control the disposition of his own body after death and that his wishes should not be frustrated by his next of kin. To encourage donations and to help meet the increasing need for organs and tissue, unnecessary and cumbersome formalities should be eliminated and only those safeguards required to protect the other varied interests involved should be included. The rights of the appropriate next of kin should be clearly provided, physicians working in this area should be protected, and the public interests in a dead body, as represented by the medical examiner, should be maintained.

---

*The conference comprises law professors, lawyers, and judges from every state; their function is to help make state laws more uniform and up to date.

The Conference of Commissioners not only greatly developed and clarified the existing laws in the United States at the time but added many new measures. It concentrated on thirteen main provisions that covered in comprehensive fashion the problems, ambiguities, and legal and medical contingencies that may arise in relation to the donation of bodies and body organs. Of crucial importance was the provision in which "the donation by the deceased is paramount to the wishes of the next of kin."

Under common law, which is in effect in most states, the next of kin generally have the right to decide on the final disposition of a body—that is, the type of funeral or burial—even to the point of going against the decedent's wishes. Ironically, under the provisions of the Uniform Anatomical Gift Act, a decedent's wishes must be carried out if body donation was specified.*

The commissioners noted that if instructions concerning donation were given in a will but the donor was an accident victim and unconscious, the donation would probably not be known until too late. They suggested that "an easily carried card" would be an excellent "written instrument" to facilitate donations. They also made recommendations that clarified existing statutes covering physicians' liability, obligations of recipient institutions (donees), revocations or amendments of gifts, and donation laws in various states.

In the case of a donation requested of survivors when the deceased had not been a prospective donor but also had not indicated a contrary wish (say, an accident victim whose heart, kidneys, or other organs could be used in transplant operations), the commissioners dealt with a number of intricate points. They established—in order of priority—six classes of persons who could authorize donations (unless there was actual notice of contrary intentions on the part of the decedent or conflicting wishes among survivors): "(1) the spouse, (2) an adult son or daughter, (3) either parent, (4) an adult brother or sister, (5) a guardian of the person of the decedent at the time of his death, (6) any other person authorized or under obligation to dispose of the body." In cases where there are contradictory indications by the decedent or if the donation is opposed by someone in the same ranking (another brother or sister, for example) or in a higher rank order in the list above, the gift cannot be accepted.

Since 1968, all states and the District of Columbia have enacted laws or revised existing ones, making it possible for people to bequeath any part

---

*This fact was noted in a book published in 1973, *Proposals for Legislative Reforms Aiding the Consumer of Funeral Industry Product & Services*: "And so we now have the irrational situation where, while one can donate one's body or parts of it and be reasonably certain that such instructions will be followed, the same certainty is not present for instructions about final disposition or the sort of funeral or memorial service, burial or cremation that one would like to have."

or all of their bodies for medical education, research, therapy, or transplantation. Institutions authorized as recipients include hospitals; medical and dental schools; universities involved in medical education and research; licensed banks and storage facilities for blood, arteries, eyes, or other human parts for use in medical education, research, therapy, and transplantation.

By the end of 1976, six of the ten Canadian provinces* had adopted the Model Human Tissue Act (the Canadian equivalent to the Uniform Anatomical Gift Act), covering about 80 percent of all Canadians. Provisions of the act give donors the right to determine the use after death of their bodies or parts of bodies for therapy, education, and research. In Canada, a bequest may be made by those who have reached the age of majority. Their statement may be signed at any time, or given orally, in the presence of at least two witnesses during a final illness.

In the United States, anyone who has reached eighteen years of age (twenty-one in some states) and is of sound mind may direct final disposition by will (without waiting for probate) or by another document signed by the person in the presence of two witnesses, also signatories. If donors are unable to sign, the will or document may be signed for them. A "uniform donor card," which fits into the donor's wallet, simplifies the problem of making anatomical gifts. Cards are available, free of charge, from a number of organizations. (See Appendix 9 for a sample card and addresses where cards may be obtained.)

Obstacles Remain

Yet, despite the growing awareness of the lack of cadavers and the adoption by states of the Uniform Anatomical Gift Act to facilitate donation, cadaver shortages continue in some areas. One reason undoubtedly is the fact that the idea of bequeathing one's body to help medical education does not yet have widespread acceptance. A 1968 Gallup Poll indicated that nearly 70 percent of all those questioned about the need for bodies in medical research had "sufficient concern to become donors." But a survey of 506 residents of Los Angeles County, conducted in 1975 for the Kidney Foundation of Southern California, found that only one-third of those questioned were in favor of donating their entire bodies for medical research or transplantation. The most frequent reasons given by those who would not want to bequeath their bodies was a fear of "experimentation" and the desire to be buried "whole."** (A majority, 54 percent, were in favor of donating specific

---

*Alberta, British Columbia, Newfoundland, Nova Scotia, Ontario, and Quebec.

**Robert Voelker, who wrote a series of articles about the funeral industry for the Pittsburgh Post-Gazette in 1972, had strong reservations about donating his body. "I didn't like the idea—not at all," he said. "My mental reaction was: If others want to do it—fine; but I don't want anyone fooling around with my body." Yet, within a month after com-

parts of their body, such as kidneys or corneas, while 29 percent expressed uncertainty, and 17 percent were not in favor of donating body parts.) Only 18 percent of those questioned in the survey knew about the uniform donor card. Even if people do express a desire to bequeath their body to a medical school, the fact is that many simply never get around to filling out the appropriate forms or documents. (Indeed, many people die intestate, never having gotten around to making out their will.)

Final Disposition: Moral and Religious Questions

Medical schools have varying policies about the final disposition of remains. Some will return them in a sealed coffin, if survivors so request. (The National Funeral Directors Association says that, unless it is contrary to the policy of the medical institution, it is possible to have a "committal service of the residue of the body" after use for medical studies has ended.) However, a physician at Kansas University Medical Center noted that "we hope they don't ask for the body. It is thoroughly used." Most schools prefer to cremate the remains and either bury them in ground set aside for this purpose by the medical school or return the remains to the family. All institutions will assume responsibility for final disposition.

The question of final disposition of the body by medical schools troubles some people on moral or religious grounds. They wonder how and in what spirit the remains are ultimately disposed of. The physician at the Kansas University Medical Center said that when ashes of several donors are buried at one time and in a single grave, university chaplains perform a commitment service "which recognizes this act of service to neighbor." Theodore Hesburgh, the priest who is president of Notre Dame University,

---

pleting the funeral series for his newspaper, he decided to become a donor. What caused him to change his mind was Ernest Morgan's *A Manual of Death Education and Simple Burial.* It stressed the need for donors, not only for bodies for medical education and research, but for eyes, kidneys, bone marrow, hearts, livers, lungs, pancreases, and skin for transplants. Morgan noted the critical need for eyes and estimated that 350,000 people, many of whom might have been helped, had gone blind in North America in the previous decade. "Somewhere along the line," said Voelker, "the uneasiness I felt about someone messing with my body began to fade. . . . The thing that struck me hardest was the thought of a blind child getting the gift of vision from my eyes." Voelker was also influenced by the fact that a "doomed" heart or kidney patient is able to add additional years to life if someone donates these organs. Buried in a grave, the badly needed heart or kidney simply "rot away." "An unused body, obviously, is worthless," Voelker wrote. "Bodies in cemeteries turn to dust. Why not help a blind child or a heart disease victim? I asked myself." He pointed out that although some people may feel uncomfortable thinking about what would happen to their bodies in medical schools, they wouldn't fare much better in a funeral home embalming room. As for cremation, Voelker came to believe that it destroys "valuable, life-saving materials." He decided to donate his body. "I wrote to the registry [the Humanity Gifts Registry of Pennsylvania] for a donor's card; filled it out and sent it back. It took less than a minute. It was signed by two witnesses, and thus became a legal document. There's another dividend. When my body goes to a medical school, or wherever it ends up, my survivors will be spared funeral and cemetery expenses."

told readers of a 1970 Ann Landers column that it is the custom for students at some Catholic medical schools to offer a Mass at the end of the semester "for the repose of the soul of the person whose body was used."

Clergy of many denominations encourage the donation of bodies for education and research as well as transplantation. Unitarians have played a leading role in the donation movement. Ever since Pope Pius XII officially approved cadaver donation,* Catholic leaders have also spoken out about helping the living after death. Hesburgh told Ann Landers's readers that far from being prohibited, giving one's body to science might rather be considered "an act of virtue, since it makes possible the training of medical students in anatomy." V. M. O'Flaherty, S.J., spiritual adviser to the Marquette School of Medicine, said in 1966: "The Church considers the arrival of the body at the medical school as final disposition, and there are therefore no further requirements to be fulfilled."

Traditional Jewish law is opposed to donating bodies to medical schools. Orthodox and Conservative Judaism generally consider dissection of the body to be mutilation, and maintain that burial must be accomplished within twenty-four hours after death. Certain exceptions may be made in case autopsy is necessary (see page 196). Solomon Freehof, a rabbi and leading legalist for Reform Judaism, has stated that "there can be little objection from the liberal point of view" if "bodies are given to a scientific institution to study, and then *are buried* after the work on them is done."

Guidelines for Donation

• People who wish to donate their body for purposes of medical education and research should make arrangements in advance with the chosen medical school, which will provide forms. (If a specific school is not named, complications may arise after death occurs.) One copy authorizing the donation is kept in the school's files; another should be kept with the donor's important papers.

• The medical school may provide donors with a uniform donor card or similar wallet-sized document so that the school can be notified immediately at time of death. The donor card, after being signed in the presence of two witnesses, becomes a legal document. It should also give the names, addresses, and telephone numbers of nearest survivors. Prospective donors should carry the card on their person at all times.** And they should tell

---

*On this subject, Pope Pius said: "On the other hand, it is equally true that medical science and the training of physicians demand a detailed knowledge of the human body, and that cadavers are needed for study. What we have just said [on the dignity of the human body] does not forbid this. A person can pursue this legitimate objective while fully accepting what we have just said. It also follows from this that a person may will to dispose of his body and to destine it to ends that are useful, morally irreproachable and even noble (among them the desire to aid the sick and suffering)."

**If donors change their mind at any time, all they need do is tear up the card and throw

their physician, lawyer, and those closest to them—family, relatives, friends, co-workers—of their intentions. (See Appendix 9 for a sample card.)

• Despite the provisions of the anatomical gift laws, many medical schools require that the next of kin also give consent to the bequest after death has occurred. (This is understandable, since few schools would want to quarrel with survivors about their wishes or to bring suit to obtain possession of a body, even though legally entitled to it.)

• Alternate plans for disposition should always be made, even though a medical school has accepted the donation. Death may occur far away from the specified donee, and in an area where local medical schools may not need bodies. Also, not all bodies are always acceptable. Medical schools do not accept the bodies of persons who have died from certain communicable diseases, such as meningitis or hepatitis. Bodies that have been autopsied, had extensive surgery, were mutilated, or had organs (except eyes) removed are unacceptable. Frequently, the very obese, the very emaciated, and the embalmed are not taken. Age is not a deterrent, nor is past or present disease except for certain infectious diseases, such as those mentioned above.

• When a donor dies, survivors should call the anatomy department of the medical school designated by the deceased, or, if no school was specified, the anatomy department of the nearest school or institution. Usually, it is preferable to have the body delivered to the medical school as soon as possible after death. Most medical schools will pay for transportation within the state or within a certain radius. Others require the estate of the deceased to pay any transportation costs.* Sometimes the school provides conveyance, or an ambulance service may be used. Often an undertaker will take the body to the school.

• If survivors wish to have a service with the body present and if embalming is suggested by the undertaker, they should ask the school whether embalming is permissible. As noted above, many schools will not accept embalmed bodies.** Undertakers usually arrange for death certificates and transporation permits. However, an undertaker may not be needed; sur-

---

it away. This automatically cancels the donation. (It would be courteous, but not legally required, to make the change in plans known to family members, physician, lawyer, and, of course, the medical school.)

*These transportation costs may be covered by the Social Security death benefit (see page 57). Where there is no surviving spouse, the medical school is legally entitled to recover the Social Security benefit to help cover the cost of the final disposition of the body.

**According to an NFDA pamphlet, "Questions and Answers on Anatomical Gifts," most medical institutions allow the holding of a funeral with the body present before it is taken to the institution for study. "This is often the case," says the pamphlet, "even at schools in states which do not grant the next of kin the right to determine if there should be a funeral with the body present before delivery to the medical institution. When a funeral is requested and permitted the funeral director will notify the medical school and should

vivors can, if they wish, obtain a death certificate from the attending physician and a transportation permit from the local board of health.

Another Alternative: Autopsy

Many people are uncomfortable at the thought of a postmortem examination, commonly called an autopsy (for a description of the procedure, see Appendix 10). Their uneasiness may be based on the belief that the body is "mutilated" during the process. They may believe that their religion forbids autopsy because it somehow prevents a "proper" burial with the body intact. Or their fears may be based on vague or unconscious sociological associations of autopsy with crime.*

In general, there is a lack of widespread support for autopsies. Indeed, some believe that postmortem procedures are only rarely warranted and too often are performed unnecessarily by hospital pathologists (physicians specially trained for the procedure) and by medical examiners. That opinion is not shared by the American Hospital Association, which has stated that the role of autopsy in both curative and preventive medicine "deserves more solid consideration than it is usually accorded." S. Raymond Gambino, M.D., a professor of pathology at Columbia University's College of Physicians and Surgeons, noted in a letter to *The New York Times* in 1976 that autopsy "has been neglected by the public, by the reimbursement agencies and by the Joint Commission on Accreditation of Hospitals. . . . There is no money provided for this service proportional to the work required. The joint commission no longer requires that a minimum percentage of deaths [in hospitals] be autopsied. Doctors are afraid to ask for autopsies for fear of malpractice suits. And the public too often refuses permission for an autopsy when it is requested."

Most people are aware that autopsy by a medical examiner and sometimes by a coroner is required by law when death occurs without an at-

---

prepare the body as required by the school." Many physicians, however, would not agree with this statement. According to Jack Davies, chairman of the Anatomy Department at Vanderbilt University School of Medicine, medical schools, unless in dire need, insist on "fresh" bodies without any embalming of any kind. This is necessary, he told Consumers Union, because conventional embalming is not adequate for medical school needs; once the veins are opened by an undertaker for arterial embalming, it is difficult, if not impossible, to reopen the veins for the procedures required for medical school use.

*The American Hospital Association manual *Postmortem Procedures* notes that "in medieval times dissection was confined mostly to criminals. . . . George II required dissection, or hanging in chains, of the bodies of all executed criminals so that 'some further terror and peculiar mark of infamy might be added to the punishment of death.' In England this act produced a deep-rooted association of the dissection of the body after death with some serious crime committed before death and strengthened public feeling against dissection of unclaimed pauper dead. . . . Even at the present time [in the United States] there is some feeling that an autopsy should be performed on the body of every executed criminal; in some states there are laws to the effect that every prison inmate, upon death, automatically becomes a coroner's case, necessitating the performing of an autopsy."

tending physician or under questionable circumstances.* Few, however, realize that autopsy can be of genuine help to medical science. One of its most important functions is to extend the horizon of medicine with the discovery of previously unsuspected diseases and causes of death. Not only can autopsy often help physicians to decipher the cause and extent of illness in cases that are clinically baffling, but the procedure can serve to train medical personnel and to improve the standards of hospital care.

When a patient dies in a hospital, an autopsy may help the staff to evaluate the diagnosis and treatment. In many cases, of course, an autopsy will produce no unexpected results. In some cases, even *after* the autopsy, it may be difficult to know with complete certainty the precise cause of death. The pathologist can state only those findings assumed to be the most likely causes. In such cases, additional specialized microscopic study may be desirable. In *The Dignity of Life*, Charles McFadden, a priest, describes other possible benefits of autopsy:

> Any deficiencies on the part of the staff immediately become obvious: Were symptoms present which were not picked up by the physicians? Was their diagnosis only partially correct? In addition to the condition which they diagnosed, was there an accompanying complication which went undetected? Would certain laboratory tests or X rays which they did not utilize have revealed the undetected complication? Is there any indication that the hospital laboratory staff is deficient or careless insofar as laboratory tests came back "negative"—and the autopsy now reveals a "positive" condition? Is there any indication that the radiology department is deficient or careless insofar as X rays which were taken did not reveal an existing condition? In a similar fashion, the autopsy report may point an accusing finger at the hospital pharmacy or the manner in which the nursing staff administered a certain drug.

McFadden points out that the dead who are autopsied do indeed serve the living. It is true, he states, "that many people in each community owe their good medical care, and even their lives, to the knowledge and skills which their hospital staff acquired as the result of autopsies."

Pathologists are now seeing new—or least newly recognized—diseases, such as certain serious viral diseases. Possible diseases from environmental factors are also a concern to pathologists. (In many instances, such research cannot be carried out with experimental animals; only autopsies on human bodies can provide the sought-after medical information.)

Religious Attitudes toward Autopsy

Attending physicians often encounter survivors who tell them that their religion prohibits autopsy. Many religions maintain that autopsy is morally

---

*The deputy chief medical examiner of New York City said some 300 deaths a year were discovered to have been homicides as a result of autopsy. Conversely, he said, in some

permissible, but only for grave medical reasons. All religions insist that the body be treated with the utmost respect and reverence during and after autopsy. Islam does prohibit Moslems from being autopsied, although under "extreme circumstances"—when there is no other way to establish the cause of death—permission would reluctantly be given. Buddhism permits autopsy; Hinduism forbids it. Since most Western religions do not forbid autopsy when there is reason to believe that medical science will benefit from the procedure, some survivors may have misconceptions about what their religious doctrine permits.

Protestantism. Although Protestantism is divided into many denominations with differing theological points of view, it can be said, in general, that Protestantism permits autopsy when there is legal and medical justification for the procedure. (Even Christian Scientists, whose religion forbids treatment by licensed physicians, may be autopsied when death occurs suddenly —without previous injury or illness—and the cause is unknown.)

Roman Catholicism. There is no ecclesiastical law prohibiting autopsy so long as there are valid reasons for the procedure—to discover the cause of death or to acquire medical knowledge.

Judaism. According to traditional Jewish law, reverent treatment of the body after death and speedy burial of the intact body are biblical precepts. On either basis, therefore, it would be possible to declare that autopsy is forbidden by Jewish law. There has been much legal discussion and differing opinions among rabbis on the question. Reform Jews have no religious objection to the procedure. Orthodox and Conservative Jews, in general, oppose it—with certain exceptions: (1) if the procedure would save other lives that are in danger; (2) in cases of hereditary disease; (3) if the decedent consented to the procedure while alive. Permission for autopsies, however, must not be given routinely; in some cases, rabbinical sanction may be needed. (This is not true if a criminal cause of death is suspected.)

Orthodox Judaism requires that autopsy procedures be kept to a minimum, preferably by simple inspection or by limited autopsy, if possible. Organs removed for examination during the procedures should be returned to the body before the body is taken away—even if this means a delay in burial —and eventually the body must be buried in a cemetery. If additional time is required for further examination of some organs removed from the body, these parts must eventually be buried in the same grave with the body. (According to Orthodox authorities, it is forbidden under Jewish law to cremate these organs.) According to Orthodox belief, "the biblical precept of burial has not been fulfilled until the last available remnant of the body has been brought to the grave."

---

cases where the district attorney's office believes it has identified a death as murder, the medical examiner finds by autopsy that the "victim" actually died of natural causes.

The attitude of Reform Judaism is to accept the survivors' decision about autopsy; if they are willing, there is no objection. The Reform position is based on the opinion of Jacob Lauterbach, a rabbi who wrote the definitive Reform statement on autopsy: "To my knowledge, no law or regulation expressly forbidding the practice of autopsy can be found in the Bible, or the Talmud or the Shulhan Aruk. It may safely be stated that in case the autopsy would not unduly delay the funeral, one could not find the least support for any objection to it in these authoritative sources of Jewish law."

Undertakers and Autopsy

Many people do not realize that a funeral with an open coffin and viewing is usually possible after an autopsy is performed at a hospital.* In some cases, however, an autopsy may be delayed, resulting in failure to release the body at the scheduled time and causing problems for the undertaker and survivors who are trying to make funeral arrangements.** Embalming can be difficult if eight hours elapse before it is begun. But even without delays, problems sometimes confront undertakers when autopsy is necessary. In some cases, they are not adequately informed by the hospital about the extent of the autopsy. Autopsy incisions may not be closed or blood vessels that would be used for injecting embalming fluid may be damaged.

Most pathologists prefer to do an autopsy before the body is embalmed. However, in some communities, pathologists permit arterial—but not cavity—embalming (see page 88) before autopsy. In rare instances, autopsies are performed in the funeral home, usually after arterial embalming is done. Arterial embalming before autopsy benefits both undertaker and pathologist. It can produce a satisfactory appearance for viewing, and the pathologist need not feel rushed to complete the autopsy and release the body to the undertaker.

Some Considerations Concerning Autopsy

• It should be remembered that a funeral with open coffin and viewing—if desired—is usually possible after autopsy.

---

*Exceptions may occur when autopsies are performed by coroners or medical examiners. When these "medicolegal" postmortem examinations are done, complete autopsies (see Appendix 9), including examination of the head, are usually mandatory.

**In 1972, through the efforts of William Reals, M.D., president of the College of American Pathologists, and Howard Raether, executive director of the NFDA, a liaison committee was established to develop understanding and cooperation between the two groups. The committee's recommendations have been approved by both the Board of Governors of the College of American Pathologists and the House of Delegates of the NFDA. Some of the recommendations approved by the liaison committee include the practice of arterial embalming prior to autopsy, except in cases where a thorough postmortem examination would be impeded; reducing the procedural delays in an effort to minimize the time interval from death to the release of the body; encouraging the use of

• Autopsy, when requested by the physician, is provided by the hospital at no cost to survivors.

• Although bequeathal of the body for autopsy can be noted on the uniform donor card (see Appendix 9) on the line following "Limitations or special wishes, if any," there is no way to know beforehand whether an autopsy will be performed after death. When death occurs in a hospital, the decision to request permission for autopsy is the physician's prerogative. Therefore, no one should assume that an autopsy will be inevitable. If autopsy is designated as the first choice on the universal donor card, a second choice should also be noted. Family, friends, physician, and lawyer should be informed about the choice of autopsy. In some cases, this might make it easier for survivors to consent to the procedure.

Listed below are a few of the most common reasons offered by survivors who refuse permission for autopsy, followed by some responses to those objections suggested by the American Hospital Association (AHA):

Disfigurement of the deceased. Incisions will not show (except in the case of medicolegal autopsies required by law); clothing will cover them the same way that most operative incisions are covered by clothing worn during life. Autopsies are performed meticulously in the interests of science and the living by specialists who do not overlook the rights of the dead and their survivors.*

Mutilation of the deceased. A surgical procedure performed on a living person is not thought of as mutilation, and a similar procedure performed on the deceased should not be thought of as mutilation either.

The deceased has suffered enough. The dead body does not suffer. An autopsy causes no pain to the subject and it may benefit others.

Perform an autopsy on someone else. If everyone responded this way, medical progress and medical education would be severely handicapped. "Everyone benefits from knowledge gained by autopsies and everyone should be willing to contribute," according to the AHA.

The deceased would not have wanted it. Was the subject ever discussed during the deceased's lifetime? If the deceased was a generous and unselfish person, then perhaps he or she would have agreed to an autopsy as a possible benefit to others.

Our religion does not permit it. In most cases this statement is likely to be incorrect. "In some communities ministers, priests, and rabbis are willing to use their influence to obtain autopsies," the AHA has said.

---

autopsy techniques that would eliminate technical difficulties for the embalmer; and encouraging both undertakers and pathologists to cooperate with and promote organ donor programs for transplantation.

*The College of American Pathologists' guidelines for professional practices states: "Every care should be taken to avoid any mutilation of a body during performance of an autopsy."

We do not care what the deceased died from. The family physician may be able to apply what was learned during autopsy to the medical care of the family in the future. In some cases, people who die are discovered by autopsy to have had a condition that could be inherited. Prompt treatment might be available to family members for an inherited abnormality that would otherwise have gone undetected.

We've heard what goes on during autopsies. According to the AHA, "It should be emphasized that hospitals today have concern for the remains of the deceased. For example, the autopsy rooms are neat and clean, and the physicians performing the autopsy conduct their examinations with dignity and respect."

There is no question that, despite disapproval of the College of American Pathologists and the American Hospital Association, physicians and hospital personnel sometimes place undue pressure on survivors to give permission for an autopsy. Charles McFadden in *The Dignity of Life* describes this:

> I have personally witnessed hospital staff members refusing to release the body to an undertaker while they came back time and time again, over a period of several hours, telling the weeping family that they were being unreasonable and selfish, that they were showing no concern for their fellowman, and that the deceased would have wanted to do whatever was possible to help the living. It is especially reprehensible when advantage is taken of the illiterate, the uneducated, or the foreigner—and his signature obtained on a consent form for an autopsy, when he has no knowledge of the nature of the form he is signing. In a word, we think that the hospital staff should express its desire to do an autopsy, explaining briefly and with no pressure the reasons for autopsies. Then—whatever be the response of the spouse, parent, or family—let it be.

A Third Way: Transplantation

Some people may prefer to donate individual organs and tissues for transfer to the living rather than bequeath their body to a medical school.* In some cases, when a body has been donated to a medical school but cannot be accepted, individual parts may be found suitable for transplant. Prospective donors can specify on the uniform donor card whether they wish to donate individual organs for possible transplantation or their body for anatomical study.

In many metropolitan areas there are eye banks, kidney foundations, and transplant centers that will supply donor cards and, when death occurs, make arrangements for transplants. After organs are removed for trans-

---

*It should be noted that individual organs—like bodies—cannot be sold. Under the law, they too are a gift.

plantation, the remains are usually returned to survivors for burial or cremation. (This is not the case when a body has been used for anatomical study; the medical school usually takes responsibility for ultimate disposition.) It may even be possible to have a conventional funeral after removal of body parts for transplant. A skilled undertaker, using embalming and restorative techniques, can prepare the body for viewing, should that be desired.

At present, more than twenty-five kinds of tissues or organs can be used for transplantation, including eye, skin, bone, tendon, bone marrow, kidney, liver, pancreas, blood vessel, lung, and heart. Some types of transplant operations—heart, lung, liver, and pancreas—are still in the area of research, although techniques are constantly improving. Others—corneal transplants, and transplants of bone, heart valves, cartilage—have been performed successfully for more than twenty years. Kidney transplantation is no longer considered experimental and is the most frequently performed organ transplant, with a high degree of success. The American Medical Association points out that it is not unusual for "a deceased donor to contribute a kidney to each of two recipients, his corneas to two blind persons and other organs and tissues to still other persons."

Problems Affecting Transplantation

Despite the increasing number of transplantations and the growing survival rate of patients, wide-ranging difficulties involving both medicine and society as a whole continue to affect the development of transplantation (see also Appendix 11):

• The medical problems of transplantation must be solved, particularly the selection of compatible donor tissue and the suppression of the phenomenon of organ or tissue rejection by the immune system of defenses of the donee (or host).

• A chronic shortage of donors means that thousands of patients die every year for lack of available organs or tissues. And, as a result of the donor shortage, it can be a difficult decision at times to select among potential recipients the one who will receive an available body part.

• The lack of a legal definition of death prevents many transplant surgeons from removing healthy organs from a dying patient whose brain activity has stopped but whose heart is still beating and whose lungs are being mechanically inflated.

• The most efficient use of available cadaver organs is severely handicapped by the lack of a fully developed nationwide communications network to synchronize information, services, and data about available donors. Without such coordination, effective cooperation among the various transplant centers is limited.

● The massive costs of research, medical training, and maintaining transplant centers raises the question of who will pay these enormous sums.*

Shortage of Organs for Transplant

Donor organs and tissues are in short supply.** For example, there are approximately 34,000 patients with kidney disease in the United States, many of them waiting for a transplant. The National Kidney Foundation in New York City estimates that at any time in the United States, there are only 2,200 donor kidneys likely to become available for 10,000 to 13,000 potential recipients. In 1977 in the New York-New Jersey area alone, about 600 people were awaiting kidney transplants.† The American Medical Association (AMA) says:

> If a kidney patient needs a transplant but has no suitable relative willing or able to donate a kidney, he may have to use dialysis for two or three years before a suitable donor kidney becomes available. The situation is so critical at the present time that many patients will die before they are able to obtain the use of even an artificial kidney, and others will die before they can get a transplanted kidney. More people die of kidney disease than are killed on our highways.

According to the National Kidney Foundation, about 54,000 people die every year because of kidney disease.

Corneas, too, are in short supply. Even though they can now be

---

*Individual costs for patients are another factor, although government assistance is now available for certain kinds of treatment and transplants. A heart transplant averaged about $36,000 in late 1975 (covering inpatient costs and immediate intensive care). A kidney transplant costs about $20,000 for surgery alone. Medicare covers about 80 percent of the costs (including use of dialysis machines) for all kidney transplant candidates, regardless of age, and the state often covers the rest.

**In his 1971 work, *Hearts*, Thomas Thompson described the tension and suffering of patients waiting in 1968 for available hearts to be transplanted at St. Luke's Hospital in Houston, Texas: "At one point in deepest autumn, more than twenty people were camped in motels . . . all waiting for new hearts. . . . The cry of an ambulance meant that somewhere in the city someone had been shot or run over or crushed in a fall, and if that someone was dead or dying, perhaps the heart would still be usable. When the ambulance broke the quiet autumn nights, the waiters—as they are called—sat up in their motel beds and switched on bedside lights and stared hard at the telephone . . . and waited to be summoned across the street to the hospital for tests."

†Early in 1977, a thirty-two-year-old New York City construction worker who had been on dialysis received a transplant from a sixteen-year-old Russian youth, killed forty-eight hours earlier in an automobile accident in Moscow. In Russia, prompt removal of organs from a dead person is permitted under a brain-death law (see Appendix 11). Only one of the youth's two healthy kidneys was needed for transplant in Moscow. On the chance that the second kidney could be used by colleagues in New York, Moscow physicians prepared the kidney for air shipment (kidneys can be preserved in a special refrigerated solution for seventy-two hours). When the kidney arrived in New York, tissue samples were taken and computer data were searched for a suitable match. After transplantation was completed, the construction worker's new kidney began functioning immediately. Six weeks later, the kidney still working well, the patient was released from the hospital.

"banked," that is, stored in eye banks indefinitely, only about half the needed donor eyes are available for transplant at any given time.

There is a continuous demand for other body parts as well. The AMA points out that there is always a great transplant need for the structural tissues of the body—bone, tendons, heart valves, fascia (the fibrous tissue that covers muscles), dura (the membrane covering the brain), and cartilage. Every year accidents and bone tumors cause extensive skeletal damage to perhaps 30,000 to 40,000 people, a number the AMA calls "staggering." Bones and joints repaired or replaced with normal tissue can often save limbs. "Up to ten to fifteen surgical procedures are possible," says the AMA, "utilizing the bones and other structural tissues from one donor."

About 13.4 million people in the United States suffer from a hearing impairment. The tiny middle-ear bones of people with hearing problems are needed for research into the cause of and cure for deafness. Some normal ear structures are also used in transplantation.

Although not needed for transplantation, human pituitary glands can be used for extraction of growth hormone to treat a specific type of short stature in children. An estimated 10,000 to 20,000 children in the United States are suffering from pituitary dwarfism. Each child needs the extract from 100 pituitary glands to stimulate normal growth for one year. Only about 1,200 children a year are being treated at designated research centers. An additional 10,000 to 50,000 children with complete or partial growth-hormone deficiency would be helped by adequate supplies of growth hormones. The National Pituitary Agency in Baltimore reports that the pituitary glands of nearly 80 percent of all people who die in the United States each year are required if treatment is to be provided for all who need it.*

In view of the rapid advances in medical science, which will make more and more transplants possible every year, and the chronic shortage of donor organs, a number of physicians, lawyers, and concerned citizens are seeking solutions to the dilemma. The Uniform Anatomical Gift Act, whose adoption by all the states was a significant advance in making bodies available to medical science, has not yet helped to substantially increase the number of donor organs.

How can more organs and tissue be made available for transplants? At present, one of the most likely sources is accident victims. There are about 100,000 accidental deaths a year in the United States. Only about one-fifth of all the victims, however, prove to be suitable donors. The rest may have been dead too long to be useful, or their organs may have been injured in

---

*To alleviate the shortage of human growth hormone, the agency has asked hospital pathologists and county medical examiners to contribute pituitary glands obtained at autopsy. Qualified investigators receive supplies of growth hormone from the National Pituitary Agency at no cost. In 1977 a commercial source of human growth hormone became available—but at substantial cost (about $2,400 per patient annually). Research continues in an attempt to find synthetic or tissue culture methods capable of yielding appreciable supplies at reasonable cost.

the accident. Then, too, permission must be obtained from survivors if the accident victim does not carry a uniform donor card. Nonetheless, thousands of accident victims have contributed vital organs to patients who needed them and thereby not only saved lives but also helped to advance medical science. (The world's first heart donor was a twenty-five-year-old woman struck and killed by a car in Cape Town, South Africa.)

How to Increase the Supply of Organs

One method of obtaining volunteers and also of making the public more aware of the need for donors has been adopted by at least twenty-eight states* and the District of Columbia. The plan, originating with Tennessee in 1973, permits drivers to indicate on their license their wish, in case of a fatal accident, to donate their body organs. Such drivers, in addition to the special notation on their driver's license, must also carry a uniform donor card, duly signed and witnessed. Thirty-five states and the District of Columbia include a donor card with a driver's license renewal form.

Ralph Porzio, author of *The Transplant Age*, suggests another voluntary system for the United States that would involve everyone registered with the Social Security Administration. "The potential donor," he says, "would carry a card that not only bears his Social Security number but also vital information such as blood and tissue type which could prove invaluable to the transplant surgeon." A Social Security information office would be the clearinghouse for information on all prospective donors. It could be reached twenty-four hours a day by medical professionals and could provide up-to-the-minute data about availability of organs, blood types, and tissue-typing to transplant teams all over the United States. The plan would be completely optional, but millions of Americans, most of whom have never given the question much thought, would be confronted with the necessity of a decision about whether or not to become donors. Porzio believes that his system, by creating a widespread awareness of the problem, would result in an increase in the available organs for transplant purposes.** Porzio maintains that a vast program of education is needed to create a large pool of volunteers.

---

*The states to adopt this plan include Alabama, Arizona, Arkansas, Colorado, Connecticut, Georgia, Hawaii, Illinois, Indiana, Kansas, Kentucky, Louisiana, Maine, Maryland, Minnesota, Mississippi, Missouri, New Hampshire, New Mexico, Oklahoma, Oregon, South Dakota, Tennessee, Texas, Virginia, Washington, West Virginia, and Wisconsin.

**Donald Longmore, in *Spare-Part Surgery*, echoes this idea in describing a universal network of donors that he envisions: "There will have to be an intensive program of public education at a fairly sophisticated level. Television, particularly programs with hospital or medical settings, will play a vital role here. To be a donor will carry a certain social importance. The small letter D that each donor has tattooed under his left arm (in invisible ultraviolet ink, if he prefers) will be increasingly seen on beaches, in clubhouse shower rooms or Turkish baths, at swimming pools—wherever people congregate in swimsuits. To some, no doubt, it will be mainly a status symbol. To many, though, it will be something more profound: the mark of the person who cares."

The proposal has also been made that people who *don't* wish to be donors carry a card or a tattoo mark to that effect—making the removal of needed organs a standard procedure for all others who die. Routine removal of organs is now common in some countries in Western Europe, among them Belgium, Denmark, France, and West Germany.* In France, for example, organs may be removed from a dead person without permission of survivors (except in the case of Moslems, victims of crimes or of accidents occurring at work, and suicides). Within the Common Market, "Eurotransplant" exchanges livers, hearts, kidneys, and other organs among ten countries. This exchange is done on the basis of matching and typing systems and by means of rapid data processing.

Some physicians believe that laws will have to be passed eventually, making it possible for doctors to remove needed organs from the dead without consent.** Blair Sadler, a lawyer who helped write the Uniform Anatomical Gift Act, prefers a voluntary approach on the part of donors. But, Sadler says, "if we get to the point where we can show that lives are being lost, I would seriously consider giving medicine the right of eminent domain."

Transplantation Centers

If and when the problem of legally defining death is resolved and other obstacles to widespread acceptance of transplantation are overcome, the logistics associated with transplantation—obtaining suitable donors and the resources for adequate service—would still have to be greatly expanded. There are already significant advances in the development of transplantation centers around the country. A number of institutions associated with

---

*Great Britain, however, has a shortage of organs for transplant. In 1975, a subcommittee of the British Transplantation Society noted the importance of the public's involvement in decisions. The role of survivors who authorize organ donations was stressed. "In particular," the committee stated, "relatives of dead patients, if available, would rather give part of their loved one's body than have it taken away. A request to use organs after death might not always increase distress of bereaved relatives. Sometimes this request was welcomed in that it provided the comfort that some good could come from the tragedy. What was needed was enthusiastic cooperation; the procedure of transplantation would then become a valuable experience for all concerned. If the public were involved, apathy would disappear."

**An example of how difficult it is to formulate such laws is illustrated in the case of a twenty-three-year-old New York City murder victim, shot in the head in 1975. The man's electroencephalogram revealed total lack of brain activity; breathing and heart rhythm were maintained by artificial means. Although doctors had obtained his mother's signed consent for kidney removal, the New York City medical examiner wanted the entire body intact for autopsy and a murder investigation as soon as the victim's heart stopped beating. Hospital officials decided to defy the medical examiner, and, when the young man's heart failed, the two kidneys were removed and successfully transplanted to two waiting patients. Later, an agreement settling such conflicts was negotiated between the city's Health and Hospitals Corporation and the medical examiner's office.

kidney-transplant work have made cooperative arrangements to share blood and tissue-typing information about prospective donors and waiting recipients. Such groups serve the areas of New England, the Middle Atlantic states, northern and southern California, New York-New Jersey, and the Mountain states.

The Northern California Transplant Bank in San Jose, located within the grounds of Santa Clara Valley Medical Center, has been organized by a group of transplant surgeons to provide "tissue to people in desperate need of human transplant material."* Potential donors to the Transplant Bank are encouraged to fill out the uniform donor card attached to the back of their driver's license. When death occurs in northern California, a human tissue bank technician removes most of the donated tissues and organs; transplant teams remove heart and kidney. "After removal of the donated tissues and organs," according to the Transplant Bank, "the body is released to the next of kin for funeral arrangements. The removal of the commonly transplanted tissues and organs does not require any alteration in the funeral arrangements."

There are also several donor clearinghouses that inform transplant centers about prospective donors.** The Living Bank in Houston, Texas, whose board of advisers includes such noted surgeons as Christiaan Barnard, Denton Cooley, and Michael DeBakey, is such a clearinghouse. It is not a storage facility for organs or bodies, but a nonprofit organization that helps people who wish to donate a part or all of their bodies after death. Potential donors complete a registration form, and the information is entered in the Living Bank's central registry. The Living Bank sends the donor and the donor's physician a copy of the form and a uniform donor card. When called at time of death (it can be reached at any hour of the day or night), the Living Bank immediately contacts the appropriate facility closest to where the death occurred—either a medical school, eye bank, or transplant center.†

The main purpose of the Medic Alert Foundation, a nonprofit organization in Turlock, California, is to assist members who have special medical

---

*The tissues the bank uses for transplantation are bone, ear (eardrum, three ossicles, and portion of the ear canal), eye (cornea and sclera), heart valve, artery, kidney, and skin.

**Airlines in the United States and Canada frequently cooperate in the shipping of tissues and organs; some of them have guaranteed immediate flight to waiting recipients. In 1969, for example, a Phoenix real estate man, awaiting a suitable kidney for a transplant operation, had a "hot line" to the University of California at Los Angeles Medical Center. Equipped with a pocket-size radio, he was given instructions to rush to the airport the moment he heard the high-pitched "beep" announcing that a suitable donor had been found. There, he was to board the first plane to Los Angeles, where an ambulance would be waiting to take him to the hospital for the operation.

†As of June 30, 1977, the Living Bank had 41,000 registered donors. It has been instrumental in the donation of 391 bodies to medical schools, and 383 corneas, 15 kidneys, 1

problems or needs not easily identifiable. For a one-time $10 membership fee, a person files medical information with the foundation. There are about 750,000 members in the United States, more than a million worldwide. Each member carries a Medic Alert medallion—a necklace or bracelet—on which is engraved the wearer's special medical status (for instance, "taking anticoagulants") and the foundation's emergency telephone number. In case of an emergency involving a Medic Alert member, medical personnel can telephone the foundation to obtain vital medical information from its central files. Information about prospective organ donors is also available in the central files, which can help speed donation after death.

In addition to the clearinghouses and the coordinated centers, there are a great number of specialized organ and tissue banks, foundations, and registries in the United States and Canada. Approximately sixty-six eye banks in these two countries store donors' eyes for transplants. The major kidney transplant centers in North America are in Ann Arbor, Baltimore, Boston, Cleveland, Denver, Indianapolis, Los Angeles, Minneapolis, Montreal, New York City, Philadelphia, Richmond, San Francisco, Seattle, and Toronto. The National Kidney Foundation helps coordinate transplants throughout the country. The Deafness Research Foundation in New York City and its National Temporal Bone Banks Center in Baltimore are both involved in research into the causes of and cures for deafness. The National Pituitary Agency accepts donations of pituitary glands. The Tissue Bank at the Naval Medical Research Institute in Bethesda has done pioneering work with skin and bone grafts. (For addresses of individual banks and registries, see Appendix 9.)

The proliferation of specialized banks—with one group soliciting corneas, another kidneys, another pituitary glands, and so on—means a great deal of costly duplication, observers maintain, since each bank has its own physical facilities, its own administrative network and staff, its own educational and public relations campaign. Moreover, although one donor body theoretically could make a specific contribution to each specialized bank, multiple contributions from an individual are rare. As a practical matter, people who wish to donate eyes, kidneys, and pituitary glands, for example, are at a disadvantage unless there is a facility in the area that can coordinate arrangements for donation of a variety of organs and tissues.

What is needed, according to some critics, is regional tissue banks in those areas where they do not already exist. These banks would, as Ernest Morgan wrote in *A Manual of Death Education and Simple Burial*, "coordinate the procurement, processing, storage and distribution of tissues for transplant and therapy, on a regional basis. Ideally such tissue banks will,

---

heart, and 1 pancreas for transplantation and research. Its donors' organs were used in research on the spinal cord, the brain, the kidney, and the spleen.

206

in the future, accept bequeathal of the entire body and dispose of the remains without expense to the family."

Medical Education, Autopsy, or Transplantation?

When considering choices—whether to donate one's body to assist medical education, or to consent to autopsy, or to donate body organs for transplantation—it should be remembered that some of these alternatives are mutually exclusive:

• If *body donation* to a medical or dental school is preferred, then this would exclude the possibility of autopsy and limit potential organ donation to the eyes.

• If *autopsy* is the first choice, then the body cannot be donated for use in medical education. But, in some cases, body organs may still be used for transplantation.

• If organ donation for *transplantation* has priority, it may still be possible for an autopsy to be performed. But only if the eyes alone are to be donated for transplantation is bequeathal of one's body for medical education then possible.

Part IV
Two Ways to Make Prearrangements for Death

18
Memorial Societies

In 1939 parishioners of the Congregational Church of the People in Seattle, Washington, formed the nation's first memorial society. Angered by exorbitant fees of undertakers and by lavish funerals, the founders of the People's Memorial Association (PMA) set out to find an alternative: simple, dignified funerals at a cost their families could afford.

A committee of volunteers from the PMA's forty charter members eventually found the key to the plan's effectiveness: a Seattle mortician who was willing to cooperate with the membership. An agreement was negotiated with the Bleitz Funeral Home, providing, among other things, the option of direct cremation, for which members would be charged a special low rate. Sympathetic to the goals of the PMA, the Bleitz firm did not pressure members to have embalming, viewing, and services with the body present. In place of these costly features of conventional funerals, the membership generally favored immediate disposition of the body, to be followed by a memorial service or meeting at some convenient time afterward.

Membership in the PMA grew slowly at first. In 1952 there were only about 650 members, but by mid-1977 the adult enrollment had reached 37,000, with some 7,500 minor children covered by family memberships. Each month 300 adults, on average, join the society. And the Bleitz Funeral Home is still affiliated with the PMA and still providing services for members at special low rates.

According to Friend Deahl, a certified public accountant and an early member of the PMA, the membership has saved a sizable sum on funeral expenses. For example, between 1965 and 1974, the decade for which Deahl has compiled data, services for 6,956 PMA members cost $1,671,735, an average of $250 a member. If conventional funerals had been arranged in regular mortuaries at average prevailing costs, Deahl told Consumers Union, the total for those services would have been well over $10 million, an average of more than $1,400 each.

211

The undertaker who made the saving possible had no regrets about his firm's longtime business arrangement. Bleitz believed that PMA members had a right to select the type of funeral arrangements they preferred. From an original fee of $50 for direct cremation, the cost for society members rose to an average of $130 during 1964 to 1974. In 1975 the firm handled about 800 funerals for PMA members and had to expand its facilities.

Growth of Memorial Societies

The memorial society did not remain for long a West Coast phenomenon. In fact, the second* memorial (or funeral**) society in the United States was organized in Brooklyn, New York, just a few months after the Seattle association was formed. But the growth of memorial societies in general was slow throughout the United States during the next decade; by 1950, only seven groups had been established.

Then the movement began to burgeon. New societies were formed in many states, particularly among Protestant religious groups, professional people, the highly educated, and the affluent.† Most of these groups patterned themselves after the PMA.

There are now some 150 memorial societies in the United States—and about 20 more in Canada—with at least 750,000 members. (Some societies count an entire family as a single membership, so these figures are, at best, rough estimates.) Membership totals are increasing steadily. The Palm Beach Funeral Society in Florida, for instance, added 1,741 new members in 1976. The Minnesota Memorial Society in Minneapolis, the only society in the state, had a membership of 12,802 by the end of 1975; 612 joined in 1976. Largest of all North American groups is the Memorial Society of British Columbia, with more than 75,000 members.

An important development in the memorial society movement came in 1963 when the Continental Association of Funeral and Memorial Societies was established. Located in Washington, D.C., with its own office and staff, the Continental Association serves as a clearinghouse for information about the nation's memorial societies. It charts their growth and acts as a unifying force among various member groups. In 1971 Canadian societies organized a comparable umbrella organization, the Memorial Society Association of Canada (with headquarters in Weston, Ontario), which works

---

*LeRoy Bowman, author of *The American Funeral,* was active in some early groups.

**The term funeral society is also used for these organizations. Neither memorial nor funeral societies should be confused with "burial societies," whose members, most of them poor, pay a few pennies a week over a period of many years for burial insurance policies to cover the cost of their funerals.

†Robert Fulton, in a 1962 survey for the National Funeral Directors Association, concluded that memorial society members had "an annual income twice that of the average American family."

closely with Continental on education and legislative projects.

Despite their growth, the concept of memorial societies remains relatively new and unfamiliar in the United States. According to a 1974 survey of attitudes toward death and funerals conducted for the Casket Manufacturers Association of America, nearly half the 1,060 respondents did not know what a memorial society was. (The same was true of many Canadians surveyed by the Consumers' Association of Canada in 1975.)

How Memorial Societies Function

Memorial societies are by no means alike. They vary in size, in their operations, and in their arrangements with mortuaries. They do share certain characteristic features, however. All are nonprofit, democratic, and cooperative. All operate on small budgets, and almost all are staffed by volunteers. Nearly all are members of the Continental Association or its Canadian counterpart. (Occasionally, an illegitimate "memorial society" is set up as a front for an undertaker; such a group usually asks a large membership fee and sometimes tries to sell members a funeral or a cemetery lot in advance of need.)

Memorial societies are, in effect, consumer movements, organized in reaction to costly and pretentious funeral and burial practices. Watchdogs of the funeral industry at the local, state, and federal level, they bring to public attention questionable practices of undertakers and related businesses, and they work for more effective regulation of the industry.* Most societies are affiliated with churches, ministerial associations, cooperatives, labor unions, or civic organizations.

Anyone may join a memorial society; there are no restrictions. Those who become members pay a one-time fee (rarely more than $20 for all members of a family and often $5 or $10 for an individual membership). To locate a memorial society, begin with the telephone directory. Look in the White Pages for "Memorial Society of" or "Funeral Society of"; in some areas a group's name may begin with the name of the locality. Some societies may be listed in the Yellow Pages under "Associations" or "Social Service Organizations." Should this prove fruitless, get in touch with the Continental Association (or its equivalent in Canada).** Lists of memorial

---

*In British Columbia, for instance, the funeral industry attempted to have introduced in the legislature a bill that would have given industry members control of the licensing apparatus and allowed them to set industry standards (which could have included, for example, compulsory embalming and cosmetology). Members of the Memorial Society of British Columbia protested so strenuously that the bill died before it was born. "Never in my many years in the legislature," said one veteran member, "have I received such a deluge of mail on one subject."

**A list of memorial societies in both countries is included in Ernest Morgan's *A Manual of Death Education and Simple Burial* (8th ed., 1977, The Celo Press, Burnsville, N.C. 28714, $2).

societies in the United States and Canada are available from both groups. Write to the Continental Association of Funeral and Memorial Societies at 1828 L Street, N.W., Washington, D.C. 20036; its telephone number is (202) 293-4821. Write to the Memorial Society Association of Canada at Box 96, Weston, Ontario M9N 3M6; its telephone number is (604) 688-6256.

The societies stress simplicity, dignity, and economy, and the right of individuals to decide the disposition of their own bodies.* All provide literature about alternatives to high-cost conventional funerals, including cremation and bequeathal of the body or body organs to medical science, and other pertinent information relating to death arrangements. They usually know which medical schools in the area need bodies and what organ transplant programs exist in community medical centers. Information that memorial societies collect is often made available to nonmembers, too, who need help in arranging the disposition of a body.

Memorial societies see their prime mission as educational: to encourage open discussion of funeral arrangements in advance of need. The societies urge people with families to discuss their wishes about disposition and services with all family members. This, they say, helps people to face the reality and inevitability of death. It may also help survivors to be better prepared for the distress and grief they will experience when death occurs.

George S. Richardson, M.D., a physician at Massachusetts General Hospital in Boston, expressed this thought in 1973, when he was president of the New England Memorial Society. The true goal of memorial societies, he said, is not a "specific price attached to a set of funeral services, but a mature decision by every person, every family, about what constitutes a truly meaningful funeral. Memorial societies provide the basic knowledge about the laws and ethics involved."

The Three Types of Memorial Societies

When a member dies, a memorial society itself does not carry out the funeral arrangements; that is up to survivors. Nor does the society prescribe or recommend specific arrangements for disposition when people join. What a society does do to assist members will depend largely on which type of memorial society it is. A contract society operates under a written agreement with at least one local mortician. A cooperating society has working arrangements—but no formal contract—with at least one mortician. An advisory society has neither contract nor verbal agreement; it serves primarily

---

*There can never be an absolute guarantee, however, that a member's instructions will be carried out. In almost all cases, survivors' wishes for disposition take precedence over the decedent's expressed desires (even if they were stated in writing while the decedent was alive). As a result, survivors may choose additional goods and services or an undertaker may persuade survivors to choose a more expensive funeral and burial.

as an information center, doing what it can to educate its members and the public at large about alternatives to high-cost funerals.

Contract Society. These groups have formal agreements with local undertakers to provide society members with prearranged services at less than regular costs. Because of the likelihood that the membership will turn to them in time of need, contract undertakers are, in effect, guaranteed sufficient volume to warrant their setting lower prices for society members. (The undertakers continue, in many cases, to conduct their regular funeral business at their normal prices.) Here is how one contract undertaker expressed his intentions in a letter to the Maryland Suburban Memorial Society:

> It has always been our desire to cooperate in every way with the Memorial Societies. We realize that your purpose is to inform all your members prior to death whom to call to be assured of their desires at a specific cost. . . .
>
> Before quoting our charges, I would like to emphasize the point that we will do what we say at the cost we quote. It is not our intention to influence, persuade or suggest changes in the minds of your members who want only cremation at the least possible cost. Nor do we want to insist on services, caskets, embalming and the like. We will expedite the wishes and desires of your members without hesitation or delay.

In contract societies, the new member is given a set of forms and literature that describes the types and prices of services available, names of the contract undertakers, and information about body and organ donation programs. After reviewing the material provided by the memorial society, the new member selects a specific plan and fills out the necessary forms. With a family membership, each adult fills out a separate form. Minor dependent children are also usually covered by the family membership.

Normally, three or four copies of each form are required, one for the member's records, one for the memorial society's files, one to be sent to the undertaker, and one for the clergy, if desired. The form with instructions should be kept with important papers (but not in a safety deposit box, which may not be readily accessible to survivors when death occurs). Most memorial societies issue identification cards for members to carry with them; the name and address of the contract undertaker should be on the card. Many memorial societies include space on the membership form for biographical data that can be used for an obituary. This ensures that the information given to newspapers is accurate and spares survivors additional stress and inconvenience at a difficult time.

Contract undertakers usually keep a separate file for the forms of memorial society members and know exactly what is to be provided when notified by survivors that a member has died. Memorial societies generally believe that survivors can expect fair treatment from a contract undertaker. If disputes arise, the societies try to mediate.

Memorial society contracts with undertakers generally offer at least two basic plans, one for direct cremation and another for direct burial. (Most groups urge that direct disposition be followed by a memorial service held a few days or weeks later.) Many contract societies have available an additional number of plans at set prices—often including a conventional funeral with viewing—and arrange with undertakers to offer extra items or services at special prices.

Total costs for either of the two basic plans rarely exceed $500, and some societies have been able to obtain much lower prices. Costs vary not only from area to area, but also from year to year, generally depending on economic conditions. Members of a contract memorial society, according to estimates made by the Continental Association, can typically save 50 percent in funeral costs, no matter what type of arrangements they make.

PMA's current contract with the Bleitz Funeral Home covers three plans: direct cremation for $192, direct burial for $275 (exclusive of cemetery costs), and "burial with service" for $417. The PMA brochure describes burial with service as including, among other things, "minimum cloth-covered casket, plus any of the following services required or requested: embalming, dressing of body, cosmetology, viewing, use of funeral home slumber room and/or chapel, transportation of body to and from local church for rosary or funeral service."

The Minnesota Memorial Society offers members four basic plans. Direct cremation for $300 and direct burial for $350 (exclusive of cemetery costs) include use of a funeral chapel, if desired, for a memorial service following disposition. For $450 a member may select direct cremation preceded by a church or funeral chapel service with the body present in a closed casket "of simple dignity." A similar option is available for direct burial (for $370, exclusive of cemetery costs). The Rochester (New York) Memorial Society distributes literature comparing the total cost of a conventional funeral and burial ($2,235)* with 1977 Rochester area costs of direct burial ($1,105, including $735 for cemetery expenses), direct cremation ($480, plus an additional $355 if interment of ashes and a marker are selected), and bequeathal of body (the standard $60 for newspaper notices and an additional $60 for clergy, sexton, and flowers).

Cooperating Society. A memorial society without a formal contract with a mortician may still be able to assist members with funeral arrangements. Such a society has an understanding or verbal agreement with at least one local funeral home. In that way, it might save survivors the task of searching for moderate-cost facilities when they are under pressure of time and so help ease the strain of making funeral arrangements.

---

*The Rochester Memorial Society gives the following breakdown for the costs of a conventional funeral and burial:

For example, the Greater Kansas City Memorial Society (300 to 400 members) has had a long-standing relationship with a cooperating mortician who offers direct cremation ($325 to society members) and direct burial ($425, exclusive of cemetery costs). Conventional funerals are also available rial society considers the arrangement to be mutually beneficial. at special low rates. Prices have remained stable since 1975, and the memo-

In Gainesville, Florida, the Memorial Society of Alachua County offers its 700 members a choice of two cooperating funeral homes. According to the society president, the undertakers' rates for the six types of funeral arrangements offered are "substantially lower" than those of competitors. The society, which is growing at the rate of 150 members a year, enables its membership to "save $500 to $1,000 on each funeral."

On the other hand, the Blackhawk Memorial Society in Davenport, Iowa, reports that its special relationship with a local mortician has deteriorated to the point that it no longer refers members to his funeral home. The reluctance of the cooperating undertaker to continue the arrangement with the society appears to be caused by pressure from other morticians, the former president of the society told Consumers Union. Blackhawk, thus far, has been unable to work out a new relationship with any undertaker in the area. But Blackhawk is still able to serve members as an advisory society.

Advisory Society. Some societies serve only in an advisory capacity, although it is rarely their wish to so limit their activities. Usually it is the failure to find a contract or cooperating undertaker that compels a society to act primarily as an information center. Frequently, morticians who agree

Funeral director (from 1975 NFDA figures for average adult complete funeral)		
Coffin	$600	
Services	385	
Facilities and hearse	300	
Total		$1,285
Miscellaneous (based on 1977 Rochester area costs)		
Newspaper notices	$ 60	
Clothing	25	
Limousine	50	
Motorcycle escort	30	
Clergy and flowers	50	
Total		$ 215
Cemetery (based on 1977 Rochester area costs)		
Single plot	$150	
Vault and setting	250	
Interment (opening and closing the grave)	150	
Flat marker	185	
Total		$ 735
Grand total		$2,235

to cooperate are subjected to pressure and ostracism from other morticians and on occasion even to disciplinary measures from the state board of funeral directors. In Massachusetts, for example, the name of an undertaker —one of seven in the state willing to work with memorial societies—was disclosed on a television program. According to the FTC, the state board then "coerced" all seven to sever their ties with the societies.

In general, resistance by undertakers to memorial societies has diminished somewhat in both the United States and Canada, but opposition is still the rule,* particularly in the South and Southwest. In some cases, resistance appears to be sanctioned by state action. In New Hampshire, for instance, undertakers have no choice about possible affiliation with memorial societies since state law prohibits contracts between morticians and groups or individuals. And in Michigan, memorial societies for many years have been unable to obtain contracts because of legal restrictions.

In a January/February 1974 article on memorial societies in *Consumer News & Views*, a newsletter published by the Michigan Consumers Council, the president of the Lansing Area Memorial Planning Society wrote:

> Michigan statute imposes a severe limitation upon those memorial societies operating in Michigan in that it prohibits contracts between groups of people and funeral establishments for funerals at less than the same rate charged everyone else. While this provision has been declared unconstitutional as an unfair restraint of trade by Attorney General Kelley, that ruling is binding only upon state agencies and has not been accepted by the Michigan Funeral Directors Association, nor has it yet been tested in court.
>
> Michigan memorial societies currently are seeking legislative removal of this prohibition not only for the benefit of our own members but for the public as well, for we believe that the competition which would then be encouraged by contracts for our members would lower funeral costs as a whole. Obviously the funeral industry agrees and this undoubtedly explains their strong opposition to this vital consumer reform.

---

*In *The Cost of Dying*, Raymond Arvio notes that it is surprising that undertakers ever cooperate with memorial societies. "They sense, correctly," he says, "that the burden of criticism they have received has emanated from memorial societies and that most of the dissent from the traditional American funerals rests among memorial society members." Why, then, do some morticians cooperate? Arvio asks. There are a number of reasons. First, a bad public image would result if all undertakers refused to cooperate with funeral "reformers." Therefore, in order to placate critics and also to procure extra business, a small percentage cooperate. In addition, some morticians, particularly those just starting out, need the business. The experience and the good will they receive from memorial societies are valuable to them, and help them to establish a reputation. Even established funeral homes benefit, since the services provided to memorial society members fill in the time between regular funerals and help to cover the overhead costs of mortuaries, whose facilities must be maintained whether or not there are funerals scheduled. Then, too, says Arvio, some undertakers are "high-minded and ethical persons who welcome an opportunity to break from the past and the reputations of their colleagues." A "handful" of such morticians actively support the work of memorial societies, emphasizing low-cost services and preplanning.

A rebuttal by the president of the Michigan Funeral Directors Association appeared in *Consumer News & Views* later in the year. Pointing out that the average funeral home in Michigan has been in business for forty-seven years—a fact that "implies some small degree of acceptance of [the] community"—the undertaker noted that "from time to time there surfaces a movement to change funeral service, as we know and understand it, to a simple disposal process. . . . Although the current movement tends to act under the banner of consumerism, the monotonous litany it chants remains pretty much unchanged down through the years." Nonetheless, the undertaker said, memorial societies can be a force for good "because they tend to remind funeral service as a profession that it must continue to police its own ranks, that in any profession there is a segment which performs at less than a professional level, and this is also true of the medical and legal professions, for example, and, for that matter, the ministry."

Some Common Themes

Memorial Services. The value of memorial meetings and services as an important part of life-affirming experiences is a recurring theme in the literature of many memorial societies. Ernest Morgan, in *A Manual of Death Education and Simple Burial*, notes that there can be many ways to conduct a memorial gathering:

> Programs can be extremely varied. A talk, a prayer, music and possibly a song reflect the more traditional procedure. Most ministers are experienced in this. Another procedure, more secular in nature, is to schedule a series of short talks by friends and relatives of the deceased, again with music included. Still a third arrangement, as commonly practiced by Friends, is a variation of Quaker worship. A period of music is followed by a few opening remarks stating the purpose of the occasion and inviting the attenders to speak as they wish. These remarks are followed by silence, interspersed with the testimony of family and friends as they feel moved to speak. Often there is song. The exact length of the meeting is not determined ahead of time.

No matter what format the meeting takes—the three types described by Morgan are open to many variations—memorial societies strongly encourage survivors to include some kind of service as part of the funeral arrangements. The service need not be planned for the same day or even week or month as the actual disposition of the remains.

Low Budgets. No payment for the expenses of disposition is ever made to a memorial society; those costs are paid directly to the undertaker at time of death. The work of memorial societies is supported by the one-time membership fee, which is barely enough to pay for mailing costs, office expenses, and educational activities. A few societies receive bequests and other financial gifts. But it is largely the unpaid work of members and volunteers that makes it possible for the societies to function and to survive financially.

There are no annual dues, and the length of an average membership is thirty years. To compensate for the cost of carrying members over many years, some societies have introduced a "records charge," usually $10, collected at time of death. It is included in the undertaker's bill and then remitted to the society. Originated by the PMA, the records charge is listed as part of each PMA funeral plan. According to Friend Deahl, the PMA considers the records charge as payable only when and if members actually make use of the arrangements worked out on their behalf by the memorial society.

Members themselves ordinarily do all the work of the organization, answering mail and phones, and maintaining records. Only a few of the larger societies have part- or full-time paid office workers. Sometimes, in the case of societies affiliated with churches, the church staff provides assistance. Officers and committees are elected from the membership every year or two, and all members are encouraged to take an active part in the society's programs.

Reciprocity. Reciprocal agreements among memorial societies are the usual practice in the United States and Canada. If a member dies while on a visit to another community, and survivors wish disposition to be arranged there, they can get in touch with the nearest memorial society in the area. If a member moves permanently to another community—one with a functioning memorial society—membership can be transferred to the new society at little or no cost. A member who spends equal time in two communities should consider joining a society in each area.

Even if there were no nearby memorial society to consult, the local society of a traveling member would assist the member or survivors with information about possible arrangements in the new locality or with advice about transportation home—for instance, would a designated medical school still accept delivery of a body from out of town?—and similar matters.

The Continental Association

Many memorial societies are offsprings of a church, a cooperative, or some other larger organization, but in some cases concerned friends and neighbors, sometimes as few as three people, have come together to organize a memorial society. For such groups, the Continental Association proves an invaluable information resource. Its Washington office will answer letters of inquiry and provide a free one-page flyer, "How to Organize a Memorial-Funeral Society."

The Continental Association publishes *Handbook for Memorial Societies,* which gives detailed instructions about how to organize and conduct the business of a memorial society (it costs $3.50). The *Handbook* contains information about negotiations with undertakers, financial arrangements, tax regulations, annual meetings, publicity, and so on. Especially important, according to Ernest Morgan, is the fact that the *Handbook* "sets forth organizational guidelines for use by new societies in writing their constitutions and by-laws. Most of these guidelines are merely suggested but a few basic ones are mandatory to membership in the Association."

The Continental Association works closely with government agencies on funeral matters. It is involved in legislation at the national level. During recent years, it has worked against passage of bills introduced in Congress that would increase veterans' burial allowances to $750 and provide a $2,500 income tax exemption for funeral expenses. The association believes that the higher the allowances and exemptions set for death costs, the more undertakers will charge for funerals.

Continental mails a bimonthly *Bulletin* to trustees and directors of member societies. In addition, it makes available to societies a model contract as a guide to negotiating with undertakers; the *Morticians Directory*, which lists the undertakers who work with memorial societies; Ernest Morgan's "Putting My House in Order," a form to help people to make plans and organize their affairs and thus lighten the burden of survivors; uniform donor cards and information about body and organ donations; a listing of educational films on death-related subjects; and two bibliographies ($1 each postpaid), *Bibliography of Funeral Reform* and *Bibliography of Death Education*.

Largely as a result of its activities, more and more new societies are being formed. Inquiries to Continental about organizing a new group average about fifteen a month. (There were twenty inquiries in all of 1969.)

The Continental Association and the Memorial Society Association of Canada both operate on budgets even smaller than those of some local memorial societies. All the work of the Canadian group is done by volunteers. Continental receives a maximum of $1 from each membership fee collected by a local group. Funds are used for the one paid employee who serves Continental as lobbyist, public relations director, editor, information director, typist, and file clerk. Whenever an article about memorial societies appears in a national magazine, it brings in thousands of inquiries about how to get in touch with a local society. Each inquiry receives a reasonably prompt reply.

The members of Continental's board of directors, elected annually, are not paid. Many of them pay part or all of their own expenses to travel to meetings. They turn over their speaking fees to Continental and plan their trips and vacations so that they can meet with local groups. From time to time small bequests are received and, on occasion, financial aid in time of emergency comes from people who believe in Continental's work. But finances are always precarious.

Memorial Societies and Direct Disposition

Nonprofit memorial societies have been on the funeral scene a lot longer than the profit-making direct disposition firms (see Chapter 16). How do memorial societies regard the "direct" firms? Do they look upon them as competition? Or do they regard them as allies in helping lower funeral costs? In general, Consumers Union found, memorial societies view these businesses favorably. However, some memorial society members point out that a number of the "direct" businesses tend to capitalize on the good will and reputations created by memorial societies. By calling themselves "societies" and charging a membership fee, critics say, the new firms deliberately create confusion among consumers about the firms' commercial status. As long as the "direct" businesses make it clear that they are profit-making operations and not cooperative volunteer groups, memorial societies in general accept them.

"We would welcome such a firm in our community," said the secretary of The Memorial Association of Central New Mexico in Albuquerque, "because a number of our members are interested in as low cost cremation as possible. Such a firm would not be in competition with our Association but, instead, would be another service we could offer our members." The secretary of the Memorial Society of Georgia said the Atlanta organization would also welcome a direct disposition firm and believed it would represent serious competition to conventional funeral establishments, which at present does not exist.

The executive secretary of The Memorial Society of Essex in Montclair, New Jersey, noted that there is a need for direct disposition firms in the large cities of Newark and Jersey City and that such an operation could not be considered as competing with the memorial society, "since we are nonprofit and exist only to provide a liaison for those who wish their remains taken care of in a simple, dignified and reasonably priced way." "Our attitude is 'more power to them,'" wrote the secretary of the Spokane Memorial Association, "but we must keep our memorial associations out there competing with them to 'keep them in line.' We feel that the principal function of a co-op is to serve as a 'pace setter,' but not to monopolize a business." And the president of the Memorial Society of Greater Philadelphia noted: "If low-cost funeral homes appear, and provide their services with dignity, we would be pleased, and if the idea became widespread we would be even more pleased, for then we might be able to close up shop and direct our volunteer effort elsewhere."

Memorial Societies and Minority Groups

As Ernest Morgan points out, "paradoxically, the people who join memorial societies are, in general, not the ones who need them most." The Continental Association and many local societies recognize their failure to attract in large numbers the poorer members of minority groups and the elderly—the chief victims of funeral exploitation. Some efforts have been made to reach minorities, but progress has been slow. In Washington, D.C., there are black contract undertakers, as there are in some areas of the South. The Los Angeles Memorial Society has distributed Spanish versions of its literature.

The desire to enroll minority members can sometimes lead memorial societies to temper certain aspects of their traditional philosophy—for example, the opposition to funerals with open caskets and viewing. Ernest Morgan points to the potential conflict between differing cultural values:

> It is not enough to have open membership; we already do. We must understand the needs, problems and feelings of people of various economic, ethnic, and religious backgrounds and meet these needs in terms of *their* feelings, not in terms of the desires of those who organized the society.
>
> In practice, this may mean that members not be required to accept the concept of simplicity, but be helped to get the kind of services they want at costs they can afford.

Friend Deahl, of the PMA, agrees that the memorial society movement has not been able "to satisfactorily reach the low-income, impoverished classes in our society." But, he says, "We'll keep trying." The PMA issued an innovative brochure aimed primarily at Hispanic people in the Seattle area. Designed to be used alongside its standard brochure, the new material, entitled "Catholics: Simple Funerals and People's Memorial Association," has been distributed by the PMA to dioceses in the western part of Washington.

The great majority of memorial society members, it is true, choose cremation or the donation of their bodies to medical science and prefer memorial meetings to conventional funeral services. But it is also true that prospective members of a memorial society need not adopt any particular philosophy or point of view. The aim of the societies is for members to be able to choose their own kind of service and at moderate cost. Because of personal preference or for religious reasons, some members of memorial societies choose conventional funerals with any number of variations and embellishments.

Memorial societies are pragmatic, realistic, consumer-oriented organizations that usually help their members to save money. They also seek to lower funeral costs for everyone in the community and to heighten consumer awareness of shoddy practices. For many members, memorial societies also help foster a healthy awareness and acceptance of the inevitability of death.

C. Murray Parkes, M.D., a distinguished British psychiatrist who is also the author of a number of works on death, in an address to the fourth annual meeting of the Continental Association in 1966, spoke of the fear that most people have of discussing death.* If people could only talk about it, he said—both their own death and that of those close to them—they might better be able to cope with distressing emotions when death occurs. Memorial societies, he said, "provide an atmosphere in which this becomes possible, to overcome the barriers to communication, to make it possible to talk about the future."

---

*Parkes, at the time of his address, was interim project director of a study on bereavement being conducted at Harvard Medical School.

19
Preneed Plans

Some people look ahead and consider making arrangements in advance to provide funds for their funeral. Those who choose to arrange for low-cost disposition through a memorial society or to donate their body to medical science will not have much financial planning to do—costs should be minimal. Those who wish to have a conventional funeral or to leave the choice to survivors may have larger financial concerns. Some people set money aside in a savings account, trust fund, or credit union account to cover funeral expenses. Some plan to have their life insurance cover funeral expenses; some buy a separate policy.

Some people prepay or prefinance funeral or burial merchandise and services through a preneed plan.* Here a buyer selects goods and services and signs a contract to pay for them in advance of need, usually on an installment basis. Preneed plans can be bought either through a preneed sales firm set up for the express purpose of merchandising such plans, or direct from a funeral home or cemetery (see page 145 for a discussion of preneed cemetery sales).

A preneed sales firm does not actually provide funeral goods and services. It serves as a sales agent for undertakers and cemeteries, seeking out and signing up preneed business for them. Typically, such an organization will advertise extensively and employ a sales staff to solicit prospective buyers, often door-to-door.

With a "flexible" preneed plan, sold directly by a funeral home or a cemetery (and by some preneed sales firms), a buyer selects goods and services and arranges to pay what they would cost if provided at the time the contract is signed. Of course, by the time the buyer dies, costs will probably have risen. So, whether there will be enough money in the plan at death to

---

*Some undertakers and some state laws refer to preneed plans as prearrangements. The term prearrangement is used here to mean the preplanning of goods and servicces. The term preneed is reserved for plans that are either prepaid or prefinanced.

cover the goods and services selected will depend on what happens to the money paid into the plan.

In most states, all money paid under a preneed plan must be deposited in a savings account or trust fund. (See Appendix 3 for information on preneed laws.) Some states require that only a percentage be deposited—for example, 50 percent in Louisiana and Mississippi, 75 percent in Pennsylvania, Utah, and Nevada, 80 percent in Missouri and Wyoming—and the remaining money may be kept by the seller, to cover administrative or sales commission costs.

Laws governing what happens to the interest on a buyer's deposited payments also vary widely. In most states, the interest that accrues remains in the fund; the practice seems to be that the accruing interest will go to offset the effects of inflation on the cost of the selected goods and services during the years until death occurs. In some states the interest goes to the seller.

Even where laws require that all payments be deposited and that all interest remain in the fund, there are no guarantees that a "flexible" preneed plan will contain enough money at need to cover the costs if prices increase appreciably.* It is therefore possible that even with a preneed plan, survivors will have to pay additional money—or they may be able to arrange for lower-priced goods or services to be provided.

Not usually available through undertakers and cemeteries are the "fixed-price" plans sold by some sales firms. While specific terms may vary, "fixed-price" plans generally guarantee that once payment is made in full, the goods and services selected will be provided at need without additional cost, despite any price increases in the interim. Some preneed sales firms claim their "fixed-price" plans provide funeral or burial services at discount prices.

Legal Problems with Preneed Plans

A number of investigations and inquiries into the sale of preneed contracts have revealed both a lack of understanding about the plans on the part of buyers and an absence of strict regulatory control of the sellers on both state and federal levels. In 1964, the Senate Subcommittee on Frauds and Misrepresentations Affecting the Elderly devoted part of its hearings to witnesses' testimony about funeral preneed schemes. The hearings revealed widespread abuse in the promotion of prefinanced funeral plans, affecting older purchasers in particular.

Laws governing the sale of preneed plans are intended as safeguards,

---

*On the other hand, it is possible that there will be more than enough, and in such cases the excess should go to the buyer's estate or to survivors. Some state laws stipulate that this be done.

but even in those states where regulatory agencies exist, there is generally inadequate enforcement of the preneed laws. Inevitably, where there is a lack of enforcement, the unscrupulous move in. A number of witnesses testified at the 1964 Senate hearings on the business dealings of dishonest promoters of funeral preneed plans. The special assistant attorney general of New Mexico was especially concerned about "promotive entrepreneurs from outside the funeral profession . . . who prey upon, or seek advantage from, elderly persons seeking security concerning their last rites on this earth." He described the case of an out-of-state group that set up a corporation in New Mexico, where the preneed laws were more lenient than in Colorado where the group had its headquarters. The company's door-to-door sales representatives used high-pressure tactics to get potential buyers —usually those in the sixty-to-seventy age group—to sign contracts for preneed funeral plans. The purchasers believed that complete funeral services were included in the plans. Yet the prepaid contract sold by the corporation for $637.50 provided only a coffin, which the president and chief stockholder admitted cost only $96.50. The assistant attorney general told the Senate committee: "Even if our elderly citizens believed they purchased merely caskets and not professional services, we were astounded at the margin of profit claimed by the vending group at the expense of elderly consumers, many of whom are on limited retirement incomes."

Four years after the Senate hearings, in 1968, the *St. Louis Post-Dispatch* reported another legal problem connected with preneed sales: "Lawyers for two preneed firms admitted in Kansas City Circuit Court that the firms had collected money for funeral contracts but failed to put enough of it into trust."* According to the 1977 summary of findings on the FTC proposed rule by the FTC's presiding officer, some sellers of preneed failed to deposit *any* of a buyer's payments into a trust or savings account.

Hugh Bernard, in *The Law of Death*, points to the potential for "fraud and wrongful use of funds while in the hands of promoters." He notes how complex and difficult this area of law and business is: "The acute and pressing regulatory problem," he says, "centers around the disposition of the funds paid in under such contracts during the period (which may be lengthy) before 'need' arises." The states have attempted to deal with this problem in a variety of ways. To administer their various preneed laws, the states use one or more of a number of agencies, such as the banking department, the insurance commission, the office of the attorney general, and the office of the comptroller. Some states have no such agency. Bernard suggests

---

*The article went on to note that "two men involved in the preneed companies . . . were released from state charges because they already faced federal prison terms for mail faud convictions in a previous business venture in Pennsylvania."

that since many preneed sales firms sell across state lines, federal regulation may be the only way to police preneed selling effectively.

The NFDA and NSM on Preneed Plans

For many years the National Funeral Directors Association opposed preneed plans on the grounds that such plans (1) involved soliciting by undertakers, which is contrary to professional ethics and (2) ignored the wishes of survivors. (The official policy of the association, however, stated that when an individual is interested in a prearranged funeral contract, "it is proper and appropriate for the [funeral] director to accede to the wishes of the client.")

A current NFDA leaflet, "The Pre-Arranging and Pre-Financing of Funerals," seems somewhat more accepting of preneed plans, especially when arranged through "careful counseling with an experienced funeral director." And, in a section headed "Those Who Survive Are Important," the leaflet urges the potential preneed buyer to involve survivors in the preneed planning:

> Before prescribing a definite kind of funeral or type of final disposition, it is always wise to consider and consult those survivors who will be most affected by the death. Grant them the opportunity to be active planning participants not just passive spectators.

The NFDA leaflet then goes on, however, to encourage the participation of survivors *at need*, and not preneed:

> This is prudent because when death comes it may have strong emotional impact upon the other members of the family. Permitting them to assist in making funeral and burial arrangements could serve as a healthy outlet for their grief and anxiety. Giving them the privilege of performing a last act of recognition, honor, and respect for the deceased will dramatize eloquently to all the reality that a life has been lived.
>
> On the other hand, if the rites or absence of them are set forth in a prearrangement agreement, survivors could be denied meeting the deep psychological and emotional needs at the time of death. Inappropriate arrangements could affect adversely the sensitivities and sensibilities of those who remain. Thus, it is important to remember while the funeral is *of* the person who has died, it is *for* those who survive.

Some critics maintain that the NFDA has disapproved of preneed contracts for another reason: When a specific sum has already been spent in advance under a preneed plan, they say, survivors tend not to spend as much for goods and services at need. Howard Raether denied this implication in an NFDA policy statement in 1963:

> Also important in the area of preneed planning, or the actual prearrangement and prefinancing of a funeral, is that such is suggested predicated on the premise that funerals arranged at the time of need are more costly and

may prove to be embarrassing and a burden on those who selected them. Those who maintain this allege people are emotionally unstable and have clouded minds when planning a funeral after death occurs.

The premise is false. Funerals are seldom selected by one person alone. There are others along if advice is necessary. Survivors are getting the kind of funerals they want and can afford. If they are not, then the entire funeral procedure should be revamped and those who have been extolling the philosophy of funeral service have not been telling the truth.

National Selected Morticians, on the other hand, has always favored funeral preneed plans. In a letter to the Senate Committee on the Aging, Wilber Krieger, of the NSM, stated in 1964:

> Honest preneed or prearrangement planning can and does serve a useful purpose to the elderly and the public at large. Funeral arrangements made in advance of death generally are unaccompanied by factors of stress which make arms-length dealing more difficult. The purchaser is able to give effect to his own preferences and to select with care the type of funeral service which meets his budgetary . . . requirements. . . .
>
> It is my belief that preneed or prearrangement planning, whether it is effected by will, contract or otherwise provides the public and particularly the elderly a greater measure of protection against the unethical funeral director or cemetery operator who exploits the bereaved. It is important, however, especially in the case of so-called preneed trusts, that there should be wholly adequate procedures to safeguard deposited funds. . . .

Preneed Plans, Pro and Con

Theoretically, there are certain advantages to preneed plans. First, buyers are arranging to pay in advance for their own funerals, thereby reducing the risk that survivors will have heavy funeral expenses at need. Second, there is the opportunity to comparison-shop among different plans and terms and to choose services most suitable to individual wishes and incomes. Third, because the transaction is not made by survivors at time of need, decisions can be made when buyers are not under severe emotional strain. Fourth, buyers have the opportunity to make known before death the type of funeral desired and may feel more secure that their wishes will be carried out because they have made the actual arrangements with an undertaker. Fifth, by prearranging and prepaying for their funeral, buyers may minimize distress and inconvenience for survivors.

In fact, however, few of these advantages necessarily hold true for preneed plans—and even where they do, a preneed plan may not be the best way to secure a given advantage. If, for example, a buyer dies before completing the payments on a preneed plan and does not have credit life insurance,* survivors will have to pay the amount outstanding—and it could be

---

*Should credit life insurance be made available as part of a preneed plan, consumers should be sure to compare the costs of the plan with and without the insurance cover-

sizable, depending on the goods and services selected and how much has already been paid on them.* Or survivors may be able to change the plan and select other, lower-cost goods and services but then another advantage of preneed plans—selecting one's own goods and services—is lost. In this connection, it should be noted that in almost every state, the right to choose the method of disposition, in most cases, remains with survivors.

The opportunity to purchase a preneed plan coolly and calmly is not guaranteed either. As the 1964 Senate hearings indicated, sales pressure may be applied by preneed salespeople. In 1968, the *St. Louis Post-Dispatch* informed its readers about the "funeral counselor" (i.e., the preneed sales representative, who is often paid on a commission basis, and who goes to people's homes to sell them preneed plans):

> He is the kind of salesman who doesn't tell you right away that he is a salesman. Rather, he comes to your house and tells you that he wants to present you with a free booklet that can be valuable to you—the sort of thing that every family needs.
>
> He shows you the booklet. It can have one of several titles. . . . One such booklet used by a preneed funeral sales firm is particularly personal. On its white cover the title is in black Spencerian writing: "My Wishes and Desires." . . .
>
> It doesn't matter particularly what the title is; the contents of such booklets are similar. And their use as come-on gifts in the sale of preneed, installment-payment funeral plans is a well-established routine.

The article went on to say that the "counselor" eventually discloses his identity and then proceeds to use tactics such as the "immediate purchase dividend" (a discount of $25 or so if the prospect accepts the offer right away). Or the "counselor" may offer a $200 check as a price discount; it is torn up if the buyer does not accept the offer then and there. In its 1973 planning memorandum the FTC observed: ". . . Prearranged funeral contracts are often sold door-to-door, with the same high-pressure tactics, deceptions, and non-delivery that attend many door-to-door sales schemes."

Whatever sales methods may be used, preneed sellers have been successful: According to the FTC presiding officer's 1977 summary of findings on the FTC proposed rule, 30 percent of prospective preneed purchasers actually sign contracts at the time they are visited by a salesperson.

Preneed contracts sold door-to-door by firms engaged in or affecting interstate commerce are regulated in at least one respect by a 1974 FTC

---

age. Prospective buyers of credit life should be aware that they may have to meet age and health requirements for insurability, but even those buyers who qualify may find the premiums prohibitively high.

*The likelihood of survivors having to meet additional expenses increases when less than 100 percent of payments is put into a trust fund or savings account and when the full interest does not remain with the account. With a "fixed-price" plan, of course, this should not happen once payments have been made in full.

trade regulation rule. This rule gives signers of a contract negotiated in their home a "cooling-off period" in which to change their mind. The rule allows purchasers of any goods and services costing more than $25 three business days to cancel the contract without penalty or fee. Buyers must be informed of this right by sellers both orally and in writing. The FTC rule also stipulates that buyers must be furnished with a *fully completed* receipt or copy of the contract at the time it is signed.

Some states have similar "cooling-off" statutes. Some preneed sales firms offer contracts allowing more than three days—some as long as thirty days. The easiest way for a prospective buyer to learn whether a particular preneed contract includes a "cooling-off" clause is to ask the seller to show it is in the contract. If the contract includes no such protection under the FTC rule or under state regulation, or if the sales firm itself does not provide an adequate "cooling-off" clause, then a buyer should consider another preneed plan.

Some Questions to Consider

The disadvantages and risks associated with preneed plans are so extensive that Consumers Union cannot recommend them at this time. Those who wish to select goods and services in advance and to minimize distress for survivors° may be able to do so by other, less risky means than with a preneed plan. Desired goods and services may be specified in instructions to survivors (see Appendix 1) or prearranged through membership in a memorial society. The necessary funds can be set aside in a savings account or made part of life insurance planning.°° Those who may still wish to purchase a preneed plan should shop around, and should consider several questions, including:

- Are the designated funeral home and—if one buys a plan from a preneed sales firm—the sales firm likely to be still in business at the time the buyer dies?
- If the buyer moves out of the area, what are the provisions for a refund or for services to be conducted at another funeral home or burial at another cemetery?
- What happens if the buyer wishes to cancel the contract for any reason? What are the provisions for a refund? Does the contract allow a switch to a lower-cost as well a higher-cost funeral?

°Conscientious survivors will, of course, check to be sure the goods and services delivered are actually those that were contracted for. But this should be less difficult than arranging for a funeral on an at-need basis.

°°Death benefits, such as the Social Security lump-sum death benefit (see Chapter 6), should be taken into account when planning for these funds. It should be noted that with a preneed plan, only a surviving spouse is eligible for the Social Security benefit.

• If payment is to be made in installments, is there a penalty if payments are not paid when due?
• If credit life insurance is available with a preneed plan, what is the premium? With plans that do not offer such insurance—or where the buyer does not buy it or does not qualify for it—what happens under the plan if the buyer dies before all payments have been made? Do survivors have a reasonable time, without penalty, to pay the balance? Do they have the option of choosing lower-cost goods and services?
• With a "fixed-price" contract, is the price guaranteed to be less than it would be if the goods and services were purchased at need? With a "flexible" contract, what percentage of payments will be put into a trust or savings account? What happens to the interest that accrues on the money?
• What items connected with final disposition does the preneed contract provide for? What items will survivors have to purchase?
• Are all goods and services specifically described in the contract? (Items such as a coffin are described generically because an undertaker cannot be sure a particular model will be manufactured at the time a buyer dies. However, such descriptions should be as specific and detailed as possible.)
• Is the contract in accordance with state laws (see Appendix 3)?

Because of the complexities of preneed laws and contracts, those who wish to buy such a plan would be wise to consult an attorney before signing anything. At the very least, buyers should familiarize themselves with their state's laws. (If there are no state laws governing preneed plans or if certain aspects are not covered, buyers can try to have the contract written so that their interests are protected.) Buyers should be sure that the contract accurately represents the transaction and should keep a copy of the contract signed by the seller, to be filed with their important papers for the benefit of survivors. Buyers should see that survivors who are likely to be responsible for carrying out the arrangements fully understand them. And those survivors who do not live with the buyer should have their own copy of the contract. Finally, buyers should ask the funeral home, cemetery, or preneed sales firm where the payments will be deposited, and check to be sure the money is being deposited in accordance with the law.

A Last Word

Two developments of the 1970s could influence the nature of the funeral marketplace for years to come. One is the Federal Trade Commission's proposed trade regulation rule concerning funeral industry practices, which will, in the commission's words, "effect vital changes in the funeral transaction" if adopted. The other is the increasing emphasis, encouraged by funeral trade associations, on the undertaker's role as a provider of "professional services" rather than a seller of merchandise. Those two developments represent opposing points of view, with widely differing economic implications for the future of the funeral industry. The FTC rule is aimed, among other things, at reducing the cost of a funeral; the insistence of the funeral industry on professional status for undertakers could contribute to increasing the cost.

By virtue of the services they provide, undertakers have long sought to identify themselves as professionals rather than as technicians and merchants. In recent years, the National Funeral Directors Association in particular has stressed the new direction for undertakers, "from preoccupation with death and the dead to a genuine concern for life and the living, from safeguarding the physical health of the survivors to safeguarding their mental and emotional health." More and more, undertakers are being urged to provide "counseling" to bereaved survivors, not only at the time of funeral arrangements but for months after the funeral as well. Counseling survivors, according to the NFDA's Howard Raether, is an ongoing process that does not end when the funeral is over.

What does counseling by undertakers involve? Vanderlyn Pine, a sociologist and an NFDA consultant, has been careful to emphasize that the undertaker does not practice therapy in the traditional psychotherapeutic sense. "The funeral service version of therapy," Pine has written, "consists of advice concerning funeral practices, the creation of a suitable atmosphere for bereavement, and the providing of counseling services aimed at helping the bereaved understand loss through death. Thus, it bears only a resemblance to traditional therapy."

In his 1975 work, *The Funeral Director and His Role As a Counselor,* Raether (with coauthor Robert Slater) described the essential steps to be followed in counseling survivors. Undertakers, he advised, should develop a method of "therapeutic procedure" that will help survivors cope with their grief. The basis of that procedure, he asserted, is "the funeral with the body present"—the conventional funeral. And from this basis the undertaker starts to build the "counseling relationship." Raether has pointed out that few people, even in the mental health field, have the special training necessary to deal with grief and bereavement. He believes that if undertakers could develop such counseling as a regular procedure, this could be "a most desirable service" of the funeral home. "We firmly believe," Raether wrote, "that it should be an integral part of funeral service today."

In discussing the objectives of post-funeral counseling, Raether wrote:

The funeral director counselor will make a periodic check . . . to determine how the family is doing both collectively and individually. It is our suggestion that the first such periodic check be made within forty-eight hours of final disposition, the second within ten days of the funeral, the third in approximately thirty days, and thereafter as frequently as is deemed necessary. Where there has been the donation of a body to medical science, a myriad of questions could be asked. The family or a member might even ask that the body be secured from the medical institution and the donation withdrawn.

The funeral director should not see himself as a trained counselor unless he has taken such training, but instead should serve as the interested resource person giving advice and counsel in those areas where he is expert and competent, serving as a listener and finally making referrals when such action is indicated. The most common referrals will be to a family pastor or doctor when they are available. By so doing, he will not only aid the family but also increase his status with the other caretaking professionals in his community.

Many survivors manage to work through their own grief without assistance; indeed, to seek help would not even occur to some of them. And yet, for a number of survivors, grief and bereavement can take a serious toll. Some may benefit from the assistance of family or friends, but often there is no one to whom to turn. Most physicians do not have the training—or the time—for "grief work." Most clergy, too, are not particularly active in "pastoral psychology." There are few mental health workers experienced in therapy for the bereaved, and there is a shortage of "outreach" programs devoted to grief counseling.

Granted the need for counselors and programs to help some survivors through their period of grief, can the undertaker effectively fill the void? Some mental health professionals believe that undertakers are equipped to do so. Others think undertakers lack the requisite education and training. For example, in twenty-three states and the District of Columbia, a person needs only a high school education and one year of mortuary science training to become a licensed undertaker or embalmer. But even if an undertaker has a limited education, that in itself may not prevent the undertaker from helping survivors with grief and bereavement. More significant may be how an undertaker chooses to counsel survivors who may not wish to have a conventional funeral. As Vanderlyn Pine wrote, "The funeral service version of therapy consists of advice concerning funeral practices, the creation of a suitable atmosphere for bereavement. . . ." That, for most undertakers, means the conventional funeral, with costly coffin, embalming, viewing, vault, and all the extras.

"The funeral industry rigidly promotes 'traditional' funerals," the FTC's presiding officer stated in his 1977 summary of findings on the FTC proposed rule. He went on: "This may not be conducive to the emotional well being of some survivors." (It may not be conducive, we would add, to the *financial* well-being of some survivors, either.) In questioning the industry's emphasis on the "traditional" funeral, the FTC presiding officer was not suggesting abandonment of conventional funeral practices. Nor does the FTC proposed rule seek to dictate how people should dispose of the dead. Rather, the proposed rule was designed "to provide the consumer with substantially more information on prices and choices, eliminate the devices used to obtain unfair leverage over the consumer, abolish the outright frauds and deceptions that have been structured into the industry, and free up the market so that the dealings between funeral director and customer will be more fair. . . ."

The industry sees it otherwise. The NFDA called the proposed rule "a veiled attempt . . . to reverse the philosophy of American funeral customs," an effort "to place a curtain between the funeral director and those he serves in a manner that would dilute effective counseling for bereaved people who seek and need such assistance." The president of one state funeral directors association said the rule focused on the marketing of the industry "as if it were a sterile test tube specimen. The result," he went on, "is an attempt to control human emotional response by regulation."

Basic Provisions of the FTC Proposed Rule

The rule would require funeral homes to furnish customers with:

• A fact sheet about legal requirements for embalming, coffins, and coffin enclosures
• An itemized list of prices for the services and merchandise offered for sale "with conspicuous disclosure of the consumer's right to select only the items desired"
• A coffin price list

- A memorandum, at the time funeral arrangements are made, that records the items selected and their respective prices

The rule would also require funeral homes that make use of institutional advertisements to include a notice that price information is available and the telephone number to call for this information.

The rule would *prohibit* undertakers from:

- routinely picking up or embalming corpses without permission from the family
- requiring those who choose direct cremation to purchase a coffin, and from refusing to make available inexpensive containers suitable for cremation
- profiting on cash-advance items—the obituary notices, cemetery charges, flowers, and the like—paid for by the undertaker and reimbursed by survivors
- misrepresenting the legal or public health necessity for or preservative utility of embalming, coffins, or burial vaults
- making untruthful and unsubstantiated claims of watertightness or airtightness of coffins and burial vaults
- bait-and-switch tactics
- disparaging a consumer's concern for price
- restricting or obstructing advertising or other disclosure of price information
- interfering with the offering of low-cost funerals, direct cremation services, or other alternative modes of disposition, preneed arrangements, and memorial society activities

Even before the FTC proposed rule was released to the public, the president of the New York State Funeral Directors Association exhorted his colleagues to "... fight every thoughtless act of intrusion by the legislature and by the consumer groups who have infiltrated it, by the private interest research groups ... in order to retain as much of our own autonomy as we can." He added: "I urge you to understand the situation. Take an accurate measurement of our opponents and prepare for the fight of our lives."

With the announcement of the proposed rule, the FTC stated that it expected "strong opposition" from "large numbers" of undertakers. Undertakers responded, as one FTC attorney noted in 1976, with "political lobbying, a huge war chest, delaying court battles and other obstructive techniques." The NFDA, in fact, hired a former FTC commissioner to help fight the proposed rule. (*The American Funeral Director* criticized this action, describing it as "a rather obvious ploy that, we suspect, did not brighten NFDA's dimmed image.")

The FTC had indicated its intent that the proposed rule should override contrary state or local laws. "Under the supremacy clause of the United

States Constitution," the FTC said, "the rule will become the supreme law of the land on the matter it covers and within the confines of the Commission's jurisdiction, pre-empting all repugnant state or local laws."

Faced with this threat to protective state and local laws, the NFDA and the National Selected Morticians petitioned the FTC to convert the proposed rule into voluntary guidelines for the industry. The guidelines would carry no penalties. The FTC denied the petition.

When hearings on the proposed rule were scheduled to be held in six cities, in order to obtain public participation in the FTC's rule-making process, the NFDA went to court. It sought a temporary restraining order and an injunction to bar the hearings, claiming, among other things, that the rule-making proceeding was outside the FTC's authority. The federal district court judge denied the NFDA's requests.

But the funeral industry was not entirely without support. The Subcommittee on Activities of Regulatory Agencies of the House Committee on Small Business heard testimony from industry and consumer representatives and held additional hearings to consider the whole matter of FTC jurisdiction over the funeral industry. In October 1976 the subcommittee issued a report sharply critical of the FTC, citing its "lack of concern" for "the problems of small business." The subcommittee declared that there is "no compelling need for federal regulation. . . . the interests of the public and small business will be better served if the funeral industry is regulated by the states."

Without question, if the FTC rule is implemented, the problems of checking some 22,500 funeral homes and processing consumer complaints around the country could be formidable. The FTC presiding officer stated in his 1977 summary of findings on the proposed rule that the individual states have a "substantial role to play in the enforcement of fair standards." He suggested that the states adopt laws or regulations similar to the FTC rule, to be enforced by state boards of funeral directors. To help ensure that state boards become sensitive to consumer needs, the FTC presiding officer urged that consumer and other representatives outside the funeral industry be included as state board members—"preferably a majority." "The continued domination of these boards by industry representatives," he said, "is the largest single deterrent to effective state consumer protection."

There is good reason to question whether state boards—no matter how constructed—would be fully effective in regulating the funeral industry in the foreseeable future. In 1973, the FTC planning memorandum called state regulation of the funeral industry "a myth"; more recently, the FTC presiding officer called it "execrable." The FTC planning memorandum pointed out that state boards seldom conduct investigative proceedings under already existing laws. "The state boards," the memorandum stated, "decide very few cases and disciplining of a funeral director is rare in the extreme, despite the fact that widespread abuses, unethical conduct, overcharging, misrepresentations and other questionable conduct have periodically been brought to light and have evoked a storm of consumer protest."

Of course, state laws and regulations should be made compatible with the terms of the FTC proposed rule. State boards should be charged with enforcing the new laws and regulations. Consumer representation—preferably a majority—should be assured on the state boards. But enforcement of the FTC rule should not have to await reform of the state boards. And reliance on ineffective state boards to enforce funeral industry regulations included in the rule could be worse than no rule at all. For consumers could be lulled into believing that the state boards were "watching out" for consumer interests. In fact, those boards have shown themselves to be almost exclusively interested in watching out for funeral industry interests. "In one or two states at any given time," the FTC presiding officer reported, "there is active consumer protection, but this tends to be short run and inconsistent."

Consumers Union believes that the FTC rule (with certain improvements) should be enforced at the federal level—at least until state and local laws and government agencies are changed to provide effective regulation. As we told the FTC in 1976 in our detailed comments on the proposed rule, FTC enforcement could be accomplished primarily through FTC regional offices. The commission has effectively used consumer protection specialists operating out of regional offices to enforce FTC statutes regulating consumer credit transactions within its jurisdiction. Similarly, consumer protection specialists could be used to police the funeral industry, conducting periodic unannounced spot checks on undertakers. Knowing they might be inspected at any time, undertakers would be encouraged to observe the provisions of the rule. The FTC would require funeral homes to present to all customers printed material covering relevant sections of the rule. Consumers would thus be better equipped to obtain fair treatment. The printed material could encourage them to complain—if they felt the need to do so— to the regional FTC office. It would then be up to the FTC to investigate and, if appropriate, to start proceedings against the alleged offender.

Implementation of the FTC rule, however, is far from certain. At this writing, the commission is about to begin consideration of whether to promulgate the rule. Whatever the commission decides, the decision is almost certain to be appealed to the courts—by the funeral industry or by public interest groups. The NFDA's chief counsel predicts that it will take until 1979 before any rule can "be effective for the consumer." A former chairman of the FTC observed that 1985 might be a more realistic date.

Where does this leave the consumer? There is the possibility that the funeral industry can muster sufficient support to ward off government regulation indefinitely. There is the likelihood that undertakers will continue to press for professional status as grief counselors—specialists in helping survivors to create a "suitable atmosphere for bereavement," while at the same time selling survivors the costly wares required for the conventional funeral. For the immediate future, then, the funeral marketplace will not be much improved.

But as people become more knowledgeable about options available for disposition after death, some funeral practices may gradually change. It is true that rituals as complex and established as funerals and burial are not readily abandoned; many people will continue to follow the customs that prevail in their families or communities. But even traditionalists may come to benefit, in terms of lowered cost, from greater understanding of the funeral marketplace. The memorial society movement is still small, but already it has helped to increase interest in low-cost cremation and low-cost burial. The development—spotty as it is—of direct cremation/direct burial firms seems to be an outgrowth of that interest. And donation to medical science is now more widely accepted.

Ultimately, it is up to the informed consumer to improve industry practices. As we said at the beginning of this book, even when appropriate governmental regulation exists, the consumer still must be informed. In the funeral marketplace, there is no better protection for the consumer than knowledge.

Appendixes

APPENDIX 1: Providing Helpful Information for Survivors

As a matter of law in almost every state, survivors generally need not be bound by a decedent's wishes concerning disposition—with the possible exception of donation of body or body organs. Most people, however, would want to take such wishes into account when making arrangements after death occurs. An effective way to make preferences known to those who will be responsible for planning disposition is a letter of instruction. In addition to describing the type of funeral desired (noting important papers concerning disposition and where they can be found), such a letter should include personal data and assist survivors with other information they may need during the period after death has occurred.

Once completed, the letter of instruction should not be placed in a safety deposit box where it might not be readily accessible immediately following death. Rather, it should be put where it can be easily located by survivors. The contents of the letter should be discussed with—and a copy given to—the family member, close relative, or trusted friend who has consented to take responsibility for arrangements after death. Other copies may be given to a physician, lawyer, or member of the clergy.

A letter of instruction should include some or all of the following:

Funeral Arrangements

(A member of a memorial society or owner of a preneed plan should give complete details, noting where relevant papers and documents are located. If there are no prearrangements, preferences, if any, should be indicated among the following choices, and in sufficient detail to be helpful to survivors.)

Burial, Cremation, or Bequeathal.
- For burial: cemetery plot or mausoleum entombment
- For cremation: urn burial, urn in niche, or scattering of remains
- For donation of body: recipient medical or dental school; include necessary forms
- For donation of body organs: recipient organization(s); include necessary forms

Conventional Funeral Service or Memorial Service.

- For conventional funeral service: type and price range of coffin; coffin to be open or closed
- For religious service: place to be held (church or denomination specified or funeral home, residence, or other)
- For nonreligious service: to be held at funeral home, residence, or elsewhere
- Service to be open for all, for relatives and friends, or for immediate family
- Details of service: person to conduct, speaker, music, flowers
- Charity to be recipient of memorial donations, if any

Personal Information

- Full name, home address (including county), home phone number
- Address and phone number of place of employment, if any
- Date and place of birth
- Citizenship
- Marital status with full name of spouse, if any; address of spouse
- Names and addresses of father and mother (including maiden name); indicate whether living or dead
- Names and addresses of children, if any

Other Helpful Information

- Name, address, and phone number of the person or persons who have consented (or are likely) to take responsibility for making arrangements after death
- List of persons to be notified when death occurs (with addresses and/or phone numbers)
- Location of will and name of executor(s)
- Location and number of safety deposit box, if any, with location of key and names of others with access to box
- Death benefits to which entitled
- Social Security number
- Service in armed forces (dates), if any, and Service Serial Number.
- For possible inclusion in obituary: other biographical information such as occupation, major employers, honors received, memberships in professional organizations

APPENDIX 2: Guidelines for Survivors

When death occurs, survivors will find their task much easier if the decedent has left a letter of instruction (see Appendix 1), even though they are not legally bound by such a letter. It will express the decedent's wishes, often specifying such details as the funeral home of choice and type of funeral service desired. If the decedent was a member of a memorial society, many of the difficult decisions required of survivors will have already been made. If the decedent was not a member of a memorial society and left no clear instructions, written or verbal, survivors will very likely have to select a funeral home and make other decisions with respect to disposition. Many details may have to be arranged in the period shortly after death. Relatives or friends may assist survivors with the tasks involved in planning disposition and arranging the affairs of the decedent.

Listed below are guidelines for some of the questions and problems that will arise. (Not all the items listed will apply in every instance, nor will they necessarily occur in the sequence given.)

Arrangements for Disposition

- If bequeathal of the body or donation of body parts is to be considered, review Chapter 17, pages 185–207.
- Select an undertaker to remove the body from the place of death. (Review Chapter 5, pages 49–55.)
- If the body must be transported from out of town, the undertaker chosen to make the arrangements should be the one in the locality where services are to be conducted. (Review "Out-of-Town Transportation," pages 118–120.)
- Decide on the type of disposition desired and the general form of the funeral. Review "The Decision about Embalming," pages 108–109, and decide whether there is to be viewing, which would necessitate embalming.
- Discuss costs with the undertaker. (Review Chapters 7, 8, and 9, pages 61–70.)
- Decide on the time and place of the funeral or memorial service, if any.
- If cremation is chosen, make the necessary arrangements with a crematory. (See "Guidelines in Arranging Cremation," pages 173–174.)
- If cremation is not chosen, decide on burial or entombment and select a

cemetery. (See "Guidelines for Choosing a Cemetery Plot or Crypt," pages 148–150.)
• Select a coffin, if one is needed. Consider what type of coffin enclosure, if any, is required. (See "Some Guidelines for Choosing a Coffin," pages 86–87, and "Guidelines for Selecting a Coffin Enclosure," page 130.)
• Decide on the inclusion or omission of flowers. (See "Flowers," pages 114–115.)
• Decide what, if any, other extras will be needed or wanted. (See "Lowering the Cost of Extra Items," pages 120–122.)
• If pallbearers are desired, notify the people chosen. (If there are those who would be chosen because of their relationship to the decedent but who cannot serve for reasons of health or age, designate them as honorary pallbearers.)
• If flowers are to be included, decide what to do wtih them after the funeral. (Many hospitals and nursing homes will accept them.)

Private and Public Notification of Death

• Notify the following persons as promptly as possible: the immediate family, very close friends, immediate supervisor at work (if the decedent was employed), lawyer, and member of the clergy, if desired.
• Prepare an obituary that can be given to the local newspaper by phone and sent to other newspapers in localities where the decedent may have lived or worked. (An undertaker may assist with preparation of the obituary. Some newspapers may also help. A member of a memorial society may have information already prepared as part of the memorial society's records.) The following material should be included in an obituary: age, cause of death, place of birth, colleges attended and degrees received, occupation and major organizations where employed, honors received, military service (if any), membership in professional organizations, immediate survivors, and time and place of funeral or memorial service.
• If a paid notice is to be inserted in the newspaper, the notice should follow the form of similar notices and be phoned to the newspaper. (An undertaker may assist with the preparation and placing of the paid notice.) If flowers are to be omitted, indicate whether there is a charity to which memorial contributions may be made.
• Make a list of other people to be notified: friends, business associates, distant relatives, and the like. Decide whether they are to be notified by phone, telegram, personal letter, or printed announcement. If an announcement is chosen, prepare the wording of the announcement and arrange to have it printed. (An undertaker may assist with the arrangements.)
• Set up a system for acknowledgment of cards, letters, and phone calls received. Decide whether there should be individual responses or a printed

card. If a card is chosen, prepare the wording of the card, and arrange to have it printed. (An undertaker may assist with the arrangements.)

Household Arrangements

• If the decedent lived alone, make sure the premises are secure (remove small valuables). Arrange for mail to be forwarded. Stop delivery of newspapers, if necessary. If utility services are no longer needed, notify the companies involved. If the premises were rented, inform the landlord of the death.

• Designate those who will accept phone inquiries and messages. (Keep a list of those who call to express sympathy.)

• If the immediate family plans to receive visitors, arrange for some other family members or friends to help with housekeeping chores (preparing meals, cleaning, and so forth).

• If there are young children in the family, arrange for other family members or friends to care for the children during the days immediately following death.

• If out-of-town family members or friends are expected, decide where they can be comfortably housed.

Business and Financial Arrangements

• If the decedent did not have an attorney, select one to handle the will and to notify the executor(s).

• Assemble all necessary papers to apply for statutory death benefits to which the decedent and survivors are entitled. (Review Chapter 6, pages 56–60.)

• Review all insurance policies held by the decedent. Arrange for immediate cancellation of those policies that are no longer applicable. Apply for payment of insurance policies, such as life insurance and accident insurance.

• Begin assembling information on the assets and liabilities of the decedent, particularly on any debts and installment purchases that carry a penalty if payment is not made. In some cases, mortgage or credit life insurance will cancel such debts.

• If there is insufficient cash to pay for immediate expenses, discuss with the decedent's lawyer the best way to raise the necessary money. (Access to bank accounts and safety deposit boxes may not be possible immediately after death.)

APPENDIX 3: Preneed Laws

In 1977 Consumers Union requested the fifty states, the District of Columbia, and the Commonwealth of Puerto Rico to provide information about their laws concerning the regulation of preneed plans and of trust funds or savings accounts established for such plans. The following table is based on the responses received. Not surprisingly, the laws vary widely in content and in style. Some are explicit and clear; others are ambiguous.

The table is divided into two parts, one covering preneed funeral plans, one covering preneed burial plans. For each are listed the department or agency, if any, that regulates preneed plans; the percentage of a preneed buyer's payments that must be deposited in either a trust fund or savings account; and whether the law specifies that the interest that accrues on the deposited money remains in the fund or account.

Although many laws require interest to remain in funeral plan or burial plan trust funds or savings accounts, the treatment of the interest varies radically. For example, some laws permit a specified portion of the interest to be withdrawn by a seller for administrative and other expenses. Some laws require interest to be refunded to the consumer in case of cancellation of the contract prior to need but let the seller retain the interest if the contract services are actually used. Some laws require the seller to refund to the estate any accrued interest that is not actually needed to pay the cost of goods and services under the contract, whereas other laws require that the interest goes to a seller, or are silent. It should be noted that some laws may permit a seller to insert a contract provision by which the consumer waives the right to receive the interest—a right that the law otherwise requires.

The laws have had to be simplified in order to be presented in this form. Referring to this table cannot take the place of reading the laws or consulting an attorney. But the table may be useful as a basic guideline for those who are thinking about purchasing a preneed plan.

FUNERAL PLANS / BURIAL PLANS

State	Funeral Plans — Department or Agency	Percent to trust	Interest	Burial Plans — Department or Agency	Percent to trust	Interest
ALABAMA1	No regulation			State Banking Department	Varies, 40–72	No
ALASKA	No regulation			No regulation		
ARIZONA	Attorney General 2	100	No	No regulation3		
ARKANSAS	Insurance Department; Bank Department, Securities Division; Burial Association Board	100	4	Insurance Department; Bank Department, Securities Division; Burial Association Board; Cemetery Board	100	4
CALIFORNIA	Board of Funeral Directors & Embalmers of Department of Consumer Affairs	100	Yes	Board of Funeral Directors & Embalmers (part) and State Cemetery Board of Department of Consumer Affairs (part)	100	Yes
COLORADO	Commissioner of Insurance	85	No	Commissioner of Insurance	85	No
CONNECTICUT	No prepayment plans permitted			No regulation		
DELAWARE	Banking Commissioner	100	Yes	No regulation		
DISTRICT OF COLUMBIA	No regulation			No regulation		
FLORIDA	Office of State Treasurer, Department of Insurance	100	Yes	Office of State Comptroller, Department of Banking & Finance	Varies, 10–25	No
GEORGIA	Comptroller General	100	Yes	Secretary of State	Varies, 5–35	No
HAWAII	Cemetery & Mortuary Board, Department of Regulatory Agencies	70	No	Cemetery & Mortuary Board, Department of Regulatory Agencies	70	No
IDAHO	Department of Law Enforcement	100	Yes	No regulation		
ILLINOIS	Comptroller	100	Yes	Comptroller	100	Yes
INDIANA	State Board of Embalmers & Funeral Directors	100	Yes	No regulation		
IOWA	Department of Justice, Consumer Protection Division	80	No	No regulation5		
KANSAS	State Board of Embalming	100	Yes	No regulation		
KENTUCKY	Banking & Securities Department	100	Yes	Banking & Securities Department	Varies, up to 110% of cost or procurement	No
LOUISIANA	Commissioner of Insurance (part)	50	Yes	Commissioner of Insurance (part); Cemetery Board (part)	50	Yes

State	Department or Agency	Percent to trust	Interest	Department or Agency	Percent to trust	Interest
MAINE	Board of Funeral Service	100	Yes	No regulation		
MARYLAND	Department of Health & Mental Hygiene	100	Yes	No regulation		
MASSACHUSETTS	No regulation			No regulation		
MICHIGAN	Board of Examiners in Mortuary Science	100	No	Cemetery Commission	Varies, 15–70	No
MINNESOTA	Board of Health, Mortuary Science Unit	100	Yes	No regulation		
MISSISSIPPI	No specific agency	50	Yes	No specific agency	50	Yes
MISSOURI	Attorney General	80	No	Attorney General	806	No
MONTANA	No specific agency	100	No	No regulation		
NEBRASKA	Department of Health	100	Yes	No regulation		
NEVADA	Department of Commerce, Insurance Division	75	Partial	Department of Commerce, Insurance Division	60	Partial
NEW HAMPSHIRE	Board of Registration of Funeral Directors & Embalmers	100	No	No regulation		
NEW JERSEY	Board of Mortuary Science	100	Yes	No regulation		
NEW MEXICO	7			No regulation		
NEW YORK	Department of Health, Bureau of Funeral Directing	100	Yes	No regulation		
NORTH CAROLINA	Banking Commission	100	Yes	Cemetery Commission	75	Yes
NORTH DAKOTA	Commissioner of Securities	100	No	Commissioner of Securities	50	No
OHIO	Board of Embalmers & Funeral Directors	100	Yes	No regulation		
OKLAHOMA	Insurance Commissioner	90	Yes	No regulation		
OREGON	None	100	Yes	None	Varies, 0–100	Varies
PENNSYLVANIA	Board of Funeral Directors	70		No regulation		
PUERTO RICO	No regulation			No regulation		
RHODE ISLAND	No regulation			No regulation		
SOUTH CAROLINA	Board of Financial Institutions	100	Yes	No regulation		
SOUTH DAKOTA	Division of Banking & Finance	100	Yes	No regulation		
TENNESSEE	Commissioner of Insurance	100	Yes	No regulation		

State	Department or Agency	Percent to trust	Interest	Department or Agency	Percent to trust	Interest
TEXAS	Banking Department	Varies, up to 90	No	No regulation		
UTAH	Securities Commission	75	Yes	No regulation		
VERMONT	No regulation			No regulation		
VIRGINIA	Board of Funeral Directors & Embalmers	100	Yes	No specific agency	40	No
WASHINGTON	Commissioner of Insurance	85	Yes	Cemetery Board	50	No
WEST VIRGINIA	Attorney General	100	Yes	No regulation		
WISCONSIN	Funeral Directors & Embalmers Examining Board	100	Yes	Burial vaults subject to Funeral Service requirements; no other regulation		
WYOMING	Insurance Department	80	Yes	No regulation		

Note: In some places where there is no specific regulation of burial plans, the law governing funeral plans is so worded that it might be found to govern "cemetery" products, if they are sold in connection with a funeral plan. In some places where there is regulation of burial plans, cemeteries run by churches, fraternal societies, and/or municipal or other public bodies are excluded, and in some places where there is regulation of burial plans, such items as grave plots, vaults, mausoleums, markers, crypts, and/or niches are excluded.

1. Legislation pending in 1977 to bring all regulation under a central authority.

2. No specific state agency is given enforcement power by law; the Attorney General has undertaken enforcement actions through Insurance Division, Corporation Commission, and Consumer Fraud Division.

3. Based on the opinion of the Attorney General that Arizona preneed funeral plan law does not apply to burial plans. If the question should ever come before a court, the court would not be forced to accept the Attorney General's opinion, but most courts accept such opinions as very persuasive.

4. Attorney General's opinion is pending on whether interest must remain in fund.

5. A recent Iowa court case indicates that where such items as burial vaults are sold as part of a preneed funeral contract, the 80 percent trust requirement of Iowa's preneed funeral law will apply.

6. Regulation applies to grave lots, markers, etc., only when sold in connection with funeral service contract.

7. Funeral homes and preneed sales firms are forbidden to sell formal preneed plans.

251

APPENDIX 4: Active Veterans Administration National Cemeteries

ALASKA
Sitka National Cemetery
P.O. Box 1065
Sitka 99835
Phone: (907) 747-8537 or 8637

ARKANSAS
Fayetteville National Cemetery
700 Government Avenue
Fayetteville 72701
Phone: (501) 443-4301, Ext. 584
Fort Smith National Cemetery
522 Garland Avenue & South 6th Street
Fort Smith 72901
Phone: (501) 783-5345
Little Rock National Cemetery
2523 Confederate Boulevard
Little Rock 72206
Phone: (501) 374-8011

CALIFORNIA
Los Angeles National Cemetery*
950 South Sepulveda Boulevard
Los Angeles 90049
Phone: (213) 478-3711, Ext. 5264,
    1327, or 1328

COLORADO
Fort Logan National Cemetery
3698 South Sheridan Boulevard

---
*Space available only for cremated remains.

Denver 80235
Phone: (303) 761-0117
Fort Lyon National Cemetery
Veterans Administration Hospital
Fort Lyon 81038
Phone: (303) 456-1260, Ext. 231

FLORIDA
Barrancas National Cemetery
Naval Air Station
Pensacola 32508
Phone: (904) 452-3357 or 4196

HAWAII
National Memorial Cemetery of
    the Pacific
2177 Puowaina Drive
Honolulu 96813
Phone: (808) 546-3190

ILLINOIS
Camp Butler National Cemetery
R.F.D. No. 1
Springfield 62707
Phone: (217) 522-5764
Danville National Cemetery
Veterans Administration Hospital
1900 East Main Street
Danville 61832
Phone: (217) 442-8000
Mound City National Cemetery
P.O. Box 128

Mound City 62963
Phone: (618) 748-9343
Quincy National Cemetery
36th and Maine Street
Quincy 62301
(Call Keokuk National Cemetery,
Keokuk, Iowa, for information)
Rock Island National Cemetery
Rock Island Arsenal
Rock Island 61201
Phone: (309) 794-6715

INDIANA
Marion National Cemetery
Veterans Administration Hospital
Marion 46952
Phone: (317) 674-3321, Ext. 392

IOWA
Keokuk National Cemetery
18th and Ridge Streets
Keokuk 52632
Phone: (319) 524-1304

KANSAS
Fort Leavenworth National Cemetery
Fort Leavenworth 66027
Phone: (913) 684-4914
Fort Scott National Cemetery
P.O. Box 917
Fort Scott 66701
Phone: (316) 223-2840
Leavenworth National Cemetery
Veterans Administration Center
4201 South 4th Street, Traffic Way
Leavenworth 66048
(Call Fort Leavenworth National
Cemetery, Kansas, for information)

KENTUCKY
Camp Nelson National Cemetery
RR No. 2, Box 250
Nicholasville 40356
Phone: (606) 885-5727
Lebanon National Cemetery

Lebanon 40033
Phone: (502) 692-3390
Mill Springs National Cemetery
R.D. No. 1, Box 172
Nancy 42544
Phone: (606) 636-6470

LOUISIANA
Alexandria National Cemetery
209 Shamrock Avenue
Pineville 71360
Phone: (318) 442-5029

MINNESOTA
Fort Snelling National Cemetery
34th Avenue, South
Minneapolis 55111
Phone: (612) 726-1127 or 1128

MISSISSIPPI
Biloxi National Cemetery
Veterans Administration Center
Biloxi 39531
Phone: (601) 388-5541
Corinth National Cemetery
1551 Horton Street
Corinth 38834
Phone: (601) 286-5782
Natchez National Cemetery
61 Cemetery Road
Natchez 39120
Phone: (601) 445-4981

MISSOURI
Jefferson Barracks National Cemetery
101 Memorial Drive
St. Louis 63125
Phone: (314) 268-8441 or 8442
Springfield National Cemetery
1702 East Seminole Street
Springfield 65804
Phone: (417) 881-9499

NEBRASKA
Fort McPherson National Cemetery

Maxwell 69151
Phone: (308) 582-4433

NEW MEXICO
Fort Bayard National Cemetery
Fort Bayard 88036
Phone: (505) 537-3686
Sante Fe National Cemetery
Box 88
Santa Fe 87501
Phone: (505) 988-6400

NEW YORK
Bath National Cemetery
Veterans Administration Center
Bath 14810
(Call Woodlawn National Cemetery,
   Elmira, New York, for information:
   (607) 732-5411)
Long Island National Cemetery
Farmingdale, L.I. 11735
Phone: (516) 249-7300 or 7301 or 7302

NORTH CAROLINA
New Bern National Cemetery
1711 National Avenue
New Bern 28560
Phone: (919) 637-2912
Raleigh National Cemetery
501 Rock Quarry Road
Raleigh 27610
Phone: (919) 832-0144
Salisbury National Cemetery
202 Government Road
Salisbury 28144
Phone: (704) 636-2661
Wilmington National Cemetery
2011 Market Street
Wilmington 28401
Phone: (919) 762-7213

OHIO
Dayton National Cemetery
Veterans Administration Center
4100 West Third Street

Dayton 45428
Phone: (513) 268-6511, Ext. 106

OKLAHOMA
Fort Gibson National Cemetery
Fort Gibson 74434
Phone: (918) 478-2334

OREGON
Roseburg National Cemetery
Veterans Administration Hospital
Roseburg 97470
Phone: (503) 672-4411
White City National Cemetery
Veterans Administration Domiciliary
White City 97501
Phone: (503) 826-2111, Ext. 351
Willamette National Cemetery
P.O. Box 66147
11800 S.E. Mt. Scott Boulevard
Portland 97266
Phone: (503) 671-4188

PUERTO RICO
Puerto Rico National Cemetery
Box 1298
Bayamon 00619
Phone: (809) 785-7281

SOUTH CAROLINA
Beaufort National Cemetery
1601 Boundary Street
Beaufort 29902
Phone: (803) 524-3925
Florence National Cemetery
803 East National Cemetery Road
Florence 29501
Phone: (803) 669-8783

SOUTH DAKOTA
Black Hills National Cemetery
P.O. Box 640
Sturgis 57785
Phone: (605) 347-3830

TENNESSEE
Chattanooga National Cemetery
1200 Bailey Avenue
Chattanooga 37404
Phone: (615) 698-4981

Memphis National Cemetery
3568 Townes Avenue
Memphis 38122
Phone: (901) 386-8311

Mountain Home National Cemetery
P.O. Box 8
Mountain Home 37684
Phone: (615) 929-7891

Nashville National Cemetery
P.O. Box 227
1050 Gallatin Road
Madison 37115
Phone: (615) 865-0741

TEXAS
Fort Bliss National Cemetery
P.O. Box 6342
Fort Bliss 79906
Phone: (915) 568-3705

Fort Sam Houston National Cemetery
1520 Harry Wurzbach Road
San Antonio 78209
Phone: (512) 221-2136 or 2137

Houston National Cemetery
10410 Stuebner Air Line Road
Rt. 2, Box 63-X
Houston 77088
Phone: (713) 447-8686

WISCONSIN
Wood National Cemetery
Veterans Administration Center
5000 W. National Avenue
Wood 53193
Phone: (414) 384-2000,
    Ext. 2776 or 2777

DEPARTMENT OF THE ARMY NATIONAL CEMETERY
Arlington National Cemetery
Arlington, Virginia 22211
Phone: (703) 695-3250 or 3253

APPENDIX 5: The Last Post Fund (Canada)

The main office of the Last Post Fund is located at 685 Cathcart Street (Room 314), Montreal, Quebec 83B 1M7. The telephone number is (514) 866-2888. Branch offices of the fund are located in:

Alberta: Calgary, Edmonton
British Columbia: Vancouver
Manitoba: Winnipeg
New Brunswick: Saint John
Newfoundland: St. John's
Nova Scotia: Halifax
Ontario: Toronto
Prince Edward Island: Charlottetown
Quebec: Montreal
Saskatchewan: Saskatoon

APPENDIX 6: Embalming and Restoration Procedures

In *Death, Here Is Thy Sting,* Coriolis (the pseudonym for a Canadian undertaker) describes in detail the process of embalming, noting that most undertakers are secretive about the procedure. In his view, undertakers fear that the public would disapprove of the procedure if they knew what is actually involved.

Essentially, says Coriolis, embalming consists of two processes: arterial embalming and cavity embalming. In the first, the body is drained of blood, and then the blood vessels are filled with a preservative fluid (usually a solution of formaldehyde in water). Coriolis notes that the fluid "is pumped in a manner not unlike the action of the heart through progressively smaller arteries and arterioles until eventually it is conducted to the walls of individual cells which it permeates. By this means, preservation of the actual tissue is secured." In cavity embalming, fluids are removed from the two main body cavities, the thorax (chest) and abdomen, and replaced with a preservative fluid (formaldehyde in water, mixed with alcohols, emulsifiers, and other substances such as embalming fluid).

Embalmers work with special equipment to facilitate the procedure. Central to the process is the embalming table, which has a "gutter" running around its perimeter in order to catch body fluids. These wastes run down to the foot of the table—two or three inches lower than the head—and then into a container or a sewer. Also essential to the procedure are the embalming machine, which pumps fluid into the body "at between five and ten pounds per square inch" and the electric aspirator, a pump that removes wastes from the abdominal and chest cavities. Embalmers also use forceps, scalpels, and trocars—large-bore injection needles—for both drawing fluids from the body cavities and injecting embalming fluids.

The first job of the embalmer, Coriolis says, is "to break up" the effects of rigor mortis by massaging limbs and joints in order that the body be positioned: legs straight together, hands crossed on the stomach, head raised and tipped slightly to the right. Then comes the difficult and detailed process of restoring the face, beginning with the "setting of the features." Plastic cusps with little picks for holding the upper and lower lids together are inserted into the eyes and the lids drawn over them. Each jawbone is pierced with needle injectors to which wires have been attached. These wires are twisted to draw the jaws together. "When the mouth has been closed to the point where the lips meet naturally, the excess wire is tucked between the teeth, out of sight," according to Coriolis.

After the body has been properly positioned, the arterial embalming begins. This is usually done in one of three locations where there is a major artery and vein in proximity. Some embalmers use all three (or other sets of blood vessels) to reach all parts of the body: axillary artery and subclavian vein near the armpits; the carotid artery and jugular vein in the neck; the femoral artery and femoral vein near the groin.

The selected artery and vein are carefully exposed, separated from the surrounding tissue, and raised. Two strings are placed under the vein and two under the artery. "The strings will be used to tie off each vessel from both directions in order that leakage may not occur after the job is completed," Coriolis says. An injection needle is inserted in the artery pointed away from the heart, while a drainage forceps is inserted in the vein directed toward the heart to allow the blood to flow from the body into the table gutter.

The injection machine then begins to pump the first batch of embalming fluid into the artery, a strong concentration designed to break up blood clots. Next, according to Coriolis, ears, legs, hands, and arms, are massaged to clear blood discolorations, and the drainage forceps is manipulated to prevent clots from interfering with the flow of blood out of the body. A second, weaker solution is then injected. It contains some reddish coloring, as does the next and usually last solution. At this point, "a firming of the facial tissues becomes evident and a pink tinge appears throughout the body," Coriolis says.

After the arterial embalming is completed, the vessels tied, and the incisions sutured, the cavity embalming begins. It is done with the trocar, which is connected to the aspirator. The trocar is inserted in a small incision near the navel and draws out blood and waste. The cavity is then filled with a very strong formalin concentrate in order to kill microorganisms and to "cook" the viscera. With this process, the embalming is completed. The body is then washed, dressed, and, if desired, the body is cosmetically "restored."

Embalming, under normal conditions, takes about two and one-half to three hours. Sometimes, however, there are special problems of restoration. A difficult case was described in *Casket & Sunnyside* by an instructor in restorative art and cosmetology at a New York college of mortuary science. In his article, the instructor discussed the particular restorative problems he had had with the body of a large thirty-four-year-old male. Working with his students in the operating room of a city mortuary, he described how he and his class corrected the corpse's disfigurements: protruding teeth that caused lip separation, a four-inch slash across the lower part of the nose, and a fractured upper jawbone.

The dental problem was the first to be solved. Using a scalpel and a screwdriver, the class was able to press two lower teeth further back into the mouth, thus creating better alignment of the teeth. But the lips remained slightly parted. This problem was solved by suturing the two lips together, a procedure that also helped to anchor the lower jaw (it could not be wired because of the fracture).

The class next turned its attention to the nose slash. One student thought it might help to excise the entire end of the nose, but, as it turned out, wax and cosmetics proved effective remedies. The wound was made to disappear by trimming the torn tissue, filling up the aperture with tufts of absorbent cotton, coating the surface with liquid sealer, and suturing the edges of the gash with nylon thread.

For the final touches, cream cosmetics were then applied. Finally, a bit of lip rouge was applied with a brush, and a light coating of drying powder was dusted over the face. Instructor and students were pleased with the results.

APPENDIX 7: Embalming Laws

In 1977 Consumers Union requested the fifty states, the District of Columbia, and the Commonwealth of Puerto Rico to provide information about their laws concerning the circumstances, if any, mandating that a body be embalmed. The following summary is based on the responses received.

In this listing, "specially prepared" is used to refer to procedures relating to the disinfecting of a body externally—such as washing the body in a disinfectant solution, closing the orifices with absorbent cotton, and wrapping the body in a clean sheet—but not embalming. It should be noted that in a few states, such as Florida and Idaho, the definition of embalming is worded in such a way that it provides for a body to be specially prepared *or* prepared by arterial and cavity injection.

By necessity, the material received by Consumers Union has been somewhat simplified for presentation in this form. The communicable diseases being referred to, for example, are often listed in a law, although they are not identified here. In addition, those planning a funeral may benefit from other provisions in embalming laws too complex to be represented here. This table, then, may serve as a useful guideline, but it should not be used in place of the laws themselves or advice of legal counsel.

Note: Some common carriers have their own regulations dictating the conditions under which a body will be accepted for transportation. These regulations may differ from the laws presented here. In addition, a body that is to be transported interstate may have to meet the requirements of the state or states through which it will pass and of the Interstate Commerce Commission. Survivors who plan to have a body transported should be sure to check on these other regulations.

ALABAMA — If a body is to be moved across the Alabama state line, it must be either embalmed or cremated.

ALASKA — A body must be embalmed if death has resulted from an unusual or highly communicable disease, or if one of a number of communicable diseases was reasonably suspected to be present. A body must be embalmed if it is to be transported into or out of the

260

state, or within the state but will not reach its destination within 24 hours after death.

ARIZONA

If a body is to be held or is to be in transit for more than 24 hours, it must be either embalmed or refrigerated. If a body is to be transported outside the state, it must be embalmed unless transportation is to be provided by an immediate family member of the decedent or by a licensed undertaker who will handle the disposition at the point of disposition and provided such exportation is made within 24 hours after death. If death is a result of a communicable disease, the body must be embalmed.

ARKANSAS

When a body is to be held any place or is to be in transit over 24 hours after death or pending final disposition, it must be either refrigerated or embalmed.

CALIFORNIA

A body must be embalmed when it is to be transferred by common carrier. If death is a result of an infectious or contagious disease, the county health officer may order the body to be embalmed.

COLORADO

When a body is to be held for more than 24 hours, it shall be either embalmed or properly refrigerated.

CONNECTICUT

When a body is to be transported over state lines by common carrier, it must be embalmed.

DELAWARE

When a body is to be kept for more than 24 hours, it must either be embalmed or placed in a hermetically sealed coffin.

DISTRICT OF COLUMBIA

A body must be embalmed if death results from a communicable disease.

FLORIDA

A body may be held in any place or in transit over 24 hours after death or pending final disposition only if the body is refrigerated, embalmed, or specially prepared.[1] When death results from a highly contagious

---

[1] By opinion of the attorney general, the same holds true if disposition of the remains takes place before 24 hours, provided the death is not the result of a highly contagious disease.

261

disease and a body is to be transported,[2] it must be embalmed.

GEORGIA Embalming is not mandatory under any circumstances.

HAWAII A body shall be embalmed, cremated, or buried within 30 hours after death, or, if death results from a communicable disease, within 30 hours after release from the Director of Health. If death results from a communicable disease and a body is to be transported by common carrier, it must be either embalmed or placed in a hermetically sealed coffin encased in an outer box.

IDAHO A body must be embalmed when it is to be transported by common carrier.

ILLINOIS If death results from a communicable disease and a body is to be transported, it must be embalmed. If a body is to be shipped by common carrier and the destination cannot be reached within 24 hours, it must be embalmed.

INDIANA A body must be embalmed if death is from a communicable disease or if it is ordered to be embalmed by the county health officer.

IOWA When death occurs from a communicable disease, a body shall be embalmed if transported and should[3] be embalmed otherwise. When death results from a cause other than a communicable disease, a body does not have to be embalmed if interment is to be made within the local health jurisdiction where the death occurred and within 48 hours after death.

KANSAS If death occurs from an infectious or contagious disease and a body is to be transported from the registration district in which death occurred or if a body

---

[2]By opinion of the attorney general, this rule appears to require embalming only when the body is to be transported to a point outside the state and not to require embalming when the body is to be disposed of in the state.

[3]According to the Board of Funeral Director and Embalmer Examiners, this is a recommendation and not a requirement.

is to be transported by common carrier, it must be embalmed. If death occurs from another cause and the body is to be transported by private conveyance within the state, it must be embalmed within 24 hours. Regardless of cause of death, if a body is not to be transported but is not buried within 24 hours of death (in some cases, longer), it must be embalmed. A body shall be embalmed if it is to be interred or deposited in any public mausoleum or private mausoleum of more than two crypts.

KENTUCKY Embalming is not mandatory under any circumstances.

LOUISIANA If a body is to be held longer than 30 hours, it must be embalmed.

MAINE If a body is to be transported by common carrier, it must be embalmed.

MARYLAND Embalming is not mandatory under any circumstances.

MASSACHUSETTS If death occurs from a highly contagious disease, a body shall not be removed until embalmed. If death occurs from a different disease dangerous to public health, a body cannot be removed unless embalmed or, if it is to be buried within 24 hours, it must be specially prepared and refrigerated. If death results from a disease or cause not dangerous to public health, a body cannot be transported unless embalmed or specially prepared and sealed in an airtight coffin or box properly sealed.

MICHIGAN If death occurs from a communicable disease and a body is to be transported, it must be embalmed. Otherwise, a body must be embalmed if the destination cannot be reached within 48 hours.

MINNESOTA Embalming is required if a body is to be transported out of state by common carrier or aircraft ambulance; or if death results from a communicable disease; or, if transported, destination will not be reached within

18 hours of death; or if moved locally and burial or cremation will not be accomplished within 72 hours. Embalming is not required if death results from non-communicable causes, transportation within the state can be accomplished within 18 hours of death, and burial or cremation will occur within 72 hours of death.

MISSISSIPPI

If final disposition is not to take place within 48 hours after death, a body must be either embalmed or refrigerated.

MISSOURI

If death results from a communicable disease and a body is to be transported by common carrier, it must be embalmed; or the body may be encased in an air-tight container that is hermetically sealed and, if death results from certain communicable diseases, specially prepared. If death results from a communicable disease and the person was subject to isolation at time of death, the body shall either be embalmed, buried, or cremated within 24 hours of death, or permanently encased in a sealed casket; if there is to be a public funeral, however, the body must be embalmed or permanently encased in a sealed casket. If death results from another cause, the body is to be transported by common carrier, and the destination cannot be reached within 24 hours, it must be either embalmed or encased in an air-tight container that is hermetically sealed.

MONTANA

If death results from a communicable disease and a body is to be transported, the body must be embalmed. If death results from another cause and the body is to be transported by common carrier and will be en route more than 8 hours or will reach its destination more than 36 hours after death, the body must be embalmed, refrigerated, or specially prepared. If death results from a cause other than a communicable disease and a body is to be transported by private conveyor and will not reach its destination within 48 hours after death, then the body must be embalmed, refrigerated, or specially prepared.

NEBRASKA If a body is to be transported intrastate by common carrier, it must be either embalmed or placed in a hermetically sealed container immediately after death. If transportation is made by privately owned conveyance under the direct supervision and responsibility of a licensed funeral director, the body must reach its destination within 24 hours following death if not embalmed and must be refrigerated (but for not more than 72 hours); if refrigerated, the body must reach its destination within 24 hours following removal from storage. Exception: If a body is placed in a metal or metal-lined hermetically sealed container immediately after death, it may be considered for the purpose of transporting the same as an embalmed body. If death occurs from a communicable disease, a body shall be promptly embalmed. If it is not embalmed, however, then the body shall be encased in a metal or metal-lined hermetically sealed container.

NEVADA A body must be buried or cremated within 18 hours after death unless it has been embalmed.

NEW HAMPSHIRE If a body is to be exposed to the public for more than 24 hours, it must be embalmed.

NEW JERSEY If a body is not to be buried or cremated within 48 hours after death, it must be either embalmed or refrigerated. If death occurs from a communicable disease and a body is not to be buried or disposed of within 24 hours after death, it must be embalmed. If death occurs from other causes and a body is to be transported by common carrier, the body must be embalmed if the destination cannot be reached within 24 hours after death.

NEW MEXICO If death is a result of a contagious disease, a body must be embalmed.[4]

NEW YORK Embalming is not mandatory under any circumstances.

[4]As this book goes to press, a substantial revision of New Mexico regulations is under consideration.

NORTH CAROLINA If death occurs from a communicable disease, and a body is to be transported out of state, the body must be either embalmed or enclosed in an air-tight container.

NORTH DAKOTA If a body is not to be buried within 72 hours after death, it must be embalmed. If death occurs from a communicable disease, a body must be embalmed unless there is no viewing and it is immediately buried. If a body is to be transported by common carrier or if it is to be transported for more than 75 miles or in interstate commerce, it must be embalmed.

OHIO Embalming is not mandatory under any circumstances.

OKLAHOMA If death results from a contagious disease or if a body cannot be disposed of within a reasonable time (before it would become a health hazard and harmful to the public), the body must be embalmed.

OREGON If a body is to be held longer than 24 hours, it must be either embalmed or refrigerated. If death is a result of a communicable disease and the body is to be transported, the body must be embalmed if it cannot reach its destination within 24 hours after death. Regardless of cause of death, if there is to be a public or private funeral to be held more than 24 hours after death, the body must be either embalmed or refrigerated.

PENNSYLVANIA If a body is to be held 24 hours after death, it shall be either embalmed, placed in a hermetically sealed container, or refrigerated, provided this does not conflict with any religious belief or medical examination.

PUERTO RICO If a body is not to be buried within 24 hours after death, it must be embalmed. If the body is to be transported and disposition cannot be completed within 24 hours after death, the body must be embalmed.

RHODE ISLAND If a body is to be shipped by common carrier, it must be embalmed. If death is a result of a communicable disease and if a public funeral is to be held somewhere other than the place of death (e.g., in a funeral home), the body must be embalmed and permanently enclosed; if not embalmed, it must be buried or enclosed in a tightly sealed outer case within 24 hours.

SOUTH CAROLINA If a body is to be shipped by common carrier, it must be embalmed.

SOUTH DAKOTA Embalming is not mandatory under any circumstances.

TENNESSEE Embalming is not mandatory under any circumstances.

TEXAS If a body is to be held in any place or is to be in transit for more than 24 hours after death and pending final disposition, the body must be either refrigerated or embalmed.

UTAH If a body is to be shipped by common carrier, it must be embalmed. If a body is to be held in any place or is to be in transit for more than 24 hours after death and pending final disposition, it must be either refrigerated or embalmed. If there is to be a public funeral and death is a result of a communicable disease, a body should be embalmed.

VERMONT Embalming is not mandatory under any circumstances.

VIRGINIA Embalming is not mandatory under any circumstances.

WASHINGTON If death is a result of a communicable disease, a body must be either embalmed or cremated. If death is a result of an infectious disease and a body is to be transferred outside the jurisdiction of the local health department or if a body is to be transported by common carrier, the body must be embalmed. If a body is to be transported pending final disposition more than 24 hours after death, the body must be embalmed.

WEST VIRGINIA A body must be embalmed if it is to be transported across state lines by a common carrier, if death is a result of an infectious or contagious disease, or if the body may cause a health problem (i.e., being held for a long time without refrigeration).

WISCONSIN If a body is to be shipped by common carrier, the body must be embalmed. Regardless of type of carrier, if a body is to be transported and if, at time of death, the person was in or subject to quarantine because of a communicable disease, the body must be embalmed.

WYOMING All bodies in the possession of a funeral director or embalmer must be buried, cremated, embalmed, or refrigerated within 36 hours after receipt thereof.

Appendix 8

APPENDIX 8: Guidelines for Direct Cremation without an Undertaker

Some members of the St. Francis Burial Society in Washington, D.C., have themselves in two instances carried out the disposition of bodies of friends and family members without using the services of an undertaker. The following guidelines are adapted from those used by the St. Francis Burial Society to help members involved in direct disposition.

Death Certificate. The death certificate is of great importance since copies must be submitted to various officials prior to disposition of the body. It must also be submitted within a certain time period to the appropriate state or county health department or vital statistics agency. The death certificate sometimes includes the burial or transit permit, which is necessary in all states to transport, bury, or cremate a body. In most states, however, this is a separate permit which must also be secured from the appropriate agency.

The death certificate should be obtained from the physician attending at death. In the place provided for the undertaker's signature on the certificate, the next of kin or the person with authority to carry out the disposition should sign his or her name. When the original death certificate is taken to or mailed to the appropriate agency, a request for a specific number of additional copies should be made (see page 59). A letter, with the decedent's name, address, date and place of death, should accompany the death certificate, together with payment for the additional copies. The letter should also state the name of the person who is serving as undertaker.

Equipment. (1) station wagon; (2) coffin;* (3) a regulation body bag, obtained from a funeral supply wholesaler; (4) two or three pairs of plastic (surgical) gloves; (5) blanket; (6) two wooden planks, 7 feet by 3 inches; (7) a pall.

Procedure. Before removing the body from the hospital (or other place of death), it is best to arrange in advance an acceptable time for removal and also to ask the crematory when it can receive the body. Timing is important,

---

*Members of St. Francis were able to borrow a coffin from the society and return it later. In such instances, the crematory should be informed in advance that the coffin will be taken away, since bodies are usually cremated within coffins or other containers.

269

because some crematories accept bodies only within certain hours. If possible, it is best to start early. Those removing the body must sign (as undertaker) a register at the hospital for removal and also the record book in the hospital morgue. At the hospital, St. Francis members found it was necessary to present the death certificate to morgue attendants.

Usually, two or three people are needed to lift the body and place it in the body bag. (St. Francis members report that a morgue attendant helped survivors to do this.) The plastic gloves were used to handle the body; the blanket was wrapped around the body bag as it went into the coffin. (The blanket and gloves helped survivors esthetically and emotionally.) The simple pall covered the coffin on the cart as it moved through the hospital halls. The two wooden planks were used to slide the coffin into the station wagon.

Cost. At the crematory, more papers must be filled out and the cremation fee paid (at the Maryland crematory it was $85). At the crematory, survivors may wish to hold a brief prayer meeting or other form of observance in memory of the deceased. According to the St. Francis members, the overall cost was minimal in each case—around $250 (in one case, the cost of interment of cremated remains was included). But the saving was not as important to the survivors as the meaning of the experience itself. The minister who accompanied one spouse described it this way:

> It was a loving labor, this with the body of our dead—hard, but without contrived distractions or phony cosmetics. Here was the power, the terror, the pain, the finality of death and the truth fully present for us. Because we were personally and fully involved, directly and naturally, we were free to grieve and move into reality. We were *in* reality, not protected from it.

APPENDIX 9: Uniform Donor Card

Uniform donor cards are available from a number of sources. Some state motor vehicle departments include them with drivers' licenses or license applications. Medical schools that accept body donations for medical education may provide prospective donors with cards. In addition, some transplant banks and transplant clearinghouses will provide cards upon request. Among them:

American Medical Association*
535 North Dearborn Street
Chicago, Illinois 60610
Attention: Order Department

Deafness Research Foundation*
366 Madison Avenue
New York, New York 10017

Eye-Bank Association of America*
3195 Maplewood Avenue
Winston Salem, North Carolina 27103

Living Bank*
P.O. Box 6725
Houston, Texas 77005

Medic Alert*
P.O. Box 1009
Turlock, California 95380

National Kidney Foundation*
116 East 27th Street
New York, New York 10016

National Pituitary Agency*
210 West Fayette Street
Suite 503
Baltimore, Maryland 21201

National Temporal Bone Banks Center
of the Deafness Research Foundation*
550 North Broadway—Room 103
The Johns Hopkins University School of
Medicine
Baltimore, Maryland 21205

Northern California Transplant Bank*
Institute for Medical Research
751 South Bascom Avenue
San Jose, California 95128

Tissue Bank at Naval Medical Research
Institute
Bethesda, Maryland 20014

Before filling out a card, it may be useful to review the summary of alternatives presented on page 207. If a prospective donor wishes to specify autopsy as a preference, that choice should be entered on the line headed *Limitations or special wishes, if any.*

---

*Will accept requests for uniform donor cards.

The uniform donor card distributed to memorial societies by the Continental Association of Funeral and Memorial Societies is pictured below.

UNIFORM DONOR CARD

OF_____

Print or type name of donor

In the hope that I may help others, I hereby make this anatomical gift, if medically acceptable, to take effect upon my death. The words and marks below indicate my desires.

I give: (a) _____ any needed organs or parts

         (b) _____ only the following organs or parts

_____

Specify the organ(s) or part(s)

for the purposes of transplantation, therapy, medical research or education;

         (c) _____ my body for anatomical study if needed.

Limitations or
special wishes, if any :_____

Signed by the donor and the following two witnesses in the presence of each other:

_____   _____

         Signature of Donor   Date of Birth of Donor

_____   _____

         Date Signed   City & State

_____   _____

         Witness   Witness

This is a legal document under the Uniform Anatomical Gift Act or similar laws.

For further information consult your local memorial society or:

Continental Association of Funeral & Memorial Societies
1828 L Street, N.W., Washington, D.C. 20036

APPENDIX 10: Autopsy Procedure

The general purpose of autopsy is to determine the cause of death as well as to provide detailed information about anatomic abnormalities that may have coexisted but not have contributed to the cause of death.

There are three types of autopsy:
• A complete autopsy includes examination of the entire body including the head. This is the most desirable from the pathologist's point of view and most apt to be productive of total information.
• A limited autopsy excludes examination of the head.
• A selective autopsy includes examination of only one or more organs of paramount concern to the interested physicians and survivors.

What follows is a detailed description of a complete autopsy:

The pathologist reads the patient's clinical record to become familiar with the medical history and the events that preceded death. Inspection of the intact body makes note of any visible abnormalities and of nutritional status.

The pathologist begins the autopsy procedure with a longitudinal incision extending from just beneath the breastbone to the lowest part of the abdomen. Two additional cuts are made, originating from the uppermost point of the original incision and progressing diagonally across the chest to each underarm. The skin and muscle layers of the chest are then dissected from the underlying ribs and folded back, exposing the thorax (chest cavity). A bone-cutting instrument is used to cut through the ribs on either side of the chest. The breastbone, together with the front portion of the rib cage, is removed, exposing the lungs and the heart.

The lungs and heart may be removed together and weighed and examined on a side table. These organs are separated and carefully cut into sections, and any abnormalities noted. Samples are taken, labeled, and placed in jars containing preservative solution for future microscopic slide preparation.

The contents of the abdominal cavity are examined next. The small and large intestines are dissected free of their attachment membranes and removed. These hollow organs are opened on a side table and inspected for any ulcerations or growths. Then the stomach and first portion of the intestine (duodenum) are removed along with the liver, gallbladder, pancreas, and spleen. The weight of each organ is recorded. The organs are then cut and inspected, and suitable sections immersed in preservative for future microscopic study.

The kidneys, ureters, and bladder are then removed. Last to be inspected and dissected are the internal reproductive organs. Once again, material for slide preparation is set aside.

Additional sections of bone, muscle, and other tissues may be taken at the discretion of the pathologist. The breastbone and ribs are replaced and the two body cavities, thorax and abdomen, are then closed. Skin flaps are restored to their original positions, and the incisions closed with thread.

The complete autopsy also includes examination of the brain. An incision is made just above one ear and extended over the crown of the head to the same point on the other side. The skull is exposed by folding the front portion of the scalp toward the face and the rear portion backward. An electric saw is used to cut through the skull along the lines formed by the scalp folds. The cut-through portion of skull is removed and the brain with its veillike coverings (meninges) is observed. Removal of the intact brain requires deft handling because of its softness and extreme fragility. This delicate tissue is then suspended in a large jar containing preservative for sectioning and future examination. The previously removed portion of the skull is then replaced, the scalp restored to its normal position, and the cut edges are stitched.

APPENDIX 11: Transplantation

As of July 1, 1977, a worldwide total of 346 heart transplants (225 in the United States) had been performed since 1967; 318 liver transplants (206 in the United States) since 1963; 57 pancreas transplants (31 in the United States) since 1966; 37 lung transplants (20 in the United States) since 1963. As of January 1977, about 44,600 kidney transplants had been performed (some 23,300 in the United States) since 1953. About 45 percent of a world-wide sample of kidney recipients were alive with functioning grafts (as of 1976). As of July 1, 1977, 77 heart recipients and 47 liver recipients (but no lung or pancreas recipients) were still alive. The longest survival periods with a functioning graft for which data were available included 20 years for a kidney (from an identical twin); 8.7 years for a heart; 7.5 years for a liver; 4.2 years for a pancreas; 10 months for a lung. There were 66 heart transplant teams throughout the world, 43 for liver, 22 for lung, and 15 for pancreas. There were 324 kidney transplant facilities worldwide (165 in the United States).

Immunology

Despite obstacles, advances are being made. There has been a gradual increase since the early kidney transplants in the long-term patient survival of first transplants from cadaver kidneys; some patients have had two, three, or four transplants. The National Institutes of Health has stated that "the outlook for significantly improving the health and longevity of man through transplantation is exceedingly hopeful if the currently imperfect rejection response can be refined."

The major problem in transplantation concerns compatibility between donor and donee (or host) tissues. The more alike the donor tissue is to the host's in terms not only of blood groups, but also of other tissue antigen compatibility—so-called histocompatibility profiling—the greater the chance that the transplanted organ will "take." If a kidney comes from an identical twin, the five-year survival rate is almost 100 percent; from a sibling, it is 85 percent, and from a parent 60 percent. The percentage drops to 50 percent or less when kidneys are from cadavers or unrelated people.

The immune response in human beings, more so than in other mammalian species where inbreeding is common, constitutes the body's primary defense system against a "foreign" protein, whether that protein is contained in a life-threatening bacterium or a life-saving kidney. Introduction of protein of different genetic composition triggers the host's immune response, generating antibody production by certain blood cells. The resultant antigen-antibody reaction leads to complex events enabling the body to destroy or render harmless—in effect, to reject—foreign protein. Close tissue matching, therefore, decreases the chances of rejection of the transplanted tissue by the host. Histocompatibility profiling has now become routine in selection of donor material. *

Since only with identical twins is there the possibility of a perfect match, drugs must be used to suppress the host's immunologic response. The success of current research into the nature of the body's immunologic system and the development of new drugs and techniques to counteract the rejection process are making significant advances possible in the transplantation of organs.

When Does Death Occur?

A crucial question confronting transplant surgeons and all of medicine today is the criterion for determining when death has occurred. The legal definition of death—whether it is cessation of brain activity or cessation of heart and lung functions—can influence the success of transplantation. If the kidneys are removed from a body after brain death has occurred but while the heart and lungs are still functioning (usually by means of a mechanical respirator), the transplant's viability is assured. Most transplant surgeons would agree with a 1975 article in the *British Medical Journal* that "good quality cadaver kidneys are obtainable only in cases where brain death occurs before the heart stops, and the surgeon removes the organs while they are still being oxygenated."

In the past, death was usually fairly simple to determine: the pulse, heartbeat, breathing, all stopped. But heart and lung function can now be continued with life-support devices. The question of when death occurs has become extremely difficult to resolve.

In 1968 a committee of Harvard University faculty members—doctors, scientists, a lawyer, a theologian, and a philosopher—"recommended a definition of irreversible coma which accepts the idea of brain death, and thus death of the individual." The American Heart Association's Committee

---

*The American Medical Association pamphlet on anatomical bequests notes that, in the case of kidney transplants, "it may be necessary to check hundreds or even a thousand donor kidneys against the body chemistry of the recipient to insure an absence of rejection."

on Ethics, professional societies, and many physicians have accepted the Harvard criteria or similar ones. (The American Medical Association, however, opposes a legal definition of death, saying it should be left to the attending physician.) Several states* have legislation specifying that legal death occurs when there has been an absence of brain waves on two electroencephalograms taken twenty-four hours apart. As protection for the patient, the Uniform Anatomical Gift Act, adopted by all states and the District of Columbia, stipulates that the doctor who pronounces the patient dead must not be involved in the transplant operation. Most hospitals, too, require more than one doctor's decision in determining death when organ transplantation is contemplated.

---

*Among them, Alaska, California, Georgia, Kansas, Maryland, Michigan, New Mexico, Oregon, Virginia.

Notes

A number of works are cited in this book with great frequency. Rather than repeat the full reference each time, we have listed them in full immediately below and again when first footnoted. Thereafter they are cited in the abbreviated style indicated below.

Hugh Y. Bernard, *The Law of Death and Disposal of the Dead* (Dobbs Ferry, N.Y.: Oceana Publications, 1966). Hereafter cited as Bernard, *The Law of Death.*

Coriolis, *Death, Here Is Thy Sting* (Toronto, Montreal: McClelland and Stewart, 1967). Hereafter cited as Coriolis, *Death, Here Is Thy Sting.*

Federal Trade Commission, *Funeral Industry Practices: Proposed Trade Regulation Rule and Staff Memorandum,* August 1975. Hereafter cited as *FTC Proposed Rule.*

Federal Trade Commission, Bureau of Consumer Protection, *FTC Survey of Funeral Prices in the District of Columbia,* 1974. Hereafter cited as *FTC Washington, D.C., Survey.*

Federal Trade Commission, Bureau of Consumer Protection, "Unfair Practices in the Funeral Industry: A Planning Report to the Federal Trade Commission" (staff memorandum), 1973. Hereafter cited as "FTC planning memorandum."

Edgar N. Jackson, *For the Living* (Des Moines: Channel Press, 1963). Hereafter cited as Jackson, *For the Living.*

Wilber M. Krieger, *Successful Funeral Service Management* (New York: Prentice-Hall, 1951). Hereafter cited as Krieger, *Successful Funeral Service Management.*

Ernest Morgan, *A Manual of Death Education and Simple Burial,* 8th edition (Burnsville, N.C.: The Celo Press, 1977). Hereafter cited as Morgan, *Manual.*

National Funeral Directors Association, *Facts and Figures of the United States,* 1976 edition. Hereafter cited as NFDA, *Facts and Figures,* 1976 ed.

U.S. Congress, House of Representatives, Subcommittee on Activities of Regulatory Agencies of the Committee on Small Business, *Regulations of*

Various Federal Regulatory Agencies and Their Effect on Small Business,
Part IV, 94th Cong., 2nd sess., March 25, April 6, June 16, and July 28, 1976.
Hereafter cited as *Hearings on Small Business, Part IV.*

U.S. Congress, Senate, Subcommittee on Antitrust and Monopoly of the
Committee on the Judiciary. *Antitrust Aspects of the Funeral Industry:
Hearing on S. Res. 262,* Part I: Funeral Directors, 88th Cong., 2nd sess.,
July 7, 8, and 9, 1964. Hereafter cited as *Antitrust Aspects, Part I.*

The notes are listed by part and by chapter. The number at the left refers to the page in the text on which sourced material appears or begins. A
key word or phrase from the text, followed by a colon, identifies the particular material being sourced.

PART I

Chapter 1

15 Lindbergh: "The Lone Eagle's Final Flight," *Time,* September 9, 1974.

Kastenbaum: Phone interview, Robert J. Kastenbaum, superintendent of Cushing
Hospital, Framingham, Mass., June 7 and September 23, 1977.

16 deaths: "Funerals: Coming to Grips With the Last Consumer Problem," *Media &
Consumer,* June 1974.

sixty-five: Phone interview, National Center for Health Statistics, December 9, 1975.

income: Phone interview, National Center for Health Statistics, August 1, 1977.

modest: "Can You Afford to Die?" *Post-Gazette,* Pittsburgh, April 10, 1972.

17 survivors: Howard C. Raether and Robert C. Slater, "United States: Dominant Pro-
file," in *The Funeral: Facing Death as an Experience of Life* (National Funeral
Directors Association, n.d.), p. 27.

uninformed: New York State College of Human Ecology, Cornell University, research project, 1974, in *Human Ecology Forum,* Vol. 5, No. 3 (Winter 1975), p. 12.

18 investment: U.S. Department of Commerce, *U.S. Industrial Outlook, 1976,* January 1976, p. 450.

arrangements: Leitz•Eagan Funeral Homes, Inc., "We Care Enough to Let You
Know" (pamphlet), 1976, n.p.

staff: U.S. Congress, House of Representatives, Subcommittee on Activities of Regu-
latory Agencies of the Committee on Small Business, *Regulations of Various Federal
Regulatory Agencies and Their Effect on Small Business: Hearings, Part III,* 94th
Cong., 2nd sess., November 13, 1975; January 21, 22, February 4, and 5, 1976, p.
370. Hereafter cited as *Hearings on Small Business, Part III;* Oregon State University
Extension Service, "When Death Comes" (pamphlet), p. 12.

overhead: "Funeral Director Explains His Profession," *The Herald Statesman,*
Yonkers, N.Y., March 9, 1976.

profits: Howard C. Raether and Robert C. Slater, "The Funeral with the Body
Present," in *Problems of Death,* edited by David L. Bender (Anoka, Minn.: Green-
haven Press, 1974), p. 133.

casket: Casket Manufacturers Association of America, "American Attitudes Toward
Death and Funerals" (booklet), p. 44.

membership: Gale Research Company, *Encyclopedia of Associations,* Vol. I: *National Organizations of the United States,* eleventh edition, 1977, Margaret Fisk,
editor.

19 income: National Funeral Directors Association, *Facts and Figures of the United States,* 1976 edition, p. 38 (The data base for the NFDA figures is the continental United States.) Hereafter cited as NFDA, *Facts and Figures,* 1976 ed.

Federated: Federated Funeral Directors of America, *Statistical Supplement for 1975,* n.p. (The data base for the FFDA figures is seventeen Midwestern and Eastern states.)

Morticians: Letter from Consumer Information Bureau, Inc., a subsidiary of NSM, June 15, 1977.

increase: Letters from Howard C. Raether, NFDA, September 2, 1976, and Consumer Information Bureau, December 8, 1975.

cost: National Foundation of Funeral Service, "Facts About Funeral Service Every Family Should Know" (pamphlet), n.d., pp. 9, 8.

delays: "F.T.C. Studies the Cost of Dying," *The New York Times,* September 26, 1976.

NFDA: R. Jay Kraeer (president of NFDA), quoted in "F.T.C. Studies the Cost of Dying," *The New York Times,* September 26, 1976.

settlement: "F.T.C. Studies the Cost of Dying," *The New York Times,* September 26, 1976.

20 ritual: Vanderlyn R. Pine and Derek L. Phillips, "The Cost of Dying: A Sociological Analysis of Funeral Expenditures," in *Social Problems,* Vol. 17, No. 3 (Winter 1970), p. 416.

wedding: Edgar N. Jackson, *For the Living* (Des Moines: Channel Press, 1963), p. 37. Hereafter cited as Jackson, *For the Living.*

Jackson: Jackson, *For the Living,* pp. 85-86.

debt: Jackson, *For the Living,* p. 86.

21 homes: NFDA, "Funeral Service: Meeting Needs . . . Serving People," edited by Robert C. Slater (Milwaukee, 1974), p. 13.

Krieger: U.S. Congress, Senate, Subcommittee on Antitrust and Monopoly of the Committee on the Judiciary, *Antitrust Aspects of the Funeral Industry: Hearing on S. Res. 262, Part I: Funeral Directors,* 88th Cong., 2nd sess., July 7, 8, and 9, 1964, p. 35. Hereafter cited as *Antitrust Aspects, Part I.*

chains: "F.T.C. Studies the Cost of Dying," *The New York Times,* September 26, 1976; FTC Bureau of Consumer Protection, "Unfair Practices in the Funeral Industry: A Planning Report to the Federal Trade Commission" (staff memorandum), p. 36. Hereafter cited as "FTC planning memorandum."

twenty-five: "FTC planning memorandum," p. 36.

funerals: NFDA, *Facts and Figures,* 1976 ed., p. 3.

colleagues: Howard C. Raether, Policy statement portion of "30 Pieces of Silver," 1963, NFDA Professional Conferences, in *Antitrust Aspects, Part I,* p. 142.

advertising: Letter from Howard C. Raether to Harold J. Rindl, January 6, 1964, reprinted in *Antitrust Aspects, Part I,* p. 47.

establishments: U.S. Department of Commerce, *1972 Census of Selected Service Industries: Area Statistics* (Washington, D.C.: U.S. Government Printing Office, 1975), p. 7.

22 secrecy: FTC Bureau of Consumer Protection, *FTC Survey of Funeral Prices in the District of Columbia,* p. 54. Hereafter cited as *FTC Washington, D.C., Survey.*

prices: Barbara Kronman, "A Death in the Family . . . A Guide to the Cost of Dying in New York City, Nassau, and Suffolk" (pamphlet) (New York Public Interest Research Group, 1974), p. 4. Hereafter cited as NYPIRG, "A Death in the Family."

23 Index: Letter from Howard C. Raether, September 2, 1976.

surveys: Letter from Howard C. Raether, September 2, 1976.

components: Letter from Howard C. Raether, September 2, 1976.

data: Phone interview, Bureau of Labor Statistics, September 22, 1977.

Labor Statistics: Phone interview, Bureau of Labor Statistics, September 22, 1977.

questionnaires: Letter to NFDA Board of Governors from Vanderlyn R. Pine, June 21, 1976, in NFDA, *Facts and Figures*, 1976 ed.

24 statistics: "FTC planning memorandum," pp. 201-3.

plots: Phone interview, Bureau of Domestic Commerce, Department of Commerce, August 26, 1976.

review: "Funerals: Coming to Grips With the Last Consumer Problem," *Media & Consumer*, June 1974.

expenditures: Phone interview, U.S. Department of Commerce Library, New York, N.Y., December 11, 1974.

$2.830 billion: U.S. Department of Commerce, *U.S. Industrial Outlook, 1977, with Projections to 1985* (Washington, D.C.: U.S. Government Printing Office, January 1977), p. 498.

establishments: U.S. Department of Commerce, *U.S. Industrial Outlook, 1977*, p. A5.

not included: U.S. Department of Commerce, *U.S. Industrial Outlook, 1977*, p. 499; *U.S. Industrial Outlook, 1976*, p. 450.

excludes: U.S. Department of Commerce, *1972 Census of Selected Service Industries*, p. A5: phone interview, Bureau of Domestic Commerce, September 12, 1977.

80 percent: Phone interview, The Cremationist of North America, May 10, 1977.

Fee: Department of Labor, *Consumer Price Index*, October 1970.

25 over-representation: Letter to NFDA Board of Governors from Vanderlyn R. Pine, June 21, 1976, in NFDA, *Facts and Figures*, 1976 ed., n.p.

underestimate: "FTC planning memorandum," pp. 199 et seq.

charge: NFDA, *Facts and Figures*, 1976 ed., pp. 10, 13.

adult: Letter from Howard C. Raether, September 2, 1976.

26 "total": NFDA, *Facts and Figures*, 1976 ed., p. 13.

Veterans: Veterans Administration, *Veterans' Burial Benefits: A Study Submitted to the Committee on Veterans Affairs, United States Senate* (Senate Committee Print No. 9), April 30, 1973, p. 15. Hereafter cited as *VA Study, 1973*.

New Jersey: "New Jersey Regulates Funeral Billing," *Caveat Emptor*, June 1973.

survey: FTC Washington, D.C., *Survey*, pp. 33-34.

27 regions: Veterans Administration, *National Cemetery System Study: A Study Submitted to the Committee on Veterans Affairs, United States Senate* (Senate Committee Print No. 24), January 21, 1974, pp. 157-77. Hereafter cited as *VA Cemetery Study, 1974*.

costs: Federated Funeral Directors of America, *Statistical Supplement for 1975*, n.p.

crematory: U.S. Department of Commerce, *U.S. Industrial Outlook, 1976*, p. 451.

inflation: "CMA Meetings Stress Raw Materials Inflation," *Casket & Sunnyside*, August 1973, p. 34.

Casket: Casket Manufacturers Association of America, "Newsletter," March 1977, p. 3.

28 coffin: "Economics of Death Outlined," *The East Hampton Star*, July 31, 1975.

predict: Doris Poté, 1972 survey for the Pre-Arrangement Interment Association, in *VA Cemetery Study, 1974*, p. 175; "What the Undertakers Often Hide from the Bereaved," *The Sunday Sun*, Baltimore, January 16, 1977.

directors: Wilber M. Krieger, *Successful Funeral Service Management* (New York: Prentice-Hall, 1951), p. 255. Hereafter cited as Krieger, *Successful Funeral Service Management*.

Haskel: Statement of Harry Haskel, Director of Health Benefit Department, International Ladies' Garment Workers' Union, New York, in *Antitrust Aspects, Part 1*, p. 182.

ILGWU: Phone interview, Death Benefit Department, ILGWU, October 1974, June 1977.

29 Rappaport: Alfred Rappaport, "The Expected Impact of Fragmented Quotation on Funeral Service Prices," February 1974 paper, reprinted in U.S. Congress, House of Representatives, Subcommittee on Business, Commerce, and Taxation of the Committee on The District of Columbia, *Funeral Financing: Hearing on H.R. 13492 and H.R. 13969*, 93rd Cong., 2nd sess., April 24, 1974, pp. 57-60. Hereafter cited as *Washington, D.C., Hearing*.

expenses: NFDA, *Facts and Figures*, 1976 ed., p. 23.

costs: FFDA, *Statistical Supplement for 1975*, n.p.

Blackwell: Roger D. Blackwell, "Price Levels in the Funeral Industry," in *The Quarterly Review of Economics and Business* (Winter 1967), p. 77.

conglomerates: "F.T.C. Studies the Cost of Dying," *The New York Times*, September 26, 1976.

30 classifications: NFDA, *Facts and Figures*, 1976 ed., p. 23.

FFDA: NFDA, *Facts and Figures*, 1976 ed., p. 23.

NSM: National Selected Morticians, "A Helpful Guide to Funeral Planning" (booklet), 1975, p. 17.

31 "package pricing": Casket Manufacturers Association of America, "American Attitudes Toward Death and Funerals," p. 35; NFDA, "What Do you *Really* Know About Funeral Costs?" (pamphlet), n.p.

Chapter 2

32 undertakers: Robert W. Habenstein and William M. Lamers, *The History of American Funeral Directing*, revised edition (Milwaukee: Bulfin Printers, 1962), pp. 592-93; NFDA, "Funeral Service: Meeting Needs . . . Serving People," p. 4.

hearing: Richard O'Keeffe, written testimony submitted to State of New York, Senate Standing Committee on Consumer Protection, *Public Hearing on Funeral Industry*, Albany, N.Y., November 17, 1975. Hereafter cited as *Albany Public Hearing*.

33 pricing: FTC, *Funeral Industry Practices: Proposed Trade Regulation Rule and Staff Memorandum*, August 1975, p. 105. Hereafter cited as *FTC Proposed Rule*.

coffin: "FTC planning memorandum," p. 109.

price: Krieger, *Successful Funeral Service Management*, p. 259.

34 Krieger: Krieger, *Successful Funeral Service Management*, p. 259.

Raether: Howard C. Raether, "The Place of the Funeral," in *Omega—The Journal of Death and Dying*, Vol. 2, No. 3, p. 140.

managers: Krieger, *Successful Funeral Service Management*, p. 262.

35 embalming: Krieger, *Successful Funeral Service Management*, p. 28.

advertisement: Quoted in Coriolis, *Death, Here Is Thy Sting* (Toronto: McClelland & Stewart, 1967), p. 39.

extras: *FTC Washington, D.C., Survey*, pp. 25-26.

36 vaults: NFDA, *Facts and Figures*, 1976 ed., p. 12.

cemetery: *Consumer Survival Kit*, adapted by John Dorfman from the television series by the Maryland Center for Public Broadcasting (New York: Praeger Publishers, 1976), pp. 291-92; FTC, "The Price of Death: A Survey Method and Consumer Guide for Funerals, Cemeteries and Grave Markers," December 1975, p. 1.

grave: *Consumer Survival Kit*, p. 291; 1974 CU spot check of cemeteries.

Chapter 3

38 Raether: Quoted in *Antitrust Aspects, Part I*, p. 156.

Jackson: Jackson, *For the Living*, p. 76.

39 advantage: Jackson, *For the Living*, p. 75.

Bowman: LeRoy Bowman, *The American Funeral* (Washington, D.C.: Public Affairs Press, 1959), p. 32. Hereafter cited as Bowman, *The American Funeral.*

essay: Vanderlyn R. Pine, "The Care of the Dead: An Historical Portrait," *Caretaker of the Dead* (New York, 1975), reprinted in *Thanatos*, Vol. 1, No. 3 (June 1976), p. 21.

goods: *Hearing on Small Business, Part III*, p. 77.

cremations: *The Cremationist of North America* (Sherman Oaks, Calif.: The Cremation Association of North America), April/May/June 1977, p. 5. Hereafter cited as *The Cremationist.*

chain: See advertisement, for example, *New York Daily News*, February 9, 1977, p. 39.

arrangement: Crestwood Memorial Chapel, "An Inexpensive Guide to Cremations and Burials" (pamphlet), pp. 1-2.

Chapter 4

43 cadavers: "Continuing Drop in Unclaimed Bodies Is Hindering Medical School Classes," *The New York Times*, October 21, 1974.

memorial: Raether and Slater, "The Funeral with the Body Present," in *Problems of Death*, edited by D. Bender, p. 135.

Great Neck: Nassau North Chapels, Inc., Great Neck, N.Y., statement dated July 6, 1972.

44 society: Continental Association of Funeral and Memorial Societies (CAFMS) brochure; Elizabeth Ogg, "A Death in the Family" (Public Affairs Committee pamphlet, 1976), p. 13.

groups: Phone interview, CAFMS, August 3, 1977.

PART II

Chapter 5

49 hospital: Robert Fulton, "A Compilation of Studies of Attitudes Toward Death, Funerals, Funeral Directors, Participated in by the Clergy, the Public, Funeral Directors, Including Critical Segments Thereof" (booklet), 1971, p. 49.

Canadian: "Funeral Arrangements: Moneymaking Venture Outdated Tradition?" *Canadian Consumer*, February 1975.

50 body-snatching: "Funeral Homes Face an Inquiry," *The New York Times*, September 9, 1974.

policy: NYPIRG, "A Death in the Family," p. 4.

NYPIRG: NYPIRG, "A Death in the Family," p. 5.

Pittsburgh: "Funeral Costs Not Easy to Get," *Post-Gazette*, Pittsburgh, October 22, 1974.

51 Maryland: Letter from Maryland Citizens Consumer Council to the FTC, June 28, 1976.

Arvio: Raymond Arvio, *The Cost of Dying and What You Can Do About It* (New York: Harper & Row, 1974), p. 46. Hereafter cited as Arvio, *The Cost of Dying.*

societies: Ernest Morgan, *A Manual of Death Education and Simple Burial*, 8th edition (Burnsville, N.C.: The Celo Press, 1977), p. 41 and insert to p. 32. Hereafter cited as Morgan, *Manual.*

52 Lutheran: Commission on Research and Social Action, The American Lutheran Church, "Appointed Once to Die" (pamphlet), July 1965, p. 3.

Johnson: Howard A. Johnson, D.D., canon theologian of the Cathedral Church of St. John the Divine, New York, statement in *Antitrust Aspects, Part I*, pp. 172-73.

Coriolis: Coriolis, *Death, Here Is Thy Sting*, pp. 75-77.

respondents: Fulton, "A Compilation of Studies and Attitudes Toward Death," p. 49.

Jewish: *The Jewish Funeral Guide*, prepared by The Joint Funeral Standards Committee of the Rabbinical Council of America and The Union of Orthodox Jewish Congregations of America, pp. 64-65.

53 Worth: Quoted in Memorial Society Association of Canada, "Church Comment on Funerals" (pamphlet), n.d., n.p.

Baiz: "Can You Afford to Die?" *Post-Gazette*, Pittsburgh, April 12, 1972.

Washington: Phone interviews with William A. Wendt, February 10, 1977, and St. Francis Burial Society, February 15, 1977; "St. Francis Burial Society" (pamphlet), n.d., n.p.; *The Virginia Churchman*, January 1977.

54 Forum: Phone interview, St. Francis Burial Society, February 15, 1977.

Minneapolis: "F.T.C. Studies the Cost of Dying," *The New York Times*, September 26, 1976.

District 65: Phone interview, District 65 of Distributive Workers of America, November, 25, 1975.

Chapter 6

56 benefits: U.S. Department of Health, Education, and Welfare, Social Security Administration, *Social Security Programs in the United States* (Washington, D.C.: U.S. Government Printing Office, 1971), p. 111; phone interview, Railroad Retirement Board, New York City, October 18, 1974; phone interview, Social Security Office, New York City, October 22, 1976; phone interview, New York State Veterans Counselor, Veterans Affairs, White Plains, N.Y., October 22, 1974.

automobile: Insurance Information Institute, "Insurance Facts," 1974 edition, p. 67.

bill: Phone interview, House Subcommittee on Consumer Protection and Finance, Washington, D.C., May 17, 1977.

Continental: Letter to John E. Moss, chairman, House Subcommittee on Commerce and Finance, from Rebecca Cohen, executive secretary, CAFMS, July 26, 1974.

57 death benefit: Phone interview, New York City Social Security Office, September 27, 1977.

payment: "Your New Social Security and Medicare Fact Sheet" (pamphlet) (Washington, D.C.: The Bureau of National Affairs, 1974), p. 3.

benefit: Veterans Administration, "Summary of Benefits for Veterans with Military Service before February 1, 1955, and Their Dependents" (booklet), revised May 1975, p. 12. Hereafter cited as Veterans Administration "Summary of Benefits . . ."

sites: Phone interview, National Cemetery System, Veterans Administration, Washington, D.C., May 17, 1977.

Morgan: Morgan, *Manual*, p. 42.

29 million: U.S. Congress, House of Representatives, Subcommittee on Cemeteries and Burial Benefits of the Committee on Veterans Affairs, *Study of the National Cemetery System: Hearing*, 94th Cong., 1st sess., May 12, 19, June 23, and July 14, 1975, p. 542. Hereafter cited as *National Cemetery System Study, 1975.*

Arlington: Veterans Administration, "Summary of Benefits . . . ," p. 13.

spouses: Cooperative Extension Service, South Dakota State University, U.S. Department of Agriculture, "After the Funeral" (pamphlet), n.d.; phone interview, New York State Division of Veterans Affairs, White Plains, N.Y., January 1, 1977.

58 application: Veterans Administration, "Summary of Benefits . . . ," p. 12.

headstone: Veterans Administration, "Summary of Benefits . . . ," pp. 12-13.

hospital: *Federal Register*, March 30, 1977, p. 16839.

$800: *National Cemetery System Study, 1975*, p. 526.

conditions: "Veterans Administration News," Washington, D.C., September 2, 1973.

application: Veterans Administration, "Summary of Benefits . . . ," p. 12.

59 papers: "Personal Finance: Steps for Widows," *The New York Times*, January 6, 1975; Walter B. Cooke Funeral Homes, "An Emergency Guide and Other Family Estate Information" (pamphlet), n.d.

60 CPP: C C H Canadian Limited, "Your Canada Pension Plan, 1977" (booklet), pp. 16-17; Jill Watt, *Canadian Guide to Death and Dying* (Vancouver/Toronto: International Self-Counsel Press, 1974), p. 117.

Canada: Watt, *Canadian Guide*, pp. 141-43.

Last Post: Watt, *Canadian Guide*, pp. 148-50.

Quebec: C C H Canadian Limited, "Your Quebec Pension Plan 1977" (booklet), p. 15.

Chapter 7

61 Danbury: Letter, Robert S. Faubel to Robert Hull, Hull Funeral Service, Danbury, Conn., September 6, 1973.

Bowman: Bowman, *The American Funeral*, p. 51.

62 itemization: *FTC Proposed Rule*, p. 109.

Bernard: Bernard, *The Law of Death*, pp. 30-31.

almanac: Bernard, *The Law of Death*, p. 31.

mandatory: *FTC Proposed Rule*, pp. 109-10.

Minnesota: Minnesota Office of Consumer Services, press release, October 24, 1975.

63 New York: *FTC Proposed Rule*, p. 109; "Rules and Regulations of the State Board of Mortuary Science of New Jersey," in *Hearings on Small Business, Part III*, p. 373.

Twenty-six: *FTC Proposed Rule*, p. 110.

departure: *FTC Proposed Rule*, p. 115.

proposal: *FTC Proposed Rule*, p. 86.

finance: "F.T.C. Studies the Cost of Dying," *The New York Times*, September 26, 1976.

payment: U.S. Congress, House of Representatives, Subcommittee on Activities of Regulatory Agencies of the Committee on Small Business, *Regulations of Various Federal Regulatory Agencies and Their Effect on Small Business, Part IV*, 94th Cong., 2nd sess., March 25, April 6, June 16, and July 28, 1976, p. 260. Hereafter cited as *Hearings on Small Business, Part IV*.

Chapter 8

64 Bowman: Bowman, *The American Funeral*, p. 30.

Ace: "Top of My Head," *Saturday Review*, March 21, 1970, p. 4.

65 belittlement: Bowman, *The American Funeral*, p. 30.

"Cadillac theory": Coriolis, *Death, Here Is Thy Sting*, p. 68.

proprietor: Coriolis, *Death, Here Is Thy Sting*, p. 68.

Glen Cove: "Religious Rites Diminishing in Funerals," *The Reporter Dispatch*, White Plains, N.Y., September 11, 1974.

Baltimore: "What the Undertakers Often Hide from the Bereaved," *The Sunday Sun*, Baltimore, January 16, 1977.

66 Highland Park: *Hearings on Small Business, Part IV*, p. 251.

Love: "Surviving Widowhood," *Ms. Magazine*, October 1974, pp. 87, 89.

67 "cheapness": Quoted in Memorial Society Association of Canada, "Church Comment on Funerals" (pamphlet), n.d., n.p.

Chapter 9

69 range: *FTC Washington, D.C., Survey*, p. 15.

coffins: *FTC Washington, D.C., Survey*, p. 41.

other means: Phone interview, Omega Funeral Service Corp., Elmsford, N.Y., March 24, 1976.

survey: "Funerals: Coming to Grips With the Last Consumer Problem," *Media & Consumer*, June 1974, p. 3.

Washington, D.C.: *FTC Washington, D.C., Survey*, pp. 6-9.

Chapter 10

71 advertisements: Minneapolis *Tribune*, November 13, 1944; Minneapolis *Star*, November 26, 1974.

appropriate: Minneapolis *Tribune*, November 13, 1974.

72 restriction: *FTC Proposed Rule*, pp. 122-32.

"Keystone": Krieger, *Successful Funeral Service Management*, p. 292.

Krieger: Krieger, *Successful Funeral Service Management*, pp. 288-89.

conditions: Coriolis, *Death, Here Is Thy Sting*, pp. 91-92.

visits: *FTC Proposed Rule*, p. 91.

gauge: Coriolis, *Death, Here Is Thy Sting*, p. 97.

73 order: Krieger, *Successful Funeral Service Management*, p. 290.

"embarrassed": Krieger, *Successful Funeral Service Management*, p. 299.

concentration: Krieger, *Successful Funeral Service Management*, p. 285.

Coriolis: Coriolis, *Death, Here Is Thy Sting*, pp. 95-98.

article: *Mortuary Management*, August 1969, p. 22.

Baltimore: "What the Undertakers Often Hide from the Bereaved," *The Sunday Sun*, Baltimore, January 16, 1977.

74 "key sales": Coriolis, *Death, Here Is Thy Sting*, pp. 96, 99.

"loaded gun": Coriolis, *Death, Here Is Thy Sting*, p. 91.

"traumatic": Raether and Slater, *The Funeral Director and His Role*, pp. 42-43.

"orientation": Raether and Slater, *The Funeral Director and His Role*, pp. 43-44.

Raether: Raether and Slater, *The Funeral Director and His Role*, p. 40.

gift: Raether and Slater, *The Funeral Director and His Role*, p. 40.

75 coercion: Raether and Slater, *The Funeral Director and His Role*, p. 44.

"lift-lid": Coriolis, *Death, Here Is Thy Sting*, p. 137.

woods: Krieger, *Successful Funeral Service Management*, pp. 246-47.

welfare: Raether and Slater, *The Funeral Director and His Role*, p. 41.

electrolytic: Krieger, *Successful Funeral Service Management*, pp. 246-47.

76 caskets: Phone interview, Casket Manufacturers Association of America, March 18, 1977.

fabrics: Krieger, *Successful Funeral Service Management*, p. 246.

"TOP SECRET": "FTC planning memorandum," p. 108.

prices: NYPIRG, "A Death in the Family," p. 6.

coffins: "Funerals: Coming to Grips With the Last Consumer Problem," *Media & Consumer*, June 1974, p. 4.

Notes

variety: Krieger, *Successful Funeral Service Management*, p. 248.

models: Pages from coffin catalogue.

"shooks": "Last Ride to Harts Island," *The New York Times*, August 14, 1974; phone interview, City Mortuary (Bellevue Hospital, New York, N.Y.) August 30, 1977.

77 differences: Sidney Margolius, *"Funeral Costs and Death Benefits"* (Public Affairs pamphlet No. 409), October 1967, p. 12.

Coriolis: Coriolis, *Death, Here Is Thy Sting*, pp. 134, 139.

"component": Testimony of John Curran, president of New York State Funeral Directors Association, *Albany Public Hearing*.

minimum: An Investigation by the New York State Temporary Commission on Living Costs and the Economy into the Practices of the Funeral Industry in the State of New York, 1974, p. 20.

testifying: Testimony of Mrs. James A. Lippke, Federation of Memorial Societies of The Greater New York Area (New York, New Jersey, and Connecticut), *Albany Public Hearing*.

coffins: *FTC Washington, D.C., Survey*, pp. 7-8.

"markup": Phone interview, Casket Manufacturers Association of America, March 18, 1977.

78 five: "FTC planning memorandum," p. 109.

unit pricing: Krieger, *Successful Funeral Service Management*, p. 262; NFDA, *Facts and Figures*, 1976 ed., p. 49.

total: *FTC Washington, D.C., Survey*, pp. 25-27.

Bi-Unit: Krieger, *Successful Funeral Service Management*, p. 265; *Washington, D.C., Hearing*, p. 7.

costs: Phone interview, Casket Manufacturers Association of America, March 18, 1977.

industry: "FTC planning memorandum," p. 109.

receptacle: *FTC Washington, D.C., Survey*, p. 33.

79 itemization: *FTC Proposed Rule*, p. 109.

fines: New York State Department of Health, news release, April 22, 1976.

Coriolis: Coriolis, *Death, Here Is Thy Sting*, pp. 89-90.

list: *FTC Proposed Rule*, pp. 110-19.

"ascending order": *FTC Proposed Rule*, pp. 93-94.

80 conversation: "Funeral Societies," *Everybody's Money*, Autumn 1970, p. 10.

bulletin: *CLF News Bulletin for Religious Liberals* (Church of the Larger Fellowship, Unitarian Universalist), April 1976, p. 1.

charts: An Investigation by the New York State Commission . . . , p. 10.

recording: An Investigation by the New York State Commission . . . , p. 10.

compensation: *FTC Proposed Rule*, p. 77.

Batesville: *Business and Society Review* (Winter 1976-77), p. 27.

81 blatant: An Investigation by the New York State Commission . . . , p. 20.

terms: Coriolis, *Death, Here Is Thy Sting*, p. 138; "FTC planning memorandum," p. 97.

techniques: *FTC Proposed Rule*, p. 81.

Washington: *FTC Washington, D.C., Survey*, p. 16.

Florida: *FTC Proposed Rule*, pp. 70-71.

buyers: *FTC Proposed Rule*, p. 71.

vulgarize: "FTC planning memorandum," p. 95.

Pawtucket: "Cost of Dying in R.I. Spirals Upward," *Providence Journal*, November 2, 1969.

reporter: "Endgame," *Los Angeles Times WEST Magazine*, October 8, 1972.

response: NYPIRG, "A Death in the Family," p. 6.

provision: *FTC Proposed Rule*, p. 82.

lining: Coriolis, *Death, Here Is Thy Sting*, p. 82.

82 color: *FTC Proposed Rule*, p. 73.

steel: Phone interview, Casket Manufacturers Association of America, March 18, 1977.

warranty: Advertisement in *Casket & Sunnyside*, September 1973; "FTC planning memorandum," p. 89.

sealer coffin: Phone interview, FTC attorney, Bureau of Consumer Protection, working on funeral industry investigation, September 26, 1977.

Raether: Raether and Slater, *The Funeral Director and His Role*, p. 41.

survey: Casket Manufacturers Association of America, "American Attitudes Toward Death and Funerals," pp. 36-38.

display: *FTC Proposed Rule*, pp. 71-74.

attorney: Phone interview, FTC attorney, Bureau of Consumer Protection, working on funeral industry investigation, September 26, 1977.

83 autopsy: "Two More Bodies Will Be Exhumed," *The New York Times*, February 9, 1976.

Jachimczyk: Thomas Thompson, *Blood and Money* (Garden City, N.Y.: Doubleday & Company, 1976), p. 150.

soil: Personal communication, September 21, 1977.

Mitford: Jessica Mitford, *The American Way of Death* (New York: Simon and Schuster, 1963), pp. 84-85.

guarantee: An Investigation by the New York State Commission . . . , pp. 16, 18.

Westchester: Phone interview, Westchester County (N.Y.) Medical Examiner, November 15, 1976.

84 "Creceptacle": "The Century Plan" (brochure), from Havey-Maloney Homes for Funerals, Inc., Yonkers, N.Y.

cardboard coffin: Phone interview, Ambrose Havey III, April 21, 1977; phone interview, Stewart Havey, February 2, 1977 (both of Havey-Maloney Homes for Funerals, Inc.).

Iowa: Phone interview, Casket Manufacturers Association of America, March 18, 1977.

coffin/vault: "Plastic Casket Sets Off a Furor in Tidewater," *Washington Post*, April 13, 1977.

"catafalque": "Plastic Casket . . . ," *Washington Post*, April 13, 1977.

transferred: "The Cut-Rate Coffin," *Newsweek*, May 10, 1976, p. 95.

cemetery: "Plastic Casket . . . ," *Washington Post*, April 13, 1977.

decomposition: *FTC Proposed Rule*, p. 68.

85 costs: Phone interview, Casket Manufacturers Association of America, March 18, 1977; "Plastic Casket . . . ," *Washington Post*, April 13, 1977.

Orlando: "The Cut-Rate Coffin," *Newsweek*, May 10, 1976, p. 95.

Virginia: "Plastic Casket . . . ," *Washington Post*, April 13, 1977.

cost: "The Cut-Rate Coffin," *Newsweek*, May 10, 1976, p. 95.

86 society: Brochure from St. Francis Burial Society; phone interview, William A. Wendt, St. Francis Burial Society, February 10, 1977; "What the Undertakers Often Hide from the Bereaved," *The Sunday Sun*, Baltimore, January 16, 1977.

Washington: *FTC Washington, D.C., Survey*, p. 44.

"agreement": An Investigation by the New York State Commission . . . , p. 20.

87 Episcopal: *Antitrust Aspects, Part I*, p. 177.

NFDA Code: NFDA, "Code of Professional Practices for Funeral Directors" (pamphlet), revised October 1972, n.p.

NSM Code: National Selected Morticians, "A Helpful Guide to Funeral Planning" (booklet), 1975, p. 17.

Chapter 11

88 process: Richard Gosse, *The Provision of Funeral and Cemetery Services in British Columbia: A Report Prepared for the Minister of Consumer Services*, 1976, p. 208. Hereafter cited as *B.C. Report;* phone interview, Jack Davies, M.D., chairman, Department of Anatomy, School of Medicine, Vanderbilt University, Nashville, Tenn., March 16, 1977.

eight hours: Prepared statement of David C. Murchison, legal counsel, National Selected Morticians, in *Hearings on Small Business, Part IV*, p. 75.

need: Phone interview, pathologist, White Plains Hospital, White Plains, N.Y., December 11, 1974.

"restoration": *B.C. Report*, pp. 207-8.

cryonics: Robert C. W. Ettinger, *The Prospect of Immortality* (Garden City, N.Y.: Doubleday & Company, 1964), p. 10.

89 embalming: Pine, "The Care of the Dead," in *Thanatos*, June 1976, p. 19.

orthodox: Joint Funeral Standards Committee of the Rabbinical Council of America and The Union of Orthodox Jewish Congregations of America, *Jewish Funeral Guide*, n.d.

common: Coriolis, *Death, Here Is Thy Sting*, p. 39.

Civil War: Coriolis, *Death, Here Is Thy Sting*, p. 26.

text: C. Strub and L. Frederick, *The Principles and Practice of Embalming* (Dallas: L. G. Frederick, 1967), p. 2.

Coriolis: Coriolis, *Death, Here Is Thy Sting*, p. 38.

appearance: Strub and Frederick, *The Principles and Practices of Embalming*, p. 2.

90 cosmetics: Jackson, *For the Living*, pp. 53-55.

identity: Jackson, *For the Living*, p. 57.

requirements: See Appendix 7.

time limit: NFDA, "Comments, Data, Views and Arguments," submitted to the FTC, reprinted in *Hearings on Small Business, Part III*, p. 297.

interstate: NFDA, "Comments, Data, Views and Arguments," p. 297.

communicable: NFDA, "Comments, Data, Views and Arguments," p. 297.

refrigeration: NFDA, "Comments, Data, Views and Arguments," p. 297.

container: See Appendix 7.

glasses: Jackson, *For the Living*, p. 57.

states: See Appendix 7.

91 brochure: Leitz•Eagan Funeral Homes, "We Care Enough to Let You Know," n.p.

New Orleans: Letter from Leitz•Eagan Funeral Homes, June 24, 1976.

inquiry: Letter from chief of Communicable Diseases, Department of Health, New Orleans, October 29, 1976.

Canadian: William A. W. Neilson and C. Gaylord Watkins, *Proposals for Legislative Reforms Aiding the Consumer of Funeral Industry Products & Services* (Burnsville, N.C.: The Celo Press, 1973), pp. 98-99. Hereafter cited as Neilson and Watkins, *Proposals.*

92 dearth: Elmer Koneman and Tate M. Minckler, "Postmortem Bacteriology," *CRC Critical Reviews in Clinical Laboratory Sciences* (Cleveland: Chemical Rubber Company, 1970), p. 6.

letter: Letter from Bacterial Diseases Division, Bureau of Epidemiology, Center for Disease Control, Atlanta, October 11, 1974.

Ives: Elizabeth J. Ives, M.D., unpublished thesis, 1959, pp. 68, 72.

purpose: Koneman and Minckler, *CRC Critical Reviews* . . . , p. 14.

questions: Koneman and Minckler, *CRC Critical Reviews* . . . , pp. 9, 14, 18.

93 letter: Letter from Elizabeth J. Ives, M.D., to Richard B. Middleton, M.D., May 15, 1973; letter from Memorial Society of Canada, Edmonton, Alberta, October 17, 1974.

bacteria: Ives, unpublished thesis, pp. 68-70.

investigators: Ives, unpublished thesis, p. 72.

insurance: Coriolis, *Death, Here Is Thy Sting*, p. 40.

dictum: Koneman and Minckler, *CRC Critical Reviews* . . . , p. 9.

infection: Ives, unpublished thesis, p. 69.

94 Frederick: Jerome F. Frederick, "The Public Health Value of Embalming," n.d.

Rose: Gordon W. Rose and Robert N. Hockett, "The Microbiologic Evaluation and Enumeration of Postmortem Specimens from Human Remains," *Health Laboratory Science*, April 1971, p. 75.

Snell: The Embalming Chemical Manufacturers Association, "Embalming: Ancient Art/Modern Science" (pamphlet), n.d., p. 11.

biochemist: Phone interviews, Dodge Chemical Company, The Bronx, N.Y., May 25, May 27, 1977.

95 editorial: "A Definitive Study Proves That Embalming Safeguards Public Health," *The American Funeral Director*, August 1973, p. 31.

mandatory: Bernard, *The Law of Death*, p. 21; *FTC Proposed Rule*, p. 56.

Bernard: Bernard, *The Law of Death*, p. 26.

Coriolis: Coriolis, *Death, Here Is Thy Sting*, p. 39.

96 contact: Letter from Bacterial Diseases Division, Bureau of Epidemiology, Center for Disease Control, Atlanta, October 11, 1974.

British Columbia: *B.C. Report*, p. 210.

Vancouver: *B.C. Report*, pp. 210-11.

study: Lyle A. Weed, M.D., and Archie H. Baggenstoss, M.D., "The Isolation of Pathogens from Tissues of Embalmed Human Bodies," in *American Journal of Clinical Pathology*, 1951, p. 1120.

significant: Weed and Baggenstoss, "The Isolation of Pathogens . . . ," p. 1115.

97 dissertation: Ives, unpublished thesis, pp. 70-72.

sterilize: Ives, unpublished thesis, p. 72.

embalmers: Ives, unpublished thesis, pp. 73-74.

contagion: Weed and Baggenstoss, "The Isolation of Pathogens . . . ," p. 1120.

98 Newfoundland: Neilson and Watkins, *Proposals*, p. 48.

Heard: "Can You Afford to Die?" *Post-Gazette*, Pittsburgh, April 12, 1972.

statement: Phone interview, Norman G. Heard, Norman Heard Funeral Home, Pittsburgh, March 25, 1977.

Toronto: Coriolis, *Death, Here Is Thy Sting*, pp. 39-40.

transmission: *B.C. Report*, p. 210.

Carr: Mitford, *The American Way of Death*, pp. 82-84.

99 conditions: Phone interview, Norman G. Heard, March 25, 1977.

Raether: *Hearings on Small Business, Part III*, p. 68.

Notes

thesis: "FTC planning memorandum," pp. 86-87.
fluid: Phone interview, Jack Davies, M.D., School of Medicine, Vanderbilt University, Nashville, Tenn., March 16, 1977.
chemical: Phone interview, Committee on Forensic Pathology, College of American Pathologists, Baltimore, March 1, 1977.
autopsy: Thompson, *Blood and Money*, pp. 160-62.
range: Phone interview, Norman Heard, March 25, 1977.
appearance: Coriolis, *Death, Here Is Thy Sting*, p. 39.
100 Gerber: Phone interview, S. R. Gerber, executive secretary, International Association of Coroners and Medical Examiners, Cleveland, Ohio, March 21, 1977.
decompose: Prepared statement of David C. Murchison, legal counsel, National Selected Morticians, in *Hearings on Small Business, Part IV*, p. 83; draft copy of Foreword, "A Manual on Postmortem Procedures," College of American Pathologists.
cadavers: Phone interview, Jack Davies, School of Medicine, Vanderbilt University, Nashville, Tenn., March 16, 1977.
101 reasons: *Hearings on Small Business, Part IV*, p. 83.
unembalmed: Statement of David C. Murchison, in *Hearings on Small Business, Part IV*, p. 83.
deterioration: NFDA, "Comments, Data, Views and Arguments," p. 298.
refrigeration: *Hearings on Small Business, Part IV*, p. 84; *Hearings on Small Business, Part III*, p. 64.
purchases: Phone interview, Bally Case & Cooler Co., Bally, Pa., March 15, 1977.
Representatives: Phone interview, Jewett Refrigerator Co., Buffalo, N. Y., March 14, 1977; phone interview, Bally Case & Cooler Co., March 15, 1977.
visitation: Phone interview, Omega Funeral Service, Elmsford, N.Y., March 24, 1976.
facilities: Phone interview, Stewart Havey, Havey-Malone Homes for Funerals, Inc., March 8, 1977.
nursing home: Phone interview, Nursing Home and Extended Care Facility of White Plains, N.Y., March 22, 1977.
Prices: Phone interview, Jewett Refrigerator Co., March 14, 1977; brochure from Bally Case & Cooler Co.
102 Westchester: Phone interview, Nursing Home and Extended Care Facility of White Plains, March 22, 1977; phone interview, McMahon Lyon & Hartnett Funeral Home, Inc., March 22, 1977.
Landers: *Chicago Sun-Times*, June 27, 1974, p. 68.
103 pamphlet: NFDA, "With the Body Present" (pamphlet), n.d.
image: Jackson, *For the Living*, p. 41.
deceased: Raether and Slater, "The Funeral with the Body Present," in *Problems of Death*, edited by D. Bender, p. 130.
recover: NFDA, "With the Body Present."
failures: Morgan, *Manual*, p. 5.
104 Christiansen: "Endgame," *Los Angeles Times WEST Magazine*, October 8, 1972.
Parting: Bowman, *The American Funeral*, p. 150.
Kliman: Phone interview, Ann Kliman, Center for Preventive Psychiatry, White Plains, N.Y., March 24, 1977.
Leviton: Phone interview, Daniel Leviton, University of Maryland, March 30, 1977.
105 Weisman: Phone interview, Avery D. Weisman, M.D., professor of psychiatry, Harvard Medical School, March 29, 1977.
climate: *Antitrust Aspects, Part I*, p. 260.

106 provisions: *FTC Proposed Rule*, pp. 18-20.

statement: Prepared statement of David C. Murchison, legal counsel, National Selected Morticians, in *Hearings on Small Business, Part IV*, p. 83.

NSM reasons: Prepared statement of David C. Murchison in *Hearings on Small Business, Part IV*, pp. 83-84.

107 Raether: *Hearings on Small Business, Part III*, pp. 67-69.

statement: NFDA, "Comments, Data, Views and Arguments," p. 299.

equipment: Phone interview, Bally Case & Cooler Co., March 15, 1977.

108 twenty hours: Phone interview, Ambrose Havey III, Havey-Maloney Homes for Funerals, Inc., April 21, 1977.

problems: Phone interview, Ambrose Havey III, April 21, 1977.

Chapter 12

110 Landers: Lincoln Heights *Bulletin News*, September 15, 1962.

clergyman: Howard A. Johnson, D.D., canon theologian of the Cathedral Church of St. John the Divine, New York, N.Y., statement, in *Antitrust Aspects, Part I*, p. 171.

embellishment: *Mortuary Management*, November 1973, p. 39.

111 bizarre: NFDA, *Facts and Figures*, 1976 ed., especially footnotes pp. 9ff.

extras: *FTC Washington, D.C., Survey*, pp. 25-26.

10 percent: Letter from The American Funeral Director, October 15, 1976.

Atlanta: *The New York Times*, March 14, 1968.

Louisiana: "Drive-Up Funeral," *The New York Times*, January 31 and April 17, 1977.

Obituaries: "Obituary Page Changes Explained," *The Reporter Dispatch*, White Plains, N.Y., August 23, 1976.

services: Joseph Gawler's Sons, Inc. (pamphlet), n.p.

112 escorts: *The New York Times*, January 22, 1977.

Heard: "Can You Afford to Die?" *Post-Gazette*, Pittsburgh, April 11, 1972.

"accommodations": *FTC Proposed Rule*, p. 49.

profits: *FTC Proposed Rule*, pp. 51-52.

motorcycle: "Kennedy's Cycle Corps Supplied Not by Police but by Mortuary," *The New York Times*, May 26, 1968.

113 in toto: *FTC Proposed Rule*, p. 53.

advances: *Washington, D.C., Hearing*, p. 10; *FTC Proposed Rule*, pp. 50-53.

overcharges: *FTC Proposed Rule*, pp. 50-51.

pallbearers: Written testimony of Richard O'Keeffe, president, Local 100 Service Employees International Union, AFL-CIO, in *Albany Public Hearing*.

notices: "Can You Afford to Die?" *Post-Gazette*, Pittsburgh, April 10, 1972.

minister: "Endgame," *Los Angeles Times WEST Magazine*, October 8, 1972.

compensation: *FTC Proposed Rule*, pp. 51-52.

hearing: Statement of J. Thomas Rosch, Bureau of Consumer Protection, FTC, in *Washington, D.C., Hearing*, p. 14.

discounts: *FTC Proposed Rule*, p. 52.

114 agents: *FTC Proposed Rule*, p. 52.

floral displays: M. Truman Fossum, "Some Observations About Trends in Expenditures for Funeral and Burial Occasions, United States, 1929-1977" (October 25, 1976), p. 2 of Summary.

establishments: Department of Commerce, Bureau of the Census, *Statistical Abstract of the United States,* 1976, p. 802. Hereafter cited as *Statistical Abstract,* 1976.

value: Letter from Society of American Florists and Ornamental Horticulturists, Alexandria, Va., October 9, 1974.

sales: *Statistical Abstract,* 1976, p. 803.

floriculture: H. Truman Fossum, "Trends in Expenditures for Funeral and Burial Occasions, United States, 1929-1977" (October 25, 1976), n.p.

40 percent: Fossum, "Trends in Expenditures...."

sales: Fossum, "Some Observations About Trends in Expenditures for Funeral and Burial Occasions, United States, 1929-1977," Table 3.

notices: "The Florists' Crusade," *Columbia Journalism Review,* March/April 1976.

overcharge: FTC Consent Order, Docket No. 9071, October 28, 1976.

Mitford: Mitford, *The American Way of Death,* p. 110.

Coriolis: Coriolis, *Death, Here Is Thy Sting,* p. 80.

115 objections: "The Florists' Crusade," *Columbia Journalism Review,* March/April 1976.

survey: "What Funeral Directors Think About Please Omit," *Florist,* September 1973, p. 48.

Press: Media Industry News Letter, November 7, 1975.

flower car: "Economics of Death Outlined," *The East Hampton Star,* July 31, 1975.

116 clothing: Phone interview, Florence Gowns, Cleveland, Ohio, March 25, 1977.

styles: Phone interview, Perfection Burial Garments, Paterson, N.J., March 25, 1977.

retail price: Phone interview, Perfection Burial Garments, March 25, 1977.

fashions: *Casket & Sunnyside,* December 1973, p. 3.

shrouds: *FTC Washington, D.C., Survey,* p. 27.

garment: Phone interview, Florence Gowns, March 25, 1977.

117 specialties: "Can You Afford to Die?" *Post-Gazette,* Pittsburgh, April 11, 1972.

hearse: "F.T.C. Studies the Cost of Dying," *The New York Times,* September 26, 1976; United States of America Before Federal Trade Commission: Report of the Presiding Officer on Proposed Trade Regulation Rule Concerning Funeral Industry Practices, July 1977, p. 98. Hereafter cited as *FTC Presiding Officer's Report.*

limousine: "Can You Afford to Die?" *Post-Gazette,* Pittsburgh, April 11, 1972.

60 percent: NFDA, *Facts and Figures,* 1976 ed., p. 7.

"comfort": "FTC planning memorandum," pp. 100-101.

names: *Mortuary Management,* November 1973, p. 20.

118 charges: *Washington, D.C., Hearing,* p. 52.

reader: Letter and enclosures, Skokie, Ill., resident, May 7, 1974.

airline shipping charges: Letter from Skokie, Ill., resident, May 7, 1974.

200,000: Letter from The American Funeral Director, October 15, 1976.

Massachusetts: "FTC planning memorandum," p. 147.

119 "bags": Phone interview, United Airlines, October 5, 1976; phone interview, American Airlines, October 6, 1976.

rates: *Casket & Sunnyside,* March 1972, p. 21.

Florida: "25,000 Bodies Shipped Last Year," *The Tampa Tribune and Times,* June 10, 1973.

domestic airlines: "FTC planning memorandum," p. 13.

"air hearse": "FTC planning memorandum," p. 13.

rail: Letter from Baggage & Express Service, Amtrak, Washington, D.C., November 29, 1976.

Sky-Pak: "25,000 Bodies Shipped Last Year," *The Tampa Tribune and Times,* June 10, 1973.

"Jim Wilson": Brochure from American Airlines.
rate: Phone interview, American Airlines, October 8, 1976.
"Air Tray": Brochure from American Airlines.
120 rule: Letter from an undertaker in New Castle, Pa., in *Changing Times* (May 1975), p. 48; "FTC planning memorandum," pp. 121-22.
compare: Joseph Bayly, *The View from a Hearse* (Elgin, Ill.: David C. Cook Publishing Co., 1969), p. 73.
New York: *FTC Proposed Rule*, p. 109.
bill: "Preplanning Funerals Offers Choice," *The Herald Statesman*, Yonkers, N.Y., March 27, 1973.
121 deduct: *FTC Washington, D.C., Survey*, p. 43.
122 certificates: *FTC Washington, D.C., Survey*, p. 28.
price: *FTC Washington, D.C., Survey*, p. 43.

Chapter 13

123 pamphlet: NFDA, "What About Funeral Costs?"
choice: *FTC Proposed Rule*, pp. 100-101.
burial: NFDA, "What About Funeral Costs?"
Rosch: *Washington, D.C., Hearing*, p. 9.
124 Egypt: *Casket & Sunnyside*, January 1974.
brochure: "FTC planning memorandum," p. 87.
remains: "FTC planning memorandum," p. 87.
Coriolis: Coriolis, *Death, Here Is Thy Sting*, pp. 119-20.
Rule 9: FTC, "Trade Practice Rules for the Concrete Burial Vault Manufacturing Industry" (statement), July 10, 1937.
125 combination: Letter from Morrison-Gottlieb, Inc., October 10, 1967.
erosion: "Funerals: Coming to Grips With the Last Consumer Problem," *Media & Consumer*, June 1974, p. 4.
letter: Letter from National Concrete Burial Vault Association, Inc., November 5, 1974.
validity: "FTC planning memorandum," p. 88.
Virginia Beach: "Plastic Casket Sets Off a Furor in Tidewater," *Washington Post*, April 13, 1977.
126 doubt: *FTC Proposed Rule*, p. 100.
surveyed: "Funeral Practices and Public Awareness," *Human Ecology Forum* (Winter 1975), p. 11.
vaults: "FTC planning memorandum," p. 100.
grave liner: Phone interview, Pine Lawn Cemetery, Farmingdale, N.Y., June 10, 1977.
receptacle: Phone interview, Pine Lawn Cemetery, June 6, 1977.
72 percent: NFDA, *Facts and Figures*, 1976 ed., p. 12.
sales: Letter from National Concrete Burial Vault Association, November 5, 1974; phone interview, National Concrete Burial Vault Association, March 17, 1977.
reduction: Phone interview, National Concrete Burial Vault Association, Inc., March 17, 1977.
retail: "Funerals: Coming to Grips With the Last Consumer Problem," *Media & Consumer*, June 1974, p. 4.
127 trend: Phone interview, National Concrete Burial Vault Association, March 17, 1977.
price brackets: Phone interview, National Concrete Burial Vault Association, March

17, 1977; brochure from American Vault and Concrete Products Corp., Detroit (1976).

range: *FTC Proposed Rule*, p. 101.

Washington: *FTC Washington, D.C., Survey*, p. 33.

$50: *FTC Washington, D.C., Survey*, p. 27.

cost: *FTC Proposed Rule*, p. 101.

NFDA literature: For example, NFDA, "What About Funeral Costs?" and "The Funeral: Facing Death as an Experience of Life" (booklet), p. 24.

mark-up: *FTC Proposed Rule*, p. 101.

list: *FTC Proposed Rule*, p. 102.

Mitford: Mitford, *The American Way of Death*, p. 59.

128 Raether: Testimony of Howard C. Raether, executive director, NFDA, before *Hearings on Small Business, Part III*, p. 70.

critical: U.S. Congress, House of Representatives, Subcommittee on Activities of Regulatory Agencies of the Committee on Small Buisiness, *Federal Trade Commission's Proposed Funeral Industry Trade Regulation Rule: Its Effect on Small Business: A Report*, October 20, 1976, pp. 20, 24. Hereafter cited as *Small Business Report*.

teams: Attorney general, North Carolina, "Consumer Protection News" (pamphlet), December 1972, p. 5.

warning: Attorney general, North Carolina, "Consumer Protection News," pp. 5-6.

129 reporter: "Cost of Dying in R.I. Spirals Upward," *Providence Journal*, November 2, 1969.

Montgomery: "FTC planning memorandum," p. 86.

manager: Letter from Memorial Park Cemetery, Kansas City, Kans., October 7, 1974.

query: Phone interview, assistant attorney general, Kansas, April 21, 1976.

law: "FTC planning memorandum," pp. 87-88.

survey: 1974 spot check by Consumers Union.

Catholic: Phone interview, Calvary Cemetery, Woodside, N.Y., March 8, 1977.

Veterans: Letter from National Cemetery System, Veterans Administration, Washington, D.C., December 19, 1975.

130 other 22: Letter from National Cemetery System, Veterans Administration, Washington, D.C., December 19, 1975.

Chapter 14

131 skyscraper: "Nashville's Choice: Six Feet Under—or 20 Stories Up," *The Wall Street Journal*, June 13, 1973; phone interview, Woodlawn of Nashville, May 13, 1977; "New Funeral Concept May Provide Answer to High Cost of Dying," *The Wall Street Journal*, October 6, 1969.

furniture: Brochure from Woodlawn of Nashville.

building: "Nashville's Choice: Six Feet Under—or 20 Stories Up," *The Wall Street Journal*, June 13, 1973; phone interview, Woodlawn of Nashville, May 13, 1977.

entombment: National Selected Morticians, "A Helpful Guide to Funeral Planning" (pamphlet), 1973, p. 19.

price: Phone interview, Woodlawn of Nashville, May 13, 1977.

132 "cross repose": Phone interview, Woodlawn of Nashville, May 13, 1977.

"bier": "Nashville's Choice: Six Feet Under—or 20 Stories Up," *The Wall Street Journal*, June 13, 1973.

Ligon: "Nashville's Choice: Six Feet Under—or 20 Stories Up," *The Wall Street Journal*, June 13, 1973; phone interview, Woodlawn of Nashville, May 13, 1977.

advance sale: "Nashville's Choice: Six Feet Under—or 20 Stories Up," *The Wall Street Journal*, June 13, 1973.

space: Phone interview, Woodlawn of Nashville, May 13, 1977.

grotto: Woodlawn of Nashville, "The Tomb of Christ" (pamphlet), n.d.

133 high-rise: "New Funeral Concept May Provide Answer to High Cost of Dying," *The Wall Street Journal*, October 6, 1969.

capacity: Phone interview, National Association of Cemeteries, March 8, 1977.

new interments: Phone interview, National Cemetery System, Veterans Administration, May 17, 1977.

National: *National Cemetery System Study, 1975*, pp. 541, 560.

promotion: *New York Daily News*, November 17, 1975; *New York Daily News*, February 7, 1977.

1 million: U.S. Congress, Senate, *Veterans Burial Benefits: A Study Submitted by the Veterans Administration to the Committee on Veterans Affairs*, Senate Committee Print No. 9, April 30, 1973, p. 5. Hereafter cited as *VA Study, 1973*.

new cemeteries: Phone interview, National Cemetery System, Veterans Administration, May 17, 1977.

134 interments: Letter from superintendent, Calvary Cemetery, New York, N.Y., March 13, 1975.

Boston: "Grave Squeeze," *Newsweek*, September 16, 1968.

Westchester: "Cemetery Space a Growing Problem," *The Reporter Dispatch*, White Plains, N.Y., February 3, 1977.

Calgary: *Candian Guide to Death and Dying*, pp. 69-70.

Baiz: "Can You Afford to Die?" *Post-Gazette*, Pittsburgh, April 13, 1972.

Peabody: ". . . and Dust to Dust," *The New York Times*, February 3, 1975.

Woodlawn: Edward Streeter, *The Story of the Woodlawn Cemetery* (New York: The Woodlawn Cemetery, n.d.), pp. 22-23.

Canada: *Canadian Consumer*, February 1975, p. 31.

135 Wells: "Undertaking with a Green Thumb," *Environmental Quality for Consumer, Ecological and Social Avenues*, August 1972, pp. 30-31.

figure: Phone interview, National Center for Health Statistics, December 9, 1975.

space: *B.C. Report*, pp. 16-17.

cremation: *The Cremationist*, p. 5.

zoning laws: *VA Cemetery Study, 1974*, p. 175.

traditional: "The Cemetery as Cultural Institution: The Establishment of Mount Auburn and the 'Rural Cemetery' Movement," in *Death in America*, edited by David E. Stannard (Philadelphia: University of Pennsylvania Press, 1975), pp. 70-72, 74-75.

survey: "American Attitudes Toward Death and Funerals," Casket Manufacturers Association of America, 1974, p. 18.

136 municipalities: Bernard, *The Law of Death*, p. 72.

laws: Bernard, *The Law of Death*, p. 72.

2,000 to 3,000: Mitford, *The American Way of Death*, p. 127.

very deep: Mitford, *The American Way of Death*, p. 127; phone interview, Pine Lawn Cemetery, Farmingdale, N.Y., June 10, 1977; phone interview, Maple Grove Cemetery, New York, N.Y., September 10, 1974.

private property: Bernard, *The Law of Death*, p. 70.

Forest Lawn: Bernard, *The Law of Death*, p. 75.

137 8,000 bodies: "Cemeteries Add Heavily to the Funeral Bill," *The Sunday Sun*, Baltimore, January 30, 1977.

precise: Phone interview, American Cemetery Association, March 28, 1977; phone interview, National Association of Cemeteries, March 8, 1977.

ACA, NAC: *VA Study, 1973*, p. 1.

two types: Robert W. Habenstein and William M. Lamers, *Funeral Customs the World Over* (Milwaukee: Bulfin Printers, 1963), p. 752.

NFDA: *The Funeral: Facing Death as an Experience of Life* (1974), p. 18.

newcomer: Phone interview, American Cemetery Association, March 28, 1977.

138 markers: *FTC Washington, D.C., Survey*, pp. 30-31.

Veterans: *VA Cemetery Study, 1974*, p. 154.

reporter: "Cost of Dying in R.I. Spirals Upward," *Providence Journal*, November 2, 1969.

"gratuities": "An Investigation by the New York State Commission . . . ," pp. 22, 23-24.

139 "modest": "Cemeteries Add Heavily to the Funeral Bill," *The Sunday Sun*, Baltimore, January 30, 1977.

prices: "What the Undertakers Often Hide from the Bereaved," *The Sunday Sun*, Baltimore, January 16, 1977.

Baltimore: "Cemeteries Add Heavily to the Funeral Bill," *The Sunday Sun*, Baltimore, January 30, 1977.

$200 burial: "Cemeteries Add Heavily to the Funeral Bill," *The Sunday Sun*, Baltimore, January 30, 1977.

inexpensive burials: Phone interview, Omega Funeral Service Corp., Elmsford, N.Y., February 10, 1977.

$170: Phone interview, Direct Cremation Co., February 10, 1977.

spot check: September 1974, Letters from Milwaukee: Arlington Park Cemetery, Highland Memorial Park Cemetery, Prairie Home Cemetery; letters from Kansas City (Kansas and Missouri): East Slope Memorial Gardens, Floral Hills Memorial Gardens, Memorial Park Cemetery; phone interview, Floral Park Cemeteries, Dean, N.J.; letter from Riverside Cemetery, Rochelle Park, N.J.; phone interview, Maple Grove Cemetery, New York, N.Y.; brochure from Kensico Cemetery, Valhalla, N.Y.; letters from Miami: Southern Memorial Park, Vista Memorial Gardens.

high: "FTC planning memorandum," p. 205.

$325: "Funerals: Coming to Grips with the Last Consumer Problem," *Media & Consumer*, June 1974.

Connecticut: *VA Cemetery Study, 1974*, p. 164.

Average: Phone interviews, National Association of Cemeteries, March 8, 1977; American Cemetery Association, March 28, 1977; National Catholic Cemetery Conference, March 25, 1977.

140 Central West: *VA Cemetery Study, 1974*, p. 152.

Seattle: *VA Cemetery Study, 1974*, p. 173.

single-plot: Mitford, *The American Way of Death*, p. 133; *VA Cemetery Study, 1974*, pp. 164-65.

sections: Habenstein and Lamers, *Funeral Customs the World Over*, p. 752; promotional literature from Kensico Cemetery, Valhalla, N.Y., Woodlawn Cemetery, The Bronx, N.Y., Highland Memorial Park, Milwaukee, Memorial Park Cemetery, Kansas City, Kans., Arlington Cemetery, Milwaukee.

"package": *FTC Washington, D.C., Survey*, pp. 31-32.

more expensive: NFDA, *The Funeral: Facing Death as an Experience of Life*, p. 26; "Cemeteries Add Heavily to the Funeral Bill," *The Sunday Sun*, Baltimore, January 30, 1977.

65 percent: "Cemeteries Add Heavily to the Funeral Bill," *The Sunday Sun*, Baltimore, January 30, 1977.

levels: "Cemeteries Add Heavily to the Funeral Bill," *The Sunday Sun*, Baltimore,

January 30, 1977.

NFDA: "Statement of the National Funeral Directors Association," in U.S. Congress, House of Representatives, Subcommittee on Cemeteries and Burial Benefits of the Committee on Veterans Affairs, *Bills Related to the National Cemetery System and to Burial Benefits: Hearings on H.R. 3103, H.R .3577, H.R. 5803, H.R. 10273, H.R. 10300, and H.R. 11140,* 94th Cong., 1st sess., December 1 and 2, 1975, January 26, February 2, and 9, 1976, p. 1319.

preconstruction: "Cemeteries Add Heavily to the Funeral Bill," *The Sunday Sun,* Baltimore, January 30, 1977.

Includes: *VA Cemetery Study, 1974,* p. 142.

141 discount: Advertisements in *Sunday News,* New York, July 11, 1976; *The New York Times,* September 30, 1975.

finished: "Cemeteries Add Heavily to the Funeral Bill," *The Sunday Sun,* Baltimore, January 30, 1977.

Milwaukee: Letter from Arlington Park Cemetery, Milwaukee, October 4, 1974.

fewer people: "Cemetery Manager Explains His Firm's Operation," *The Reporter Dispatch,* White Plains, N.Y., March 10, 1976.

require: Letter from National Concrete Burial Vault Association, November 5, 1974.

more expensive: *FTC Proposed Rule,* p. 100.

spot check: Phone interview, Floral Park Cemeteries, Dean, N.J., October 10, 1974; letter from Floral Hills Funeral Home and Cemetery, Kansas City, Mo., October 8, 1974.

liner: *FTC Washington, D.C., Survey,* pp. 27, 33.

wooden enclosures: Phone interview, National Catholic Cemetery Conference, March 25, 1977.

advertisement: *The New York Times,* April 12, 1975.

spot check: Phone interview, Kensico Cemetery, Valhalla, N.Y., September 10, 1974; Floral Park Cemeteries, Dean, N.J., October 10, 1974; brochure from Prairie Home Cemetery, Milwaukee, October 8, 1974.

142 gravedigger: "FTC planning memorandum," pp. 164-65; "Cemeteries Add Heavily to the Funeral Bill," *The Sunday Sun,* Baltimore, January 30, 1977.

operation: "FTC planning memorandum," p. 165.

Baltimore: "Cemeteries Add Heavily to the Funeral Bill," *The Sunday Sun,* Baltimore, January 30, 1977.

Hartford: "Hartford Gravediggers Return to Work After a Six-Week Strike," *The New York Times,* September 7, 1977.

survey: *FTC Washington, D.C., Survey,* p. 34.

spot check: Letters from Memorial Park Cemetery, Kansas City, Kans., October 7, 1974; Floral Hills Funeral Home and Cemetery, Kansas City, Mo., October 8, 1974; Arlington Park Cemetery, Milwaukee, October 4, 1974 and Prairie Home Cemetery, Milwaukee, October 7, 1974; letter from Vista Memorial Gardens, Miami, October 22, 1974.

Oregon: Oregon State University Extension Service, "When Death Comes," p. 3.

Central West: *VA Cemetery Study, 1974,* p. 168.

Maryland: *VA Cemetery Study, 1974,* p. 165.

Terkel: Studs Terkel, *Working: People Talk About What They Do All Day and How They Feel About What They Do* (New York: Pantheon Books, 1974), p. 508.

143 Seattle: *VA Cemetery Study, 1974,* p. 173.

standard size: Bernard, *The Law of Death,* pp. 84-85; "FTC planning memorandum," p. 166.

Mausoleums: Ferncliff Cemetery Association, Ferncliff Mausoleums, Hartsdale, N.Y., Rules and Regulations, January 1, 1976.

wording: Bernard, *The Law of Death*, p. 85.

markers: Mitford, *The American Way of Death*, p. 127; "FTC planning memorandum," p. 166.

Terkel: Terkel, *Working*, pp. 505-6.

Monument Builders: Phone interview, Monument Builders of North America, March 21, 1977.

FTC: "FTC planning memorandum," p. 166.

brochure: Brochure from Highland Memorial Park Cemetery, Milwaukee.

144 markers: Oregon State University Extension Service, "When Death Comes," p. 5; *FTC Washington, D.C., Survey*, p. 31; Alverda Lynch, "Facts About Funerals" (pamphlet), South Dakota State University Cooperative Extension Service, p. 4.

average size: Phone interview, Monument Builders of North America, December 23, 1975.

granite: Phone interview, Monument Builders of North America, March 21, 1977.

Washington: *FTC Washington, D.C., Survey*, p. 31.

spot check: Letter from Memorial Park Cemetery, Kansas City, Kans., October 7, 1974.

interment: *FTC Washington, D.C., Survey*, p. 30.

embalming: "What to Do If Decomposition Renders Mausoleum Miasmatic," *Casket & Sunnyside*, February 1975; letter from assistant attorney general, Kansas, September 9, 1977, enclosing Kansas statute 28-9-4, which states, "No dead body shall be interred or deposited in any public mausoleum or private mausoleum of more than two crypts unless the body has first been embalmed in compliance with recognized embalming practice."

decorations: Ferncliff Cemetery Association, Hartsdale, N.Y., Rules and Regulations; brochure from Prairie Home Cemetery, Milwaukee.

problems: "What to Do If Decomposition Renders Mausoleum Miasmatic," *Casket & Sunnyside*, February 1975.

145 Louisville: "Cemetery's Rule: Service or Expense?" *Courier-Journal*, Louisville, February 24, 1976.

146 Bernard: Bernard, *The Law of Death*, p. 75.

high-pressure: Attorney general, North Carolina, "Consumer Protection News," pp. 5-7.

147 fraud: "Docket: Cemetery Firms Fined fo Deceptive Practices," *Consumer Reports*, March 1975, p. 155.

schemes: "FTC planning memorandum," pp. 171-74.

Vietnam: *VA Cemetery Study, 1974*, p. 176.

plot: "FTC planning memorandum," pp. 169-70.

Bernard: Bernard, *The Law of Death*, p. 71.

Code: "FTC planning memorandum," pp. 174-75; "National Association of Cemeteries: Consumer's Code for Veterans' Programs," *VA Cemetery Study, 1974*, p. 55.

148 transfer: "Cemeteries Add Heavily to the Funeral Bill," *The Sunday Sun*, Baltimore, January 30, 1977.

New York: Letter from New York State Funeral Directors Association, October 8, 1975, enclosing law; "FTC planning memorandum," p.70.

inflation: "FTC planning memorandum," p. 168.

trust: FTC, "The Price of Death."

reduction: "Cemeteries Add Heavily to the Funeral Bill," *The Sunday Sun*, Baltimore, January 30, 1977.

149 time-payment: "Cemeteries Add Heavily to the Funeral Bill," *The Sunday Sun*, Baltimore, January 30, 1977.

twenty cemeteries: NYPIRG, "A Death in the Family," p. 7.

10 percent: "Cemeteries Add Heavily to the Funeral Bill," *The Sunday Sun*, Baltimore, January 30, 1974.

endowment: FTC, "The Price of Death," p. 16.

150 requirements: Bernard, *The Law of Death*, p. 84.

restrictive: FTC, "The Price of Death," p. 19.

smaller fees: FTC, "The Price of Death," p. 20; letter from employee of an independent memorial dealer, November 2, 1976.

Mausoleums: Bernard, *The Law of Death*, p. 84; Ferncliff Cemetery Association, Hartsdale, N.Y., Rules and Regulations.

PART III

Chapter 15

155 process: Paul E. Irion, *Cremation* (Philadelphia: Fortress Press, 1968), p. 24.

450 crematories: Phone interview, Cremation Association of North America, September 15, 1977.

80 percent: Phone interview, Cremation Association of North America, May 10, 1977.

owned: Habenstein and Lamers, *The History of American Funeral Directing*, p. 589.

Arlington: *VA Cemetery Study, 1974*, p. 34.

chamber: Irion, *Cremation*, pp. 37, 43.

gas: Phone interview, Cremation Association of North America, September 15, 1977; phone interview, Fresh Pond Crematory, Middle Village, N.Y., September 13, 1977.

draft control: Irion, *Cremation*, p. 37.

no crematories: Phone interview, Cremation Association of North America, September 9, 1977.

oxidation: Irion, *Cremation*, p. 37.

156 container: *FTC Proposed Rule*, p. 44; Irion, *Cremation*, p. 37.

removed: Irion, *Cremation*, p. 37; "FTC planning memorandum," p. 146.

fiber glass: Irion, *Cremation*, pp. 41-42.

excessive smoke: Letter in *Pharos*, official journal of the Cremation Society of Great Britain and the International Cremation Federation, August 1974, p. 100.

memorial service: Irion, *Cremation*, p. 36.

committal room: Irion, *Cremation*, p. 36.

catafalque: Irion, *Cremation*, p. 36; Cremation Society's *Handbook and Directory of Crematoria*, 7th edition (Hollingbourne, Maidstone, Kent: The Cremation Society of Great Britain, 1975), p. 62. Hereafter cited as *Cremation Handbook*.

floor: Phone interview, Cremation Association of North America, September 9, 1977.

curtain: Irion, *Cremation*, p. 36.

Irion: Irion, *Cremation*, p. 42.

cremations in U.S.: *The Cremationist*, p. 5.

157 cremations in Canada: *The Cremationist*, p. 5.

West Coast: *The Cremationist*, p. 5.

total cremations: *The Cremationist*, p. 5.

Canada: *B.C. Report*, p. 16.

Japan: *B.C. Report*, p. 17.

Tokyo: Charles J. McFadden, *The Dignity of Life: Moral Values in a Changing Society* (Huntington, Ind.: Our Sunday Visitor, 1976), p. 181.

Great Britain: *Cremation Handbook*, p. 98.

Australia: *Pharos*, August 1974, p. 113; *Choice* (Journal of the Australian Consumers' Association), January 1974, p. 4.

New Zealand: *B.C. Report*, p. 17.

Scandinavian: *Pharos*, August 1974, p. 133.

74 percent: *FTC Proposed Rule*, p. 41.

Fulton: Fulton, "A Compilation of Studies of Attitudes Toward Death," p. 21.

crematories: *The Cremationist*, p. 5; *Pharos*, August 1974, pp. 135-36.

158 11.8 percent: *The Cremationist*, p. 5.

16 percent: *The Cremationist*, p. 5.

South Atlantic: *The Cremationist*, p. 5.

North Carolina: Associated Press dispatch, December 26, 1974.

private: Associated Press dispatch, December 26, 1974.

reasons: Associated Press dispatch, December 26, 1974.

direct: Crestwood Memorial Chapel, "An Inexpensive Guide to Cremations and Burials" (pamphlet, n.d.), p. 1.

Philadelphia: Letter from member of Memorial Society of Greater Philadelphia, May 30, 1974; correspondence from Memorial Society of Greater Philadelphia, September 12, 1977.

costly charges: "$95 Cremation Costs Widow $897 Extra," *Detroit Free Press*, February 6, 1972.

160 charge: "FTC planning memorandum," p. 118.

Florida: "Consumer Information: Facts About Funerals" (leaflet) (Florida Board of Funeral Directors and Embalmers in cooperation with Office of the Attorney General and Division of Consumer Services, Department of Agriculture, n.d.), n.p.

Philbrick: " 'Cash and Carry' Cremation Stirs Price War Complaints," *The New York Times*, October 6, 1975.

New York: Phone interview, Walter B. Cooke Funeral Homes, March 17, 1977.

Miami: "FTC planning memorandum," pp. 112-13.

minimal: "FTC planning memorandum," p. 119.

161 Irion: Irion, *Cremation*, p. 43.

inclination: Habenstein and Lamers, *The History of American Funeral Directing*, p. 589.

Raether: Raether and Slater, *The Funeral Director and His Role*, p. 67.

NSM literature: National Selected Morticians, "A Helpful Guide to Funeral Planning" (pamphlet), 1975, p. 19.

plan: Crestwood Memorial Chapel, "An Inexpensive Guide to Cremations and Burials" (pamphlet, n.d.), pp. 1, 7.

pamphlet: NFDA, "Considerations Concerning Cremation" (pamphlet), 1974.

162 threat: *FTC Proposed Rule*, p. 42.

Tennessee undertaker: Testimony of Robert P. Shackelford, Tennessee Funeral Directors Association, in *Hearings on Small Business, Part IV*, p. 21.

Chicago: Testimony of Robert H. Miller, executive director, National Funeral Directors and Morticians Association, in *Hearings on Small Business, Part IV*, pp. 24, 26.

Washington: *FTC Washington, D.C., Survey*, p. 20.

163 survivors': "FTC planning memorandum," p. 118.

flower: Irion, *Cremation*, pp. 36-37.

simple container: *FTC Proposed Rule*, p. 44.

complaints: *FTC Proposed Rule*, p. 43.
requirement: *FTC Proposed Rule*, pp. 42-43.
164 coffin: *FTC Proposed Rule*, pp. 42-43.
coffins: *FTC Proposed Rule*, pp. 44-48.
Maryland: "What the Undertakers Often Hide from the Bereaved," *The Sunday Sun*, Baltimore, January 16, 1977.
"monopolist": *FTC Proposed Rule*, pp. 44-48.
forbid: Yaffa Draznin, *How to Prepare for Death* (New York: Hawthorne Books, 1976), p. 14.
conservative: Draznin, *How to Prepare for Death*, p. 14.
Mormons: Draznin, *How to Prepare for Death*, p. 15.
Orthodox: Irion, *Cremation*, p. 88.
Washington: *FTC Washington, D.C., Survey*, pp. 22-23.
license: "Switching Coffins Costs Mortician His License," *The New York Times*, December 20, 1975.
165 religions: *B.C. Report*, p. 15; *Cremation Handbook*, p. 76.
opposition: Irion, *Cremation*, p. 73.
"pagan": Irion, *Cremation*, p. 86.
resurrection: Irion, *Cremation*, p. 74.
Shaftesbury: Irion, *Cremation*, p. 80.
England: Irion, *Cremation*, p. 88.
denominations: *Cremation Handbook*, p. 76.
Catholic: Irion, *Cremation*, pp. 74-78.
statement: Prepared statement of Gene S. Hutchens, president, Missouri Funeral Directors Association, in *Hearings on Small Business, Part III*, p. 371.
spokesman: "Cemetery Manager Explains His Firm's Operation," *The Reporter Dispatch*, White Plains, N.Y., March 10, 1976.
166 repeal: *Cremation Handbook*, p. 74.
opposition: McFadden, *The Dignity of Life*, p. 181.
1963: McFadden, *The Dignity of Life*, p. 181.
England: *Cremation Handbook*, p. 77.
reasons: McFadden, *The Dignity of Life*, p. 181.
diocese: Draznin, *How to Prepare for Death*, p. 15.
bishops: McFadden, *The Dignity of Life*, p. 181.
spokesman: "Cemetery Manager Explains His Firm's Operation," *The Reporter Dispatch*, White Plains, N.Y., March 10, 1976.
rites: McFadden, *The Dignity of Life*, pp. 181-82.
167 Orthodox: Solomon Freehof, *Contemporary Reform Responsa* (Cincinnati: Hebrew Union College Press, 1975), p. 133; Irion, *Cremation*, pp. 89-90.
Conservative: "Mourning and Funerals" (Summary of decision of Committee on Jewish Law and Standards of The Rabbinical Assembly, n.d.), p. 12; Irion, *Cremation*, p. 89.
Irion: Irion, *Cremation*, p. 91.
laws: Irion, *Cremation*, p. 93; Bernard, *The Law of Death*, p. 82.
instructions: Bernard, *The Law of Death*, p. 15.
168 permit: Irion, *Cremation*, p. 98.
laws: Bernard, *The Law of Death*, p. 82.
conceal: Bernard, *The Law of Death*, p. 82.
physician: Irion, *Cremation*, p. 98.

Notes

foul play: Irion, *Cremation*, pp. 96-98.
authorization: Irion, *Cremation*, pp. 95, 98.
two states: *FTC Proposed Rule*, pp. 46-47.
Massachusetts: *FTC Proposed Rule*, p. 47.
Michigan: *FTC Proposed Rule*, p. 46.
enforced: *FTC Proposed Rule*, pp. 46-47.
Washington: *FTC Washington, D.C., Survey*, p. 22.
East Hampton: "Economics of Death Outlined," *The East Hampton Star*, July 31, 1975.
Bernard: Bernard, *The Law of Death*, p. 83.
169 "suitable casket": Irion, *Cremation*, p. 41.
seven states: *FTC Proposed Rule*, p. 46.
rule: *FTC Proposed Rule*, pp. 44-48.
Indiana: Phone interview, Cremation Association of North America, August 24, 1977.
ordinances: Bernard, *The Law of Death*, pp. 83-84.
scattering: Irion, *Cremation*, pp. 47-48; *The Cremationist*, p. 12.
suggests: Irion, *Cremation*, p. 41.
New Jersey: *FTC Proposed Rule*, p. 47.
pulverization: *The Cremationist*, p. 12.
170 California: "As Burial Costs Go Up, So Does the Popularity of Scattering Ashes," *The Wall Street Journal*, September 25, 1973.
disapproval: "As Burial Costs Go Up, So Does the Popularity of Scattering Ashes," *The Wall Street Journal*, September 25, 1973.
ashes: Irion, *Cremation*, p. 47.
policy: *The Cremationist*, p. 15.
burial: "As Burial Costs Go Up, So Does the Popularity of Scattering Ashes," *The Wall Street Journal*, September 25, 1973.
lawyer: Bernard, *The Law of Death*, p. 84.
charges: NFDA, "The Funeral: Facing Death as an Experience of Life," p. 26; phone interview, Walter B. Cooke Funeral Homes, New York, N.Y., March 17, 1977.
grinder: "As Burial Costs Go Up, So Does the Popularity of Scattering Ashes," *The Wall Street Journal*, September 25, 1973.
Irion: Irion, *Cremation*, pp. 47-48.
171 Washington: *FTC Washington, D.C., Survey*, p. 21.
charge: *FTC Washington, D.C., Survey*, p. 21.
transporting: "Economics of Death Outlined," *The East Hampton Star*, July 31, 1975.
deliver: "Economics of Death Outlined," *The East Hampton Star*, July 31, 1975.
parcel post: "FTC planning memorandum," p. 112.
urns: *The Cremationist*, pp. 4, 13, 16.
Service: *Hearings on Small Business, Part IV*, p. 249.
South Dakota: Alverda Lynch, "Facts About Funerals" (pamphlet) (Brookings, S.D.: Cooperative Extension Service, U.S. Department of Agriculture, South Dakota University, n.d.), p. 4.
charge $25: "FTC planning memorandum," p. 121.
172 bronze: *The Cremationist*, advertisements, pp. 4, 8, 9, 15, 16.
price: Irion, *Cremation*, p. 46.
several people: Oregon State University Extension Service, "When Death Comes," p. 5.

304

columbarium: Oregon State University Extension Service, "When Death Comes," p. 5.
facings: *The Cremationist*, p. 8; FTC, "The Price of Death," p. 19.
Inscriptions: FTC, "The Price of Death," p. 19.
cost: NFDA, "The Funeral: Facing Death as an Experience of Life," p. 26.
Baltimore: "What the Undertakers Often Hide from the Bereaved," *The Sunday Sun*, Baltimore, January 16, 1977.
shelves: Irion, *Cremation*, p. 46.
"urn garden": Irion, *Cremation*, p. 46.
private property: Oregon State University Extension Service, "When Death Comes," p. 4; "Family Plots: Homely History Amid Sprawl," *The New York Times*, May 22, 1977.
plot: "Economics of Death Outlined," *The East Hampton Star*, July 31, 1975.
vaultlike: Oregon State University Extension Service, "When Death Comes," p. 5.
crematories: Irion, *Cremation*, p. 45; NFDA, "Considerations Concerning Cremation," 1974.
173 $270: "Scatter His Ashes at Liberty's Feet," *New York Post*, February 4, 1977.
$250: "His Airy Way of Living Turns to Ashes," *New York Post*, September 22, 1975.
Portland: "As Burial Costs Go Up, So Does the Popularity of Scattering Ashes," *The Wall Street Journal*, September 25, 1973.
societies: Oregon State University Extension Service, "When Death Comes," p. 5.
canister: Oregon State University Extension Service, "When Death Comes," p. 4.
Atlantic: "Economics of Death Outlined," *The East Hampton Star*, July 31, 1975.
pilot: "His Airy Way of Living Turns to Ashes," *New York Post*, September 22, 1975.
viewing: *FTC Washington, D.C., Survey*, p. 24.
174 unmarked: "Planning and Paying for Funerals" (Agricultural Extension Service, University of Minnesota, September 1969), p. 23.
storage: Oregon State University Extension Service, "When Death Comes," p. 5.
Hartsdale: "Resting in Style at Ferncliff," *The New York Times*, April 10, 1977.

Chapter 16

175 $250: The Telophase Society of America, "Complete Cremation Services" (pamphlet) (San Diego, 1973).
name: "New Firm Offers Cremation Service to Cut Death Costs," *Evening Tribune*, San Diego, April 26, 1971.
founded: "Low-Cost Funeral Firm Battles Legislative Bills," *The San Diego Union*, February 10, 1974; "A Move to Embalm 'Cremation Clubs,'" *Business Week*, September 21, 1974.
fee: Phone interview, Telophase, February 18, 1977.
members: Phone interview, Thomas B. Weber, president, Telophase, April 12, 1977; phone interview, Thomas B. Weber, Telophase, February 24, 1977; phone interview, Telophase, February 18, 1977.
branches: Phone interview, Thomas B. Weber, Telophase, February 24, 1977.
grosses: Phone interview, Thomas B. Weber, Telophase, February 24, 1977.
children: Phone interview, Telophase, February 18, 1977.
Weber: Letter from Thomas B. Weber, Telophase, October 28, 1974.
176 brochure: The Telophase Society of America, "Complete Cremation Services" (pamphlet) (San Diego, 1974).
"barbaric": "Death Minus Boloney," *The Star News*, San Diego, April 5, 1973;

Notes

"New Firm Offers Cremation Service to Cut Death Costs," *Evening Tribune*, San Diego, April 26, 1971.

opposition: "Cheap Cremation Wins a Lease on Life," *Business Week*, August 12, 1972, p. 31.

847 licensed: "Cheap Cremation Wins a Lease on Life," *Business Week*, August 12, 1972, p. 31.

Neptune: "The Boom in Low-Cost Funerals," *The San Francisco Bay Guardian*, June 9, 1977.

attacks: "A Move to Embalm 'Cremation Clubs,'" *Business Week*, September 21, 1974.

177 commitment: "Trend to Cremations on Incline," *Times-Advocate*, Escondido, Calif., February 16, 1973; Telophase, "Complete Cremation Services," 1973.

lobbying: "A Move to Embalm 'Cremation Clubs,'" *Business Week*, September 21, 1974.

funeral directors: Phone interview, Telophase, February 18, 1977.

refrigeration: Phone interview, Telophase, February 18, 1977.

own crematory: Phone interview, Thomas B. Weber, Telophase, October 7, 1977.

court actions: Phone interview, Thomas B. Weber, Telophase, April 12, 1977; phone interview, Telophase, February 18, 1977.

judge: Decision of Judge Lester Van Tatenhove, Superior Court of the State of California in and for the County of Orange, April 14, 1977.

battles: Phone interview, Thomas B. Weber, Telophase, April 12, 1977.

head: Phone interview, Thomas B. Weber, Telophase, April 12, 1977; phone interview, Telophase, February 18, 1977.

178 unanimity: "High-Cost Funeral Productions Threatened by Extinction," *California Business*, December 14, 1972.

California: "High-Cost Funeral Productions Threatened by Extinction," *California Business*, December 14, 1972.

health regulations: Open letter from president of Telophase to members and friends of the society, March 1974.

179 Spohn: Phone interview, director, Department of Consumer Affairs for the State of California, April 13, 1977.

rules: Amendment to Administrative Rule and Regulation 77.5, effective February 28, 1974; phone interview, Omega Funeral Service, White Plains, N.Y., October 15, 1974.

Askew: "Death Minus Boloney," *The Star News*, San Diego, April 5, 1973.

California: "Brown Places 60 on California Regulatory Boards as 'Lobbyists for People' Instead of Special Interests," *The New York Times*, February 7, 1977.

Florida: Phone interview, National Cremation Society, Largo, Fla., March 21, 1977.

Society: Phone interview, National Cremation Society, March 21, 1977; opinion filed in the Supreme Court of Florida, June 4, 1976.

support: Phone interview, National Cremation Society, March 21, 1977.

editorial: "Join Club or Else," *St. Petersburg Times*, August 13, 1976.

dissent: Dissent opinion, offered in *The Telophase Society of Florida, Inc., et al.*, v. *State Board of Funeral Directors and Embalmers, etc.*, June 4, 1976.

181 Morgan: Letter from Ernest Morgan, February 15, 1975.

Omega: Phone interview, Omega Funeral Service, White Plains, N.Y., October 15, 1974.

"total service": Price list from Omega Funeral Service.

$350: Phone interview, Direct Cremation Company, New York City, February 10, 1977; "Some Commonly Asked Questions About Direct Cremation (leaflet of Direct Cremation Co., 1965).

306

law: "FTC planning memorandum," p. 147.

Freeport: "Do-It-Yourself Funerals: Breaking the Barriers Is Difficult," by Phyllis Austin, reprinted in *Hearings on Small Business, Part IV*, p. 94.

182 Maryland: Phone interview, St. Francis Burial Society, February 15, 1977.

accounts: *St. Francis Burial Society Quarterly*, Winter 1975-76, pp. 6-9; *St. Francis Burial Society Quarterly*, Fall 1976, pp. 6-8.

checklist: *St. Francis Burial Society Quarterly*, Fall 1976, p. 7.

conventional: Literature from Omega Funeral Service, White Plains, N.Y., Crestwood Memorial Chapel (New York City), Walter B. Cooke Funeral Homes (New York City).

pastor: *St. Francis Burial Society Quarterly*, Fall 1976, p. 7.

183 low-cost: *Business Week*, September 21, 1974, p. 89; *FTC Presiding Officer's Report*, pp. 87-88.

three states: Findings of Consumers Union survey of memorial societies, February 1975.

thirty: "A Move to Embalm 'Cremation Clubs,'" *Business Week*, September 21, 1974.

large cities: Responses to 1975 Consumers Union survey from: Memorial Society of Georgia, Atlanta, Ga.; Chicago Memorial Association; Greater Cincinnati Memorial Society; The Greater Kansas City Memorial Society, Kansas City, Mo.; Memorial Society of Greater Philadelphia; Pittsburgh Memorial Society; Memorial and Planned Funeral Society, St. Louis, Mo.

Seattle: Letter from Friend A. Deahl, People's Memorial Association, Seattle, Wash., February 10, 1975.

letter: Letter from Greater Louisville Funeral Society, Inc., Louisville, Ky., February 12, 1975.

Omega: Omega Funeral Service, "Simplicity, Dignity, Reverence" (brochure) (White Plains, N.Y., n.d.), n.p.

Direct Cremation: "Some Commonly Asked Questions About Direct Cremation" (Direct Cremation Co.).

184 Societies: Responses to 1975 Consumers Union survey from: Tucson Memorial Society, Inc., Tucson, Ariz.; The Memorial Association of Central New Mexico, Inc., Albuquerque, N.M.; Western Nevada Funeral Society, Reno, Nev.; Northwest Arkansas Memorial Society, Fayetteville, Ark.; Blackhawk Memorial Society, Davenport, Iowa; Northeastern Indiana Memorial Society, Inc., Fort Wayne, Ind.; The Memorial Society of Essex, Montclair, N.J.; The Raritan Valley Memorial Society, East Brunswick, N.J.

Westchester: Yellow Pages, Westchester, N.Y., Telephone Directory, 1977.

archaic ritual: "Opposition Stiffens to Funeral Spectacles," *California Business*, December 14, 1972.

Chapter 17

185 bill: "Four Medical Examiners Block Autopsy Bill in Albany," *The New York Times*, July 6, 1977; "Albany Bill on Cadavers Causes Protest from Medical Examiners," *The New York Times*, July 4, 1977; "Continuing Drop in Unclaimed Bodies Is Hindering Medical School Classes," *The New York Times*, October 21, 1974; phone interview, Burton S. Sherman, M.D., professor of anatomy, Downstate Medical Center, Brooklyn, N.Y., June 2, 1977.

amendment: "Four Medical Examiners Block Autopsy Bill in Albany," *The New York Times*, July 6, 1977.

Nassau: "Albany Bill on Cadavers Causes Protest from Medical Examiners," *The New York Times*, July 4, 1977.

Sherman: Phone interview, Burton S. Sherman, June 2, 1977.
186 dissection: Phone interview, Burton S. Sherman, June 2, 1977.
thwarted: "Continuing Drop in Unclaimed Bodies Is Hindering Medical School Classes," *The New York Times*, October 21, 1974.
twenty or thirty: "Continuing Drop in Unclaimed Bodies Is Hindering Medical School Classes," *The New York Times*, October 21, 1974.
four students: "Medical Education," *Medical World News*, November 8, 1974, p. 10; CU's medical consultants.
shortage: Phone interview, Burton S. Sherman, June 2, 1977.
programs: Morgan, *Manual*, p. 59.
Davies: Letter from Jack Davies, School of Medicine, Vanderbilt University, Nashville, Tenn., November 3, 1976; "U.S. Schools Share Cadavers," *Medical World News*, April 19, 1976, p. 23.
187 Yale: "U.S. Schools Share Cadavers," *Medical World News*, April 19, 1976, p. 23.
Boston area: "The Cadaver Boom," *Newsweek*, April 17, 1972, p. 63.
Detroit: "The Cadaver Boom," *Newsweek*, April 17, 1972, p. 63.
California: Letter to the Editor from David S. Maxwell, School of Medicine, UCLA, *Medical World News*, June 14, 1976, p. 105.
Emory: "U.S. Schools Share Cadavers," *Medical World News*, April 19, 1976, p. 24.
Virginia: "U.S. Schools Share Cadavers," *Medical World News*, April 19, 1976, p. 24.
Illinois: Phone interview, Burton S. Sherman, June 2, 1977.
Bernard: Bernard, *The Law of Death*, p. 45.
statutes: Bernard, *The Law of Death*, pp. 45, 48; Neilson and Watkins, *Proposals*, p. 14.
glamour: "The Cadaver Boom," *Newsweek*, April 17, 1972, p. 63.
188 laws: "The Uniform Anatomical Gift Act," *Journal of the American Medical Association*, Vol. 206, No. 11, December 9, 1968, p. 2501.
open-ended: "The Uniform Anatomical Gift Act," *JAMA*, December 9, 1968, p. 2503.
wills: "The Uniform Anatomical Gift Act," *JAMA*, December 9, 1968, p. 2503.
legislation: "The Uniform Anatomical Gift Act," *JAMA*, December 9, 1968, p. 2501.
article: "The Uniform Anatomical Gift Act," *JAMA*, December 9, 1968, p. 2503.
189 measures: "The Uniform Anatomical Gift Act," *JAMA*, December 9, 1968, p. 2503.
decedent's wishes: "The Uniform Anatomical Gift Act," *JAMA*, December 9, 1968, p. 2503.
recommendations: "The Uniform Anatomical Gift Act," *JAMA*, December 9, 1968, pp. 2503-4.
six classes: "The Uniform Anatomical Gift Act," *JAMA*, December 9, 1968, p. 2505.
laws: American Medical Association, "Donation of Bodies or Organs for Transplantation and Medical Science" (pamphlet, n.d.), n.p.
book: Neilson and Watkins, *Proposals*, p. 15.
190 Institutions: Morgan, *Manual*, pp. 53-56.
Canadian: Letter from Memorial Society of British Columbia, Vancouver, B.C., November 27, 1976.
postmortem: Neilson and Watkins, *Proposals*, p. 56.
disposition: *Trusts & Estates*, April 1966, p. 264; Morgan, *Manual*, p. 56; promotion material from Medic Alert Foundation.
shortages: NFDA, "Questions and Answers on Anatomical Gifts" (pamphlet, n.d.), p. 1.
Gallup: Copy of 1968 poll, sent by the Gallup poll, Princeton, N.J., March 7, 1975.

California: "Organ Donations Backed in Survey," *The New York Times*, November 22, 1975.

reasons: "Organ Donations Backed in Survey," *The New York Times*, November 22, 1975.

majority: "Organ Donations Backed in Survey," *The New York Times*, November 22, 1975.

Post-Gazette: "A Reporter Donates His Body," *Media & Consumer*, February 1973, p. 15.

policies: NFDA, "Questions and Answers on Anatomical Gifts" (pamphlet, n.d.), front page.

191 "committal": NFDA, "Questions and Answers on Anatomical Gifts" (pamphlet, n.d.), p. 2.

physician: "Lower High Cost of Living," *National Catholic Reporter*, November 5, 1971.

schools: American Medical Association, "Donation of Bodies or Organs for Transplantation and Medical Service" (pamphlet, n.d.), n.p.; School of Medicine, Vanderbilt University, "The Ultimate Gift" (pamphlet, n.d.), n.p.

responsibility: AMA, "Donation of Bodies or Organs for Transplantation and Medical Science."

religious: AMA, "Donation of Bodies or Organs for Transplantation and Medical Science"; "Lower High Cost of Living," *National Catholic Reporter*, November 5, 1971.

Hesburgh: "Is a Catholic Good for Research?" *Chicago Sun-Times*, May 11, 1970, p. 46.

Voelker: "Can You Afford to Die?" *Media & Consumer*, February 1973, p. 15; "Less Costly Burials Push May Backfire," *Post-Gazette*, Pittsburgh, April 14, 1972.

192 Unitarians: Bowman, *The American Funeral*, p. 185.

approved: McFadden, *The Dignity of Life*, pp. 175-76.

virtue: "Is a Catholic Good for Research?" *Chicago Sun-Times*, May 11, 1970, p. 46.

O'Flaherty: "Cadaver Crisis," *America*, October 29, 1966, p. 515.

donor card: AMA, "Donation of Bodies or Organs for Transplantation and Medical Science."

Pius: McFadden, *The Dignity of Life*, pp. 175-76.

tear up: AMA, "Donation of Bodies or Organs for Transplantation and Medical Science."

193 consent: Draznin, *How to Prepare for Death*, p. 20.

alternate: School of Medicine, Vanderbilt, University, "The Ultimate Gift."

transportation costs: Phone interview, Social Security Office, New York, N.Y., October 27, 1976.

survivors: Draznin, *How to Prepare for Death*, pp. 19-20.

pamphlet: NFDA, "Questions and Answers on Anatomical Gifts" (pamphlet, n.d.), p. 2.

194 uneasiness: American Hospital Association, "Postmortem Procedures" (Chicago, 1970), pp. 52, 63, 68.

AHA: AHA, "Postmortem Procedures," p. 10.

support: "The Postmortem Examination: Scientific Necessity or Folly?" *JAMA*, Vol. 233, No. 5, August 4, 1975, pp. 441-43.

Gambino: Letter to the Editor: "Neglected Autopsy," *The New York Times*, February 19, 1976.

Davies: Phone interview, Jack Davies, School of Medicine, Vanderbilt University, Nashville, Tenn., March 16, 1977.

manual: AHA, "Postmortem Procedures," p. 68.

Notes

195 discovery: AHA, "Postmortem Procedures," pp. 12-14.
results: AHA, "Postmortem Procedures," p. 14.
benefits: McFadden, *The Dignity of Life*, pp. 177-78.
serve: McFadden, *The Dignity of Life*, p. 177.
viral: AHA, "Postmortem Procedures," p. 8.
environmental: AHA, "Postmortem Procedures," p. 9.
prohibits: AHA, "Postmortem Procedures," p. 63.
300 deaths: "Four Medical Examiners Block Autopsy Bill in Albany," *The New York Times*, July 6, 1977.
196 Islam: Phone interview, Islamic Center, New York, N.Y., July 28, 1977.
Buddhism: *Collier's Encyclopedia*, 1976 ed., Vol. 23, p. 368.
Hinduism: *Collier's Encyclopedia*, 1976 ed., Vol. 23, p. 368.
Protestantism: AHA, "Postmortem Procedures," pp. 66-67.
Christian Scientists: Phone interview, First Church of Christ, Scientist, New York, N.Y., July 27, 1977; phone interview, First Church of Christ, Scientist, Office of Committee on Publications for the State of New York, New York, N.Y., July 29, 1977.
Catholicism: AHA, "Postmortem Procedures," p. 66.
precepts: Solomon Freehof, *Reform Responsa* (New York: Ktav, 1960), p. 115.
Reform: Freehof, *Reform Responsa*, p. 131.
Orthodox: AHA, "Postmortem Procedures," pp. 64-66.
minimum: AHA, "Postmortem Procedures," pp. 64-65.
remnant: AHA, "Postmortem Procedures," p. 65.
197 Lauterbach: Freehof, *Reform Responsa*, p. 116.
viewing: AHA, "Postmortem Procedures," p. 56.
problems: AHA, "Postmortem Procedures," pp. 56-57.
pathologists: AHA, "Postmortem Procedures," p. 58.
rare instances: AHA, "Postmortem Procedures," p. 58.
"medicolegal": AHA, "Postmortem Procedures," p. 46.
liaison: College of American Pathologists and NFDA, "Postmortem Procedures" (draft copy of manual).
198 no cost: AHA, "Postmortem Procedures," p. 51.
Disfigurement: AHA, "Postmortem Procedures," p. 52.
Mutilation: AHA, "Postmortem Procedures," p. 52.
suffered: AHA, "Postmortem Procedures," p. 53.
someone else: AHA, "Postmortem Procedures," p. 53.
deceased: AHA, "Postmortem Procedures," p. 53.
religion: AHA, "Postmortem Procedures," p. 54.
guidelines: College of American Pathologists, galley proof of *Professional Practices, Guidelines for Pathologists*, Section A 1961.
199 physician: AHA, "Postmortem Procedures," p. 54.
heard: AHA, "Postmortem Procedures," p. 54.
pressure: "Postmortem Procedures," p. 119.
McFadden: McFadden, *The Dignity of Life*, p. 179.
organs: AMA, "Donation of Bodies or Organs for Transplantation and Medical Science."
specify: AMA, "Donation of Bodies or Organs for Transplantation and Medical Science."
metropolitan: Morgan, *Manual*, pp. 53-57.
gift: NFDA, "Questions and Answers on Anatomical Gifts," p. 1.

200 remains: AMA, "Donation of Bodies or Organs for Transplantation and Medical Science."

responsibility: AMA, "Donation of Bodies or Organs for Transplantation and Medical Science."

funeral: NFDA, "Questions and Answers on Anatomical Gifts," p. 2.

25 kinds: AMA, "Donation of Bodies or Organs for Transplantation and Medical Science"; Morgan, *Manual*, pp. 53-54; material sent by Northern California Transplant Bank, San Jose, Calif.; Virgil Smirnow, "The Real Truth About Kidney Transplants" (booklet) (Washington, D.C.: Virgil Smirnow Associates, 1973), p. 15.

research: AMA, "Donation of Bodies or Organs for Transplantation and Medical Science."

Others: AMA, "Donation of Bodies or Organs for Transplantation and Medical Science."

American Medical: AMA, "Donation of Bodies or Organs for Transplantation and Medical Science."

compatible: Irving Ladimer, "The Challenge of Transplantation" (booklet) (The Bronx, N.Y.: Public Affairs Committee, 1970), pp. 4, 6.

shortage: "Transplants: Shortage of Donors Is Still Acute," *The New York Times*, May 29, 1977.

definition: Ladimer, "The Challenge of Transplantation," pp. 14-15.

network: Morgan, *Manual*, p. 57.

201 costs: Ladimer, "The Challenge of Transplantation," pp. 17-19.

34,000 patients: Phone interview, End Stage Renal Disease Medical Information System, Rockville, Md., August 10, 1977.

2,200 donor: Phone interview, End Stage Renal Disease Medical Information System, August 10, 1977.

600 people: "Transplants: Shortage of Donors Is Still Acute," *The New York Times*, May 29, 1977.

AMA: AMA, "Donation of Bodies or Organs for Transplantation and Medical Science."

54,000 people: Kidney Foundation of New York, Inc. (an affiliate of the National Kidney Foundation), promotion material.

corneas: Phone interview, Eye Bank for Sight Restoration, New York, N.Y., February 5, 1975, June 9, 1977.

assistance: Ladimer, "The Challenge of Transplantation," pp. 19-20.

heart: Phone interview, News Bureau, Stanford University Medical Center, Palo Alto, Calif., August 11, 1977.

kidney: Phone interview, End Stage Renal Disease Medical Information System, August 10, 1977.

Medicare: David Dempsey, "Transplants Are Common: Now It's the Organs That Have Become Rare," *The New York Times Magazine*, October 13, 1974; Alan Anderson, Jr., "Dialysis or Death," *The New York Times Magazine*, March 7, 1976.

St. Luke's: Thomas Thompson, *Hearts* (Greenwich, Conn.: Fawcett Publications, 1971), pp. 185-86.

construction worker: "New Yorker Gets Russian's Kidney," *The New York Times*, February 24, 1977; "Kidney Transplant," *The New York Times*, April 3, 1977; "Transplants: Shortage of Donors Is Still Acute," *The New York Times*, May 29, 1977.

dialysis: AMA, "Donation of Bodies or Organs for Transplantation and Medical Science."

202 tissues: AMA, "Donation of Bodies or Organs for Transplantation and Medical Science."

13.4 million: Phone interview, New York University Deafness Research and Training Center, New York, N.Y., September 19, 1977; Morgan, *Manual*, p. 53.

pituitary: Phone interview, The National Pituitary Agency, Baltimore, Md., August 11, 1977.

accidental: Ladimer, "The Challenge of Transplantation," p. 12.

one-fifth: Ladimer, "The Challenge of Transplantation," p. 12.

alleviate: Phone interview, The National Pituitary Agency, August 11, 1977; "Human Growth Hormone," *The Medical Letter*, Vol. 19, No. 14, July 15, 1977, p. 57.

203 permission: Ladimer, "The Challenge of Transplantation," p. 12.

Cape Town: Thompson, *Hearts*, p. 294; *Encyclopædia Britannica, 1968 Yearbook*.

Tennessee: *Journal of the American Medical Association*, November 10, 1975, p. 583; U.S. Department of Transportation, Federal Highway Administration, "1976 Driver License: Administration Requirements and Fees," February 1976.

states: U.S. Department of Transportation, Federal Highway Administration, "1976 Driver License: Administration, Requirements and Fees," February 1976.

Thirty-five: "Transplants: Shortage of Donors Is Still Acute," *The New York Times*, May 29, 1977.

Porzio: Ralph Porzio, *The Transplant Age* (New York: The Vantage Press, 1969), p. 49.

program: Porzio, *The Transplant Age*, pp. 49-50.

Longmore: Donald Longmore, *Spare-Part Surgery* (Garden City, N.Y.: Doubleday & Co., 1968), p. 185.

204 tattoo mark: Dempsey, "Transplants Are Common: Now It's the Organs That Have Become Rare," *The New York Times Magazine*, October 13, 1974.

Europe: "The Shortage of Organs for Clinical Transplantation: Document for Discussion," *British Medical Journal*, February 1, 1975, p. 253; Jesse Dukeminier, Jr., LL.B., and David Sanders, M.D., M.P.H., "Organ Transplantation: A Proposal for Routine Salvaging of Cadaver Organs," *New England Journal of Medicine*, August 22, 1968, p. 418.

Moslems: Dukeminier and Sanders, "Organ Transplantation: A Proposal for Routine Salvaging of Cadaver Organs," *New England Journal of Medicine*, August 22, 1968, p. 418.

"Eurotransplant": Ladimer, "The Challenge of Transplantation," p. 21.

Sadler: Dempsey, "Transplants Are Common: Now It's the Organs That Have Become Rare," *The New York Times Magazine*, October 13, 1974.

advances: Phone interview, End Stage Renal Disease Medical Information System, August 10, 1977.

Britain: "The Shortage of Organs for Clinical Transplantation: Document for Discussion," *British Medical Journal*, February 1, 1975, p. 254.

victim: "Medical Examiner Defied in Transplant of Kidney," *The New York Times*, March 8, 1975; "Bronx Judge Says 'Brain Death' Is the Legal End of Human Life," *The New York Times*, April 26, 1975.

205 Northern California: Material sent by Northern California Transplant Bank, San Jose, Calif., January 31, 1975.

removal: Material sent from Northern California Transplant Bank, January 31, 1975; phone interview, Northern California Transplant Bank, August 8, 1977.

Living Bank: Material sent by The Living Bank, Houston, Tex.

donors: Phone interview, The Living Bank, Houston, Tex., August 10, 1977.

Medic Alert: Phone interview, Medic Alert Foundation, Turlock, Calif., August 11, 1977.

tissues: Material sent by Northern California Transplant Bank, January 31, 1975.

Airlines: "Radio to Call Kidney Patient for Transplant," *Los Angeles Times*, April

13, 1969.

206 eye-banks: Phone interview, New York Eye Bank, August 11, 1977.

centers: Smirnow, "The Real Truth About Kidney Transplants," p. 19.

helps coordinate: Phone interview, End Stage Renal Disease Medical Information System, August 10, 1977.

deafness: Phone interview, The Deafness Research Foundation, New York, N.Y., October 11, 1977.

Pituitary: Morgan, *Manual*, p. 54.

Bethesda: Nancy Rosenberg and Reuven K. Snyderman, *New Parts for People* (New York: W.W. Norton and Co., 1969), pp. 72-73; Morgan, *Manual*, p. 54.

proliferation: Morgan, *Manual*, p. 57.

Morgan: Morgan, *Manual*, p. 57.

PART IV
Chapter 18

211 PMA: The People's Memorial Association, "The People's Memorial Association" (brochure), Seattle, Wash.

Bleitz: "The People's Memorial Association."

membership: Phone interview, People's Memorial Association, August 22, 1977.

300 adults: Phone interview, People's Memorial Association, August 22, 1977.

Affiliated: People's Memorial Association, "Plans for Simpler Funerals" (leaflet).

expenses: Information verified by Friend A. Deahl, People's Memorial Association, January 1, 1976.

212 cost: Phone interview, Friend A. Deahl, August 8, 1977.

Brooklyn: Phone interview, Continental Association of Funeral and Memorial Societies, Washington, D.C. (CAFMS), October 14, 1977.

"burial societies": "Poor Southerner's Way of Death: Paying Pennies a Week to Depart in Style," *The New York Times*, March 2, 1975.

1950: Phone interview, CAFMS, August 23, 1977.

burgeon: Phone interview, CAFMS, August 23, 1977.

societies: Phone interview, CAFMS, August 3, 1977.

estimates: Phone interview, CAFMS, August 4, 1977.

Palm Beach: Phone interview, CAFMS, August 4, 1977.

Minnesota: Phone interview, CAFMS, August 4, 1977.

Largest: Letter from First Memorial Services Ltd., Vancouver, B.C., April 29, 1975.

movement: Morgan, *Manual*, p. 33.

Canada: Morgan, *Manual*, p. 33 and insert to p. 33.

Fulton: Fulton, "A Compilation of Studies of Attitudes Toward Death," p. 20.

213 survey: Casket Manufacturers Association of America, "American Attitudes Toward Death and Funerals," p. 43.

Canadian: *Canadian Consumer*, February 1975, p. 31.

vary: Morgan, *Manual*, pp. 29-31.

members: Morgan, *Manual*, p. 31.

illegitimate: Morgan, *Manual*, p. 31.

movements: Arvio, *The Cost of Dying*, pp. 28-29.

affiliated: Morgan, *Manual*, p. 29.

no restrictions: Morgan, *Manual,* pp. 29, 31; Arvio, *The Cost of Dying,* p. 50; phone interview, CAFMS, August 3, 1977.

British Columbia: Phone interview, Memorial Society of British Columbia, Vancouver, B.C., September 7, 1977.

214 Write: Morgan, *Manual,* insert to p. 33.

literature: Arvio, *The Cost of Dying,* p. 30.

medical schools: Phone interview, CAFMS, August 11, 1977.

mission: Morgan, *Manual,* p. 30.

Richardson: "Funeral and Memorial Societies," *Harvard Medical Alumni Bulletin,* March/April 1973, p. 14.

arrangements: Morgan, *Manual,* p. 31.

contract: "The People's Memorial Association."

cooperating: Phone interview, former president, Blackhawk Memorial Society, Davenport, Iowa, August 11, 1977.

advisory: Morgan, *Manual,* p. 31.

215 formal agreements: "The People's Memorial Association"; Arvio, *The Cost of Dying,* pp. 46-47.

letter: Letter from W.W. Chambers, president, W.W. Chambers Co., Inc., to the Maryland Suburban Memorial Society, Silver Spring, Md., August 22, 1974.

forms: People's Memorial Association, "Plans for Simpler Funerals."

copies: Arvio, *The Cost of Dying,* p. 151.

undertakers: Phone interview, CAFMS, August 10, 1977.

disputes: Phone interview, CAFMS, August 22, 1977.

216 plans: Morgan, *Manual,* p. 32; Arvio, *The Cost of Dying,* p. 36.

service: Findings of CU survey of memorial societies, February 1975.

prices: Findings of CU survey of memorial societies, February 1975.

$500: Phone interview, CAFMS, August 10, 1977.

50 percent: Phone interview, CAFMS, August 10, 1977.

plans: Brochure from Bleitz Funeral Home, Seattle, Wash.

Minnesota: Brochure from Minnesota Memorial Society, Minneapolis, Minn.

Rochester: Material from Rochester Memorial Society, Inc., Rochester, N.Y.

Cooperating: Findings of CU survey of memorial societies, February 1975.

breakdown: Material from Rochester Memorial Society, Inc., Rochester, N.Y.

217 Kansas City: Phone interview, Greater Kansas City Memorial Society, Kansas City, Mo., August 11, 1977.

Florida: Phone interview, Memorial Society of Alachua County, Gainesville, Fla., August 11, 1977.

Blackhawk: Phone interview, former president, Blackhawk Memorial Society, Davenport, Iowa, August 11, 1977.

ostracism: "FTC planning memorandum," pp. 27-29.

FTC: *FTC Proposed Rule,* p. 135.

218 opposition: "Co-operatives Offer Low-Cost Funerals," *National Observer,* January 26, 1970; findings of CU survey, February 1975.

Lansing: "Memorial Societies Inform and Assist," *Consumer News & Views,* January/February 1974, p. 1.

Arvio: Arvio, *The Cost of Dying,* p. 45.

New Hampshire: NFDA, "The Pre-Arranging and Pre-Financing of Funerals" (leaflet), September 1977.

219 rebuttal: "Funerals: The Last Consumer Decision," *Consumer News & Views,* November/December 1974, pp. 1, 8.

services: Morgan, *Manual*, p. 13.
payment: Morgan, *Manual*, p. 31.
fee: Morgan, *Manual*, p. 29.
bequests: Morgan, *Manual*, p. 29.
dues: CAFMS, *Handbook for Funeral & Memorial Societies*, pp. IV-1.
220 "records charge": Phone interview, Friend Deahl, August 8, 1977; CAFMS and Memorial Society Association of Canada, *Handbook for Funeral & Memorial Societies*, pp. IV-2.
Deahl: Phone interview, Friend Deahl, August 8, 1977.
work: Morgan, *Manual*, p. 29.
officers: CAFMS, *Handbook for Funeral & Memorial Societies*, pp. I-4.
Reciprocal: Morgan, *Manual*, p. 35.
moves: Morgan, *Manual*, p. 31.
equal time: Morgan, *Manual*, p. 35.
assist: Phone interview, CAFMS, August 11, 1977.
offsprings: CAFMS, *Handbook for Funeral & Memorial Societies*, pp. XI-1.
flyer: CAFMS, "How to Organize a Memorial-Funeral Society."
Handbook: Morgan, *Manual*, p. 33; phone interview, CAFMS, August 4, 1977.
221 Morgan: Morgan, *Manual*, p. 34.
legislation: Material sent by CAFMS, August 26, 1977.
higher: Letter submitted by CAFMS to Subcommittee on Commerce and Finance, U.S. House of Representatives, about National No-Fault Motor Vehicle Insurance, July 26, 1974.
Bulletin: Morgan, *Manual*, p. 34.
new societies: Material from CAFMS, August 26, 1977.
budgets: Phone interview, CAFMS, August 22, 1977.
$1: Phone interview, CAFMS, August 22, 1977.
article: Phone interview, CAFMS, August 22, 1977.
directors: Material sent by CAFMS, August 26, 1977.
aid: Phone interview, CAFMS, August 22, 1977.
222 Non-profit: "The People's Memorial Association"; "A Move to Embalm 'Cremation Clubs,'" *Business Week*, September 21, 1974, p. 89.
businesses: Findings of CU survey of memorial societies, February 1975.
New Mexico: Letter from Memorial Association of Central New Mexico, Inc., March 14, 1975.
Georgia: Letter from Memorial Society of Georgia, Atlanta, Ga., February 19, 1975.
Essex: Letter from Memorial Society of Essex, Montclair, N.J., February 28, 1975.
Spokane: Letter from Spokane Memorial Association, Spokane, Wash., February 8, 1975.
Philadelphia: Letter from Memorial Society of Greater Philadelphia, Philadelphia, Pa., March 3, 1975.
Morgan: Morgan, *Manual*, p. 36.
223 minority: Phone interview, CAFMS, August 8, 1977.
Los Angeles: Phone interview, CAFMS, August 8, 1977.
conflict: Morgan, *Manual*, p. 36.
Deahl: Letter from Friend A. Deahl, August 8, 1977.
brochure: "Catholics, Simple Funerals and People's Memorial Association" (brochure published by People's Memorial Association); phone interview, Friend Deahl, August 8, 1977; phone interview, People's Memorial Association, August 22, 1977.

majority: Phone interview, board member, CAFMS, Rochester, N.Y., August 22, 1977.

conventional: Arvio, *The Cost of Dying*, pp. 35-36.

224 Parkes: "Proceedings: Fourth Annual Meeting of the Continental Association of Funeral and Memorial Societies, Inc.," May 13-16, 1966 (Chicago, Ill.: Continental Association, 1966), p. 20; Ira O. Glick, Robert S. Weiss and C. Murray Parkes, *The First Years of Bereavement* (New York: John Wiley & Sons, 1974), flyleaf of book.

director: "Proceedings: Fourth Annual Meeting of the Continental Association of Funeral and Memorial Societies, Inc.," p. 18.

Chapter 19

225 funeral expenses: Morgan, *Manual*, p. 43; U.S. Congress, Senate, Subcommittee on Frauds and Misrepresentations Affecting the Elderly of the Special Committee on Aging, *Preneed Burial Service: Hearing*, 88th Cong., 2nd sess., May 19, 1964, pp. 24, 27. Hereafter cited as *Hearing on Preneed Burial Service*.

installment: Bernard, *The Law of Death*, p. 57.

plans: Bernard, *The Law of Death*, p. 61.

agent: "Prepaid Funeral Plans Grow," *St. Louis Post-Dispatch*, February 4, 1968.

226 most states: *Hearing on Preneed Burial Service*, p. 25.

percentage: See Appendix 3.

remain: See Appendix 3.

seller: See Appendix 3.

discount: "Prepaid Funeral Plans Grow," *St. Louis Post-Dispatch*, February 4, 1968.

hearing: *Hearing on Preneed Burial Service*, pp. 3, 21.

safeguards:*Hearing on Preneed Burial Service*, p. 9.

227 New Mexico: *Hearing on Preneed Burial Service*, pp. 3-5, 16.

problem: "Funeral Payment Path Is Complex," *St. Louis Post-Dispatch*, February 6, 1968.

deposit: *FTC Presiding Officer's Report*, pp. 48-49.

Bernard: Bernard, *The Law of Death*, pp. 56-57.

administer: NFDA, "The Pre-Arranging and Pre-Financing of Funerals."

agency: NFDA, "The Pre-Arranging and Pre-Financing of Funerals."

article: "Funeral Payment Path Is Complex," *St. Louis Post-Dispatch*, February 6, 1968.

228 federal regulation: Bernard, *The Law of Death*, p. 56.

opposed: Testimony of Thomas H. Clark, general counsel of NFDA, *Antritrust Aspects, Part I*, p. 135; Policy Statement Portion of "30 Pieces of Silver," by Howard C. Raether, 1963 NFDA Professional Conferences, reprinted in *Antitrust Aspects, Part I*, p. 139.

policy: *Hearing on Preneed Burial Service*, p. 23.

leaflet: NFDA, "The Pre-Arranging and Pre-Financing of Funerals."

Raether: Policy statement portion by Howard C. Raether, reprinted in *Antitrust Aspects, Part I*, p. 139.

229 Krieger: Letter from W. M. Krieger to Harrison A. Williams, Jr., member, Special Committee on Aging, U.S. Senate, June 3, 1964, reprinted in *Hearing on Preneed Burial Service*, p. 20.

230 survivors: *Hearing on Preneed Burial Service*, p. 22.

pressure: *Hearing on Preneed Burial Service*, p. 21.

"funeral counselor": "How Prepaid Funerals Are Sold," *St. Louis Post-Dispatch*, February 5, 1968.

door-to-door: "FTC planning memorandum," p. 161.
30 percent: *FTC Presiding Officer's Report*, p. 47.
231 "cooling-off": *FTC Presiding Officer's Report*, p. 47.
Social Security: Phone interview, Social Security Office, New Rochelle, N.Y., September 9, 1977.

A Last Word

233 changes: *FTC Proposed Rule*, p. 150.
new direction: NFDA, "Funeral Service: Meeting Needs . . . Serving People," pp. 4, 7.
Counseling: Raether and Slater, *The Funeral Director and His Role*, pp. 1, 12.
Pine: *FTC Presiding Officer's Report*, p. 125.
234 steps: Raether and Slater, *The Funeral Director and His Role*, p. 5.
integral: Raether and Slater, *The Funeral Director and His Role*, p. 77.
check: Raether and Slater, *The Funeral Director and His Role*, p. 76.
235 education: NFDA, "Funeral Service: Meeting Needs . . . Serving People," pp. 10, 11.
Pine: *FTC Presiding Officer's Report*, p. 125.
"traditional": *FTC Presiding Officer's Report*, p. 131.
rule: *FTC Proposed Rule*, pp. 6-7.
NFDA: NFDA, "An Analysis with Comments of the 'Proposed FTC Trade Regulation Rule and Staff Memorandum,'" *The Director*, October 1975, p. 1A.
sterile: *Hearings on Small Business, Part III*, p. 371.
rule: *FTC Proposed Rule*, pp. 14-31.
236 thoughtless act: "Convention Reports," *The American Funeral Director*, August 1974.
"strong opposition": *FTC Proposed Rule*, p. 149.
attorney: "Lawyer Attacks Funeral Industry," *The Reporter Dispatch*, White Plains, N.Y., July 21, 1976.
commissioner: CAFMS, *Bulletin*, December 1976, p. 17.
ploy: CAFMS, *Bulletin*, December 1976, p. 17.
supremacy clause: *FTC Proposed Rule, 16 CFR Part 453*, Notice of Proceeding, p. 29.
237 threat: *FTC Presiding Officer's Report*, pp. 2-8.
additional: *Small Business Report*, p. 1.
report: *Small Business Report*, pp. 29-31.
need: *Small Business Report*, pp. 15, 29.
summary: *FTC Presiding Officer's Report*, p. 133.
domination: *FTC Presiding Officer's Report*, p. 134.
"a myth": "FTC planning memorandum," p. 17.
"execrable": *FTC Presiding Officer's Report*, p. 135.
state boards: "FTC planning memorandum," p. 23.
238 one or two: *FTC Presiding Officer's Report*, p. 133.
enforcement: Consumers Union, "Comments on Funeral Industry Practices Trade Regulation Rule," April 22, 1976, pp. 62-64.
consideration: *FTC Presiding Officer's Report*, p. 8.
1979: "High Cost of Dying," *Washington Star*, March 26, 1976 in *Hearings on Small Business, Part IV*, p. 248.

Permission to Quote

Consumers Union wishes to acknowledge its appreciation to the following authors, individuals, organizations, publishers, and publications for permission to use selected materials from their works:

American Hospital Association for "Postmortem Procedures." Copyright ©1970 by the American Hospital Association.

American Journal of Clinical Pathology for "The Isolation of Pathogens from Tissues of Embalmed Human Bodies," by Lyle A. Weed, M.D., and Archie H. Baggenstoss, M.D., December 1951. Reproduced with permission from the *American Journal of Clinical Pathology*, 21: 1114-1120, 1951. Copyright © 1951 by American Society of Clinical Pathologists.

British Medical Journal for "Contemporary Themes: The Shortage of Organs for Clinical Transplantation: Document for Discussion," February 1, 1975. Copright © 1975 by *British Medical Journal*.

California Business for "Opposition Stiffens to Funeral Spectacles," by Stephen Kaplan, December 14, 1972. Copyright © 1972 by *California Business.*

W. W. Chambers, Chambers Funeral Home, personal communication.

Consumer News & Views for "Memorial Societies Inform and Assist," by Rev. Robert E. Green, January/February 1974, and "Funerals: The Last Consumer Decision," by Joseph Peterson, November/December 1974. Copyright © 1974 by Michigan Consumers Council.

The Courier-Journal for "Cemetery's Rule: Service or Expense?" by Larry Werner, February 24, 1976. Copyright © 1976, *The Courier-Journal,* Louisville, Kentucky. Reprinted with permission.

CRC Critical Reviews in Clinical Laboratory Sciences for "Postmortem Bacteriology," by Elmer W. Koneman, M.D., January 1970. Copyright © 1970 by Chemical Rubber Company.

Detroit Free Press for "$95 Cremation Costs Widow $897 Extra," by Jim Schutze, February 6, 1972. Copyright © 1972 by *Detroit Free Press.* Reprinted with permission.

Everybody's Money for "Funeral Societies," Autumn 1970. Reprinted with permission from the Autumn '70 issue of *Everybody's Money,* the consumer magazine for credit union members, published by Credit Union National Association, Madison, Wisconsin 53701.

Robert S. Faubel for personal communication.

Robert Fendell for personal communication.

Index

Index

Burial, *see* Funerals and burial
Burial clothes, 35, 116-17
  See also Shrouds
Burial costs, *see* Funeral and burial costs
Burial enclosures, *see* Coffin enclosures;
  Grave liners; Vaults
Burial societies, 40, 53-54, 85-86, 134, 182,
  212

Cadavers, for medical research:
  organs for transplantation, 199-207
  shortage of, 43, 186-88
  Uniform Anatomical Gift Act, 188-90,
    202, 204
  See also Donation of body or organs
California Business, 178
California Funeral Directors Association,
  178
Calvary Cemetery (New York City), 133-34
Canada Pension Plan, 60
Canadian Consumer, 49
Carr, Jesse, 98-99
Cash advances, 112-14, 236
Casket & Sunnyside, 116-17, 124, 144
Casket Manufacturers Association of
    America:
  on coffin prices, 27, 73, 77-78
  on coffin types, 76
  survey of attitudes, 18, 82, 135, 213
Caskets, *see* Coffins
Catafalque, 156
Catholic Church:
  on autopsy, 196
  on cremation, 165-66
  on donation of body or organs, 191-92
  on simple funerals, 67
"Catholics: Simple Funerals and People's
    Memorial Association," 223
Cemeteries, 36, 131-51, 172
  Arlington National Cemetery, 57-58,
    155
  coffin enclosures, 36, 123-30, 141-42,
    150
  costs, 24, 26, 36, 138-44
  decorations, 144-45
  embalming requirement, 145
  memorials, 143-44

National Cemetery System, 57, 129-30,
    133, 147
  opening and closing graves, 142-43, 144
  perpetual care of graves, 138, 139,
    149-50
  plots, 138, 139-40
  regulation of, 136
  sales tactics, 145-48
  shortage of space, 133-35
  types of, 137
  See also Mausoleums
Cemetery Board (California), 177
Center for Disease Control, 92, 96
Children, participation in funeral and
  viewing, 104-5
Christiansen, Peter Hans, 104
Churches, assisting in arranging funerals,
  38-39, 52-54, 68
Clergy:
  assisting in arranging funerals, 38-39,
    52-54, 68
  honoraria, 113
Clothes, *see* Burial clothes; Shrouds
Coffin enclosures, 36, 123-30
  choosing, 130, 150
  costs of, 126-28, 141-42
  legal aspects of, 36, 129, 235, 236
  sales tactics, 128-29
  types of, 126
Coffins, 33-34, 71-87, 145
  choosing, 86-87
  display room, 72-75, 78, 81-82, 86
  eternal rest bed vault, 84-85
  for cremation, 84, 155-56, 163-64,
    168-69, 173, 236
  guarantees and warranties, 82-83
  kits, 86
  legal aspects of, 163, 168-69, 235
  mail order, 53, 85-86
  pricing of, 27-28, 69-70, 72-74, 76-79,
    235
  protection of body, 82-84, 236
  sales tactics, 79-82
  types and styles, 75-76
  unconventional, 84-85
College of American Pathologists, 100,
    197-98, 199

324

on funeral home profits, 19
on funeral pricing, 19, 28-29
on preneed plans, 229
National Temporal Bone Banks Center, 206
Naval Medical Research Institute Tissue Bank, 206
Neptune Society, 176
New England Memorial Society, 214
New Jersey State Board of Mortuary Science, average cost of funeral, 26
New York Public Interest Research Group, 22, 50, 76, 81, 149
New York State College of Human Ecology, 17, 126
New York State Funeral Directors Association, 62, 236
New York Times, The, 134-35, 141, 194
NFDA, *see* National Funeral Directors Association
Niches, 42, 138, 169, 172
Northern California Transplant Bank, 205
Notices, death, 35, 111
NSM, *see* National Selected Morticians
Nursing homes, 101-2
NYPIRG, *see* New York Public Interest Research Group

Obituaries, 111
See also Death notices
Office of Consumer Affairs, Montgomery County (Maryland), 129
O'Flaherty, V. M., 192
Omega Alpha Society, 53
Omega Funeral Service Corporation, 181, 183
Organ banks, 204-7
Organs, donation of, *see* Donation of body or organs

Package pricing, *see* Unit Pricing
Pallbearers, 35
Palm Beach Funeral Society, 212
Parkes, C. Murray, 224
Peabody, D. W., 134-35
People's Memorial Association, 183-84, 211-12, 216, 220, 223

Perpetual care of graves, 138, 139, 149-50
Philbrick, W. L., 160
Photographs, 110, 111
Pierce Brothers, 178
Pine, Vanderlyn, 25, 39, 233-34, 235
Planning in advance, 41-45, 85-86
See also Memorial societies; Preneed plans
Plaques, 143, 150, 172-73
Plots, cemetery, *see* Cemeteries
Police escorts, 112
Portrait memorialization, 110, 111
Porzio, Ralph, 203-4
Post-Gazette (Pittsburgh), 190-91
"Postmortem Bacteriology," 92, 93
Postmortem Procedures, 194
Pre-Arrangement Interment Association of America, 137
"Pre-Arranging and Pre-Financing of Funerals, The," 228
Preneed plans, 40, 45, 225-32
choosing, 231-32
for crypts, 131-32, 145-51
for eternal rest bed vault, 85
for grave markers, 128-29
for plots, 36, 137, 145-51
for vaults and other coffin enclosures, 128-29, 130
legal aspects of, 226-28, 232
pro and con, 229-31
See also Planning in advance
Preservation, 34, 69
See also Embalming
Press (Pittsburgh), 115
Price itemization, 62-63, 79, 120-21, 235
Principles and Practice of Embalming, The, 89
Proposals for Legislative Reforms Aiding the Consumer of Funeral Industry Product & Services, 189
Prospect of Immortality, The, 88
Protestantism:
on autopsy, 196
on cremation, 164-65
Providence Journal, 138
Psychology of Funeral Service, 91
Public Health Service, 92, 96

331

Index

"Public Health Value of Embalming,
   The," 94
Public Interest Research Group, *see* New
   York Public Interest Research Group
"Putting My House In Order," 221

Quakers, 52
Quebec Pension Plan, 60
"Questions and Answers on Anatomical
   Gifts," 193-94

Rabbinical Assembly, The, Committee on
   Jewish Law and Standards, 167
Rabbinical Council of America, 52-53
Raether, Howard:
   on alternative funerals, 161
   on autopsy, 197-98
   on cemeteries, 128
   on coffin sales, 74-75, 82
   on counseling survivors, 233, 234
   on embalming, 99, 107
   on funeral pricing, 23
   on grief therapy, 34-35, 38, 43
   on preneed plans, 228-29
   on price advertising, 21
   on viewing, 34-35
Railroad Retirement Board, 56
Rappaport, Alfred, 29
Reals, William, 197-98
Religious views, 52-54
   on autopsy, 185, 195-97
   on covering coffin, 87
   on cremation, 52, 164-67, 170
   on donation of body or organs, 191-92
   on embalming, 89, 95
   on memorial services, 104
   on shrouds, 116
   on simple funerals, 52-53, 67
   on viewing, 104
Research, medical, *see* Cadavers, for medical research; Donation of body or organs
Restoration, 19, 88-90
Richardson, George S., 214
Richmond Memorial Parks, Inc., 147
Rochester Memorial Society (New York),
   216-17

Rosch, J. Thomas, 113, 123
Rose, Gordon, 94

Sadler, Blair, 204
St. Francis Burial Society, 53-54, 85-86,
   182
St. Louis Post-Dispatch, 227, 230
Saturday Review, 64-65
Scattering of cremated remains, 42,
   169-70, 172-73, 174
Service Corporation International, 29, 114,
   171
Services, *see* Graveside services; Memorial
   services
Shaftesbury, Lord, 165
Sherman, Burton, 185-86
Shrouds, 116, 135, 145
   See also Burial clothes
Sky-Pak, 119
Slater, Robert, 43, 234
Snell, Inc., Foster D., 94-95
Social Security, 41, 43, 57, 59, 61, 193,
   203, 231
Societies, memorial, *see* Memorial soci-
   eties; Names of individual societies
Society of American Florists, 114-15
Society to Honor the Dead, 54
Spare-Part Surgery, 203
Spohn, Richard, 179
Spokane Memorial Association, 22
Star (Minneapolis), 71
State Society for Cremation (Florida), 180
Strub, C., 89
Successful Funeral Service Management,
   34, 35, 72
Synagogues, assisting in arranging funer-
   als, 38-39, 52-54, 68

Telophase Society, 175-79, 184
Terkel, Studs, 142, 143
Thompson, Thomas, 99, 201
Times (St. Petersburg), 180
Tips, 138
Tombstones, 128, 137, 143-44, 150
"Tower Gardens," 139
Transplant Age, The, 203-4
Transplantation, *see* Donation of body o1

332

Index